Intertemporal Macroeconomic Models, Money and
Rational Choices

Also by Giuseppe Chirichiello

DYNAMIC OPTIMIZATION: Models in Economic Theory

ELEMENTS OF MICROECONOMIC THEORY (*co-author*)

THE ISSUE OF THE INTEGRATION BETWEEN PRICE THEORY AND
MONETARY THEORY: An Introductory View

MACROECONOMIC MODELS AND CONTROVERSIES

THREE LECTURES ON MONETARY THEORY (*co-editor*)

Intertemporal Macroeconomic Models, Money and Rational Choices

Giuseppe Chirichiello
Professor of Economics
University of Rome
Italy

First published in Great Britain 2000 by
MACMILLAN PRESS LTD
Houndmills, Basingstoke, Hampshire RG21 6XS and London
Companies and representatives throughout the world

A catalogue record for this book is available from the British Library.

ISBN 0–333–77814–6

First published in the United States of America 2000 by
ST. MARTIN'S PRESS, INC.,
Scholarly and Reference Division,
175 Fifth Avenue, New York, N.Y. 10010

ISBN 0–312–23218–7

Library of Congress Cataloging-in-Publication Data
Chirichiello, Giuseppe.
Intertemporal macroeconomic models, money, and rational choices / Giuseppe
Chirichiello.
p. cm.
Includes bibliographical references and index.
ISBN 0–312–23218–7
1. Macroeconomics—Mathematical models. 2. Monetary policy—Mathematical
models. I. Title.
HB172.5 .C4558 2000
339'.01'5118—dc21

99 086836

This book is printed on paper suitable for recycling and made from fully managed and sustained
forest sources.

10   9   8   7   6   5   4   3   2   1
09   08   07   06   05   04   03   02   01   00

Printed and bound in Great Britain by
Antony Rowe Ltd, Chippenham, Wiltshire

Contents

List of Figures

Preface

Intertemporal macroeconomics relies on microeconomics and general equilbrium analysis to describe choices of agents over period of time, perhaps infinitely long. In particular, the formal modelling of individual choices uses the methods of dynamic optimization or optimal control theory. To this, methods of dynamic macroeconomics, that is of growth theory, are linked and the effects of policy interventions are then examined as the interaction between decisions of agents and policy interventions. This way of approaching macroeconomics sustains a fundamental change of perspective, with respect to the conventional macroeconomics originated from the IS/LM–AD/AS Keynesian foundations. The idea is that macroeconomics is not only concerned with short-run and the state of the effective demand but also is concerned with long-run and intertemporal allocation of economie's resources. Economic policy interventions, therefore, are reconsidered in relation to the effects on rate of growth and capital accumulation. Two basic approaches can be pointed out: models of infinitely-lived agents (Cass-Ramsey-Koopmans approach) and models of overlapping-generations (Allais-Fisher-Samuelson approach). This book explores both the approaches, by first presenting the major issues of the 'real' models of growth and the role of fiscal policies. However, whereas results about real models of growth and fiscal policies are well-established, more controversial are the questions concerning monetary models and monetary policies. Indeed, money may be or may not be a source of instability and changes in growth rate of money stock may be or may not be 'superneutral' according to the way monetary economy and/or monetary policy are modelled. The book offers a framework and a systematic exploration of these and related questions in both basic models, and also in models of endogenous growth. The book has originated from advanced courses I taught to students of a research group of which I was co-ordinator in the 1990s. The original Italian manuscript was finished in the 1996; the book is the result of a revised translation of that work. I want to thank Cora Hahn for her professional job of thoroughly revising my translation and turning the manuscript into a more readable work. I dedicate the book to my mother Nigro Antonia.

Introduction

Intertemporal macroeconomics provides a completely new paradigm with respect to conventional AD/AS macroeconomics, originating from Keynesian models. Since new answers to traditional questions continue to appear in the professional journals, this book offers an assessment and a step toward standardization of intertemporal macroeconomics. It ideally consists of two parts. A first part covers Chapter 1 to Chapter 3 and is concerned with basic intertemporal models. The second part covers Chapter 4 to Chapter 6 and is concerned with more complex and controversial subjects, such as monetary models and endogenous growth models, the latter also extended to monetary economies. The book is organized as follows. Chapter 1 contains a review of descriptive models of growth. Section 1.1 examines the Harrod-Domar 'Keynesian' model of growth, which could be considered a bridge between conventional macroeconomics and actual dynamic macroeconomics. Sections 1.2 to 1.6 discuss neoclassical (Solow's) model by revisiting the issues of existence, stability and efficiency of steady state, and the golden rule and its importance for the efficiency of steady state. Two of these sections are devoted to the comparative analysis of changes in propensity to save and to the comparison of stylized facts and prescriptions of the neoclassical model.

Chapter 2 deals with aggregate intertemporal microfounded models. It sheds light on the fundamental change in macroeconomics: the view that macroeconomics, like microeconomics, deals with interactions over time between rational agents. Section 2.1 demonstrates Ramsey's optimal saving rule for a single 'pure-saver' agent. As in Ramsey, this problem is initially formulated as a variational problem, but it is then reformulated as an optimal control problem. Optimal control is the methodology applied to dynamic choices in the rest of the book.

In section 2.2 Ramsey's optimal saving rule is extended to the economy as a whole, by proposing a peculiar model where income is not distributed to agents by the market. This model serves as tool to examine in sections 2.3 and 2.4 the existence, stability and efficiency of optimal steady state paths. The remainder of Chapter 2 examines the dynamics, efficiency and the effects of fiscal policy in a decentralized competitive economy.

Chapter 3 deals with overlapping generations models. Section 3.1 presents Fisher's optimal saving rule for a single agent. Sections 3.2 and 3.3 are devoted to a close examination of the properties of the saving function from the microeconomic point of view. Basic microeconomic methodology, even the dual approach, is applied here to highlight the microfoundations of the aggregate saving function on which the pure-exchange aggregate model and the growth model of competitive economy with overlapping generations are built. Sections 3.4 to 3.15 examine the dynamics, efficiency and the effects of fiscal policies. In particular sections 3.9 to 3.15 offer an extensive analysis of taxation, social security, and public debt and deficit.

Chapter 4 deals with intertemporal monetary models with an infinite horizon. Section 4.1 contains a basic descriptive monetary model. In three subsections (4.1.1–4.1.3), dynamics, stability and the existence of a steady state are examined using various hypotheses of forming expectations. Section 4.2 revises Cagan's model of monetary instability and prepares the ground for subsequent issues. Section 4.3 considers the monetary model with optimizing agents (Sidrauski). In this framework three issues are considered: the superneutrality of money (section 4.4), the welfare effects of inflation (section 4.5), and self-generating hyperinflation phenomena (section 4.6). Finally, the appendix to Chapter 4 presents alternative models of monetary economy with an infinite horizon.

Chapter 5 examines alternative approaches to a monetary economy with overlapping-generations. Section 5.1 considers the basic pure exchange model, which offers a framework for discussing issues regarding the foundations of money. Section 5.2 examines the dynamics of the basic model through the 'reflected offer curve'. Section 5.3 extends the model to the production of goods and the accumulation of physical capital, and it examines dynamics. The remaining sections are devoted to problems of monetary theory. Section 5.4 considers an economy with storage technology and the non-dominance of money in nominal interest rate when there is a market for private credit. Section 5.5 shows the inefficiency of seignorage policy. Section 5. 6 reconsiders the optimum quantity of money problem in the overlapping generations model when money enters into the utility function. Sections 5.7 to 5.10 examine alternative overlapping generations models of a money economy (cash-in-advance constraint; transaction costs approach; legal restrictions approach) and the effects of monetary policy.

Chapter 6 offers an introduction to endogenous growth models. Sections from 6.2 to 6.4 examine a basic framework for endogenous growth derived from (i) models with constant-returns-of-scale and human capital; (ii) models with externalities; (iii) models of non-competitive economies. Sections 6.5 and 6.6 examine taxation and public spending policies. Sections 6.7 to 6.11, devoted to monetary economies and to an examination of the effects of monetary policy on growth, offer an innovative synthesis of issues. The book makes extensive use of mathematics. However, it presumes only a basic knowledge of calculus. Essentials tools such as difference and differential systems of equations, stability and saddle-path stability–instability and the theory of optimal control are presented in mathematical appendixes at the end of the book.

1
Descriptive Models of Growth

1.1 Harrod-Domar model as prototye of growth models

The Harrod-Domar model of growth (Harrod 1939; Domar, 1946) is a dynamic extension of the simple real (moneyless) Keynesian model. It is built on the following assumptions:

a) production technology admits constant returns of scale. In particular, it is assumed that technology has fixed coefficients v and u for inputs of capital K and labour L;
b) aggregate consumption function C is the canonical long-run Keynesian consumption function. This function is assumed to have constant and identical marginal and average propensity to consume. Aggregate savings function S, therefore, also has constant and identical marginal and average propensity to save;
c) capital stock and labour grow over the time. Capital grows because of investments, labour grows because of population growth. Both these circumstances impart to the model a dynamic character.

Mathematically, conditions (a) ~ (c) correspond to the following equations:

$$
\begin{aligned}
K &= vQ \\
L &= uQ \\
S &= sQ \\
\dot{K} &= I \\
\dot{L} &= nL
\end{aligned}
\qquad \text{(A)}
$$

The first and second equations of (A) define requirements of current capital K and labour L as proportions of current production Q, in accordance with respective technical coefficients v and u. The third and fourth equations define saving function S, which has a constant propensity to save s, and capital accumulation over time $dK/dt = \dot{K}$ derived from current investments I. The fifth equation defines changes of labour over time $dL/dt = \dot{L}$ which is proportional to the existing labour force. The growth rate of population n is exogenously given. Equilibrium requires that both goods and labour markets clear simultaneously at every instant. This happens when investments are equal to savings $\dot{K} = sQ$ and the labour requirement is equal to the availability of labour, $L = \dot{L}/n = uQ$. Since $K = vQ$, then $v\dot{Q} = sQ$, so that equilibrium paths are described by the system of two homogeneous differential equations

$$\dot{Q} - (s/v)Q = 0$$

$\dot{L} - nL = 0$, together with the condition $L(t) = uQ(t)$

Each equation of the system depends solely on the variable to which equilibrium refers and therefore can be solved apart. Starting from the first equation, given the initial condition $Q(0) = Q_0$, the equilibrium path of goods market is the exponential function $Q(t) = Q_0 e^{(s/v)t}$. Along this path the output at every instant equals effective demand and output grows at the rate:

$$\dot{Q}/Q = (s/v)Q_0 e^{(s/v)t}/Q_0 e^{(s/v)t} = s/v$$

This rate is the *warranted rate* of growth (Harrod, 1939). An economy which grows at the warranted rate of growth has no lack of effective demand. The second equation of the differential system solves for the path of instantaneous availability of the labour force. Given an initial condition $L(0) = L_0$, the labour force's availability path is the exponential function $L(t) = L_0 e^{nt}$. The additional condition dictated by the technical requirement $L(t) = uQ(t)$ is a restriction on the set of solutions. An output path satisfying such condition is a full-employment path. It corresponds to

$$Q(t) = L(t)/u = (L_0/u)e^{nt} = Q_0^1 e^{nt}$$

where Q_0^1 is the initial output which, when realized, utilizes the entire labour force L_0 at t_0. In order for an economy starting at full-employment output Q_0^1 to run full-employment forever, it must grow at the rate

$$\dot{Q}/Q = Q_0^1 n\, e^{nt}/Q_0 e^{nt} = n$$

This is the *natural rate* of growth (Harrod, 1939). Full employment equilibrium at every instant requires

$$Q_0 e^{(s/v)t} = Q_0^1 e^{nt}$$

That is, an economic system starting at some instant from full employment $Q_0 = Q_0^1$ will remain forever at full employment if, from that instant on, the warranted rate of growth is equal to the natural rate of growth. An economy which at each instant equalizes warranted and natural rates of growth is said to follow a balanced path growth. One important aspect of the Harrod-Domar model is that the magnitudes s, v, n on which a balanced growth solution depends are freely assigned parameters. There is no necessity for them to assume the values required for balanced growth. One can also assume s and v vary, by admitting some mechanism that generates the required values for s and v. Yet the lack of such a mechanism is an important theoretical characteristic of the Harrod-Domar model in which growth follows a 'knife-edge' path. We can give the knife-edge issue a formal and a diagrammatic representation in terms of capital accumulation. The equilibrium of goods market $v\dot{Q} = sQ$ can be reproposed as $\dot{K} = (s/v)K$. Given full-employment steady state capital stock K^*, deviations from the steady state capital stock are described by $\dot{K} = s/v[K(t) - K^*]$. In the phase plane $(K, \dot{K})$ this equation plots a straight line which has a slope s/v and intercepts the horizontal axis at point $K(t) = K^*$, as depicted in Figure 1.1.

Since s/v is positive, deviations from the steady state move in the same direction as the sign of $[K(t) - K^*]$, so that if $K(t) - K^* \gtrless 0, \dot{K} \gtrless < 0$. An economic system following the warranted rate accumulates or decumulates physical capital, depending on the starting position steady state K^*.

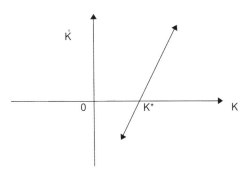

Figure 1.1 A phase diagram in the phase plane $(K, \dot{K})$ in Harrod-Domar model

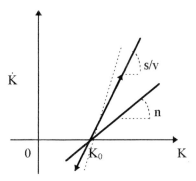

Figure 1.2   Natural and waranted growth paths in Harrod-Domar model

On the other hand, from $K = (v/u)L$, or $\dot{K} = (v/u)\dot{L}$, by rewriting $\dot{K} = (v/u)L(\dot{L}/L)$ we can also write $\dot{K} = nK$. This describes capital accumulation for an economy whose output grows at a natural rate of growth. If this economy starts at steady state full-employment position K^*, its deviations of capital stock from steady state are described by the equation $\dot{K} = n[K(t) - K^*]$. In the phase plane $(K, \dot{K})$ this equation plots a straight line having slope n which intercepts the horizontal axis at point $K(t) = K^*$, as depicted in Figure 1.2.

Figure 1.2 combines warranted and natural paths of capital accumulation. For a system starting at $K = K^*$ there are three possibilities:

a) when natural rate of growth n coincides with warranted rate of growth s/v, the two paths have the same slope in phase plane $(K, \dot{K})$. Since they also intercept the horizontal axis at the same points, the two paths coincide in the entire plane. The economic system will follow the balanced growth path $s/v = n$ indefinitely without unemployment and/or lack of effective demand;

b) when natural rate of growth n is greater than warranted rate of growth $n > s/v$, the line of the natural growth path for $K > K^*$ lies entirely above the line of warranted growth. Starting from $K = K^*$, an economy experiencing no overproduction will have a growth rate lesser than natural growth rate. This economy then will leave the full-employment path and never return to it. It will experience permanent unemployment;

c) when natural rate of growth n is lower than warranted rate of growth $n < s/v$, the line of the natural growth path for $K > K^*$ lies entirely below the line of the warranted growth. Starting from $K = K^*$ an economy experiencing full-employment will have overproduction. It will experience permanent insufficient effective demand.

Except for case (a) , the Harrod-Domar model predicts that an economy starting at full employment finds itself on a knife-edge. It risks turning into a path of permanent unemployment or a path of permanent lack of effective demand. Another important point is that growth *à la* Harrod-Domar does not exhibit any tendency to stay or converge toward a steady state. The instability of the steady state is trivially derived by noticing that by virtue of $s/v > 0$ it follows that $\lim\limits_{t \to +\infty} K(t) = \lim\limits_{t \to +\infty} K_0 e^{(s/v)t} = +\infty$.

1.2   Neoclassical growth model

The Harrod-Domar model already shows that admitting a multiplicity of production processes is the same as admitting a range of values $v_1, v_2, ...,$ v_n for the capital coefficient v. However, if we abandon the hypothesis of a fixed capital/labour ratio, the nature of the problem of growth changes in respect to the Harrod-Domar model. Assuming a flexible capital/labour ratio the question becomes: is there a capital coefficient v such that warranted rate of growth s/v and natural rate of growth n coincide for any values s and n? A way to recognize that v can assume an infinite number of values or a continuum of values is to represent technology by means of a production function. With this kind of technology, the neoclassical answer (Solow, 1956; Swan, 1956) to the query of existence of required values for v is that if the production function is *well-behaved*, whatever the rate of growth, it is always possible to find a capital requirement v which equalizes warranted rate of growth to natural rate of growth. This equality makes it unnecessary to distinguish between the natural and the warranted rate of growth. One can speak of growth rate of output *tout-court*. We shall examine below the meaning of a *well-behaved* production function. For the moment let us look at the problem of growth. Assume technology represented by a production function. The neoclassical growth model (which, we observe, keeps the basic Keynesian framework) can be written

$$Q = F(K, L)$$
$$S = sQ$$
$$\dot{K} = I$$
$$\dot{L} = nL \qquad\qquad\qquad\qquad\qquad\qquad (A)$$

Goods market equilibrium $I = \dot{K} = sF(K, L)$ is also a full-employment equilibrium if at each instant $L(t) = L_0e^{nt}$. Therefore, the family of full employment equilibrium trajectories is described by the relationship

$$\dot{K} - sF(K(t), L_0e^{nt}) = 0$$

With given n, this is a non linear ordinary first-order differential equation in K(t). We can not say much about its integral, except to state the general conditions that ensure the existence of solutions to this differential equation (see Mathematical Appendix). However, by introducing further restrictions we may describe the nature of admissible solutions. In particular, we can restrict the search for steady state growth or a uniform or balanced growth rate. Steady state growth is characterized by the following conditions

1. each relevant variable grows at constant rate;
2. the constant growth rate is the same for every variable.

That is, since by assumption $\dot{L}/L = n$, the condition for steady state is

$$\dot{Q}/Q = \dot{K}/K = n$$

Ultimately, by limiting the search for a balanced growth path is the same as adding these two extra dynamic conditions to the system. Thus model (A) is reformulated as follows

$$\dot{K} - sF(K, L) = 0$$
$$\dot{L} = nL$$
$$\dot{Q} = nQ$$
$$\dot{K} = nK \qquad\qquad\qquad\qquad (B)$$

Reformulation (B) accounts only for the subset of economies which display balanced growth. Moving from the system (A) to (B) does not mean aiming at a more 'realistic' description of the paths of the economy but only facilitates checking that the set of economies displaying balanced growth is not empty. It is worth noting that this way of dealing with the question of the existence of a balanced growth path can be rephrased by echoing Harrod-Domar's methodology. More exactly we can ask the following question:

> Given a system that evolves by accumulating physical capital at natural rate $\dot{K}/K$ $= \dot{L}/L = n$ and that is endowed with a flexible technology of production F(K, L), what conditions must the production technology satisfy so that the warranted growth s/[K/F(K, L)] = s/v(K, L) is equal to the natural rate of growth n?

After introducing the necessary changes, it is trivial to show that this question is just another way of asking the question about the existence of balanced growth path. Indeed, if $\dot{K} = nK$, the balanced growth condition is $nK = sF(K, L)$ which requires the equality between the natural and the warranted rate of growth, that is $n = s/v(K, L)$. To deduce balanced growth solutions, therefore, let us refer to the model (B). From $Q(t) = F(K(t), L(t))$ it follows that

$$\dot{Q} = F'_k \dot{K} + F'_L \dot{L} \text{ where } F'_K = \partial F/\partial K \text{ and } F'_L = \partial F/\partial L.$$

From the balanced growth conditions for K and L we obtain $nQ = F'_K nK + F'_L nL$, that is $Q = F'_K K + F'_L L$. This condition is met only if the production function is homogeneous of degree one. Therefore, we can state the following proposition:

If an economy admits a production function technology characterized by a constant return of scale there is at least one balanced growth path.

When population growth rate is exogenous, steady state growth and balanced growth can be used as synonymous because warranted rate of growth is exactly equal to the natural rate of growth. Indeed, with production function technology, warranted growth is $sF(K, L)/K$.
The definition of output growth rate also gives $sF(K, L)/K = (F'_K \dot{K} + F'_L \dot{L})/F(K, L)$, or using the steady state growth condition $\dot{K}/K = \dot{L}/L = n$ the output rate of growth is $sF(K, L)/K = (F'_K \dot{K} + F'_L \dot{L})n/F(K, L)$. But production function is homogeneous of degree one, so that $sF(K, L)/K = F(K, L)n/F(K, L) = n$, that is:

A system that evolves by accumulating physical capital at natural rate $\dot{K}/K = \dot{L}/L = n$ and is endowed with a production function F(K, L) homogeneous of degree one has a warranted rate of growth exactly equal to the natural rate of growth n.

We have so far proved that in order for a balanced growth path to exist it is sufficient to admit a degree–one homogeneous production function. It should be noted that a well-behaved production function must satisfy the following conditions

1. $\partial F/\partial K > 0$, $\partial F/\partial L > 0$, $\partial^2 F/K^2 < 0$, $\partial^2 F/\partial L^2 < 0$ (marginal products are both positive and decreasing);
2. $\alpha Q = F(\alpha K, \alpha L)$, $\forall \alpha > 0$ (constant return of scale) ;
3. a) $F(0, L) = F(K, 0) = 0$;   b) $\lim_{K \to 0} \partial F/\partial K = +\infty$; $\lim_{L \to 0} \partial F/\partial L = +\infty$; $\lim_{K \to 0} \partial F/\partial K = 0$; $\lim_{L \to 0} \partial F/\partial L = 0$

[both capital and labour are prerequisites to production and the isoquants have asymptotes equal to the axes in the plane (L, K)].

Conditions 1 and 2 are standard in basic economics. Conditions 3 (a) and (b) are known as Inada conditions (Inada, 1964). From a well behaved production function, by putting $\alpha = 1/L$ we obtain a per capita production function $q = f(k)$ which inherits the following conditions

a) $\partial F/\partial K = Lf'(k)\partial(K/L)/\partial K = f'(k)$;
b) $\partial F/\partial L = \partial(Lf(k))/\partial L = f(k) + L\partial f/\partial L = f(k) - K(L/L^2)\partial f/\partial k = f(k) - f'(k)k$
c) $f(0) = 0; f'(k) > 0; f''(k) < 0; \lim_{K\to 0} f'(k) = 0; \lim_{K\to 0} f'(k) = +\infty$;

1.3   Neoclassical model in per capita terms: dynamics, the golden rule and dynamic efficiency

Any economy which has a well-behaved aggregate production function can be represented in per capita terms. Consider again the aggregate neoclassical growth model with a well-behaved production function. If we divide every equation for the instantaneous labour force,

$$q = f(k)$$
$$s_{pc} = sf(k)$$
$$i = \dot{k} + nk$$
$$s_{pc} = i$$

where s_{pc} indicates per capita savings. From the equilibrium condition in the goods market $sf(k) = \dot{k} + nk$, the dynamics in per capita terms becomes

$$\dot{k} = sf(k) - nk (°)$$

Graphically this condition is depicted and can easily be interpreted from an economics point of view in Figure 1.3.

Since equilibrium presupposes equality between savings and investments, the term $sf(k)$ also measures ongoing investments. Conversely, since $i = \dot{k} + nk$ indicates per capita investments, the term nk describes investments occurring when $\dot{k} = 0$, that is break-even investments. In Figure 1.3 a positive distance between the curve of current investments and the line of break-even investments indicates a positive accumulation $\dot{k} > 0$, whereas their intersections indicate steady states $\dot{k} = 0$.

Figure 1.3 exhibits two intersections, the origin $k = 0$ and a point of positive per capita capital stock $k^* > 0$. Mathematically, this is demonstrated as follows. When $k = 0$ we have $sf(0) - n0 = 0$ because $f(0) = 0$. To show that there exists $k^* > 0$, let us define the function

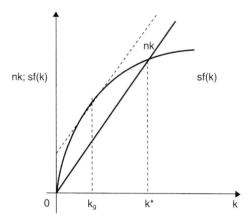

Figure 1.3 Capital accumulation, steady state and golden-rule capital stock in neoclassical (Solow's) model

$z(k) = sf(k) - nk$, which is the excess of current per capita investments over break-even investments. Its first derivative is $z'(k) = sf'(k) - n$, so $z'(k) \gtrless 0$ according to $sf'(k) \gtrless n$. Graphically (in Figure 1.3) this means that when the slope of the line tangent to the curve of current investments is greater than or equal to the slope of the line of break-even investments, we have $dk/dk \geq 0$. Capital accumulation stops, that is $dk/dk = 0$, where $z'(k) = 0$. this happens when $sf'(k) = n$ and the line tangent to the curve of current investments is parallel to the line of break-even investments. Per capita capital stock corresponding to this point of tangency is maximum. It is called the golden rule capital stock and it must be positive $k_g > 0$. If it were not positive, we would have $k_g = 0$, that is $f'(0) = n/s$. But this can not be true because $f'(0) = +\infty$ by Inada conditions and $0 < k_g < +\infty$. Per capita capital k_g is maximum since $z''(k) = sf''(k) < 0$. If we consider per capita steady state capital stock $k^* \neq 0$ it follows that $z(k*) = 0 < z(k_g)$ and, therefore, $k_g < k^*$ which means $k^* > 0$. Note that we can exclude $k^* = +\infty$ because it would imply, according to Hopital's rule, $\lim_{k^* \to +\infty} f(k^*)/k^* = \lim_{k* \to +\infty} f'(k^*) = 0$, which is a contradiction because $f(k^*)/k^* = n > 0$. We can conclude that $0 < k^* < +\infty$.

Stability of the solution $k^* > 0$ can be examined locally by a linear approximation (see Mathematical Appendixes). By defining $d = k - k^*$, the deviations from the steady state, a linear approximation of k^* corresponds to

$$\dot{d} = [sf'(0)]d$$

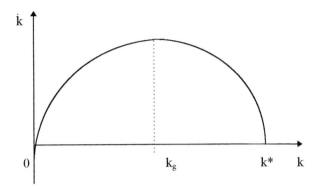

Figure 1.4 A phase diagram in the phase plane (k,k̇) in neoclassical model

which is a first-order homogeneous linear differential equation. Given an initial condition $d_0 = k_0 - k^*$, the unique solution is $d(t) = d_0 e^{[sf'(0)]t}$. Convergence to $d(t) = 0$ as $t \to +\infty$ requires $sf'(0) < 0$, or $sf'(k^*) - n < 0$ This condition is verified because $f(k)$ is concave and its dominion is $[0, +\infty]$. Thus the system converges to the steady state. Figure 1.4 shows the function $\dot{k} = z(k)$ in the phase plane $(k, \dot{k})$.

The fundamental equation of the dynamics of an economy allows us to deduce the dynamics of consumption. If the equilibrium condition is rewritten as

$$\dot{k} + nk = sf(k) + f(k) - f(k) = f(k) - (1 - s)f(k)$$

per capita consumption is $c = (1\text{-}s) f(k)$, so that along the equilibrium path we have

$$c = f(k) - nk - \dot{k}$$

If capital stock is at golden rule level $k = k_g$, then $c'(k_g) = f'(k_g) - n = 0$.

Moreover, $c''(k_g) = (1 - s)f''(k_g) < 0$. In the set of per capita capital stocks where $\dot{k} = 0$, the golden rule capital stock maximizes per capita consumption. Therefore, for any other stationary value of per capita capital stock $c'(k) > \le c'(k_g)$ according to $k \le > k_g$, that is $c'(k) > \le 0$ when $k \le > k_g$. The behaviour of propensity to consume $c'(k)$ along a steady state path is represented graphically in Figure 1.5.

The line parallel to the horizontal axis corresponds to $f'(k_g) = n$. By virtue of this condition we can write $c'(k) = f'(k) - f'(k_g)$. This corresponds to the distance between the curve of the marginal product of per capita

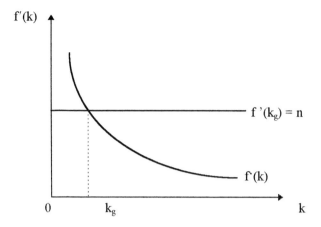

Figure 1.5   Golden rule and dynamic inefficiency

capital and the line $f'(k_g) = n$. Due to Inada conditions $f'(0) = +\infty$ and $f'(+\infty) = 0$, the marginal product of capital curve approximates the horizontal axis asymptotically, as in Figure 1.5. Figure 1.5 shows that, with respect to the null value $c'(k_g) = 0$ at the golden rule value, the propensity to consume $c'(k)$ is positive to the left of intersection E, or is positive for $k < k_g$, and negative for $k > k_g$. An economic system aiming for a capital stock at steady state greater than the golden rule stock must pay for this large accumulation by reducing consumption below the golden rule level. The negative value of propensity to consume tells us that it is possible to increase consumption by reducing capital stock toward the level of the golden rule.

This shows that the region $[k_g, +\infty]$ is a region of *dynamic inefficiency*, a concept worth examining from another point of view. Consider Figure 1.6.

Figure 1.6 has been obtained from Figure 1.3 by superimposing the output curve $f(k)$. Since the $sf(k)$ curve is the locus of current investments, the difference between the points on the $f(k)$ curve and the points on the $sf(k)$ curve corresponds to per capita consumption. A line tangent to $f(k)$ curve at k_g may slope more or less than a line tangent to the same curve at k^*. In Figure 1.6 illustrates the case where $f'(k^*) < n$ and $k_g < k^*$, which is the same result as in Figure 1.5.

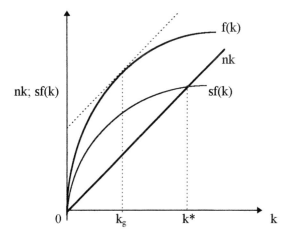

Figure 1.6   An alternative representation of golden rule and dynamic inefficiency

1.4   Changes in propensity to save and the effects on growth

The evolution of an economic system and the stability of steady state $k = k^*$ enable us to perform some comparative dynamic exercises. In particular we are interested in the effects of an increase in propensity to save s on per capita capital stock, output and consumption at the steady state. However, it is useful first to consider the global picture of growth obtained if we assume that Solow's model (without technical progress) is descriptive of the real growth of an economy. The economy depicted by Solow's model shows a growth path with the following characteristics:

a) per capita capital stock tends toward a constant magnitude;
b) per capita output and consumption, the principal indicators of living standard, also tend toward constant values;
c) since per capita variables approximate a steady state, aggregate variables (consumption, output and capital stock of the entire community) approximate a balanced growth path.

The activity of the economy, therefore, proceeds without imbalances and grows at the same rate as the population. The parameters of Solow's model that can not be chosen by agents are: (1) – technology, stationary over time because the production function is assumed not to be dependent on time; (2) – saving propensity, assumed to be constant in the long run; and (3) – growth rate of the population, assumed to be exogenously constant.

As a matter of fact, technology changes because of technical progress, and propensity to save can be changed by policies. Even the growth rate of population is changeable because couples make choices about the number of children they want based on their standard of living (see Barro and Sala-I-Martin, 1995). However, here we shall limit ourselves to asking whether changes in propensity to save lead to changes in the growth path. Specifically, we are asking whether changes in the propensity to save lead up to a positive rate of growth in per capita variables. This point is of practical importance because if the effective economy evolves according to Solow's model, there is hope that in the long run individual standards of living will not fall even when the population increases. Yet it is also important to know whether individual standard of living can be increased by influencing in some way individual attitudes toward saving. Solow's model gives a negative answer. Indeed, the model can not replicate situations in which per capita output grows. For example, let us suppose that propensity to save increases from s to s_1. With the aid of Figure 1.7 we see that since an increase of saving propensity to s_1 causes an increase in the per capita saving, the curve $sf(k)$ of current per capita investment shifts to the left in the plane $[k, sf(k)]$. The higher curve $s_1f(k)$ determines a new intersection with the line nk at point $k_1^* > k$.

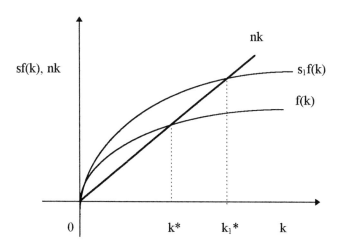

Figure 1.7 Effects from an increase in propensity to save

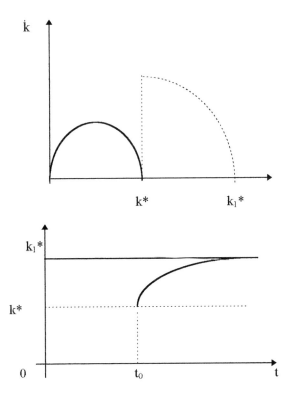

Figure 1.8 and *Figure 1.9*   Effects of an increase in propensity to save on capital accumulation

The transition from k^* to k_1^* is gradual. At the beginning, per capita capital starts to grow, so in the open interval $[k^*, k_1^*[$ we have $\dot{k} > 0$. But at point $k = k_1^*$ the positive effect on growth disappears. Therefore, the positive effect of the increase in the propensity to save on growth is only temporary. The effect on the stationary per capita capital stock, however, is permanent, since $k_1^* > k^*$. Both these effects are shown in Figures 1.8 and 1.9.

Mathematically, to evaluate the effect of a change in propensity to save on per capita steady state consumption we must evaluate the sign of derivative

$$dc/ds = dc/dk(dk/ds) = f'(k)(dk/ds) - n(dk/ds) = [f'(k) - n](dk/ds)$$

Since $dk/ds > 0$, steady state per capita consumption can be larger, the same, or less, depending on whether the marginal product of capital is greater, equal or less than the population growth rate. In fact the final effects on per

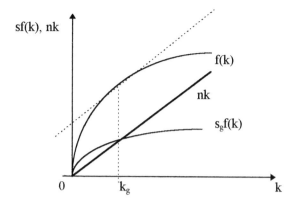

Figure 1.10   The golden rule propensity to save

capita consumption c depends on the sign of $[f'(k) - n]$. We can now answer the question of whether for the community it always pays that individuals become more parsimonious, or whether there is an 'optimal' propensity to save. It pays for the community to adopt the propensity where $dc/ds = 0$ so that the steady state capital stock is at the golden rule level. To be more precise, consider Figure 1.10 where the per capita production function $f(k)$ is compared to the break-even investment line nk.

We already know that the distance $f(k) - nk$ indicates the per capita consumption required to keep per capita capital stock unchanged. Graphically the maximum distance is located at a point where the line parallel to nk is tangent to $f(k)$ curve. If a community chooses the propensity to save s_g so that the $s_g f(k)$ curve intersects the nk line at point $k = k_g$ (where line tangent to $f(k)$ is parallel to nk), then the corresponding steady state is at golden rule state since $f'(k_g) = n$. Per capita consumption is maximum when $s = s_g$ and per capita capital stock is dynamically efficient. The transitional dynamics is similar to that depicted in Figure 1.11.

In Figure 1.11 whether or not it pays for a community to go through state $s = s_g$ can not be deduced from the model. Indeed the answer depends on the way households evaluate consumption loss measured by segment AB relative to consumption gain measured by segment BD. Since these segments compare consumption at different instants, we need a criterion to evaluate losses and gains from consumption reallocation over time. In addition, we need a procedure for discounting future consumption gain in order to compare it with current consumption loss. This problem is dealt with by optimal growth models, which we will consider in subsequent chapters. At the moment we will complete the dynamic

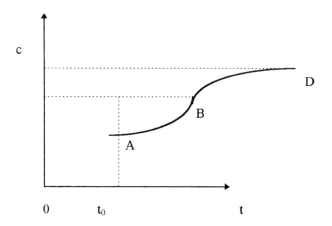

Figure 1.11   The trade-off between current and future consumption

comparative analysis by following Romer's (1996) examination of the effects of changes in propensity to save on per capita output f(k). We already know that dk/ds > 0. Since df(k)/ds = f'(k)dk/ds, df(k)/ds > 0. However we do not know the expression of dk/ds. By differentiating sf(k) = n with respect to s we obtain

$$sf'(k)dk/ds + f(k) = n(dk/ds)$$

Since dk/ds[n − sf'(k)] = f(k)(dk/ds) = f(k)/n − sf'(k), by substituting it follows that

$$df(k)/ds = [f(k)f'(k)]/n − sf'(k)$$

This expression can be reinterpreted in terms of the elasticity of steady state per capita production with respect to propensity to save

$$\varepsilon_{q,s} = [s/f(k)[df(k)/ds] = s/f(k)[f'(k)f(k)/n − sf'(k)]$$

By substituting for sf(k) its stationary value nk, we get

$$\varepsilon_{q,s} = nkf'(k)/nf(k) − sf(k)f'(k) = kf'(k)/f(k) − kf'(k),$$

that is

$$\varepsilon_{q,s} = \frac{\dfrac{kf'(k)}{f(k)}}{1 − \dfrac{kf'(k)}{f(k)}}$$

The magnitude $\dfrac{kf'(k)}{f(k)}$ is the elasticity of per capita production with respect to per capita capital.

Letting $\alpha_k = kf'(k)/f(k)$ we have $\varepsilon_{q,s} = \alpha_k/1 - \alpha_k$. In a competitive system, $kf'(k)$ is the real income paid to capital input so that α_k is the output share of capital input, and $\alpha_k < 1$. For example, suppose that propensity to save increases by 20 per cent (for instance from 20 per cent to 24 per cent). If we take the share of industrialized countries, which is estimated about 1/3 of output, the effect on output of the assumed increase in propensity to save is about 10 per cent because $\varepsilon_{q,s} = \frac{1}{2}$. This exercise suggests that a significant increase in the propensity to save s determines only a relatively moderate increase in output $f(k)$. A related point is the change in speed of the convergence to steady state after an increase in s.

The derivative of the fundamental equation of motion with respect to per capita capital k is

$$\frac{d\dot{k}}{dk} = (sf'(k) - n) = \frac{sf(k)f'(k)}{f(k)} - n = \frac{nkf'(k)}{f(k)} - n = (\alpha_k - 1)n$$

Thus, the linear approximation in a neighbourhood of steady state $k = k^*$ is

$$\dot{k} = (\alpha_k - 1)n(k - k^*) = -(1 - \alpha_k)n(k - k^*)$$

and the speed to which the system reduces distance $(k - k^*)$ is the coefficient $(1 - \alpha_k)n$. The linear differential equation in the distance $d = k - k^*$ is $\dot{d} = -(1 - \alpha_k)n\,d$, which has the solution $d(t) = d(0)e^{-(1-\alpha_k)nt}$.

This solution can be calibrated to see how economies approximate their steady states. For the sake of realism this kind of operation must also account for other factors so far ignored, such as technological progress and depreciation, as well as the rate of growth of population. A calibration of this equation offered by Romer (1996) takes into account technological progress and depreciation. As we shall see, the equation of motion in this case is $\dot{d} = -(1 - \alpha_k)(n + \omega + \delta)d$, where ω is the rate of growth of technological progress and δ is the rate of depreciation. Romer's calibration proposes the values $n = 0.02$; $\omega + \delta = 0.04$; and $\alpha_k = 1/3$. The speed of convergence each year is about 4 per cent of the remaining distance from k^* and q^*. After a year the former increase of the 20 per cent in propensity to save determines an increase in the output of $0.04 \times 0.10 = 0.4$ per cent above the previous path. Approximating by means of Father Pacioli's rule, we can state that a 50 per cent reduction of distance from k^* and q^* takes about $(0.69/0.04) + 0.35 = 17.6$ years. After that time it approximates asymptotically 10 per cent of output over the previous steady state value. From a practical point of view, therefore, not only do increases in propensity to save induce moderate increases in production, but they also display their effects very slowly.

1.5   Solow's model with technological progress

Solow's basic model can also include technological progress. Much technological knowledge comes from specifically designed R&D activity which employ resources. The extension of Solow's basic model, however, considers only exogenous technological progress which can assume various forms. Technological innovations may spread over the entire capital stock and labour force, or introduced only through new capital goods and a newly employed labour force. When innovations are spread over the entire capital stock and labour force, they are classified as capital and/or labour saving innovations if they obtain the same amount of output with less input of either capital or labour. Innovations which do not save any input are called neutral technical progress. The exact definition of neutral technical progress depends on the meaning given to the terms capital saving and labour saving.

According to Hicks (1932), Solow (1963), and Harrod (1942), given a production function unchanging over time, technical progress can be classified as:

a) Innovation Hicks-neutral, if it leaves the marginal rate of substitution between inputs unchanged. The general production function admitting technological progress is $Q = F(K, L, t)$ which specializes $Q = T(t)F(K, L)$, where $T(t)$ is an index of technological progress. Therefore, Hicks-neutral technological progress can also be defined as product augmenting, since

$$\dot{Q} = \dot{T}F(K, L) > 0, \text{ with } \dot{T} \geq 0;$$

b) Innovation Harrod-neutral, if for a given capital/labour ratio it leaves the relative input share on output unchanged, that is if, for K/L given, the ratio

$$\frac{KF_k/F(K, L)}{LF_L/F(K, L)} = \frac{KF_K}{LF_L}$$

remains unchanged over time. Harrod-neutrality requires the following production function

$$Q = F(K, A(t)L)$$

where $A(t)$ is an index of technological progress with $\dot{A} \geq 0$. Harrod-neutral technological progress is also called labour augmenting since innovation has the same effect as an increase of labour input;

c) Innovation Solow-neutral, if it leaves the relative share of inputs LF_L/KF_K unchanged for given L/K. This form of technological progress requires a production function $Q = F(B(t) K, L)$ where $B(t)$ is the index of technological progress and $\dot{B} \geq 0$. Solow-neutral technological progress is called capital augmenting since innovation has the same effect as an increase of capital input.

With an exogenous given rate of technological progress, the only technological progress consistent with a steady state solution is labour-saving Harrod-neutral technological progress. To illustrate this, let us consider the production function $Q = F(B(t)K, A(t)L)$. Since it is homogeneous of the first order, we can write the average product of capital in terms of efficiency units $Q/B(t)K = F[1, A(t)/B(t) (L/K)]$, that is $Q/K = B(t)F[1, A(t)/B(t)(L/K)]$. By assuming that the innovation of both inputs grows exponentially, $A(t) = A(o)e^{\omega t}$; $B(t) = B(o) e^{bt}$, the growth rates of the technological efficiency of labour and capital are respectively $\dot{A}/A = \omega \geq 0$, $\dot{B}/B = b \geq 0$. Therefore,

$$Q/K = B(o)e^{bt}F[1, A(o)/B(o)e^{(\omega-b)t}L/K]$$

By normalizing $A(o) = B(o) = 1$ we can write $Q/K = e^{bt}h(L/Ke^{\omega-b)t})$. In a steady state this becomes

$$Q/K = e^{bt}h[L(o)e^{nt}/K(o)e_k^g e^{(\omega-b)t}] = e^{bt}h(e^{(n-g_k+\omega-b)t})$$

The capital steady state rate of growth is $g_k = sQ/K$. Since propensity to save s is constant Q/K must be constant. This condition is verified when

a) $b = 0$ and $g_k = n + \omega$, that is if technological progress is labour-augmenting and the capital steady state rate of growth is $n + \omega$; or

b) $d(Q/K)/dt = 0$. This requires a Cobb-Douglas production function (when the production function is Cobb-Douglas, technical progress can always be expressed in the labour-augmenting form, see Barro and Sala-i-Martin, 1995, pp. 54–5).

An outstanding feature of Solow's model is that it admits a steady-state solution. If we want to preserve this feature we must assume labour-augmenting technological progress. Therefore, by assuming the production function $Q = F(K, A(t)L)$, Solow's aggregate model with technological progress becomes:

$Q = F[K, A(t)L]$
$S = sQ$
$\dot{K} = I$
$\dot{L} = nL$
$\dot{A} = \omega A$

At equilibrium we have $\dot{K} = sF[K, A(t)L]$, and by dividing both sides of the equality by L, since $\dot{K}/L = \dot{k} + nk$ dynamic per capita equilibrium becomes

$\dot{k} = sF[k, A(t)] - nk$

Now output per worker $F[k, A(o)e^{\omega t}]$ depends also on the level of technological knowledge $A(o)e^{\omega t}$ so it is more convenient to rewrite the model in terms of *effective* labour units $L_e = A(t)L$. Thus $Q/AL = F(K/AL, 1)$, or $q_e = f(k_e)$. By considering a constant depreciation rate of capital $\delta > 0$, the dynamic equilibrium in the original aggregate variables is

$\dot{K}(t) = sF[K(t), A(t)L(t)] - \delta K(t)$

which in terms of effective labour units is equivalent to

$\dot{K}/A(t)L(t) = sF[K(t)/A(t)L(t), 1] - \delta K(t)/A(t)L(t)$.
Since $\dot{K}(t)/A(t)L(t) = \dot{k}_e + (n + \omega)k_e$ we have $\dot{k}_e = sf(k_e) - (n + \omega + \delta)k_e$

The only formal difference with respect to Solow's basic model is per capita capital expressed in terms of effective labour units k_e. Steady state growth rate is $n + \omega + \delta$. Steady state per capita capital stock k_e^* is such that

$sf(k_e^*) = (n + \omega + \delta) k_e^*$

Graphically we obtain the picture in Figure 1.12, which is the same as Figure 1.4. Per capita capital in effective labour units k_e^* is located at the intersection between the line of break-even investments per effective labour units and the investments curve per effective labour units.

The qualitative features of Solow's model, when the technological progress is labour-augmenting, are unchanged with respect to the basic model. It is useful, however, to calculate the growth rates of per capita variables in this different context explicitly. Per capita consumption, capital and output are respectively

$c = C/L = (C/AL)A = c_e A; k = K/L = (K/AL)A = k_e A;$
$q = (Q/AL)A = q_e A$

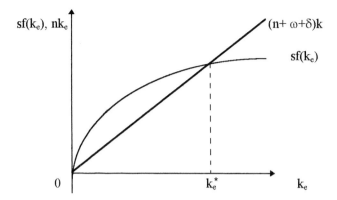

Figure 1.12 The neoclassical model with technological progress

By differentiating each variable with respect to time t we have

$$\dot{c} = \dot{c}_e + \dot{A}; \, \dot{k} = \dot{k}_e + \dot{A}; \, \dot{q} = \dot{k}_e + \dot{A}$$

When in the steady state $\dot{c}_e/c_e = \dot{k}_e/k_e = \dot{q}_e/q_e = 0$, it follows that $\dot{c}/c = \dot{k}/k = \dot{q}/q = \omega$. Solow's model now admits a positive growth rate in per capita magnitudes but this growth is exogenous since the positive rate coincides with the growth rate of technological progress which in the model is given exogenously.

1.6 Stylized facts and the neoclassical growth model

Kaldor's (1963) well-known contribution listed stylized facts about growth in several countries for different periods. The relevant stylized facts are

1. capital to output ratio K/Q tends to be constant;
2. output per capita exhibits sustained rate of growth, that is a rate of growth which does not tend to decrease over time;
3. capital to labour ratio tends to increase over time;
4. different economies at different times show different paths of the capital to output ratio as well as different rates of growth.

   How do many of these stylized facts fit Solow's model? Surely Solow's model replicates fact 1 since the capital to output ratio changes over time according to

$$\frac{d(K/Q)}{dt} = \frac{K}{Q}(\frac{\dot{K}}{K} - \frac{\dot{Q}}{Q}).$$ Since $\dot{K}/K = \dot{Q}/Q = n$ then $d(K/Q)/dt = 0$

Fact 2 must be evaluated taking into consideration the inference in Solow's model that the growth rate of per capita output is null $\dot{q}/q = 0$. This rate is positive when the exogenous rate of technological progress is positive. But since exogenous technological progress is unexplained fact 2 also remains unexplained.

Fact 3 is not reproduced in Solow's model. Similar to fact 2, it must be compared to rate $d(K/Q)/dt$ which we have just seen is null. Finally, fact 4 refutes the uniformity of growth rates which is implied in Solow's model when it refers to different countries and different periods. Empirically (Barro and Sala-I-Martin, 1995) the variability of growth rates for different countries seems due to

1. a positive correlation between growth of per capita income and rate of investment I/K: the greater the I/K is, the greater the $\dot{q}/q$;
2. a positive correlation between per capita income and education level and skill of workers: the greater the skill, education and workmanship, the greater the $\dot{q}/q$;
3. a negative correlation between per capita income growth rate and population growth rate: the greater rate of growth of income, the less the rate of growth of population;
4. a positive correlation between per capita income growth rate in a single country and both the growth rate in the world economy and the degree of openness to international trade

The explanation of correlations 1–4 is high on the research agenda in growth theory.

References

Allen, R.G.D. (1967) *Macroeconomic Theory, A Mathematical Treatment* (London: Macmillan).
Barro, R. and X, Sala-I-Martin. (1995) *Economic Growth* (New York: McGraw-Hill).
Burmeister, E. and A.R. Dobell (1970) *Mathematical Theories of Economic Growth* (New York: Macmillan).
Domar, E.D. (1946) 'Capital Expansion, Rate of Growth and Employment', *Econometrica*, 14, pp. 137–47
Hahn, F.H. and R.C.O Matthews (1964) 'The Theory of Economic Growth: A Survey', *Economic Journal*, 74, pp. 825–832.

Harrod R.F. (1939) 'An essay in dynamic theory', *Economic Journal*, 49, pp. 14–33.

Harrod, R.F. (1942) *Toward a Dynamic Economics: Some Recent Development of Economic Theory and their Application to Policy* (London: Macmillan).

Hicks, J.R. (1932) *The Theory of Wages* (London: Macmillan).

Inada, K.I. (1964) 'On a Two-Sector Model of Economic Growth: Comments and a Generalisation', *Review of Economic Studies*, 30, pp. 119–27.

Kaldor, N. (1963) 'Capital Accumulation and Economic Growth', in F.A. Lutz, and D.C. Hague, (eds) *Proceedings of a Conference Held by the International Economic Association* (London: Macmillan).

Phelps, E.S. (1961) 'The Golden Rule of Accumulation: A Fable for Growthmen', *American Economic Review*, 51, pp. 638–43.

Phelps, E.S. (1965) 'Second Essay on the Golden Rule of Accumulation', *American Economic Review*, 55, pp. 793–814.

Phelps, E.S. (1966) *Golden Rules of Economic Growth* (New York: Norton).

Romer, D. (1996) *Advanced Macroeconomics* (New York: McGraw-Hill).

Swan, T.W. (1956) 'Economic Growth and Capital Accumulation', *Economic Record*, 32, pp. 334-61.

Swan, T.W. (1963) 'Growth Models of Golden Ages and Production Function' in K. E. Berrill, (ed.), *Economic Development with Special Reference to East Asia* (London: Macmillan).

Solow, R.M. (1956) 'A Contribution to the Theory of Economic Growth', *Quarterly Journal of Economics*, 70, pp. 65–94.

Solow, R.M. (1957) 'Technical Change and the Aggregate Production Function', *Review of Economic Studies*, 39, pp. 312–20.

Solow, R.M. (1962) 'Technical Progress, capital Formation and Economic Growth', *American Economic Review*, 52, pp. 76–86.

Solow, R.M. (1963) *Capital Theory and the Rate of Return* (New York: North-Holland).

2
Aggregate Intertemporal Microfounded Models with Infinite Horizon

2.1 Ramsey's optimal saving rule and individual choices

Solow's model is of a great theoretical interest in a discussion of dynamic efficiency but does not specify any criteria for ascertaining whether a saving behaviour based on the golden rule propensity to save $s = s_g$ is optimal. This would require a theory of optimal individual saving. Modern theory offers the competing approaches of Ramsey (1928) and Fisher (1930). We shall begin here with Ramsey's approach. His distinctive assumption is that a consumer's objective is to maximize over a given horizon a utility functional which depends on an instantaneous utility function. Since instantaneous utility exhibits decreasing marginal utility of consumption, the individual has an incentive not to concentrate all the consumption in the current period, but to distribute it over time as uniformly as possible. In this intertemporal re-allocation, a rational agent must compare the marginal rate of substitution between current consumption and saving to what will be earned as future utility from future consumption. The optimal saving condition is dictated by the Ramsey-Keynes rule, according to which saving, or a wealth accumulation path, is optimal if the growth rate of marginal utility is equal to the difference between the utility discount rate and the real rate of return of saving.

Before adopting this rule as the criterion for assessing optimality of growth for the entire economy we should prove that it is an optimal rule for the choices of an individual 'pure saver'. By pure saver we mean an agent whose only goal at every instant is to decide which part of his wealth should be allocated to current consumption and which to future wealth. The latter choice is desirable not *per se* but because more wealth permits the agent to obtain greater future income and therefore greater future consumption. By limiting our initial study to the choices of a *rentier*, who has only accumulated wealth as source of income, we can isolate, so to speak, *in vitro* the phenomenon of saving and the incentives on which it is based (the desire to stabilize consumption over time). Let $c(t)$ and $a(t)$ be the consumption and real wealth of an agent at instant t and let us assume

1. that wealth $a(t)$ generates income over time depending on a real rate of return $\rho(t)$. For the sake of simplicity, we assume a uniform real rate of return over time ρ, so that the disposable real resources at every instant are $q(t) = \rho a(t)$;
2. that the consumer has no other source of income but the return on wealth. In each period resources $q(t)$ can be destined either to consumption or to increasing real wealth. Consequently, the instantaneous constraint to an individual's choices is
   $$c(t) + \dot{a}(t) = q(t);$$
3. that the initial wealth at $t = 0$, $a(0) = a_o$, is given and that the consumer-saver wishes at some future instant $t = T$ to have given real wealth $a(T) = a_1$.

The objective of the consumer-saver is to choose a path of consumption, and therefore of savings, that maximize the utility functional

$$V(T) = \int_0^T e^{-\beta t} u[c(t)] dt$$

The instantaneous utility function $u(c)$ depends on the current consumption $c(t)$ and has the following properties:

1. for each $c(t) > 0$, $u'(.) > 0$, $u''(.) < 0$ (marginal utility of consumption is positive and decreasing);
2. utility function satisfies conditions similar to Inada conditions for the production function, that is
   $$u(0) = 0; \lim_{c \to 0} u'(c) = +\infty; \lim_{c \to +\infty} u'(c) = 0;$$
3. an intertemporal rate of preference of the agent is represented by a discount factor $1 > \beta > 0$, . This shows that immediate consumption is preferable to future consumption.[1]

The control problem of the individual consumer-saver, then, takes the form:

$$\max_{\{c(t)\}} V(T) = \int_0^T e^{-\beta t} u[c(t)] dt$$
$$c(t) + \dot{a}(t) = \rho a(t)$$
$$a(0) = a_o \; ; \; a(T) = a_1$$

This is a classical problem of the calculus of variations (see Mathematical Appendixes). Euler's equation for this problem is

$$\rho\,e^{-\beta t}u'(c) - \frac{d}{dt}[-e^{-\beta t}u'(c)] = 0$$

Letting $\dot{u}'(c) = \frac{du'(c)}{dt}$, we obtain the optimal saving rule

$$\dot{u}'(c)/u'(c) = (\beta - \rho)$$

This is the formal expression that proves the accumulation of wealth (saving) is optimal when the growth rate of marginal utility of consumption is equal to the difference between the utility discount factor and the real rate return of saving. We now have an exact criterion for assessing the optimality of an accumulation activity. Before extending this optimality rule to the economic system, however, it may be worthwhile to reflect for a moment upon the link between this rule and Fisher's rule. Fisher's optimal saving rule requires equality between the intertemporal rate of substitution of consumption and the real interest rate, or equality between the intertemporal preference rate and the real interest rate. We shall show that, if Fisher's intertemporal rate of substitution is redefined in terms of the rate of temporal preference, Ramsey's optimal saving rule admits Fisher's rule as a particular case.

First, let us rewrite Euler's equation as

$$\dot{u}' - (\beta - \rho)u'(c) = 0$$

Given β and ρ, this is a differential homogeneous equation in the marginal utility of consumption. The solution is $u'(c(t)) = u'(c(0))e^{(\beta-\rho)t}$. This relationship may also be rewritten as

$$e^{\rho\triangle t} = \frac{u'(c(0))e^{\beta\triangle t}}{u'(c(t))}$$

Now optimality of saving reads as the equality between the return of postponed consumption (by abstention from current consumption and by substituting it with future consumption at the instant $t + \triangle t$) and the return of one unit of current consumption allocated to savings. With this reinterpretation the right hand term of the equation indicates the marginal rate of substitution of consumption, and Fisher's intertemporal preference rate (Koopmans, 1967b) is given by

$$\frac{u'[c(0)]\,e^{\beta\triangle t}}{u'[c(t)]} - 1 = \gamma$$

We must now emphasize that both the real interest rate ρ and the intertemporal preference rate β are *instantaneous rates*, so that if we refer a real interest rate δ and an intertemporal preference rate γ to a discrete period of time $\triangle t$, it must be true that

$$e^{\rho \triangle t} = (1 + \delta)^{\triangle t}; \quad \frac{u'[c(0)] \, e^{\beta \triangle t}}{u'[c(t)]} = (1 + \gamma)^{\triangle t}$$

which for $\triangle t = 1$ are equivalent to

$$e^{\rho} = (1 + \delta); \quad \frac{u'[c(0)] \, e^{\beta}}{u'[c(t)]} = (1 + \gamma)$$

Therefore Ramsey's rule for optimal saving for $\triangle t = 1$ becomes

$$(1 + \delta) = (1 + \gamma)$$

which is exactly Fisher's rule, or the equality $\delta = \gamma$ between the real rate of interest and the intertemporal rate of preference for a time interval of unit length.

2.2 Ramsey's rule and optimality of growth: a model of an economy with stationary population

Ramsey's optimal saving rule offers a criterion for distinguishing the optimal paths for an economic system. In the equilibrium growth models, the feasible paths for an economy are the balanced growth paths. A balanced growth path has growth rate the same for all relevant variables. For detecting this path here we shall construct a macroeconomic model which, in a certain sense, is the aggregate equivalent of the pure *rentier* savings microeconomic model of section 2.1. Consider an economy populated by $L(t)$ identical agents. Let $C(t)$ be the aggregate consumption. Identical agents' individual consumption is also the per capita consumption $C(t)/L(t) = c(t)$. Therefore, the behaviour of a representative agent is the same as that of other agents, and also, apart from a factor of scale, the same as that of the economy. By assuming an infinite time horizon, the utility functional of the infinitely lived representative agent is

$$V = \int_0^{\infty} e^{-\beta t} \, u[c(t)] \, dt,$$

A typical agent participates in production by supplying inelastically both the labour and accumulated capital. The disposable income of each agent is a share $q(t)$ of uniformly distributed production. A share remunerates every type of input and the amount of real income distributed Y(t) is proportional to the population, that is labour force, $Y(t) = L(t)q(t)$. By virtue of the exhaustion principle, $Y(t) = L(t)q(t) = Q(t)$. Moreover, since production function is homogeneous of degree one, $Q(t) = f(k(t)L(t))$, the real income of a representative agent q(t) coincides with per capita output $q(t) = Q(t)/L(t) = f(k(t))$.[2] In this particular economy, a single agent's savings decision immediately affects capital accumulation. In fact identity between per capita consumption and individual consumption entails:

$$q(k(t)) - c(t) = s(t) = \dot{k}$$

This condition, a consequence of an instantaneous constraint, is also the equation of capital accumulation in a neoclassical economy which has a stationary population $\dot{L}/L = n = 0$ and is in equilibrium at each instant. For this particular economy we can choose the optimal path of accumulation by solving the optimal control problem

$$\max_{\{c(t)\}} V = \int_0^\infty e^{-\beta t} u[c(t)]dt$$

$$\dot{k} - f(k(t)) - c(t)$$

$$k(0) - k_0; 0 < c(t) < +\infty; k(t) \geq 0; \lim_{t \to \infty} e^{-\beta t} u'[c(t)]k(t) = 0$$

This is an optimal control problem with a transversality condition (see Mathematical Appendixes). It is convenient here to solve it as continuum Lagrangian maxima problem. This method is undoubtedly familiar to the reader and it also can highlight the reasons for the transversality condition

$$\lim_{t \to \infty} e^{-\beta t} u'[c(t)]k(t) = 0.$$

A continuum of problems of Lagrangian maxima consists of forming the Lagrangian

$$L = V + \int_0^\infty \lambda(t)[f(k(t)) - c(t) - \dot{k}(t)]dt =$$

$$\int_0^\infty \{e^{-\beta t} u[c(t)] + \lambda(t)[f(k(t)) - c(t) - \dot{k}(t)]\}dt$$

Integrating by parts, the term $\lambda(t)\dot{k}(t)$ yields

$$-\int_0^\infty \lambda(t)\dot{k}(t)\,dt = -[\lambda(t)k(t)]_0^\infty + \int_0^\infty \dot{\lambda}(t)k(t)dt$$

$$= \lambda(0)k(0) - \lim_{t \to \infty} \lambda(t)k(t) + \int_0^\infty \dot{\lambda}(t)k(t)dt$$

By substituting this into the original Lagrangian we obtain a modified Lagrangian

$$L^* = \int_0^\infty \{e^{-\beta t}\, u[c(t)] + \lambda(t)[f(k(t)) - c(t)] +$$
$$\dot{\lambda}(t)k(t)\}dt + \lambda(0)k(0) - \lim_{t\to\infty} \lambda(t)k(t)$$

Lagrangian L^* is more manageable than the original one, because it does not contain $\dot{k}$. However the maximum problem for L^* does not have a definite solution if the component $\lim_{t\to\infty} \lambda(t)k(t)$ does not converge. We can see that even if the optimal control problem has no explicit terminal condition for per capita capital stock, this condition can be imposed by restricting per capita capital stock to economically meaningful values. This adds the constraint $k(t) \geq 0$ which by virtue of the Kuhn-Tucker theorem, also involves complimentary–slackness conditions $\lim_{t\to\infty} \lambda(t) \geq 0$ and $\lim_{t\to\infty} \lambda(t)k(t) = 0$. The latter condition is a transversality condition for $\lambda(t) = e^{-\beta t}u'[c(t)]$. Therefore by assuming the validity of a transversality condition, given $k(0) = k_0$ we can limit to solve

$$\max_{\{c(t),k(t)\}} L^* = \int_0^\infty \{e^{-\beta t}\, u[c(t)] + \lambda(t)[f(k(t)) - c(t)] + \dot{\lambda}(t)k(t)\}dt$$

By differentiating L^* with respect to its arguments, and L with respect to $\lambda(t)$, first-order necessary conditions for a maximizing the Lagrangian are

$$\partial L^*/\partial c(t) = e^{-\beta t}u'[c(t)] - \lambda(t) = 0$$
$$\partial L^*/\partial k(t) = \lambda(t)\,f'(k(t)) + \dot{\lambda}(t) = 0$$
$$\partial L/\partial \lambda(t) = f(k(t)) - c(t) - \dot{k}(t)] = 0$$

Equivalently, the same problem can be solved by applying Pontryagin's maximum principle with a transversality condition. By forming the Hamiltonian $H(t) = e^{-\beta t}\, u[c(t)] + \lambda(t)[f(k(t)) - c(t)]$, we obtain the following canonical first-order necessary conditions for the optimal control

$$\partial H/\partial c(t) = e^{-\beta t}\, u'[c(t)] - \lambda(t) = 0$$
$$\partial H/\partial \lambda(t) = \dot{k}(t) = f(k(t)) - c(t)$$
$$\partial H/\partial \lambda(t) = \dot{\lambda}(t) = -\lambda(t)\,f'(k(t))$$
$$\lim_{t\to\infty} \lambda(t)k(t) = 0$$

The next section considers the economic meaning of these conditions and their relation to Euler's equation.

2.3   The economic significance of optimality conditions and Euler's equation

The first-order necessary conditions of the optimal control problem of the section 2.2 describe dynamics that seem puzzling because the economic significance is not evident. Indeed a condition $\dot{\lambda}(t)$ indicating time changes of co-state variable whose meaning has not yet been specified is added to the condition defining per capita capital accumulation $\dot{k}$. We note from the first necessary condition for the optimal control that

$$\lambda(t) = e^{-\beta t} u'[c(t)]$$

Instantaneous optimal $\lambda(t)$ is the discounted marginal utility. In addition we can identify the co-state variable $\lambda(t)$ as the shadow price of saving, that is, in the aggregate perspective, the shadow price of capital accumulation. Therefore $\lambda(t)$ also indicates the increase of the utility functional following the increase of instantaneous per capita capital $k(t)$. It follows that $\lambda(t) = e^{-\beta t} u'[c(t)]$ indicates the equality between the increase in the utility over time from consumption and the increase in the utility over time from the availability of new capital stock. The other necessary condition

$$\dot{\lambda}(t) = -\lambda(t) f'(k(t))$$

indicates that the rate of return from transforming consumption into capital as input of production must be equal at each instant to the gain of utility over time. Finally, since there is a non-satiety condition, the transversality condition excludes from optimality those choices which from a given instant involve an indefinite accumulation of capital stock, or on the contrary involve the end of capital accumulation because the desire to consume disappears.

It is interesting, now, to reconsider first-order conditions in terms of Ramsey's optimal saving rule. By differentiating $\lambda(t) = e^{-\beta t} u'[c(t)]$ with respect to time we find

$$\dot{\lambda}(t) = -\beta e^{-\beta t} u'[c(t)] + e^{-\beta t} \dot{u}'[c(t)]$$

which compared to $\dot{\lambda}(t) = -\lambda(t) f'(k(t))$ gives Euler's equation

$$\frac{\dot{u}'[c(t)]}{u'[c(t)]} = \beta - f'(k(t))$$

When markets are competitive, the marginal product of capital $f'(k(t))$ coincides with the real rate of interest $\rho(t)$, so that necessary conditions for optimality imply Ramsey's rule

$$\frac{\dot{u}'[c(t)]}{u'[c(t)]} = \beta - \rho(t)$$

2.4   Existence, stability and efficiency of optimal steady state

Having acquired a criterion for the optimality of capital accumulation, we are now able to examine the dynamics of optimal growth by simply deducing paths of per capita consumption implicit in the first-order necessary conditions of a representative agent's optimal control problem. In order to do that, we need to make some calculations. In Euler's equation the term $\dot{u}'$ indicates changes in the marginal utility over time. By taking the first derivative of marginal utility with respect to time we can write $\dot{u}'(c(t) = u''(c(t))\, \dot{c}$, so that Euler's equation becomes

$$\frac{u''(c(t))}{u'(c(t))}\, \dot{c} = \beta - f'(k(t))$$

By defining the elasticity of marginal utility as

$$\sigma(c(t)) = -\frac{u''(c(t))c(t)}{u'(c(t))}$$

and by substituting $\sigma(c(t))$ in Euler's equation we obtain

$$\dot{c}(t) = \frac{c(t)}{\sigma(c(t))}[f'(k(t)) - \beta]$$

In other words an economic system which 'chooses' per capita consumption that generates optimal saving at every instant, necessarily places itself on a trajectory where per capita consumption grows in proportion to the difference between marginal productivity of capital and the discount factor of utility. The coefficient is the consumption weighted by the elasticity of the marginal utility. In general, the dynamics of a system with a stationary population and a capital accumulation that is optimal in the sense of Ramsey-Keynes rule is reducible to the differential equations

$$\dot{k}(t) = f(k(t)) - c(t)$$

$$\dot{c} = \frac{c(t)}{\sigma(c(t))}[f'(k(t)) - \beta]$$

We can analyze conditions for the existence, stability and efficiency of feasible steady states for this system. As we know (see Mathematical Appendixes), the evolution of a dynamic system can be studied by

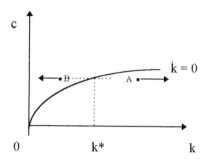

Figure 2.1   Dynamics of per capita capital stock

considering steady states and the direction of paths outside the steady states. Steady states or stationary solutions correspond to states where $\dot{k}(t) = 0$ and $\dot{c}(t) = 0$. The locus of points in the plane (k, c) corresponding to the equation $\dot{k}(t) = 0$ is simply the per capita output function reproduced in figure 2.1.

The direction of motion outside this locus can be found by considering points (k, c) which have per capita capital different from the steady state. When $k > k^*$ then $f(k) > f(k^*)$, and given $c(t) = c^*$ we have $f(k) - c^* > f(k^*) - c^* = 0$. This implies $\dot{k} > 0$ and, therefore, points like A in figure 2.1 move toward increasing per capita capital. At point A in figure 2.1 this direction is indicated by a vector applied in A that points in the same direction as that of the horizontal axis. Similarly since $f(k) < f(k^*)$, when $k < k^*$, $\dot{k} < 0$ and the motion at points like B in figure 2.1 is in the opposite direction to that of the horizontal axis. Let us now consider the $\dot{c} = 0$ locus, which corresponds to points (k, c) where $f'(k) = \beta$.

This is the equation of a line in plane (k, c) which is parallel to vertical axis, as shown in figure 2.2.

When $k < k^*$, since $f'(k)$ is decreasing we have $f'(k) > \beta$ and $\dot{c} > 0$. Consumption increases at points like B located to the left of k^* in figure 2.1 and the direction of a vector applied at B is the same as the positive direction of the vertical axis. By the same token, the direction of the motion at points like A in figure 2.1 is opposite to the positive direction of the vertical axis. Combining together the two loci into a unique picture we obtain figure 2. 3.

By assigning initial conditions [k(0), c(0)] there is only one path which describes dynamic equilibrium. However, since only the initial condition of per capita capital stock is given, there are in principle an infinity of initial values of consumption that might be considered. As figure 2.3

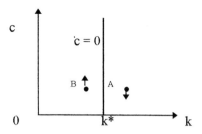

Figure 2.2 Dynamics of per capita consumption

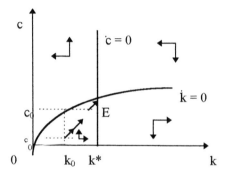

Figure 2.3 Dynamics of per capita consumption and capital stock

suggests, there is only one initial consumption from which the system can move toward the steady state. This is so because the steady state is a saddle point and dynamic equilibrium must satisfy the transversality condition. We will demonstrate in detail the nature of a saddle point of the steady state in a model less restrictive than the present one.[3] At this point we will only give a brief illustration of the methodology that will be used extensively in the rest of the book. By a linear approximation in a neighborhood of the steady state, we obtain

$$\dot{k} = f'(k^*)(k - k^*) - (c - c^*)$$
$$\dot{c} = \frac{c^* f''(k^*)}{\sigma^*}(k - k^*)$$

The characteristic equation of the system is $\mu^2 - f'(k^*)\mu + \dfrac{c^* f''(k^*)}{\sigma^*} = 0$ whose discriminant is $\Delta = f'(k^*)^2 - 4\dfrac{c^* f''(k^*)}{\sigma^*} > 0$. Since $f'(k*) > 0$ and $f''(k*) < 0$ the roots are real and have opposite sign.

Let $\mu_1 > 0$. and $\mu_2 < 0$. By imposing the condition excluding divergent paths, the only convergent path is

$$c(t) - c^* = \frac{\sigma^*}{c^* f''(k^*)} [k(t) - k^*]$$

$$c(0) - c^* = \frac{\sigma^*}{c^* f''(k^*)} [k_0 - k^*]$$

The results obtained can be summarized as follows: an economic system with stationary population that obeys Ramsey-Keynes' optimal saving rule will undergo an evolution that admits only one economically meaningful asymptotically stable steady state.

To complete our discussion, we have to examine dynamic efficiency of the steady state solution. Let us consider the dynamic equation of per capita consumption. Since $\sigma(t) > 0$ and $c(t) > 0$, the direction of consumption changes over time $\dot{c}$ depends on the sign of $f'(k) - \beta$. Therefore, consumption increases, is constant or decreases according to $f'(k) \gtrless \beta$.

Graphically in the plane $(k, f'(k))$ condition $f'(k) - \beta$ is the distance between the curve of the marginal product of capital and a line parallel to horizontal axis passing through the given value β as pictured in figure 2.4

Figure 2.4 is similar to figure 1.5 of Solow's model. The significant difference here is that the steady state is at the intersection with the β-constant line. To prove dynamic efficiency we must find where steady state k^* locates in respect to golden age per capita capital k_g. Golden age $k = k_g$ solves $f'(k_g) = n$. Since population is stationary, golden age requires $f'(k_g) = 0$. This can also be found directly since $\dot{k} = 0$ implies $c(k) = f(k)$. At

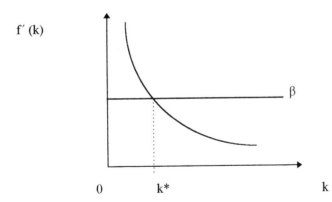

Figure 2.4 Efficiency of steady state

golden age per capita steady state, consumption is maximum, that is k_g is such that $c'(k_g) = f'(k_g) = 0$. When the production function is well-behaved, from Inada conditions it follows that $f'(k_g) = 0$ is possible only when $k_g = +\infty$. Therefore the steady state solution is efficient when $0 < k^* < +\infty$. Efficiency of the steady state in optimal growth models, then, requires only that the solution be meaningful from the economic standpoint.

2.5   Optimal growth model for a decentralized competitive economy

In the previous pages optimal growth paths were described only for a specific economic system. Is it possible to extend the same conclusions to other economic systems? Many of the conditions hypothesized for the former case can be changed without changing the conclusions. First, we can consider a population growing at a constant rate $\dot{L}/L = n > 0$. Second, we can assume a perfectly competitive economy where production decisions are decentralized to a large number of firms, each so small that it cannot influence prices or the evolution of accumulation by itself. Finally, we can disregard the hypothesis that a household's income is derived from uniform income distribution and admit on the contrary that labour and capital receive market remuneration. These modifications involve changes in description of both household behaviour and firm's behaviour.

We shall begin with household behaviour. A household is now considered a dynasty where over the years new births increase the number of family members. In this way we can introduce growth of population without altering the basic structure of the starting model. In fact, increase in the number of family members coincides with the growth of population described by the evolution of the labour force $L(t) = L(0)e^{nt}$. Let us assume the number of households (i.e. dynasties) is stationary over time $H(t) = H$. The members of a single household in each period are the adults of that household $L(t)/H = (L(0)/H)e^{nt}$. Given per capita consumption $c(t)$, a household's consumption is $c(t)[L(t)/H] = [L(0)/H]c(t)e^{nt}$. Likewise, given the individual utility function, a household's instantaneous utility function is $[L(0)/H]u(c(t))e^{nt}$ and the functional objective of a single household is

$$V = [L(0)/H] \int_0^{+\infty} e^{nt}e^{-\beta t}u[c(t)] \, dt$$

A household's income comes from two sources

a) labour income: all members of a household, as formerly, offers their labour inelastically, so that a household's total supply of labour is $L(t)/H$. Since markets are competitive, an individual household assumes that the real wage of each member is given, so that a household's labour income is $w(t)[L(t)/H] = [L(0)/H]w(t)\,e^{nt}$;

b) capital income: capital stock owned by a single individual $k(t)$ is rented to a firm at market price. Each household member receives quasi-rents amounting to $\rho(t)k(t)$ so that $\rho(t)k(t)[L(t)/H] = [L(0)/H]\,\rho(t)k(t)\,e^{nt}$ is the household's capital income.

At each instant t a household's disposable resources are allocated to consumption or saving. The latter indirectly enhances future consumption opportunities by accruing per capita capital. Physical capital is the only possible form in which a household can accumulate saving. A household's savings $s_h(t)$ and its accumulated capital stock $\dot{k}_h(t)$ are related as $s_h(t) - nk_h(t) = \dot{k}_h(t)$. Thus a household member's per capita capital accumulates according to $s_h(t)\,[H/L(t)] - nk(t) = \dot{k}(t)$. A single household's saving is

$$s_h(t) = [L(0)H]w(t)e^{nt} + [L(0)/H]\rho(t)k(t)e^{nt} - [L(0)/H]e^{nt}c(t)$$

The accumulation of a household's members per capita capital obeys the condition

$$\dot{k}(t) = w(t) + k(t)[\rho(t) - n] - c(t)$$

This condition does not preclude that a household could dissipate its wealth over a long period, even over its entire temporal horizon. For the sake of consistency, when households dissipate wealth we must require that dissipation does not exceed initial stock of wealth. Mathematically this means that household's budget constraint must further satisfy the condition

$$[L(0)/H]e^{nt}\int_0^{+\infty}[c(t) - w(t)]e^{-\int_0^\infty[\rho(\tau)-n]d\tau}dt = [L(0)/H]k(0)e^{nt}$$

which in per capita terms is simply

$$\int_0^{+\infty}[c(t) - w(t)]e^{-\int_0^\infty[\rho(\tau)-n]d\tau}dt = k(0)$$

This is known as the 'no-Ponzi-game' condition which states that the excess of consumption over labour income for the entire temporal horizon must be financed by the initial per capita capital stock. This condition limits admissible budget constraints to the subset which further satisfies the transversality condition $\lim\limits_{t\to\infty} k(t)\, e^{-\int_0^t [\rho(\tau)-n]d\tau} = 0$. The no-Ponzi -game condition and the transversality condition are equivalent.[4]

The representative household chooses the optimal path of consumption $c(t)$ by solving the optimal control problem

$$\max V = [L(0)/H]\int_0^{+\infty} e^{nt}\, e^{-\beta t}u[c(t)]dt$$

$$\dot{k}_h = [L(0)/H]e^{nt}\{w(t) + k(t)[\rho(t) - n] - c(t)$$

$$k_h(0) = [L(0)/H]k_0;\; \lim\limits_{t\to\infty}[L(0)/H]k(t)\, e^{n-\int_0^\tau [\rho(\tau)-n]d\tau} = 0$$

Similarly, it can be assumed that the household's objective is to maximize representative individual's welfare.

We adopt the last assumption by formulating the problem

$$\max V = \int_0^{+\infty} e^{-\beta t}\, u[c(t)]dt$$

$$\dot{k} = w(t) + k(t)[\rho(t) - n] - c(t)$$

$$k(0) = k_0;\; \lim\limits_{t\to\infty} k(t)\, e^{-\int_0^t [\rho(\tau)-n]d\tau} = 0$$

First-order conditions for this optimal control problem are

$$e^{-\beta t}\, u'[c(t)] - \lambda(t) = 0$$

$$\dot{k} = w(t) + k(t)[\rho(t) - n] - c(t)$$

$$\dot{\lambda}(t) = -\lambda(t)[\rho(\tau) - n]$$

From the first and the last condition we get

$$-\beta u'[c(t)] + \dot{u}'[c(t)] = -u'[c(t)][\rho(t) - n]$$

so that again we get Euler's equation

$$\frac{\dot{u}'[c(t)]}{u'[c(t)]} = n + \beta - \rho(t)$$

This is the modified golden rule and coincides with the 'pure' Ramsey-Keynes optimal saving rule when $n = 0$.

Concerning firms, production and prices, we make the following assumptions. Firms are finite number F each having access to a production function technology $Q_f = F(K_f, L_f)$ identical for all the firms. The production function admits constant return of scale. Inputs of capital and work are bought from households, at rent price for capital $\rho(t)$ and at real wages w(t) for work. The objective of a firm is to maximize profit over a given horizon. The instantaneous profit function is

$$\pi_f(t) = Q_f(t) - w(t)L_f(t) - \rho(t)K_f(t)$$

Given the discount rate $\delta(t) = \int_0^{+\infty} \rho(t)dt$, the objective functional of a single firm becomes

$$\prod_f = \int_0^{+\infty} e^{-\delta(t)} \pi_f(t)dt$$

By virtue of first degree homogeneity of the production function, the profit function can also be written in per capita terms. Intertemporal choices of representative firms are, therefore, solutions of the following constrained optimal control problem

$$\max_{\{k_f(t),\, L_f(t)\}} \int_0^{+\infty} e^{-\delta(t)} L_f(t)[q_f(t) - w(t) - \rho(t)k_f(t)]dt$$
$$\text{sub}: \quad q_f(t) = f(k_f(t)) \qquad \text{for } t \in [0, +\infty]$$

First order necessary conditions for the maximum of the f-th firm are

$$f'(k_f(t)) - \rho(t) = 0$$
$$f(k_f(t)) - \rho(t)k_f(t) - w(t) = 0$$

Since firms have identical technology and markets are competitive, it easy to go from the micro to the macro level. Indeed

- global output is $Q(t) = \sum_{f=1}^{F} Q_f(t) = \sum_{f=1}^{F} L_f(t)f(k_f(t));$
- from competitiveness and the first of the necessary conditions for a maximum profit it follows that $k = k_f$ each f;
- from the first and the second conditions for maximum profit it follows $f'(k(t)) = \rho(t)$; and $f(k(t)) - k(t)f'(k(t)) = w(t)$; and
- by definition of the aggregate production $Q(t) = L(t)f(k(t))$.

Thus, the production sector of the economic system and prices of capital and labour services are described by the following conditions:

$$q(t) = f(k(t))$$
$$f'(k(t)) = \rho(t)$$
$$f(k(t)) - k(t)f'(k(t)) = w(t)$$

2.6   Equilibrium and dynamics of a competitive economy

Equilibrium requires that output not consumed is demanded by households as physical capital. Therefore, in the aggregate, the equilibrium becomes

$$I(t) = Q(t) - C(t) = \sum_{h=1}^{H} s_h(t)$$

Since $\sum_{h=1}^{H} s_h(t) = L(t)[\dot{k} + nk]$ and $Q(t) - C(t) = L(t)[f(k(t)) - c(t)]$,   the aggregate equilibrium condition in per capita terms becomes $f(k(t)) - c(t) = \dot{k}(t) + nk(t)$, or

$$\dot{k}(t) = f(k(t)) - c(t) - nk(t)$$

This is ultimately the same dynamic equation as that of Solow's model.

We have already specified the behaviour of households. If we also take into account first-order conditions of their optimal problem, the equilibrium dynamics of decentralized competitive economy is described by the differential equations

$$\dot{k}(t) = f(k(t)) - c(t) - nk(t)$$

$$\dot{c}(t) = \frac{c(t)}{\sigma(t)}[f'(k(t)) - (n + \beta)]$$

$$k(0) = k_0; \quad \lim_{t \to \infty} k(t)\, e^{-\int_0^t [f(k(\tau)) - n]d\tau} = 0$$

where the second equation takes account of Euler's equation $\frac{u''(t)c(t)\dot{c}(t)}{u'(t)c(t)} = n + \beta - \rho(t)$ together with the competitiveness condition $\rho(t) = f'(k(t))$. We will study the dynamics of this system by examining the phase curves in the phase plane (k, c).

First, let us consider the locus $\dot{k} = 0$. In the phase plane (k, c) the corresponding equation is $c(k) = f(k) - nk$. It has the following properties:

1. $c'(k) = f'(k) - n$; $c(0) = f(0)$; and $c''(k) = f''(k)$. Consequently, $c(k)$ starts from the origin, because $c(0) = f(0) = 0$. Moreover, due to the Inada condition $f'(0) = +\infty$, $c(k)$ increases at the origin, reaches its maximum at $k = k_g$ where $f'(k_g) - n = 0$, and increases when $k < k_g$, and decreases when $k > k_g$;
2. $c(k)$ crosses the horizontal axis at point $(k^{**}, 0)$, where k^{**} verifies $f(k^{**}) - nk^{**} = 0$, and is concave over the entire interval $[0, k^{**}]$ since $f''(k) < 0$ for $k \geq 0$.

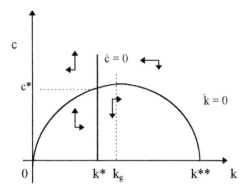

Figure 2.5   Dynamics of a competitive economy

It is easier to study the locus $\dot{c} = 0$ because it corresponds to equation $k = k^*$, where k^* is such that $f'(k^*) - (n + \beta) = 0$. Notice that $f'(k_g) - n < f'(k^*) = (n + \beta)$. Since $f'(k)$ decreases, $k^* < k_g$. Therefore, the line $k - k^*$ locates to the left of the golden rule capital stock k_g where per capita consumption c is maximum. Putting all this information together we obtain figure 2.5.

Qualitative information about the characteristic curves are inferred by assigning orientation to the points out of the loci $\dot{k} = \dot{c} = 0$. Let us denote $c(k)$ the $\dot{k} = 0$ locus and note that we can write $\dot{k} = c(k) - c$. Thus $\dot{k} > 0$ for $c < c(k)$, that is k increases at points where c is below the $c(k)$ curve and decreases at points above the $c(k)$ curve. On the other hand, for the $k = k^*$ locus the same considerations of the model with stationary population are still valid. Thus the orientation of the points out of the phase curve that pass through the steady state is that indicated by the arrows in figure 2.5 in each of the four sectors the plane (k, c) is divided by the $\dot{k} = 0$, $\dot{c} = 0$ curves. Since $1/\sigma(t) \neq 0$, figure 2.5 also shows there are at least three steady states corresponding to the points $(0, 0)$, $(k^{**}, 0)$, (k^*, c^*), where $k^{**} > 0$; $k^* > 0$, $c^* > 0$. The picture suggests that there are paths pointing to (k^*, c^*), because two regions have arrows pointing toward this solution.

To verify this conjecture we must study the stability of solution (k^*, c^*). Linear approximation around the steady state gives

$$\dot{k} = [f'(k^*) - n](k - k^*) - (c - c^*)$$
$$\dot{c} = \frac{c^* f''(k^*)}{\sigma^*}(k - k^*)$$

where dependence on t is understood. The Jacobian matrix of this system is

$$
\begin{bmatrix}
f'(k^*) - n & -1 \\
\dfrac{c^*f''(k^*)}{\sigma^*} & 0
\end{bmatrix}
$$

and $\det J = \dfrac{c^*f''(k^*)}{\sigma^*} < 0;\ \operatorname{tr} J = f'(k^*) - n = \beta > 0.$

The associated characteristic equation is

$$
\mu^2 - \operatorname{tr}J\mu + \det J = \mu^2 - \beta\mu + \frac{c^*f''(k^*)}{\sigma^*} = 0
$$

Since $\dfrac{c^*f''(k^*)}{\sigma^*} < 0$ and $\triangle = \beta^2 - 4\dfrac{c^*f''(k^*)}{\sigma^*} > 0$ we can apply Descartes' rule and deduce that one root is positive. This is the mathematical confirmation that (k^*, c^*) is a saddle point and therefore it admits only one convergent path. We can now proceed by deducing the equation of the unique path convergent to the steady state (k^*, c^*). Let μ_1 and μ_2 be the roots of the characteristic equation, and let be $\mu_1 > 0$.

The general solution of the dynamic system (see Mathematical Appendixes) is

$$
k(t) = k^* + a_1 v_{11} e^{\mu_1 t} + a_2 v_{21} e^{\mu_2 t}
$$
$$
c(t) = c^* + a_1 v_{12} e^{\mu_1 t} + a_2 v_{22} e^{\mu_2 t}
$$

Here a_1 and a_2 are arbitrary constants, that must be determined. The v_{ij} are the components of eigenvectors $(v_{11}, v_{12})^T$ and $(v_{21}, v_{22})^T$ associated with eigenvalues μ_1 and μ_2. The set of eigenvectors associated with μ_1 and μ_2 must contain the (column) eigenvectors $v_1 = (\mu_1 \dfrac{\sigma^*}{c^*f''(k^*)}, 1);\ v_2 = (\mu_2 \dfrac{\sigma^*}{c^*f''(k^*)}, 1).$[5] By substituting, the solution to the linearized dynamic system becomes

$$
k(t) = k^* + a_1 \mu_1 \frac{\sigma^*}{c^*f''(k^*)} e^{\mu_1 t} + a_2 \mu_2 \frac{\sigma^*}{c^*f''(k^*)} e^{\mu_2 t}
$$
$$
c(t) = c^* + a_1 e^{\mu_1 t} + a_2 e^{\mu_2 t}
$$

Arbitrary constants a_1 and a_2 are now determined by admitting that it is possible to exclude paths which diverge from steady state from the set of optimal paths. This is the same as imposing $\lim_{t \to \infty} k(t) - k^* = \lim_{t \to \infty} c(t) - c^* = 0$, that is

$$\lim_{t\to\infty} [a_1\mu_1 \frac{\sigma^*}{c^*f''(k^*)}e^{\mu_1 t} + a_2\mu_2 \frac{\sigma^*}{c^*f''(k^*)}e^{\mu_2 t}] = 0$$

$$\lim_{t\to\infty} a_1 e^{\mu_1 t} + a_2 e^{\mu_2 t} = 0$$

Since μ_1 is positive, these two conditions are verified only if $a_1 = 0$. In this case the convergent solution is

$$k(t) = k^* + a_2\mu_2 \frac{\sigma^*}{c^*f''(k^*)}e^{\mu_2 t}$$

$$c(t) = c^* + a_2 e^{\mu_2 t}$$

For $t = 0$ and $k(0) = k_0$ from the first condition we get $a_2 = \frac{c^*f''(k^*)}{\sigma^*\mu_2}(k_0\text{-}k^*)$, so that

$$c(0) - c^* = \frac{c^*f''(k^*)}{\sigma^*\mu_2}[k_0 - k^*]$$

Therefore, the only convergent path corresponds to the equation

$$c - c^* = \frac{c^*f''(k^*)}{\sigma^*\mu_2}[k - k^*]$$

This is the equation of a line which passes through the origin and has a positive slope. Deprived of steady state, it describes two half-lines with opposite orientations. The direction of movement depends on the sign of $k - k^*$, that is $c < c^*$ if $k < k^*$, and vice-versa. Since steady state is a saddle point, the stable path is an asymptote in respect to the characteristic curves. This can be deduced by considering the limit

$$\lim_{t\to\infty} \frac{c(t)}{k(t)} = \lim_{t\to\infty} \frac{c^* + a_1 e^{\mu_1 t} + a_2 e^{\mu_2 t}}{k^* + a_1\mu_1 \frac{\sigma^*}{c^*f''(k^*)}e^{\mu_1 t} + a_2\mu_2 \frac{\sigma^*}{c^*f''(k^*)}e^{\mu_2 t}}$$

which can be rewritten

$$\lim_{t\to\infty} \frac{c^* e^{-\mu_1 t} + a_1 + a_2 e^{(\mu_1-\mu_2)t}}{k^* e^{-\mu_1 t} + a_1\mu_1 \frac{\sigma^*}{c^*f''(k^*)} + a_2\mu_2 \frac{\sigma^*}{c^*f''(k^*)}e^{(\mu_1-\mu_2)t}}$$

This limit is $\frac{c^*f''(k^*)}{\mu_2}$ when $a_1 = 0$, that is, it coincides with the slope of the line convergent to steady state (k^*, c^*). The dynamics of the system are depicted in figure 2.6

The possibility of excluding from the optimal path those divergent from the single meaningful steady state (k^*, c^*) becomes a property of optimal dynamic equilibrium models due to the assumed validity of the

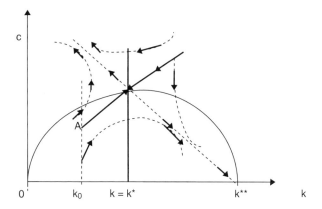

Figure 2.6 Saddle path dynamics of steady state

transversality condition. To see this let us refer to the following formulation of transversality condition $\lim_{t\to\infty} e^{-\beta t} u'[c(t)]k(t) = 0$. Since $\beta > 0$, we can exclude paths for which $u'[c(t)] \to \infty$ and $k(t) \to \infty$. However we cannot exclude paths that entail $k(t) \to k \neq k^*$ and $c(t) \to 0$. Suppose then that $\lim_{t\to\infty} k(t) \neq k^*$. In this case we must have $\lim_{t\to\infty} k(t) = 0$ or $\lim_{t\to\infty} k(t) = k^{**}$. In the phase plane (k, c) paths that do not converge to steady state (k*, c*) will evolve as indicated in figure 2.6, so that they cross the vertical axis c and take the value c = 0, or they cross the horizontal axis at k** where c= 0.

The null value of per capita consumption violates Euler's equation, which is a necessary condition for optimality. In effect, given the Inada conditions, when $c(t) \to 0$ Euler's equation would imply $\mu'/\lim_{c\to 0} u' = 0$ but instead we must have $\dot{u}'/u'(0) > 0$. We can also add that $c(t) = f(0) = 0$ for k= 0. By virtue of the uniqueness of the path associated with a given initial condition, it is not optimal for the economy, given $k(0) = k_0$, to choose an initial consumption $c(0) = c_0$ corresponding to a path which asymptotically entails $\lim_{t\to\infty} k(t) = 0$ or $\lim_{t\to\infty} k(t) = k^{**}$. Therefore, an economy that keeps a transversality condition and reflects optimal choices of rational agents will choose an initial consumption on the only path which converges toward an economically meaningful steady state (k*, c *).

Another point to be considered concerns the dynamic efficiency of the steady state. So far we have referred to the transversality condition $\lim_{t\to\infty} e^{-\beta t} u'[c(t)]k(t) = 0$. But in the optimal control problem we have

formulated the transversality condition as $\lim_{t\to\infty} k(t)e^{-\int_0^t[p(\tau)-n]d\tau} = 0$.
Therefore the validity of the previous reasoning depends on the
equivalence between these two formulations of the transversality
condition. We will demonstrate this equivalence exists and that it entails
convergence of the component $e^{-\int_0^t[\rho(\tau)-n]d\tau}$, which in turn implies
dynamic efficiency of the stable steady state path. The equivalence
between the two transversality conditions is shown as follows. The
magnitude $e^{-\int_0^t[\rho(\tau)-n]d\tau} = \lambda(t)$ is the shadow price of household savings. It
evolves over time according to

$$\dot{\lambda}(t) = d[e^{-\int_0^t[\rho(\tau)-n]d\tau}]/dt = -[\rho(t)-n]\,e^{-\int_0^t[\rho(t)-n]d\tau} = -[\rho(t)-n]\lambda(t)$$

This condition, together with $\lambda(t) = e^{-\beta t}u'[c(t)]$, is a necessary condition
for the optimal control problem of households. Therefore the transversality condition can also be written as

$$\lim_{t\to\infty} \lambda(t)k(t) = \lim_{t\to\infty} e^{-\beta t}u'(c(t))k(t) = \lim_{t\to\infty} k(t)e^{-\int_0^t[\rho^t(\tau))-n]d\tau} = 0.$$

Let us now refer to the transversality condition $\lim_{t\to\infty} k(t)e^{-\int_0^t[\rho(\tau)-n]d\tau} = 0$.
Competitiveness of the economy entails $\rho(t) = f'(k(t))$. When $\lim_{t\to\infty} k(t)$ is
finite, in order for $\lim_{t\to\infty} e^{-\int_0^t[p(\tau)-n]d\tau} = 0$, as the transversality condition
requires, $f'(k) > n$. This is the same as the condition for dynamic efficiency
$0 < k < k_g$. This completes our examination of the existence, stability and
efficiency of the steady state of a competitive economy.

2.7   Central planner optimum: Pareto optimality and dynamic efficiency

In this section we discuss the concept of dynamic efficiency in more
detail. Up to now we have adopted Phelps-Koopmans' criterion (Phelps,
1966; Koopmans, 1965), subsequently generalized by Cass (1972). This
efficiency criterion excludes from optimal steady states those states
entailing over-accumulation of per capita capital. However microeconomic models of static general (Walrasian) equilibrium uses Pareto-
optimality as the efficiency criterion. According to Walrasian tradition, a
general equilibrium state is efficient if the allocation of resources is a
Pareto-optimum. An allocation of resources is a Pareto-optimum if by
reallocating the given resources the welfare of at least one agent can not be

increased without lowering the welfare of any other agent. Two equivalent methods are generally adopted for detecting conditions for Pareto-optimum. Both methods assume a central-planner economy where a benevolent central-planner, who has complete information about preferences and technology of the economy, is in charge of reallocating available resources. A benevolent central-planner solves the optimal programming problem of maximizing community welfare under the constraint of available resources and technology. In pursuing this goal, the central-planner can

a) maximize a social welfare function which depends on individual utility of agents; or
b) maximize the utility of one agent, given the utility level of the other agents.

In a disaggregate context with heterogeneous preferences, methodo-logy (a) can be considered the same as (b). However, methodology (a) seems to be more appropriate in an aggregate context where it is assumed that there is a representative agent. Therefore, we shall assume that the central-planner wants to maximize the welfare functional over the set of feasible intertemporal per capita consumption allocations, subject to the rule of accumulation of per capita capital stock. Thus, the central-planner solves the following optimal control problem

$$\max V = \int_0^{+\infty} e^{-\beta t} u[c(t)]dt$$
$$\dot{k} = f(k(t)) - nk(t) - c(t); \ k(0) = k_o; 0 < c(t) < \infty;$$
$$k(t) \geq 0; \lim_{t \to +\infty} e^{-\beta t} u'[c(t)]k(t) = 0$$

This command optimal control problem is similar to the one of representative households in a decentralized competitive economy. This similarity shows that optimal paths of a competitive economy also are Pareto-optimal intertemporal allocations. There is a substantial analogy to the well-known second theorem of welfare economics, which states that a Pareto optimum can be obtained as a competitive equilibrium. However, because of the intertemporal context, the analogy is only partial. Indeed, to the static equality between relevant substitution and transformation rates, we must add the intertemporal condition that the rate of growth of population must be lesser than the real rate of interest.

2.8   Comparative dynamics: changes in technology and in preferences

In the Ramsey model with an infinite temporal horizon, exogenous parameters outside agents' choices are preferences and technology, as in Solow's model. Comparative dynamic exercises permit the evaluation of the effects of changes in preferences and technology. We bear in mind that dynamic comparative analysis, by analogy to static comparative analysis, consists of comparing two dynamic systems which differ for the value assigned to any parameter. However, in a dynamic context, in addition to the steady state, transitional paths to a steady state are also influenced by changes in parameters. Therefore, we need to distinguish between the impact effects, which are a response, instant by instant, of the relevant magnitudes and the long-run effects, which are a response of steady states. The following differential equations account for once and for all changes of parameters of a dynamic competitive economy

$$\dot{k}(t) = f(k(t), a) - c(t) - nk(t)$$
$$\dot{c}(t) = [c(t)/\sigma(t)][f'(k(t), a) - n + \beta)]$$
$$k(0) = k_0; \ \lim_{t \to \infty} k(t) \, e^{-\int_0^t [f'(k(\tau)) - n] d\tau} = 0$$

The equations include a parameter, a, whose changes indicate changes in technology. To be concise we will deal only with the long run effects, by considering steady state system

$$c = f(k, a) - nk$$
$$f'(k, a) = n + \beta$$

By differentiating totally with respect to technological parameter a, we get

$$dc = [f'_k(dk/da) + f'_a - n(dk/da)]da$$
$$[f''_k(dk/da) + f''_a]da = 0$$

From the second equation we obtain $dk/da = -f''_a/f''_k$. By substituting into the first equation we get

$$dc/da = -(f''_a/f''_k)(n - f'_k) + f'_a = -\beta(f''_a/f''_k) + f'_a$$

We distinguish technological shocks that do or do not modify steady state per capita capital stock. When $dk/da = 0$ we have $dc/da = f'_a$. Therefore, if a technological shock appears as an increase of per capita output, it leaves unchanged steady state per capita capital but allows for a large steady state

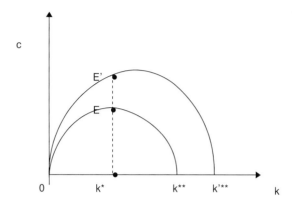

Figure 2.7 Effects of a technological shock that leaves unchanged steady state capital stock

per capita consumption. Graphically this new situation is indicated by point E' in figure 2.7

Conversely, a technological shock that increases per capita output $f'_a > 0$ and also entails a larger marginal product of capital $f''_a > 0$ has a positive final effect on per capita steady state consumption $dc/da > 0$ even greater than in the previous case. Graphically this new steady state corresponds to point E' in figure 2.8

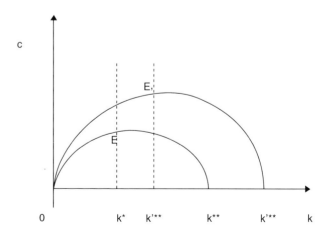

Figure 2.8 Effects of a technological shock that changes steady state capital stock

So far comparative analysis, by referring to once and for all changes, traces comparative static analysis. However, this is unsatisfactory since, in a growth context, it is more appropriate to handle technological changes as a process. In another section we shall deal with technological changes as a technological process. At the moment is more useful to extend the previous dynamic comparative analysis to changes in preferences, represented by the parameter β. Let us differentiate the steady state system with respect to β

$$dc/d\beta = (f'_k - n)(dk/d\beta)$$
$$d\beta = f''_k d\beta (dk/d\beta)$$

From the second equation we obtain $dk/d\beta = 1/f''_k < 0$. By substituting into the first equation we get

$$dc/d\beta = (f'_k - n)/f''_k$$

Therefore, an increase of the utility factor discounting β entails both less steady state per capita capital stock and less steady state per capita consumption. The situation described in Figure 2.9 corresponds to a shift to left of the locus $c = 0$, so that a new steady state equilibrium is at point E'.

We can give also an intuitive illustration of the impact–effects of an increase of β. In figure 2.9, since the steady state is on the stable branch of a saddle point, the location of E' to the left of E requires that the location of the new stable branch be to the left. Thus, initial consumption must jump to the value required for the economy to follow the new convergent path. It follows that initially per capita consumption increases but after some time it approximates the new steady state consumption by

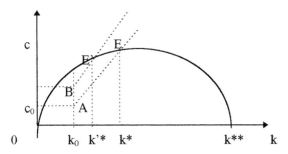

Figure 2.9 Effects of an increase in the utility factor discounting and transitional dynamics

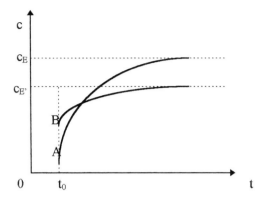

Figure 2.10 Dynamics of per capita consumption after an increase in the utility factor discounting

following a path below that of the original path. This is pictured in figure 2.10

It is evident that, with the necessary changes, figure 2.10 is similar to figure 1.7 (see chapter 1) which shows the effects of a decrease in propensity to save in the Solow's model. Contrary to Solow's model, here propensity to save is variable, $s(k, c) = [f(k) - c]/f(k) = 1 - [c/f(k)]$. By differentiating with respect to time we obtain

$$\dot{s} = -[\dot{c}f(k) - cf'(k)\dot{k}]/f(k)^2 = -[c/f(k)][(\dot{c}/c) - \alpha_k \dot{k}/k]$$

Rates $(\dot{c}/c)$, and $(\dot{k}/k)$ are variable along the transition paths, so they can have any combination of signs.

Consequently even $\dot{s}$ can be positive or negative. Thus in models of optimal growth the direction of changes in propensity to save has no particular significance. On the other hand, in these models steady state equilibrium is efficient. Therefore the question of greater or lesser propensity to save, so important in Solow's model for choosing dynamic efficient steady states, becomes irrelevant in the model under consideration.

2.9 Effects of fiscal policy in the model of competitive economy

By including government in the model of a decentralized competitive economy we are able to analyze the effects of alternative fiscal policies on optimal consumption and capital accumulation paths. A government decision regarding taxation and public spending is not dependent on the choices of private agents. Therefore taxation and government spending are exogenous parameters for private agents. However, this does not mean that government decisions are totally arbitrary. Like any other agent, a government runs a budget constraint which limits its set of feasible actions. Mathematically a government budget constraint differs in different fiscal regimes. It is useful to distinguish:

a) on the side of taxation, between
   a_1 – lump-sum taxation; and
   a_2 – proportional taxation on income of factors of production;
b) on the side of spending, between
   b_1 – public spending entirely financed by taxation, and
   b_2 – public spending financed by deficit. Deficit, in turn, can be financed by an interest-bearing public debt (bonds) or by a barren debt (money).

The simplest case to analyze is government spending financed entirely by lump-sum taxation. Assuming the absence of initial debt, the government's instantaneous budget constraint in per capita real terms is

$$g(t) = G(T)/L(t) = T(t)/L(t) = \theta(t)$$

government spending $g(t)$ is assumed to be devoted exclusively to public consumption, so it does not affect the future output of the economy. However, government spending does affect the utility of the representative agent. Therefore the utility functional of the representative agent must be modified, since the current consumption bundle is now composed of private consumption and government-provided goods. Taxation, on the contrary, affects a household's disposable income and therefore affects savings. These influences affect the description of a household's behaviour. The household budget constraint including taxation becomes

$$s_h(t) = [L(0)/H]e^{nt}[w(t) + \rho(t)k(t) - c(t) - \theta(t)]$$

and household capital accumulation is

$$\dot{k}_h(t) = [L(0)/H]e^{nt}\{w(t) + [\rho(t) - n]k(t) - c(t) - \theta(t)\}$$

This in per capita terms equals

$$\dot{k}(t) = w(t) + [\rho(t) - n]k(t) - c(t) - \theta(t)$$

The household functional is now

$$V = [L(0)/H\}] \int_0^{+\infty} e^{(n-\beta)t} v[c(t), g(t)] dt$$

The rate of substitutability between private and public consumption can be defined by reconsidering consumption as a 'composite' basket $c_c(t)$ (Barro, 1981, 1989). We assume this composite basket

$$c_c(t) = c(t) + \delta g(t), \text{ where } 0 \le \delta \le 1.$$

Trivially, since instantaneous utility is $v(c_c(t))$, $\partial v/\partial c = dv/dc_c$ and $\partial v/\partial g = (dv/dc_c)\delta$, the marginal rate of substitution between private and public consumption is $(\partial v/\partial g)/(\partial v/\partial c) = \delta$. A common assumption excludes any interaction between private consumption and public consumption, that is $\partial^2 v/\partial c \partial g = \partial^2 v/\partial g \partial c = 0$. An instantaneous utility function having this property is the separable additive function

$$v[c(t), g(t)] = u(c(t)) + u_g(g(t))$$

For this utility function one deduces $\dfrac{\partial v/\partial g}{\partial v/\partial c} = \dfrac{u'}{u'_g}$. When $\dfrac{u'}{u'_g} = \delta$, the previous case is included as a particular case. Thus, if we assume that marginal utility of private consumption is not influenced by public spending we can refer to the utility functional of a representative household as

$$V = [L(0)/H][\int_0^{+\infty} e^{(n-\beta)t} u(c(t) dt + \int_0^{+\infty} e^{(n-\beta)t} u_g(g(t)) dt]$$

Since the second component of the functional depends on public goods, a representative household can maximize $V(.)$ by maximizing only the component referring to private consumption. Therefore, the household optimal control problem is

$$\max V = \int_0^{+\infty} e^{-\beta t} u(c(t) dt$$

$$\dot{k}(t) = w(t) + [\rho(t) - n]k(t) - c(t) - \theta(t)$$

$$k(0) = k_0; \; \lim_{t \to \infty} k(t) e^{-\int_0^t [\rho(\tau) - n] d\tau} = 0$$

In a competitive economy prices of inputs are $f'(k(t)) = \rho(t)$; $f(k(t)) - k(t) f'(k(t)) = w(t)$. Due to the government budget constraint $g(t) = \theta(t)$, the necessary conditions for optimal control give the dynamic equations

$$\dot{k}(t) = f(k(t)) - c(t) - g(t) - nk(t)$$

$$\dot{c}(t) = \frac{c(t)}{\sigma(t)}[f'(k(t)) - (n + \beta)]$$

These, together with the initial condition of per capita capital stock and the transversality condition, describe the intertemporal equilibrium of an economy. We are now able to ascertain how public spending influences the dynamics of per capita private consumption. The hypothesized fiscal policy acts as a withdrawal from the households resources. Let us suppose $g(t) = g$ and consider a steady state solution. Now the locus $\dot{k} = 0$ is $c = f(k) - g - nk$, whereas the locus $\dot{c} = 0$ is the same $k = k^*$ as in the absence of government. With respect to the case where there is no government intervention the locus $\dot{k} = 0$ differs for the amount of government spending. The corresponding curve in Figure 2.11 shows that, for equal per capita capital stock, per capita consumption is uniformly reduced by the amount of taxation θ, equal to public spending g, and government spending entirely crowds out private spending.

Figure 2.11 can also be used to illustrate the effects of increases in public spending. Indeed the locus $\dot{k} = 0$ located higher in the plane (k, c) corresponds to $g(t) = g = 0$, so that when $g > 0$ steady state equilibrium passes from point E to point E'. We can also distinguish impact effects from long-run effects. To do this, assume the economy is at steady state E. We already know that when public spending permanently increases, per capita consumption responds by instantaneously jumping to the level needed to locate the system on the unique path convergent to the new

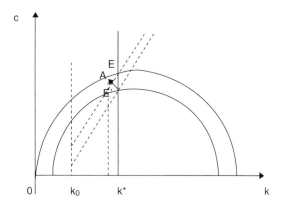

Figure 2.11   Effects of an increase in government spending

steady state. The economy, then, does not show impact effects. The case is different when the initial position differs from the steady state or the increase in public spending is transitory. In the latter simpler case, suppose $g(t) = g(t_0) = g(T) = g > 0$ and $g(t) = 0$ for $t > T$. During the interval $[t_0, T]$ the economy accumulates capital according to the rule

$$\dot{k}(t) = f(k(t)) - c(t) - g - nk(t)$$

Consumption $c(t)$ at instant t_0 must locate at a level from which dynamics follows the path convergent to the steady state for $g = 0$. For example, let us suppose that in Figure 2.11 the economy is at E and that the instantaneous jump of consumption leads the system precisely to E′, the steady state which prevails when $g(t) = g > 0$. We know that ultimately $g(t) = 0$ at $t > T$. Hence, forces operating at point E′ will push the system toward, for example, point A, from which the path convergent to steady state E departs. The dynamics of capital accumulation runs according to Figure 2.12.

Let us now examine the case of public deficit financed by an issue of government bonds. Let $b(t)$ be per capita public debt in real terms and $d(t)$ per capita government deficit in real terms. When the population grows at rate n, the relationship between growth of per capita public debt and deficit is [6]

$$\dot{b}(t) = d(t) - nb(t)$$

At every instant the per capita public deficit has two components, primary deficit $g(t) - \theta(t)$ and per capita interest service on current debt $\rho(t)b(t)$, that is

$$d(t) = [g(t) - \theta(t)] + \rho(t)b(t)$$

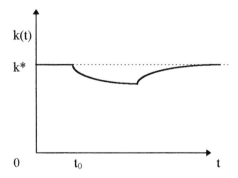

Figure 2.12 Dynamics of per capita capital stock

Therefore the equation for accumulation of public debt is

$$\dot{b}(t) = g(t) - \theta(t) + [\rho(t) - n]b(t)$$

This equation, together with a transversality condition, gives rise to a government intertemporal constraint. Indeed, as in the case of households, it is reasonable to exclude from feasible spending and taxation those paths which show indefinite accumulation of public debt over time. On the other hand, initial debt $b(0)$ is a historical fact. If, as is plausible, $b(0) > 0$, government can play a game which involves indefinite maintenance of the initial debt. To do this is sufficient to generate a primary surplus for the amount needed so that $b(t) = b(0)$ for every t. To exclude both indefinite accumulation of debt and rolling over the initial debt, government spending and taxation programmes must satisfy

$$\int_0^\infty [\theta(t) - g(t)]e^{-\int_0^t [\rho(\tau) - n]d\tau} dt = -b(0)$$

which is equivalent to transversality condition $\lim_{t\to\infty} b(t)e^{-\int_0^t [\rho(\tau)-n]d\tau} = 0^7$.

Debt financing of the deficit further modifies a household's budget constraint. Indeed a public debt which bears positive interest provides households with another instrument, besides physical capital, for accumulating savings. For a household the relationship between savings and accumulation of wealth is

$$\dot{k}_h(t) + \dot{b}_h(t) = s_h(t) - n[k_h(t) + b_h(t)]$$

Household savings s_h is the surplus of disposable income net of per household taxation $\theta_h(t)$. Since $\theta_h(t) = [L(0)/H]e^{nt}\theta(t)$; $k_h(t) = [L(0)/H]e^{nt}k(t)$; and $b_h(t) = [L(0)/H]e^{nt}b(t)$, the relationship for the accumulation of per capita wealth becomes

$$\dot{k}(t) + \dot{b}(t) = w(t) + [\rho(t) - n][k(t) + b(t)] - c(t) - \theta(t)$$

Necessary first-order conditions for optimal control of a representative agent, the exclusion of 'Ponzi-game' and competitiveness of the economy allow us to describe the dynamics of a decentralized system through the equations

$$\dot{k}(t) + \dot{b}(t) = f(k(t)) + [f'(k(t)) - n]b(t) - c(t) - \theta(t) - nk(t)$$

$$\dot{b}(t) = g(t) + [f'(k(t)) - n]b(t) - \theta(t)$$

$$\dot{c}(t) = \frac{c(t)}{\sigma(t)}[f'(k(t)) - (n + \beta)]$$

$$k(0) = k_0, b(0) = b_0, \lim_{t\to\infty} k(t)e^{-\int_0^t [\rho(\tau)-n]d\tau} = 0, \ \lim_{t\to\infty} b(t)e^{-\int_0^t [\rho(\tau')-n]d\tau} = 0.$$

However, private agents know that government does not play the Ponzi game so we can substitute $\dot{b}(t)$ into the relationship of growth of wealth and the dynamics of the system becomes

$$\dot{k}(t) = f(k(t)) - c(t) - g(t) - nk(t)$$

$$\dot{c}(t) = \frac{c(t)}{\sigma(t)}[f'(k(t)) - (n + \beta)]$$

With the appropriate transversality condition for per capita capital stock, this system is identical to the one where government spending is entirely financed by taxation. This identity seems to be the most effective way to demonstrate 'Ricardian neutrality' or 'Ricardian equivalence' (reproposed by Barro, 1974). Indeed, a given path of public spending g(t) has exactly the same influence on per capita capital accumulation and on per capita consumption paths independent of whether government spending is financed by public debt or by lump-sum taxation. This assertion has been debated on both theoretical and empirical grounds (Barro 1974; Bernheim 1987).

In order to verify its theoretical soundness we must determine whether the Ricardian equivalence is valid under all fiscal regimes and, in particular, whether it is valid when taxation is not lump-sum. Let us suppose that taxation is proportional to incomes from capital, labour and the interest on public debt. Let θ_k be the tax rate as a percentage of income from physical capital and bonds which are perfect substitutes for savings. Furthermore let θ_L be the tax rate on income from labour and x be the per capita lump-sum transfer. The households budget constraint now is

$$[L(0)/H]e^{nt}[\dot{k}(t) + \dot{b}(t) + c(t)] = [L(0)/H]e^{nt}\{(1 - \theta_L(t))w(t) +$$
$$[\rho(t)(1 - \theta_k(t)) - n][k(t) + b(t)] + x(t)\}$$

which gives the following equation for accumulation of per capita wealth

$$\dot{k}(t) + \dot{b}(t) = (1 - \theta_L(t))w(t) + [\rho(t)(1 - \theta_k(t)) - n][k(t) + b(t)] + x(t) - c(t)$$

The objective of the representative household is to maximize the welfare of its representative member, so that the problem of representative households reduces to the optimal control problem

$$\max V = \int_0^{+\infty} e^{-\beta t}u[c(t)]dt$$

$$\dot{k}(t) + \dot{b}(t) = (1 - \theta_L(t))w(t) + [\rho(t)(1 - \theta_k(t)) - n][k(t) + b(t)] + x(t) - c(t)$$

$$k(0) = k_0; b(0) = b_0; \lim_{t\to\infty} k(t)e^{-\int_0^t [\rho(\tau)(1-\theta_k)-n]d\tau} = 0;$$

$$\lim_{t\to\infty} b(t)e^{-\int_0^t [\rho(\tau)(1-\theta_k)-n]d\tau} = 0$$

The equation for government accumulation of the per capita debt is

$$\dot{b}(t) = d(t) - nb(t)$$

but now the per capita deficit is

$$d(t) = g(t) + x(t) + \rho(t)b(t) - \theta_L(t)w(t) - [\theta_k(t)\rho(t)][k(t) + b(t)]$$

First-order necessary conditions for the optimal control problem of a representative agent are

$$u'(c(t)) = \lambda(t)$$
$$\dot{k}(t) + \dot{b}(t) = (1 - \theta_L(t))w(t) + \{\rho(t)\}[1 - \theta_k(t)] - n\}[k(t) + b(t)] + x(t) - c(t)$$
$$- \beta\lambda(t) + \dot{\lambda}(t) = -\lambda(t)\{\rho(t)[1 - \theta_k(t)] - n\}$$

Eulers equation is

$$\dot{u}'[c(t)]/u'[c(t)] = n + \beta - \rho(t)[1 - \theta_k(t)]$$

From the equation for government accumulation of per capita public debt, the dynamic equations of a competitive economy reduce to

$$\dot{k}(t) - f(k(t)) \quad c(t) \quad g(t) \quad nk(t)$$
$$\dot{c}(t) = \frac{c(t)}{\sigma(t)}\{[1 - \theta_k(t)]f'(k(t)) - (n + \beta)\}$$

The equation of accumulation of capital no longer coincides with that for a dynamic system with lump-sum taxation. The steady state is

$$c = f(k) - nk - g$$
$$f'(k) = \frac{n + \beta}{1 - \theta_k}$$

Since $1-\theta_k < 1$ it follows that $f'(k) > n + \beta$ and since $f'(k)$ is decreasing, this means that $k < k^*$, where k^* is steady state per capital when taxation is lump-sum, with or without public debt. With respect to a system with lump-sum taxation, then, the locus $\dot{c} = 0$ locates to left in plane (k, c) as shown in Figure 2.13.

Taxation proportional to income influences both accumulation and steady state levels of per capita capital stock and consumption so the Ricardian neutrality is refuted. From this refutation an active policy for capital accumulation becomes admissible. In fact, let us suppose $\theta_k < 0$. A negative tax rate indicates a subsidy to capital that is financed through debt. In this case the steady state condition on consumption yields $1 - \theta_k > 1, f'(k) < f(k^*)$, hence $k > k^*$.

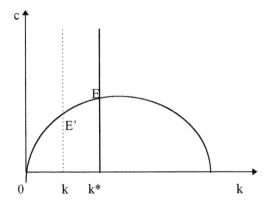

Figure 2.13 Effects of taxation proportional to incomes from factors

A government policy of transfers proportional to capital can lead to steady state characterized by both greater per capita consumption and per capita capital. However this can also lead the economy to a state of *dynamic inefficiency* in which capital stock is over-accumulated. For this to occur the government need only fix the subsidy rate $\theta_k < 0$ such that $f'(k) < f'(k_g)$, that is $-\theta_k > (\beta/n)$. Obviously, this condition must be qualified according to the ways subsidies to capital are financed. Indeed, while the conclusions remain true when subsidies are financed through taxation on consumption, they must be reconsidered when taxation weighs on labour income. We shall not go more deeply into these problems. We shall merely note that a probability of dynamic inefficiency due to a policy of capital incentive is greater when the population growth rate is lower and the rate of temporal preference is higher, situations that are empirically observable in most developed countries.

Another comment can be added if we look at transversality conditions, for both the households and the government and if we refer to the interest rate net of taxation. An economically meaningful steady state requires $f'(k) > n/(1 - \theta_k)$. However this condition is not sufficient to exclude inefficient dynamic equilibria, as it was in the absence of taxation. Indeed, nothing prevents the government from fixing a rate of incentives such that steady state per capita capital verifies $n > f'(k) > n/(1 - \theta_k)$. This condition includes $-\theta_k > (\beta/n)$ and hence the possibility that a steady state is dynamically inefficient.

2.10   The model of a competitive economy with technological progress

In this section we briefly describe the model of a competitive economy that incorporates labour-saving technological progress. In this case the aggregate production function is $Q(t) = F(K(t), A(t)L(t))$ where $A(t)$ is the technological progress index and the growth rate is $\dot{A}(t)/A(t) = \omega$. Degree one homogeneity of the production function allows us to express the variables in terms of effective labour units $L_e(t) = A(t)L(t)$, so that the production sector is described by the following equations

$$q_e(t) = f(k_e(t))$$
$$f'(k_e(t)) = \rho(t)$$
$$f(k_e(t)) - k_e(t)f'(k_e(t)) = w(t)$$

The disposable income of the representative household comes from labour and capital. In terms of effective units of labour we have, respectively, $w(t)[L_e(t)/H]$ and $\rho(t)k_e(t)[L_e(t)/H]$. A representative household accumulates effective capital according to the relationship

$$\dot{k}_{hc}(t) = s_{hc}(t) \quad (n + \omega)k_{hc}(t)$$

where $s_{he}(t) = [L(0)/H\ ]e^{(n+\omega)}[w(t) + \rho(t)k_e(t) - c_e(t)]$. It follows that in terms of effective units of labour per capita capital accumulates according to $\dot{k}_e(t) = w(t) + [\rho(t) - (n + \omega)]\, k_e(t) - c_e(t)$. The consumption of a households representative member in terms of effective units is $c_e(t) = c(t)/A(t)$. Thus the representative household solves the following optimal control problem

$$\max V = \int_0^{+\infty} e^{-\beta t}u[c_e(t)]dt$$
$$\dot{k}_e = w(t) + [\rho(t) - (n + \omega)]k_e(t) - c_e(t)$$
$$k_e(0) = k_{e0}; \ \lim_{t \to \infty} k_e(t)\ e^{-\int_0^t [\rho(t) - (n+\omega)]d\tau} = 0$$

From first order conditions for the optimal control, we find that the dynamics of a competitive system in terms of effective units of labour are described by the following equations

$$\dot{k}_e(t) = f(k_e(t)) - c_e(t) - (n + \omega)k_e(t)$$
$$\dot{c}_e(t) = \frac{c_e(t)}{\sigma(t)}[f'(k_e(t)) - (n + \omega + \beta)]$$

If we put $n + \omega = \eta$ and rewrite the dynamic system as

$$\dot{k}_e(t) = f(k_e(t)) - c_e(t) - \eta k_e(t)$$
$$\dot{c}_e(t) = \frac{c_e(t)}{\sigma(t)}[f'(k_e(t)) - (\eta + \beta)]$$

We deduce that the dynamic system in terms of effective units of labour is indistinguishable in form from one without technological progress. Therefore, even the characteristics of the paths of a competitive economy remain the same.

Notes

1. Suppose, for example, consumption follows the path c(t) = c every t. Admit also that the utility function is time stationary and exhibits positive intertemporal preference, in other words for equal consumption present utility is greater than future utility. Therefore for t > 0 we have $e^{-\beta t}u$ (c) $< e^{-\beta 0}u(c)$, that is $e^{\beta t} > 1$. This amounts to $\beta t \log_e e > 0$ which for t > 0 calls for $\beta > 0$.

2. If the production function is homogeneous of degree one, Euler's theorem holds:

   $$Q(t) = [\partial F/\partial K(t)]K(t) + [\partial F/\partial L(t)]L(t)$$

   Being L(t)q(t) real income distributed to workers, the exhaustion principle for output entails

   $$L(t)q(t) = [\partial F/\partial K(t)]K(t) + [\partial F/\partial L(t)]L(t)$$

   that is L(t)q(t) = Q(t), so that q(t) = Q(t)/L(t).

3. The analytical details to which we refer are contained in section 2.6, which presents stability analysis of a competivite system.

4. Multiplying both sides of budget constraint by $e^{-\int_0^T [\rho(\tau)-n]d\tau}$ and considering that $d[e^{-\int_0^T [\rho(\tau)-n]d\tau}]/dt = -[\rho(\tau) - n]e^{-\int_0^T [\rho(\tau)-n]d\tau}$, with some further calculations the budget constraint becomes

   $$[k(t)e^{-\int_0^T [\rho(\tau)-n]}]_0^T = \int_0^T w(t)e^{-\int_0^T [\rho(\tau)-n]d\tau}dt - \int_0^T c(t)e^{-\int_0^T [\rho(\tau)-n]d\tau}dt.$$

   For $T \to \infty$ it is

   $$k(0) - \lim_{T\to\infty} k(T) e^{\int_0^T [\rho(\tau)-n]d\tau} = \int_0^{+\infty} c(t)e^{-\int_0^{+\infty}[\rho(\tau)-n]d\tau}dt - \int_0^{+\infty} w(t)e^{-\int_0^{+\infty}[\rho(\tau)-n]dt}dt$$

   Therefore $k(0) = \int_0^{+\infty} c(t)e^{-\int_0^{+\infty}[\rho(\tau)-n]d\tau}dt - \int_0^{+\infty} w(t)e^{-\int_0^{+\infty}[\rho(\tau)-n]dt}dt$

   if $\lim_{T\to\infty} k(T)e^{-\int_0^T [\rho(\tau)-n]d\tau} = 0$.

5. To find these eigenvectors associated with μ_1 e μ_2 we must consider respectively the systems of equations

$$[f'(k^*) - n]v_{11} - 1 = \mu_1 v_{11}$$

$$\frac{c^* f''(k^*)}{\sigma^*} v_{11} = \mu_1$$

$$[f'(k^*) - n]v_{21} - 1 = \mu_2 v_{21}$$

$$\frac{c^* f''(k^*)}{\sigma^*} v_{21} = \mu_2$$

Since the characteristic determinant is null, the solutions for v_{11} and v_{21} can be obtained either from the first or the second equation in each system.

6. By definition, $d(t)$ is the change of $B(t)/L(t)$ over time. Therefore:

$$d(t) = \frac{\dot{B}L - B\dot{L}}{L^2} = \frac{\dot{B}}{L} + \frac{B}{L}\frac{\dot{L}}{L} = \dot{b} + nb$$

7. This obtains as follows: Multiply the espression of $b(t)$ by $e^{-\int_0^t [\rho(\tau) - n] d\tau}$ so that $d(e^{-\int_0^t [\rho(\tau)-n]d\tau})/dt = -[\rho(\tau) - n]e^{-\int_0^t [\rho(\tau)-n]d\tau}.$

By integrating it follows that $-b(0) =$

$$\int_0^\infty [\theta(t) - g(t)] \, e^{-\int_0^t [\rho(\tau)-n]d\tau} \, dt \quad \text{if } \lim_{t\to\infty} b(t) e^{-\int_0^t [\rho(\tau)-n]d\tau} = 0$$

References

Abel, A. and O. Blanchard, (1983) 'An Intertemporal Equilibrium Model of Saving and Investment', *Econometrica*, 51, pp. 675–92.

Arrow, K. (1951) 'An Extension of the Basic Theorems of Classical Welfare Economics', in J. Newman, (ed.) *Proceedings of the Second Berkeley Symposium on Mathematical Statistics and Probability* (Berkeley: University of California Press).

Arrow, K. and M. Kurz (1970) *Public Investment, the Rate of Return, and Optimal Fiscal policy* (Baltimore: Johns Hopkins Press).

Azariadis, C. (1993) *Intertemporal Macroeconomics* (Oxford: Basil Blackwell).

Barro, R. (1974) 'Are Government Bonds Net Wealth?', *Journal of Political Economy*, 82, pp. 379–402.

Barro, R. (1981) 'Output Effects of Government Purchases', *Journal of Political Economy*, 89, pp. 1085–121.

Barro, R. (1989) 'The Neoclassical Approach to Fiscal Policy', in R. Barro, (ed.) *Modern Business Cycle Theory* (Cambridge MA: Harvard University Press).

Barro, R. and X. Sala-I-Martin, (1995) *Economic Growth* (New York: McGraw-Hill).

Bernheim, B.D. (1987) 'Ricardian Equivalence: Theory and Evidence', *NBR Macroeconomics Annual*, 2, pp. 263–304.

Blanchard, O. and S. Fischer (1989) *Lectures on Macroeconomics* (Cambridge MA: Mit Press).

Cass, D. (1965) 'Optimum Growth in an Aggregative Model of Capital Accumulation', *Review of Economic Studies*, 32, pp. 233–40.

Cass, D. (1966) 'Optimum Growth in an Aggregative Model of Capital Accumulation: A Turnpike Theorem', *Econometrica*, 34, pp. 833–50.

Cass, D. (1972) 'On Capital Overaccumulation in the Aggregative, Neoclassical Model of Economic Growth: a Complete Characterization', *Journal of Economic Theory*, 4, pp. 200–23.

Chiang, A. (1992) *Elements of Dynamic Optimization* (New York: McGraw-Hill).

Chirichiello, G. (1997) 'Modelli descrittivi di crescita: una rivisitazione (Descriptive Growth Models: A Revisitation)', *Temi di Teoria Economica, saggi provvisori*, n. 1, serie didattica, Roma.

Debreu, G. (1954) 'Valuation Equilibrium and Pareto Optimum', in *Proceedings of the National Academy of Sciences*, 40, pp. 588–92.

Debreu, G. (1959) *Theory of Value* (New York: Wiley).

Dorfman, R. (1969) 'An Economic Interpretation of Optimal Control Theory', *American Economic Review*, 59, pp. 817–31.

Fisher, I. (1930) *The Theory of Interest* (New York: Macmillan).

Intriligator, M., *Mathematical Optimization and Economic theory* (Englewood Cliffs: Prentice-Hall).

Kamien, M. and N. Schwartz, (1981) *Dynamic Optimization: The Calculus of Variations and Optimal Control in Economics and Management* (New York: North-Holland).

Koopmans, T.C. (1965) 'On the Concept of Optimal Economic Growth', in *The Economic Approach to Development Planning* (Amsterdam: North-Holland).

Koopmans, T.C. (1967a) 'Objectives, Constraints and Outcomes in Optimal Growth Models', *Econometrica*, 35, pp.1 – 15.

Koopmans, T.C. (1967b) 'Intertemporal Distribution and Optimal Aggregate Economic Growth', in *Ten Economic Studies in the Tradition of Irving Fisher* (New York: Wiley).

Malinvaud, E. (1953) 'Capital Accumulation and Efficient Allocation of Resources', *Econometrica*, 21, pp. 233–68.

Phelps, E.S. (1961) 'The Golden Rule of Accumulation: A Fable for Growthmen', *American Economic Review*, 51, pp. 638–43.

Phelps, E.S. (1965) 'Second Essay on the Golden Rule of Accumulation', *American Economic Review*, 55, pp. 793–814.

Pontryagin, L.S.,V.G. Botlyanskii, R.V. Gamkelidze, and Mischenko, E.F. (1962) *The Mathematical Theory of Optimal Processes* (New York: Wiley-Interscience).

Ramsey, F.P. (1928) 'A Mathematical Theory of Saving', *Economic Journal*, 38, pp. 543–59.

Romer, D. (1996) *Advanced Macroeconomics* (New York: McGraw-Hill).

Solow, R.M. (1956) 'A Contribution to the Theory of Economic Growth', *Quarterly Journal of Economics*, 70, pp. 65–94.

Turnovsky, S.J. (1995) *Methods of Macroeconomic Dynamics* (Cambridge MA: Mit Press).

Weizsäcker, C.C. (1965) 'Existence of Optimal Programs of Accumulation for an Infinite Time Horizon', *Review of Economic Studies*, 32, pp. 85–104.

3
Intertemporal Models of Overlapping Generations

3.1 Fisher's optimal saving rule and individual choices

Fisher's optimal saving rule (Fisher, 1930), like Ramsey's rule, can be adopted as the criterion for distinguishing the optimal paths in the set of feasible paths of a growing economy. To deduce Fisher's rule we start by considering the optimal saving problem of a single agent. The model we shall adopt considers a consumer-saver who makes choices over time sequentially. This model, ultimately similar to that of individual demand in a temporary equilibrium context, allows us to deduce a saving theory. Its optimality requisites satisfy Fisher's optimality intertemporal rule, the equality between the intertemporal marginal rate of substitution for consumption and the rate of interest (see Chapter 2).

The sequential view supporting Fisher's approach implies a change in mathematical methods with respect to Ramsey's approach. Since now time is discrete the proper dynamics is represented by system of difference equations. To begin with, let a rational individual have a time horizon consisting of two periods, present and future. Preferences are described by utility function $U(c_t, c_{t+1})$, where c_t and c_{t+1} are present and future consumption. Apart from the properties of positive and decreasing marginal utilities, we also assume that the utility function is strictly separable on present and future consumption. Exogenous endowments at time t and t + 1 are (e_t, e_{t+1}); the real rate of interest accruing savings at the beginning of period t+1 (or, equivalently, at the end of period t) is ρ_{t+1}. At time t, the consumer choice problem is a conventional constrained maximum problem

$$\max U(c_t, c_{t+1})$$
$$\text{sub } c_t + (1/1 + \rho_{t+1})c_{t+1} = e_t + (1/1 + \rho_{t+1})e_{t+1}$$

To simplify we put $R_{t+1} = (1 + \rho_{t+1})$ the interest factor. The Lagrangian multiplier is indicated by λ. Optimal consumption over the two periods must satisfy the budget constraint as well as the first-order necessary conditions

$$U'(c_t) = \lambda$$
$$U'(c_{t+1}) = \lambda(1/R_{t+1})$$

By eliminating λ it follows that

$$U'(c_t)/U'(c_{t+1}) = R_{t+1}$$

which is the familiar equality between the intertemporal marginal rate of substitution between current and future consumption and the interest factor. Let us now consider the first-order necessary conditions as an implicit function

$$F(c_t, c_{t+1}, R_{t+1}) = U'(c_t)/U'(c_{t+1}) - R_{t+1} = 0$$

By admitting that $F(.)$ can solve for c_t we obtain

$$c_t - f(c_{t+1}, R_{t+1}).$$

By substituting this into the budget constraint we have

$$g[c_{t+1}, R_{t+1}, e_t + (1/R_{t+1})e_{t+1}] =$$
$$e_t + (1/R_{t+1})e_{t+1} - f(c_{t+1}, R_{t+1}) - (1/R_{t+1})c_{t+1} = 0$$

If we solve $g(.)$ for c_{t+1} and rewrite the disposable income $y(R_{t+1}, e_t, e_{t+1}) = e_t + (1/R_{t+1})e_{t+1}$, and since endowment (e_t, e_{t+1}) exogenously predetermined, optimal present and future consumption are functions that depend only on the interest factor

$$c_t = c[R_{t+1}, y(R_{t+1})]$$
$$c_{t+1} = c_1[R_{t+1}, y(R_{t+1})]$$

The necessary condition for optimal choices of current and future consumption can be formulated in terms of Fisher's optimal saving rule. To do this, let us specify the consumer's scale of preferences. When time extends to the future, individual preferences can also express an intertemporal preference. This indicates that the increases in utility are evaluated not only 'quantitatively' but also according to the *moment* at which increases in consumption are enjoyed by the consumer. In this sense the intertemporal preference measures the impatience of the consumer waiting for the consumption that has been postponed to future. Consumer impatience can also be expressed as the fraction of the increase in current utility she/he is ready to forgo to receive an increase in future utility. If $0 < \beta_{t+1} < 1$ indicates the fraction of marginal utility $U'(c_t)$ of current consumption that consumer is willing to accept in return for a unit of marginal utility $U'(c_{t+1})$ of future consumption, then $U'(c_t) = \beta_{t+1}U'(c_{t+1})$. Magnitude β_{t+1} becomes a discount factor because relates marginal utilities valued at different instants. Its reverse can be expressed as the sum of unity and an unknown magnitude $1/\beta_{t+1} = 1 + (1/\beta_{t+1} - 1)$ where $(1/\beta_{t+1}) - 1$ measures the implicit discount rate applied by the consumer. This implicit discount rate γ_{t+1} is

$$\gamma_{t+1} = (1/\beta_{t+1}) - 1 = [U'(c_t)/U'(c_{t+1})] - 1 = [U'(c_t) - U'(c_{t+1})]/U'(c_{t+1})$$

The rate γ_{t+1} is Fisher's rate of temporal preference and $1 + \gamma_{t+1}$ is the intertemporal rate of substitution of current for future consumption, so the necessary condition for the optimal allocation of consumption over time becomes

$$1 + \gamma_{t+1} = R_{t+1}$$

or

$$\gamma_{t+1} - \mu_{t+1}$$

which is the Fisher rule for optimal saving that requires that the rate of temporal preference and the rate of interest be the same. The same conclusions are reached by assuming a utility function $U(c_t, c_{t+1}) = U(c_t) + \beta_{t+1}U(c_{t+1})$. The fact that optimal intertemporal allocation of consumption can be traced back to Fisher's optimal saving rule suggests that it is possible to assume that the consumer chooses optimal (real) saving s_t. As usual, current (real) savings is the difference between current endowment and current consumption $s_t = e_t - c_t$. Given the path of endowments, the feasible set of consumption in the two periods in terms of savings is $c_t = e_t - s_t$ and $c_{t+1} = e_{t+1} + s_t R_{t+1}$. These conditions are both equivalent to an intertemporal budget constraint for the consumer.[1] A choice of optimal intertemporal allocation of consumption, therefore, is also a choice of current savings s_t which solves the maximum problem

$$\max U(e_t - s_t, e_{t+1} + s_t R_{t+1})$$

By indicating U'_{si} partial i-th derivative, $i = 1, 2$, the first order condition for a maximum is

$$U'_{s1} + U'_{s2} = 0$$

Since $U'_{s1} = -U'(c_t)$ and $U'_{s2} = R_{t+1}U'(c_{t+1})$, the condition $-(U'_{s1}/U'_{s2}) = 1$ can be written as $(1 + \gamma_{t+1})/R_{t+1} = 1$, that is, the equality between the interest factor and the intertemporal preference factor $\gamma_{t+1} = \rho_{t+1}$. The necessary condition for a maximum can be written as the implicit function

$$S(s_t, R_{t+1}, e_t, e_{t+1}) = U'_{s1}(e_t - s_t,) + U'_{s2}(e_{t+1} + s_t R_{t+1}) = 0$$

If we admit s_t solves for $S(.)$ we obtain

$$s_t = s(R_{t+1}, e_t, e_{t+1})$$

which is the individual optimal savings function.[2]

3.2   Properties of the individual saving function

In this section we study the savings function by applying conventional microeconomic methodology of individual demand functions. We start from the premise that it is unimportant to describe intertemporal individual choices through the function

$$s_t = s[R_{t+1}, y(R_{t+1})]$$

or through the functions

$$c_t = c[R_{t+1}, y(R_{t+1})] \text{ and } c_{t+1} = c_1[R_{t+1}, y(R_{t+1})]$$

Therefore, to study saving function, we can consider only the savings function expressed in terms of current consumption

$$s[R_{t+1}, y(R_{t+1})] = e_t - c[R_{t+1}, y(R_{t+1})]$$

The link between savings and interest rate is deduced simply by considering the sign of the derivative

$$ds/dR_{t+1} = -[\partial c/\partial R_{t+1} + (\partial c/\partial y)_3 \partial y/\partial R_{t+1}] = (-\partial c/\partial R_{t+1}) + (\partial c/\partial y)(e_{t+1}/R_{t+1}^2)$$

This allows for a straightforward exercise of basic microeconomics. The response of savings to an increase of interest factor R_{t+1} looks like the familiar response of a demand function for good to increase of its price. The first term on the right $(-\partial c/\partial R_{t+1})$ measures the substitution effect and the second term on the right $(\partial c/\partial y)(e_{t+1}/R_{t+1}^2)$ measures the income effect. Moreover, since the interest factor R_{t+1} is also the relative price of present consumption c_t in terms of future consumption c_{t+1}, it is easy to deduce the sign of both substitution and income effects. If c_t is a gross-substitute with respect to c_{t+1} then $\partial c/\partial R_{t+1}$ is negative. In addition, if c_t is normal good, $\partial c/\partial y$ is positive. Therefore, under the admitted normality conditions, both the substitution and income effects of an increase in interest rate are positive and the final effect is positive $ds/dR_{t+1} > 0$.

Let us now consider the properties of savings function which is defined over the open interval $]0, \infty[$. Since the allocation of consumption $(c_t, c_{t+1}) = (e_t, e_{t+1})$ belongs to the dominion of the saving function, we can find $\bar{R}_{t+1}$ such that $c_t = c[\bar{R}_{t+1}, y(\bar{R}_{t+1})] = e_t$, and $c_{t+1} = c_1[\bar{R}_{t+1}, y(\bar{R}_{t+1})] = e_{t+1}$ that is

$$s[\bar{R}_{t+1}, y(\bar{R}_{t+1})] = 0$$

The increasing monotonicity admitted for savings function implies that $s[R_{t+1}, y(R_{t+1})] > 0$ if $R_{t+1} > \bar{R}_{t+1}$ whereas $s[R_{t+1}, y(R_{t+1})] < 0$ if $R_{t+1} < \bar{R}_{t+1}$. Furthermore, by assuming that savings is a normal good, the savings curve is as pictured in Figure 3.1.

The shape of the savings curve in Figure 3.1 is a consequence of the assumed smoothness of current consumption function. However, the hypothesis that current and future consumption are gross substitutes is fairly strong, because it constrains both the relationship between present and future consumption and also the relationship between future consumption and interest rate. From basic single agent demand theory, we know that to have gross substitutability between present and future consumption after a change of interest rate there must be an income effect on future consumption less than the substitution effect. Since this condition is not guaranteed, nor is it guaranteed that current consumption is a normal good, nor that between present and future consumption there is a strict link of substitutability, a backward-bending savings curve appears admissible. When the savings curve is backward-bending there can be multiple values for $\bar{R}_{t+1}$ (possibly a continuum) such that $s[(\bar{R}_{t+1}, y(\bar{R}_{t+1})] = 0$, as shown in Figure 3.2.

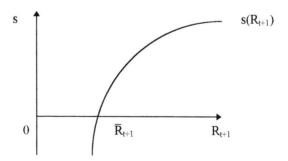

Figure 3.1   Normal individual saving curve

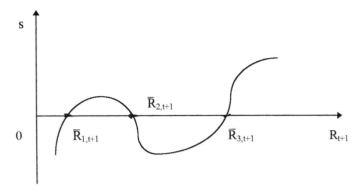

Figure 3.2   A backward-bending individual saving curve

The individual saving model that has been described can be applied to the case of a consumer-worker. For example a life-cycle approach can be shown by admitting the additional choice between leisure time and working time, limited only to the current period t. Current period t, therefore, can be interpreted as the period of youth whereas future period $t + 1$ is the period of retirement. Let $T - l_t$ indicate leisure in the period of youth and w_t indicate the current real wage, which is given to the single agent. The problem of choices for a young consumer-worker can be formulated as

$$\max U(c_t, c_{t+1}, T - l_t)$$
$$\text{sub } c_t + (1/R_{t+1})c_{t+1} = w_t l_t$$

This formulation can also be applied when labor supply is a rigid share of disposable time. In this case the savings function of a consumer-worker can be obtained directly as the solution to the problem

$$\max U(w_t l_t - s_t, R_{t+1} s_t)$$

so that the savings function is

$$s_t = s(R_{t+1}, w_t)$$

3.3   Further thoughts about the saving function: a dual approach to optimal individual saving

The sign of derivative ds/dR_{t+1} is worth further examination. In deducing the admissible sign we referred to present and future consumption as gross-substitutes. ds/dR_{t+1} in the interpretation we offered coincides with the negative net substitution effect on *current* consumption due to an increase of interest rate. Ultimately it coincides with the negative intertemporal substitution effect of current and future consumption. This is also implied by the basic relationships of individual demand theory. Indeed, in reference to a compensated function $c^c(.)$ of current consumption

$$\partial c^c/\partial R_{t+1} = \partial c/\partial R_{t+1} + (\partial c/\partial y)\partial y/\partial R_{t+1}, \text{ so that } ds/dR_{t+1} = -\partial c^c/\partial R_{t+1}.$$

This identification requires a clear theoretical explanation of the compensated consumption function. Let us consider the dual problem of the individual consumer. This problem consists of minimizing expenditure over the two periods of horizon subject to a given utility level

$$\min c_t + (1/R_{t+1})c_{t+1}$$
$$\text{sub } \overline{U} - U(c_t, c_{t+1}) = 0$$

Forming Lagrangian $L = c_t + (1/R_{t+1})c_{t+1} + \mu[U - \overline{U}(c_t, c_{t+1})]$, first-order conditions are

$$1 - \mu U'(c_t) - 0$$
$$(1/R_{t+1}) \quad \mu U'(c_{t+1}) - 0$$
$$\overline{U} - U(c_t, c_{t+1}) = 0$$

which reduce to

$$R_{t+1} = U'(c_t)/U'(c_{t+1})$$
$$\overline{U} = U(c_t, c_{t+1})$$

By solving this system we have the compensated functions of present and future consumption

$$c_t^c = c^c(R_{t+1}, U)$$
$$c_{t+1}^c = c_1^c(R_{t+1}, U)$$

The properties of these functions straightforwardly follow from the basic dual theory of the individual demand function. In particular, consider the direct problem when life income $y(R_{t+1}, e_t, e_{t+1}) = e_t + (1/R_{t+1})e_{t+1}$ is exactly equal to minimum expenditure $E = c^c(R_{t+1}, U) + (1/R_{t+1})c_1^c(R_{t+1}, U)$. Since ordinary consumption functions satisfy the budget constraint, the equality $E(.) = y(.)$ implies

$$c^c(R_{t+1}, U) + (1/R_{t+1})c_1^c(R_{t+1}, U) = c[R_{t+1}, y(R_{t+1})] +$$
$$(1/R_{t+1})c_1[R_{t+1}, y(R_{t+1})]$$

that is

$$c^c(R_{t+1}, U) = c[R_{t+1}, y(R_{t+1})]$$
$$c_1^c(R_{t+1}, U) = c_1[R_{t+1}, y(R_{t+1})]$$

from which follows

$$\partial c^c / \partial R_{t+1} = \partial c / \partial R_{t+1} + (\partial c / \partial y)(\partial y / \partial R_{t+1}) = -(ds/dR_{t+1})$$

which is what we conjectured intuitively. We can express the effect of an increase in interest rate on savings as the sum of substitution and income effects on the *savings*. From the definition of individual saving function $\partial s / \partial y = -\partial c / \partial y$ and, therefore,

$$\partial c^c / \partial R_{t+1} - (\partial c / \partial y)(\partial y / \partial R_{t+1}) = -[ds/dR_{t+1} + (\partial s / \partial y)(\partial y / \partial R_{t+1})]$$

The term in brackets on the right hand is the change in compensated saving $\partial s^c / \partial R_{t+1}$, so that

$$ds/dR_{t+1} = \partial s^c / \partial R_{t+1} - (\partial s / \partial y)\partial y / \partial R_{t+1}$$

which is what we wanted to demonstrate.

A final link between the Fisher's approach and Ramsey's original analysis emerges if we consider the dual problem directly as a choice of optimal savings. The constraints on feasible consumption and the assumption that total utility over the entire time horizon is given, lead to the following problem

$$\min \overline{U} - U(e_t - s_t, e_{t+1} + s_t R_{t+1})$$

The first-order necessary condition is similar to the that of the primal problem $U'_{s1} + U'_{s2} = 0$.

This is the formulation we obtain when we assume, as in Ramsey's approach, that the consumer-saver's objective is to minimize distance from a given 'Bliss point' $\overline{U}$. This interpretation of the dual problem is confirmed if we realize that in the dual approach the Bliss point is the indirect utility level. However, indirect utility changes as the interest rate changes. This implies that the optimal way a current utility can approach a Bliss point is trivially indicated by the change in indirect utility with respect to the change in interest rate. In formal terms, let indirect utility $V(R_{t+1}) = U[e_t - s_t(R_{t+1}), e_{t+1} + s_t(R_{t+1})R_{t+1}]$. The first derivative is

$$V'(R_{t+1}) = (\partial U / \partial c_{t+1})\{[-(\partial U / \partial c_t)/(\partial U / \partial c_{t+1}) + (R_{t+1})]ds/dR_{t+1} + s(R_{t++1})\}$$

The necessary condition for optimal saving yields

$$-(\partial U / \partial c_t)/(\partial U / \partial c_{t+1}) + R_{t+1} = 0. \quad \text{Therefore}$$

$$V'(R_{t+1}) = (\partial U / \partial c_{t+1}) s(R_{t+1})$$

Because variations are infinitesimal, this coincides with Ramsey's dictum which says that: '[the] rate of saving multiplied by marginal utility should always equal bliss minus actual rate of utility enjoyed.' (Ramsey, 1928, p. 537)

3.4 Intertemporal consumption allocation and Fisher's rule in an aggregative model with overlapping generations. A pure exchange economy

Fisher's theory of individual saving gives a microeconomic structure to an aggregate model of an economy. The microeconomic structure is similar to that of a Walrasian general equilibrium model, yet here it is the entire economy which assumes a structural form similar to that of a microeconomic agent. This perspective also implies a change in the objective assigned to macroeconomics. Indeed, now the conventional objective of determining the amount of resources used is replaced by the allocation of resources. A basic contribution to this change in direction is Samuelson's overlapping generations model (1958) which considers population as a sequence of generations. At every instant t a new generation appears in the economy, substituting and partially over-lapping former generations. Each generation is assumed to live only two periods t and t + 1. Thus at each period two generations cohabit, the one composed of old people (in number L_{t-1}) and the other composed of young people (in number L_t). Total population at instant t is $L_{t-1} + L_t$. It is assumed that the population grows at constant rate n, so current generation L_t is a multiple (1 + n) of former generation, $L_t = (1 + n)L_{t-1}$.

In this section we consider only a 'pure loan-consumption' economy, which is the same to a Walrasian pure-exchange economy. The basic assumptions and notations are the following. At each instant t the economy has Q_t real resources whose temporal sequence $\{Q_t\}_{t=1}^{\infty}$ is exogenously given. These resources consist of a unique homogeneous perishable good. Agents are indexed $h = 1, .., L_{t-1}; h = 1, ...L_t$. An allocation of consumption c^t at t is an allocation of consumption between individuals of two generations

$$c^t = (c_{11}^t, ..., c_{1L_t}^t, c_{21}^t, ..., c_{2L_{t-1}}^t)$$

An intertemporal allocation of consumption is a sequence of allocations of consumption at each $t\{c^t\}_{t=1}^{\infty}$. An intertemporal allocation of consumption is feasible if allocation of consumption c^t is feasible at each t. An allocation of consumption at t is feasible if c^t verifies

$$\sum_{h=1}^{L_t} c_{1h}^t + \sum_{h=1}^{L_{t-1}} c_{2h}^t = Q_t$$

In a decentralized economy endowments are held by individuals. A sequence of endowments for an individual born at instant t is a couple (e_{1h}^t, e_{2h}^{t+1}), so that, if the endowment of both generations is (q_1^t, q_2^t), the global endowment Q_t at t of a decentralized economy is

$$Q_t = \sum_{h=1}^{L_t} e_{1h}^t + \sum_{h=1}^{L_{t-1}} e_{2h}^{t-1} = q_1^t + q_2^t$$

Consequently, a feasible consumption allocation of a decentralized economy at t verifies

$$\sum_{h=1}^{L_t} c_{1h}^t + \sum_{h=1}^{L_{t-1}} c_{2h}^t = \sum_{h=1}^{L_t} e_{1h}^t + \sum_{h=1}^{L_{t-1}} e_{2h}^t$$

In a private ownership economy, allocation of resources occurs through a market mechanism which guides individual rational choices among feasible consumptions for each generation and for the entire temporal horizon. Let us consider an economic system where generations with the same individual preferences succeed one another. For simplicity we assume each household consists of a single individual. The objective of generic individual h of the older generation is simply to consume the entire disposable endowment. This objective is based on a rational choice which can easily be deduced. Indeed, the objective of older people is still to maximize utility over the entire temporal horizon subject to the constraint of disposable resources. Since the older persons residual horizon coincides with current period, the h-th older person solves the constrained maximization problem

$$\max U_h(c_{2h}^t)$$
$$\text{sub } c_{2h}^t = e_{2h}^t$$

which has the trivial solution $c_{2h}^t = e_{2h}^t$. Total current consumption of the older generation is

$$\sum_{h=1}^{L_{t-1}} c_{2h}^t = c_2^t$$

On the contrary, the h-th individual of younger generation has a two-period time horizon. She/he solves a constrained maximization problem similar to that of Fisher's saver

$$\max U_h(c^t_{1h}, c^{t+1}_{2h})$$
$$\text{sub } c^t_{1h} + (1/R_{t+1})c^{t+1}_{2h} = e^t_{1h} + (1/R_{t+1})e^{t+1}_{2h}$$

By solving this problem we obtain current and future individual consumption functions $c_{1h}(R_{t+1}); c_{2h}(R_{t+1})$.

Thus, the total current and future consumption functions of the younger generation are

$$\sum_{h=1}^{L_t} c_h(R_{t+1}) = c_1(R_{t+1}); \quad \sum_{h=1}^{L_t} c_{2h}(R_{t+1}) = c_{21}(R_{t+1})$$

Since these are behavioral functions, they presuppose some market transactions. But individuals hold the same good. Transaction activity, therefore, must have some rational motivation. Following Samuelson, we assume that exchanges between two individuals are pure-credit consumption contracts where the two parts agree to give each other the consumption good. The originator commits himself to give back in the future period R_{t+1} units of the consumption good in exchange for one unit of current consumption. Substantially, individuals exchange consumption in two subsequent periods at relative price R_{t+1}. In this context given current endowments $(q^t_1, q^t_2) = (\sum_{h=1}^{L_t} e^t_{1h}, \sum_{h=1}^{L_{t-1}} e^{t-1}_{2h})$, a competitive equilibrium at t is a pair consisting of the interest factor R_{t+1} and the consumption allocation c^t which verify

$$c_1(R_{t+1}) + c_2(R_{t+1}) = q^t_1 + q^t_2$$

An intertemporal competitive equilibrium is a sequence of competitive equilibria at each t, that is a pair of sequences of consumption and interest factors $\{c^t\}^\infty_{t=1}, \{R_{t+1}\}^\infty_{t=1}$ so that

$$c_1(R_{t+1}) + c_2(R_{t+1}) = q^{t-1} + q^t \quad (t = 1, 2, ...\infty)$$

It is convenient to re-write competitive equilibrium conditions in terms of individual saving functions

$$\sum_{h=1}^{L_t} s_{1h}(R_{t+1}) + \sum_{h=1}^{L_{t-1}} [e^t_{2h} - c_{2h}(R_{t+1})] = 0$$

Since $c_{2h}(R_{t+1}) = e_{2h}^t$, competitive equilibrium is a *generational autarkic* equilibrium. It implies

$$\sum_{h=1}^{L_t} s_{1h}(R_{t+1}) = s(R_{t+1}) = 0$$

In the class of generational autarkic equilibria, therefore, we can distinguish two types of competitive equilibria, depending on whether or not $s_{1h}(R_{t+1})$ is identically equal to zero. When $s_{1h}(R_{t+1}) = 0, \forall h$, the competitive equilibrium, is also *individually autarkic*. This second kind of equilibrium implies that a competitive equilibrium in which no exchange takes place is admissible. However, a market mechanism can reach competitive equilibria that are Pareto-superior to the individually autarkic one. This is possible in economies where young people have different intertemporal preferences. These young people can stipulate mutually advantageous pure-loan agreements because the more impatient individual can anticipate future consumption and the more patient individual can enjoy greater future consumption. Let us suppose for example that at instant t only two young people have different intertemporal preferences. In this case a competitive equilibrium is individually autarkic for all agents except for the two agents with different intertemporal preferences for which the equilibrium is also an equilibrium of transactions. Figure 3.3a shows this equilibrium, where segment R*A must be regarded as exactly equal to segment R*B. Similarly, in Figure 3.3b, where individual saving functions decrease over some intervals, is depicted the possibility of a continuum of equilibria. Figure 3.3b shows a set of equilibria between R_0^* and R_1^* on the assumption that individual saving functions s_{1h} and s_{1k} are symmetric in respect to the horizontal axis, and that for $j \neq h, k$ and $R_{t+1} \in [R_0^*, R_1^*]$ we have $s_{1j}(R_{t+1}) = 0$.

Figure 3.3 shows that the basis on which the market acts in 'choosing' Pareto-superior from the set of feasible equilibria is dissimilarity between agents intertemporal preferences. Figure 3.3 also shows that an overlapping generations-competitive system where young people's preferences are heterogeneous admits multiple equilibria, of which at least one (two in Figure 3.3b) is sub-optimal in the Pareto sense. This demonstrates that individually autarkic competitive equilibria do not exhaust the feasible allocations. However this does not apply to the economy described up to now because the preferences of individuals of the same generation are the same. To show that feasible allocations other than individual autarky exist let us consider the set of feasible stationary allocations. At least one feasible stationary allocation that is not

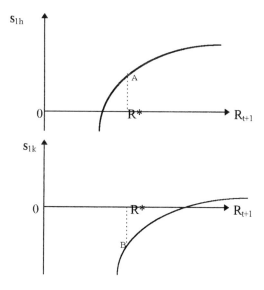

Figure 3.3a   Competitive equilibrium not individually autarkic

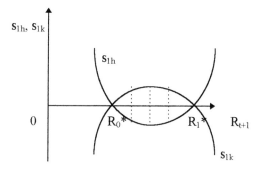

Figure 3.3b   A continuum of competitive equilibria not individually autarkic

necessarily reached as competitive equilibrium can be identified by taking into account a rate of population growth n. This is the famous 'Samuelson paradox'. The stationary allocation is socially desirable because it is a Pareto optimum.

3.5 Pareto optimum steady state and the Samuelson's paradox

The notion of feasibility applied to stationary allocations of consumption gives

$$L_t c^y + L_{t-1} c^0 = L_t e_1 + L_{t-1} e_2$$

Since $L_t = (1+n)L_{t-1}$, the former equation becomes

$$c^y + (1/1+n)c^0 = e_1 + (1/1+n)e_2$$

A feasible stationary allocation is a Pareto-optimum when consumption of one generation cannot be increased without reducing consumption of the other generation. As we already know, the set of Pareto-optimum allocations is the same as the set of solutions of a benevolent central planner problem whose aim is to maximize social welfare. The social welfare index is assumed to be the weighted sum of individual utilities. Since along a steady state path the central planner assigns to individual utilities the same weight and assumes that individual utility refers to the entire temporal horizon, and since generations have stationary preferences, the objective of the central planner is to maximize the life-cycle utility function of the representative individual $U(c^y, c^0)$. This is the utility function of representative young people over succeeding generations.[3] It is assumed to be separable. The central planner's disposable resources for reallocating consumption between generations are those of the economy along a steady state path. Therefore the central planner problem is

$$\max U(c^y, c^0)$$
$$\text{sub}: \ c^y + (1/1+n)c^0 = e_1 + (1/1+n)e_2$$

First-order necessary conditions require that

$$U'(c^y) = \lambda; \ U'(c^0) = (\lambda/1+n)$$

from which the optimal steady state condition is

$$U'(c^y)/U'(c^0) = (1+n)$$

This is the same as the golden rule in a pure exchange economy. The question that now arises is whether a competitive economy is capable of allocating resources between generations according to the golden rule. For an answer, we start by considering the representative young person in a competitive system confronted with a continuum of budget constraints depending on the value of R. The set of feasible R is the interval of positive real number $0 < R < +\infty$.[4] Since $(1 + n) \geq 1$, Samuelson's 'biological' interest factor $R_B = (1 + n)$ evidently belongs to the feasible set, that is $R_B \in]0 + \infty[$. When competitive equilibrium is at $R^* = R_B$ the representative young person solves the problem

max $U(c^y, c^0)$

sub $c^y + (1/1 + n)c^0 = e_1 + (1/1 + n)e_2$

which is exactly the same problem as that of the central planner. In general in the interval $]0, +\infty[$ R^* can assume multiple values. However, there is no reason why competitive equilibrium must always occur at the biological interest factor R_B. But $R^* = R_B$ is a necessary condition for Pareto-optimum. Consequently, the set of competitive steady states where $R^* \neq R_B$ are Pareto-inefficient.

To understand this inefficiency, let us imagine the economy is at competitive equilibrium $s(R^*) = 0$ with $R^* \neq R_B$, and then suddenly it changes from a decentralized to a command economy. Assume the central planner fixes the interest factor at the biological level R_B. Following Gale (1973) the two possible steady states which can occur after this change are

a) the classical case, where $s(R_B) < 0$;
b) the Samuelson case, where $s(R_B) > 0$.

In Figure 3.4a the classical case requires $R^* > R_B$, whereas the Samuelson case in Figure 3.4b requires $R^* < R_B$

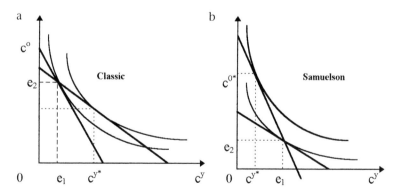

Figure 3.4a The classic case in terms of consumption choices
Figure 3.4b The Samuelson case in terms of consumption choices

Figure 3.4 uses the fact that competitive equilibrium is individually autarkic equilibrium. It is located where the budget line $c^0 = -R^*c^y + (R^*e_1 + e_2)$ is tangent to an indifference curve at the autarky point (e_1, e_2). On the contrary, steady state Pareto- optimum (c^{*y}, c^{*0}) is located where the line of resources constraint $c^0 = -(1+n)c^y + [(1+n)e_1 + e_2]$ is tangent to an indifference curve. Gales classification (1973) is important for separating steady states that can be reached as competitive equilibria from those that can not.

The complicated case where the representative young person's saving function is 'backward-bending' and there are multiple competitive equilibria becomes even more complicated when there are multiple optimal steady states. To simplify, we can limit ourselves to the case where smooth utility functions generate a unique optimal steady state. Saving function $s(R)$, then, is also regular, so that there is a unique value $R = R^*$ which yields $s(R^*) = 0$. Any other steady state, and particularly the Pareto-optimum with $R_B \neq R^*$, is not feasible for the market. Indeed, a state different from competitive equilibrium would appear as *disequilibrium* rather than equilibrium but, due to the way a competitive market mechanism works, it is impossible to observe this along a stationary path. This is an obverse face of multiplicity of equilibria which Samuelson described as 'surprising' or paradoxical. The paradox is that a state which we know to be Pareto-efficient can not be reached as an equilibrium of a competitive market. The classical steady state R_B^c is depicted in Figure 3.5a; Samuelson steady state R_B^s is depicted in Figure 3.5b.

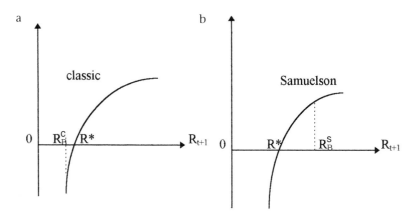

Figure 3.5a The classic case in terms of aggregate saving function
Figure 3.5b The Samuelson case in terms of aggregate saving function

If each of the $s(R_B)$ states in Figure 3.5, were imposed upon a system that is competitive in all other aspects, these states would be visible only for short time despite the fact that they are steady states. Indeed the market tends to eliminate states where $s(R) \neq 0$ because it regards them as disequilibria. It would seem that a competitive system can suffer from a kind of auto-immunization disease. The economic system tends to consider its own constituents extraneous bodies and does not recognizes an efficient state as equilibrium. However for different reasons classical and Samuelson steady states can not be reached through the market. When $s(R_B) < 0$, the younger generation want to consume more than it has, as Figure 3.5a shows. If the corresponding transactions were realized through the market, or, in other words, if $R = R_B$ in some way were fixed, leaving individuals the task of reallocating consumption, the following situation would occur. A pure-consumption-loan contract with the older generation would require that one unit of current consumption be exchanged for the promise to receive R_B units in the future. This, however, is a kind of transaction that the older generation never accept voluntarily since its credit expires when they have passed away. Forced reallocation of consumption would increase the welfare of the young at the expense of the old. On the contrary, in the Samuelson case $s(R_B) > 0$ the younger generation would agree to exchange R_B units of future consumption for each unit of current consumption. The counterpart is the older generation whose members can not honour repayment of the loan because it no longer exists in the future. However, if the counterpart of the younger generation were a still living agent and capable of honouring loans to the elders of previous generation, the young would *freely* sign a contract with $R = R_B$. In this case passing from competitive state $R = R^*$ to the steady state $R = R_B$ would increase the welfare of the older generation without reducing that of the younger one.

This can also be demonstrated in another way. Suppose that the central planner, hearing of a possible Samuelson case imposes intergenerational transfers. These consists of a social security system which levies a constant fraction of the resources of the young and gives back the entire amount levied to old. To be exact, let us assume that the state $s(R_B) > 0$ is set at instant $t = \tau$. From that instant on and for all future periods the central planner orders a fixed per capita levy α on the young, giving back to them the per capita equivalent of the amount levied when they are old. The central planners budget at each instant $t = \tau, \tau + 1,...$ is balanced since comparison between total levies and total transfers implies

$$\alpha L_t = \alpha(1 + n)L_{t-1}$$

At $t = \tau$ and ever after the representative young person solves the problem

$$\max U(c^y, c^0)$$
$$\text{sub } c^y + (1/1 + n)c^0 = e_1 + e_2$$

Among first-order necessary conditions for this problem $U'(c^y) - U'(c^0)(1 + n) = 0$ must be verified and it follows that

$$U'(c^y)/U'(c^0) = (1 + n)$$

The optimal consumption path of a representative young person obeys the golden rule and, therefore, is Pareto-optimal. We can compare the level of utility enjoyed along the competitive path and the level of utility enjoyed along the path with redistribution. In these two cases the maximum utility level is the indirect utility function, that is

$$U[e_1 - s(R^*), e_2 + s(R^*)R^*] = U[e_1, e_2]$$
$$U[e_1 - \alpha, e_2 + (1 + n)\alpha]$$

We can approximate the redistribution scheme for infinitesimal α by starting from a competitive situation for $\alpha - 0$. The linear approximation near $\alpha = 0$ gives

$$U[e_1 - \alpha, e_2 + (1 + n)\alpha] = U[e_1, e_2] + [-U'(e_1) + U'(e_2)(1 + n)]\alpha =$$
$$U[e_1, e_2] + U'(e_2)[-U'(e_1)/U'(e_2) + (1 + n)]\alpha$$

At the competitive equilibrium we must have $U'(e_1)/U'(e_2) = R^*$. Therefore the gain of the utility obtained by each individual after the change of the system is

$$U[e_1 - \alpha, e_2 + (1 + n)\alpha] - U[e_1, e_2] = [(1 + n) - R^*]\alpha\, U'(e_2)$$

Since $\alpha > 0$, this utility gain is positive when $(1 + n) - R^* > 0$, that is if $n > \rho^*$. Hence, in the Samuelson case competitive equilibrium is inefficient. In general we can say that some feasible steady state allocations can be reached through non-market redistribution schemes, but only in the Samuelson case is the redistribution scheme justifiable because of market failure.

However, there is still the question of whether a non-competitive steady state selected by the central planner is convergent. This question can not be answered here since no dynamics for disposable resources has been specified. We shall consider this problem in a model that admits capital accumulation. At the moment, let us try to describe market failure from another point of view. When we distinguished individually autarkic equilibria in the set of competitive equilibria, we pointed out that individually autarkic equilibria are inefficient if agents preferences are heterogeneous. In fact they are sub-optimal compared to the generationally autarkic equilibria that are not individually autarkic. The market was able to guide the economy from an inefficient equilibrium to the efficient one because of the differences of intertemporal preferences of at least two individuals. For allocation of consumption between generations a market is in a situation similar to that when it must reallocate consumption of the same generation with only two individuals who have different intertemporal preferences.

To exploit this comparison we need only adapt the previous model. Assume that each generation is composed of only one individual and that the separable utility function shows a Fisher rate of intertemporal preference. The first hypothesis reduces comparison between generations to comparison between individuals. The second hypothesis clearly distinguishes the difference in preferences between the young and the old. The problem now is to allocate consumption between two individuals with different intertemporal preferences. Trivially, for the young we put

$$U(c^y, c^0) = U(c^y) + \beta_y U(c^0) \text{ with } \beta_y > 0$$

whereas for the old we put

$$U(c^0) = U(c^0) + \beta_0 U(c^{0+1}) \text{ with } \beta_0 \equiv 0$$

Notwithstanding the obvious difference between the intertemporal preference rates $\beta_y \neq 0$, the economy remains at individually autarkic equilibrium. This shows how the market mechanism fails. In the Samuelson case the market mechanism does not create enough incentives for the young to exploit all the opportunities for exchange.

3.6   Growth model of a competitive economy with overlapping generations

The model of a pure-exchange economy can only be considered a useful reference. To describe a more realistic economy we must also take into account the production of goods and the accumulation of capital. In this section we do this by following Diamond (1965). We assume an economy where production is decentralized and firms operate in competitive markets. The production sector is the same as in the optimal growth model where there are F firms, labelled by index $f = 1, ..F$. Productive technology is represented by a stationary production function, assumed to be continuous, concave, homogeneous of degree one and, for the sake of simplicity, identical for each firm. Capital and labour inputs K_f^t, L_f^t are bought by firms from individuals. Each agent of the younger generation is endowed with only one unit of work, inelastically supplied to firms at the current real wage w_t. On the contrary, the old are endowed with the entire capital stock K_t existing at the beginning of each period t. Property rights on the capital stock are inelastically supplied to the young at the current price on capital market. Therefore, income of the old is the amount of quasi-rents paid by firms for the use of capital at user-price ρ_t, and capital stock K_t sold entirely to the young at the current unit price. The objective of a single firm, by virtue of the homogeneity of degree one of the production function, is to maximize profit by solving at each t

$$\max \pi_f^t = L_f^t[f(k_f^t) - w_t - \rho_{t+1}k_f^t]$$
$$\{L_f^t, k_f^t\}$$

First-order necessary conditions imply $k_f^t = k_t$ each $f = 1, ..F,$ and $\rho_{t+1} = f'(k_t)$; $w_t = f(k_t) - k_t f'(k_t)$. Agents behaviour is described as follows. The young have only labour as a source of income, so the first period constraint is $c_{1h}^t + k_{1h}^{t+1} = w_t$. Because of lack of income in the retirement period, future resources are derived only from saving s_{ht}, held in the form of physical capital k_{1h}^{t+1}. Thus, the second-period constraint is $c_{2h}^{t+1} = R_{t+1}k_{1h}^{t+1}$. An h-th young agent solves the constrained maximum problem

$$\max U(c_{1h}^t, c_{2h}^{t+1})$$
$$\text{sub } c_{1h}^t + k_{1h}^{t+1} = w_t$$
$$c_{2h}^{t+1} = R_{t+1}k_{1h}^{t+1}$$

Let consumption function of the young and the desired capital stock function be

$$C_1(R_{t+1}, w_t) = \sum_{h=1}^{L_t} c_{1h}(R_{t+1}, w_t); \text{ and } K_{t+1}(R_{t+1}, w_t) = w_t L_t - C_1(R_{t+1}, w_t).$$

The old simply consume the entire disposable income. Let consumption of the old and the existing capital stock they hold be

$$C_2^t = \sum_{h=1}^{L_{t-1}} c_{2h}^t; K_t = \sum_{h=1}^{L_{t-1}} k_{2h}^t$$

Aggregate demand is $(C_1^t + C_2^t + (K_{t+1} - K_t))$. Since the labour market is at equilibrium at each instant, $\sum_{f=1}^{F} L_f^t = L_t$, total production is $Q_t = \sum_{f=1}^{F} L_f^t[f(k_t)] = L_t f(k_t)$. Therefore, the equilibrium condition of the goods market, which requires equality between aggregate demand and total production, is

$$(C_1^t + C_2^t) + (K_{t+1} - K_t) = L_t f(k_t)$$

Instantaneous equilibrium condition for the goods market implicitly contains an equation for the dynamics of per capita capital. Per capita variables defined in terms of the young are

$$c_2^t/1 + n = C_2^t/L_{t-1}; \; c_1^t = C_1^t/L_t; \; k_{t+1}(1 + n) = K_{t+1}/L_t; \; k_t = K_t/L_t = k_{2t}/1 + n.$$

Equilibrium in per capita terms becomes

$$c_1^t + (c_2^t/1 + n) + k_{t+1}(1 + n) - k_t = f(k_t)$$

By taking into account budget constraints and competitive prices, the equilibrium condition becomes

$$k_{t+1} = s(R_{t+1}, w_t)/(1 + n) = (1/1 + n)s[1 + f'(k_{t+1}), f(k_t) - k_t f'(k_t)]$$

For a given initial per capita capital stock k_0, the competitive dynamic equilibrium is a sequence $\{k_t\}_{t=0}$ that verifies this basic dynamic equation. It is a first-order difference equation in k_t which we shall now study.

3.7   Existence and stability of equilibrium

Let us consider again the equilibrium condition in the implicit form

$$Z(k_t, k_{t+1}) = k_{t+1} - (1/1 + n)s[1 + f'(k_{t+1}), f(k_t) - k_t f'(k_t)] = 0$$

Assume $Z(.)$ is defined in the set $\{(k_t, k_{t+1}) : k_t \geq 0, k_{t+1} \geq 0\}$, and has continuous partial derivatives. If conditions of the implicit functions theorem are met we can solve $Z(.)$ for one of its arguments. The forward-looking solution for k_{t+1}, defines a single-valued function which we call $k_{t+1} = E(k_t)$. The necessary condition for this solution is $\partial Z/\partial k_{t+1} = (1 + n) - (\partial s/\partial R_{t+1})f''(k_{t+1}) \neq 0$. This holds everywhere, except when $(\partial s/\partial R_{t+1})f''(k_{t+1}) = 1 + n$ which requires $\partial s/\partial R_{t+1} < 0$. Therefore, the assumption that current and future consumption are gross substitutes $\partial s/\partial R_{t+1} \geq 0$ is sufficient to ensure $\partial Z/\partial k_{t+1} \neq 0$. The function $k_{t+1} = E(k_t)$

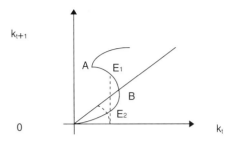

Figure 3.6 Multiple temporary equilibria

in the phase plane (k_t, k_{t+1}) depicts the dynamics of the economy. Its first derivative is

$$E' = -(\partial Z/\partial k_t / \partial Z/\partial k_{t+1}) = -\frac{(\partial s/\partial w_t)k_t f''(k_t)}{(1+n) - (\partial s/\partial R_{t+1})f''(k_{t+1})}$$

By assuming saving is a normal good $0 < \partial s/\partial w_t < 1$, the numerator is negative. The sign of the denominator depends on the sign of the $\partial s/\partial R_{t+1}$. If the saving function is smooth $\partial s/\partial R_{t+1} \geq 0$, the denominator is positive. Consequently the phase curve $E(k_t)$ in the plane (k_t, k_{t+1}) is increasing and verifies $E(0) = 0.$[5] However, since it is impossible to exclude the 'backward-bending' saving function, even an overlapping-generations model with production and capital accumulation can admit, as the pure exchange model, multiple temporary equilibria, as shown by point E_1 and E_2 on segment AB of $E(k_t)$ curve in Figure 3.6.

The model implies neither convexity nor concavity of the phase curve. As shown in Figure 3.6 the phase curve can be either convex or concave without violating the assumptions of the model (Galor and Ryder, 1989). This implies that if steady states exist, they can be multiple. Since $E'(k_t)$ is continuous, convexity or concavity of the phase curve can be ascertained by studying the sign of the second derivative

$$E''(k_t) = \frac{d(-\partial Z/\partial k_t / \partial Z/\partial k_{t+1})}{dk_t}$$

This study shows that the expression for the second derivative $E''(k_t)$[6] contains terms having a third derivative of the production function and a second derivative of the saving function. Any sign assumed for these derivatives implies severe restrictions on technology and preference to be acceptable.

Let us now refer to steady state. A steady state is a per capita capital stock $k_t = \bar{k}$ such that

$$\bar{k} = s[1 + f'(\bar{k}), f(\bar{k}) - \bar{k}f'(\bar{k})]/(1 + n), \quad \text{that is} \quad \bar{k} = E(\bar{k})$$

Therefore, steady state is a fixed point for function E(k). Since we already know that $k = 0$ is a steady state, in seeking the fixed points of function E(k) we can limit ourselves to the economically significant values $k > 0$. By virtue of this restriction we can rewrite the steady states as $\bar{k} = E(\bar{k})/\bar{k}]\bar{k}$ so that by considering the function

$$D(k) = [(E(k)/k) - 1]k$$

a steady state is a zero for the function D(k), that is $D(k) = 0$. Clearly for $k > 0$ the zeros of D(k) are the same as those for $F(k) = [(E(k)/k) - 1]$, so that the existence of steady states becomes the problem of the existence of zeros for F(k) function.

In geometric terms, function F(k) is the distance of the intersections between the lines leaving from the origin of the phase plane and intersecting the E(k) function at points $k > 0$, and the line $k = k$ which is a $45°$ line. Studying the properties of F(k), for $k \to \infty$ and for $k \to 0$ we obtain

a) $\lim_{k \to \infty} F(k) = -1$

Indeed it is

$$\left[\lim_{k \to \infty} [E(k)/k] \leq \lim_{k \to \infty} [w/(1 + n)k] = \lim_{k \to \infty} [f(k)/(1 + n)k] - \lim_{k \to \infty} [f'(k)/(1 + n)] \right].$$

From Inada's condition $f'(\infty) = 0$ and by applying Hospital's rule $\lim_{k \to \infty} [f(k)/(1 + n)k] = (1/1 + n)f'(\infty) = 0.$

b) $\lim_{k \to 0} F(k) = e > 0$

When $k \to 0$, since $E(0) = 0$, application of Hospital's rule gives $\lim_{k \to 0} [E(k)/k] = \lim_{k \to 0} E'(k) = E'(0).$

By assuming $E'(0) > 1$ and by putting $E'(0) - 1 = e > 0$, we can write $\lim_{k \to 0} F(k) = e > 0.$

Since F(k) is continuous, it will take all the values in the interval $[-1, e]$, so that there is at least a point $\bar{k}$ where $F(\bar{k}) = [E(\bar{k})/\bar{k}] - 1 = 0$. This point is a steady state equilibrium since it verifies $\bar{k} = E(\bar{k})$. This result can be enforced to guarantee the uniqueness of the steady state by assuming that phase curve $E(k_t)$ is strictly concave. Indeed, in this case if we admit $E(\overline{k}_1) = \overline{k}_1$ and $E(\overline{k}_2) = \overline{k}_2$ for two values $\overline{k}_2 > \overline{k}_1 > 0$, strict concavity of function $E(k)$ would imply

$$E(0) - E(\overline{k}_1)]/\overline{k}_1 > E(0) - E(\overline{k}_2)/\overline{k}_2 > E(\overline{k}_1) - E(\overline{k}_2)/(\overline{k}_2 - \overline{k}_1),$$

that is, by taking on account that $E(0) = 0$

$$[E(\overline{k}_1)]/\overline{k}_1] - 1 < [E(\overline{k}_2) - E(\overline{k}_1)/(\overline{k}_2 - \overline{k}_1)] - 1 = 0$$

which contradicts $[E(\overline{k}_1)]/\overline{k}_1] - 1 = 0$. This can be used to count the number of steady states. If the steady states are an integer number $m > 1$, and $E'(0) > 1$ then there must be $m - 1 = 2n$ for any integer $n \geq 0$. In the opposite case it would be $m-1 = 2n +1$ with $n \geq 0$, from which it would follow $m = 0$ for $n = 0$, which is a contradiction to the fact $m > 1$.

Therefore, when $E'(0) > 1$ steady states are odd number $m = 2n + 1$, where n is a positive integer or null. Abandoning condition $E'(0) > 1$ does not guarantee that at least one steady state exists. Indeed, this condition is essential in the demonstration of the existence of zeros for function $F(k)$. When $E'(0) < 1$ the number of steady states can be either null or an even number, that is $m = 2n$ where n is a positive integer or null. In fact with $E'(0) < 1$, if $m > 0$ there must be $E'(k) > 1$ at least at one steady state. Since ultimately $\lim_{t \to \infty} E'(\overline{k}) < 1$, when there is a steady state $\overline{k}$ with $E'(\overline{k}) > 1$ there must also be another steady state k^* with $E'(k^*) < 1$.

The condition that the first derivative of the phase curve at steady states must be less than one is also important for the study of stability. For that reason, let us assume for the time being that the system has a unique steady state k^*. A linear approximation in a neighborhood of k^* gives the equation

$$k_{t+1} - k^* = E'(k^*)(k_t - k^*)$$

Since $E'(k^*)$ is constant, this is a homogeneous first-order differential equation for the variable $k_t - k^*$ whose solution is

$$k_t - k^* = (k^\circ - k^*)[E'(k^*)]^t$$

The condition for convergence to k^* is $E'(k^*) < 1$. This is a condition for global stability when the steady state is unique, that is when $E'(0) > 1$ is also verified. When there are multiple steady states, a stability condition must be valid in a neighbourhood of each of the admissible steady states. In such cases, when $E'(0) > 1$, among the $m = 2n + 1$ admissible steady states, there are $j = 1, ..n + 1$ that verify $E'(\overline{k}_j) < 1$ and they are asymptotically stable, whereas the remaining $i = 1, ..n$, verify $E'(\overline{k}_i) > 1$

and are unstable. Figure 3.7 shows the variety of cases admitted by the overlapping generations growth model.

To understand Figure 3.7 remember that up to now we have excluded the backward-bending saving function. When saving function is backward-bending the locus $E(k_t)$ does not correspond (except that locally) to a one-to-one function of k_t so that there are values of k_t to which a set of values of k_{t+1} corresponds. In this case stable points do not necessarily remain isolated. Unstable and stable points can share points in some neighbourhood so that it is impossible to distinguish points from which there are forces pushing toward a stable point or pushing away from unstable point. Figure 3.7 represents these possible cases.

An important characteristic of the overlapping generations growth model, which we shall not consider here, is that it admits cyclical solutions (see Azariadis, 1981, 1993; Benhabib and Day, 1982; Farmer, 1986; Grandmont, 1985; Sargent, 1987).

3.8   Efficiency of steady-state equilibrium

As we have seen, the extension of the overlapping generations model to an economy with production and capital accumulation not only does not solve the problem of multiple equilibria but adds the problem of the impossibility of distinguishing dynamic forces emanating from a given temporary equilibrium. It is also necessary to verify whether and how dynamic efficiency of competitive allocations is affected by the inclusion of capital accumulation. Pareto-optimal allocations are the solutions to the maximum problem of the central planner. In the present context the objective function of the central planner is still the utility function (separable and stationary) of a representative of the young generation. Relevant modification refers to the central planners resources constraint.

By considering per worker variables, the constraint is

$$f(k_t) = c_1^t + c_2^t/(1+n) + k_{t+1}(1+n) - k_t$$

This constraint reflects feasible uses of the available resources. The choice for the central planner is between current consumption of the young and capital accumulation. For the time being, we assume that the central planner has a finite time horizon T. Initial capital stock $k_0 > 0$ and terminal capital stock $k_T > 0$ are given. With these assumptions, the central planner problem is to solve the constrained maximum problem

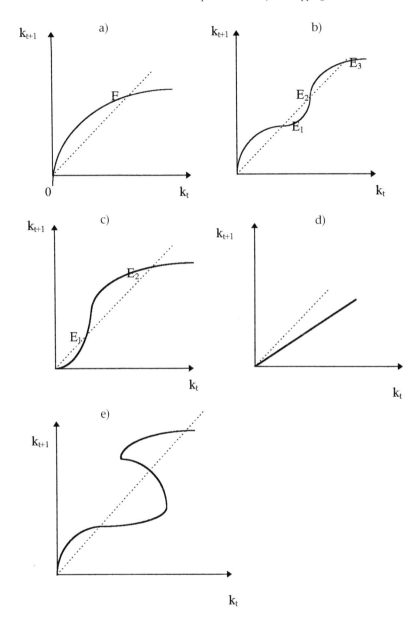

Figure 3.7 Possible cases of steady state equilibria

$$\max \sum_{t=0}^{T} U(c_1^t, c_2^{t+1})$$

$$\text{sub} \quad f(k_t) = c_1^t + (c_2^{t+1}/1 + n) + k_{t+1}(1 + n) - k_t$$

$$k_0 > 0; \; k_T > 0$$

The central planner problem can be also formulated as a discrete optimal control problem

$$\max \sum_{t=0}^{T} U(c_1^t, c_2^{t+1})$$

$$k_{t+1} = (1 + n)^{-1}[f(k_t) + k_t - c_1^t - c_2^{t+1}(1 + n)^{-1}]$$

$$k_0 > 0; \; k_T > 0$$

In this formulation, by virtue of the maximum principle for the case of discrete time (see Mathematical Appendixes) first-order necessary conditions are

$$U(c_1^t) - \lambda_{t+1}(1 + n)^{-1} = 0$$

$$U(c_2^{t+1}) - \lambda_{t+1}(1 + n)^{-2} = 0$$

$$\lambda_t = \lambda_{t+1}(1 + n)^{-1}[1 + f'(k_t)]$$

and the terminal condition is $\lambda_T = 0$.

From the first and second condition we get

$$\frac{U'(c_1^t)}{U'(c_2^{t+1})} = 1 + n$$

From the first and last conditions we get

$$\frac{U'(c_1^t)}{U'(c_1^{t+1})} = \frac{1 + f'(k_{t+1})}{1 + n}$$

The first of these two conditions requires the equality between intertemporal substitutions marginal rate of consumption and the growth factor of the population which has already been indicated as equivalent to the golden rule of a pure exchange economy. It gives the central planner the criterion for optimal redistribution of consumption from the youth to the elderly of the current young generation. The second condition gives the central planner the criterion for optimal capital accumulation, which equalizes the intertemporal substitutions rate of consumption and the transformation rate which is measured by the ratio between the return of accumulation and the growth rate of population. The latter is the equality that market *can not achieve* because it presupposes transactions between living agents and agents who have not yet been born.

However, we cannot ignore that in the long run the central planner could make only competitive allocations. To analyze long-run tendencies we must examine the steady state allocations a central planner can make, and then compare them to steady state allocations that the market can make. As we already know steady state consumption allocation is a sequence $\{c^t\}_{t=1}^{\infty}$ so that $c^t = c$ at each t. For a system with population growing at constant rate n and stationary technology, a feasible steady state verifies $c = f(k) - kn$. where $c = c_1 + c_2/1 + n$. In the set of feasible steady states, the central planner selects an optimal steady state by solving the problem

$$\max U(c_1, c_2)$$
$$\text{sub } c_1 + c_2/1 + n = f(k) - kn$$

If λ is the Langrage multiplier, necessary first-order conditions for the maximum are

$$U'(c_1) = \lambda$$
$$U'(c_2) = \lambda/1 + n$$
$$f'(k) = n$$

These conditions in terms of marginal rate of substitution are

$$\frac{U'(c_1)}{U'(c_2)} = (1 + n) = 1 + f'(k)$$

which is the golden rule. By also imposing competitiveness condition $R = 1 + f'(k)$, we find that an optimal competitive steady state requires the equality between competitive interest factor R and biological interest factor $1 + n$. This, however, is a mere coincidence.

3.9   Stability of planner's optimum

We shall now consider stability of the steady state for the dynamic system governed by a central planner. The dynamic system deduced from first-order necessary conditions boils down to a system of difference equations

$$k_{t+1} = (1 + n)^{-1}[f(k_t) + k_t - c_1^t] - c_2^t(1 + n)^{-2}]$$
$$U'(c_1^t) = U'(c_2^{t+1})[f'(k_t) + 1]$$
$$U'(c_2^{t+1})(1 + n) = U'(c_1^t)$$

Since $U''(c_2^{t+1}) < 0$, the last equation can be solved for c_2^t.[7] This system admits the optimal steady state solution $(c_1^*, c_2(c_1^*), k^*)$ already defined.[8] A linear approximation in the neighbourhood of steady state yields

$$k_{t+1} - k^* = (1+n)^{-1}[1 + f'(k^*)](k_t - k^*) + [1 + (U''(c_1^*)/U''(c_2^*))](c_1^t - c_1^*)$$

$$c_1^t - c_1^* = (1+n)^{-1}[1 + f'(k^*)](c_1^{t+1} - c_1^*) + [U'(c_1^*)/U''(c_1^*)(1+n)^{-1}f''(k^*)]$$
$$(k_{t+1} - k^*)$$

By solving for $c_1^{t+1} - c_1^*$ and $c_1^t - c_1^*$ and by substituting we obtain the following second order difference equation for the variable $k_t - k^*$

$$(k_{t+2} - k^*) - a(k_{t+1} - k^*) + (k_t - k^*) = 0$$

where $a = 2 + \dfrac{U'(c_1^*)f''(k^*)}{U''(c_1^*)(1+n)[1 + f'(k^*)]}\{1 + \dfrac{f'(k^*)U''(c_1^*)(1+n)[[1 + f'(k^*)]}{U'(c_1^*)f''(k^*)}$

$$+\dfrac{U''(c_1^*)]}{(1+n)^2 U''(c_2^*)}\} > 0$$

The associated characteristic equation is $p(\lambda) = \lambda^2 - a\lambda + 1 = 0$. Since $a > 2$, the discriminant $\triangle = a^2 - 4$ is positive and both roots λ_1, λ_2 are real. Moreover the equation shows two variations. By Descartes rule both roots are positive, so for the stability we must ascertain whether $\lambda_i < 1$ for $i = 1, 2$. We do this by considering the value of $p(\lambda)$ when $\lambda = 1$, and we obtain $p(1) = 2 - a < 0$. Therefore, the largest root, say λ_1, verifies $\lambda_1 > 1$ so that the steady state is a saddle point. This qualification of steady state also allows us to give a normative significance to steady state even in the case of finite horizon. Indeed, optimum steady state, has the 'turnpike' property originally demonstrated for Ramsey's optimal model with infinite horizon (Cass, 1966). To deduce a turnpike property for the command economy let us explicitly write the dynamic of deviations from the steady state. We have

$$k_t - k^* = a_1\lambda_1^t + a_2\lambda_2^t$$

In the model we are considering this equation is subject to initial and final conditions $a_1 + a_2 = k_0 - k^*$; $a_1\lambda_1^T + a_2\lambda_2^T = k_T - k^*$. Since steady state is a limiting-state, the time needed to reach it is in general much longer than time horizon assumed by a central planner, so that for finite $t = T$ we have $k_T - k^* < 0$. When calendar time elapsed t becomes sufficiently long, the distance from T tends to become infinite. Deviations from steady state of per capita capital stock, by virtue of the stability of the steady state, tend to become null. Therefore we must have $a_2 = 0$. Let us also suppose that when the central planner takes the command, initial per capita capital

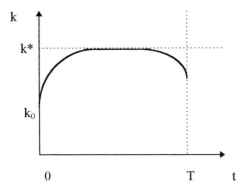

Figure 3.8 The turnpike property

stock is less than terminal capital stock, so that $k_0 - k^* < 0$ and $a_1 < 0$. Under these conditions, the economy appears under-capitalized and the central planner will modify consumption allocation in order to change capital stock evolution so that it approximates k_T in an optimal way over time. This is described by $k_t - k^* = a_1 \lambda_1^t$. If T is sufficiently long, distance $k_t - k^*$ tends to nullify rapidly, and becomes $k_T - k^*$ near to k_T. The path described by the turnpike theorem in plane (t, k_t) is shown in Figure 3.8.

In addition to the normative significance, the turnpike theorem has another implication. A system with finite horizon driven by a central planner usually stays a short distance from a steady state. This justifies approximating infinite horizon programmes as limits for solutions of programmes with a finite horizon and also supports the validity of formulating the central planner problem as a programme over finite horizon T.[9]

3.10   Fiscal policies and public expenditure

Government policy is put into effect through public spending and taxation. For the h-th agent fiscal policy is a quadruple of parameters $\{g_{1h}^t, g_{2h}^{t+1}, \theta_{1h}^t, \theta_{2h}^{t+1}\}$ relative to public spending and taxation for each period on the horizon. We assume lump-sum taxation $\theta_{1h}^t = \theta_1^t; \theta_{2h}^{t+1} = \theta_2^{t+1}$. For the sake of symmetry it is also useful to assume $g_{1h}^t = g_1^t; g_{2h}^{t+1} = g_2^{t+1}$. With a balanced budget policy, the government budget constraint at every instant is $\theta_1^t L + \theta_2^{t+1} L_{t-1} = G_t$. This constraint in per capita terms is

$$\theta_1^t + (1/1 + n)\theta_2^t = g_1^t + (1/1 + n)g_2^t = g_t$$

We assume identical preferences for agents of each generation and that private consumption marginal utility is not influenced by public spending. Therefore, the instantaneous utility function for the young is $U(c_1^t, c_2^{t+1}) + U(g_1^t, g_2^{t+1})$ and for the old $U(c_2^{t+1}) + U(g_2^{t+1})$. However, since g_1^t and g_2^{t+1} are parameters, a representative young solves the maximum problem

$$\max \quad U(c_1^t, c_2^{t+1})$$
$$\text{sub} \quad c_1^t + k_{t+1} = w_t - \theta_1^t$$
$$c_2^{t+1} = R_{t+1}k_{t+1} - \theta_2^{t+1}$$

On the contrary, the problem of the representative old person consists of consuming the entire disposable income, so that $c_2^t = R_t k_{2t} - \theta_2^t$. Taking into account the government balanced budget constraint $\theta_1^t + (1/1 + n)\theta_2^t = g_t$, the competitive equilibrium condition in per capita terms at time t is

$$c_1^t + (c_2^t/1 + n) + g_t + k_{t+1}(1 + n) - k_t = f(k_t)$$

Similarly, by considering the optimal saving function of the young $s_t(R_{t+1}, w_t - \theta_1^t, \theta_2^{t+1})$ and the competitive price system, the equilibrium condition at t is

$$k_{t+1} = (1/1 + n)s_t[1 + f'(k_{t+1}), f(k_t) - k_t f'(k_t) - \theta_1^t, \theta_2^{t+1}] - (1/1 + n)g_t$$

This is the fundamental dynamic equation of Diamond's model with taxation and a government balanced budget policy. Stationary fiscal policy is defined as the quadruple $(g_1, g_2, \theta_1, \theta_2)$ so that

$$\theta_1 + (1/1 + n)\theta_2 = g_1 + (1/1 + n)g_2 = g.$$

It is now possible to ascertain the redistributive effects of taxation and public spending, the effects of financing a temporary deficit spending by public debt, and the effects of intergenerational transfers such as those in social security systems. Let us start by assuming a balanced budget policy with public spending g financed by taxing only the young $g = \theta_1$ (or, even by taxing both generations, but with the tax burden greater for the young). Under these conditions the temporary equilibrium condition is

$$k_{t+1} - (1/1 + n)s[1 + f'(k_{t+1}), f(k_t) - k_t f'(k_t) - \theta_1] + (\theta_1/1 + n) = 0$$

which, solved for k_{t+1} gives the function

$$k_{t+1} = E(k_t, \theta_1)$$

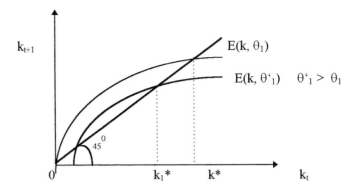

Figure 3.9   Effects of an increase of tax rate on the young generation

This describes the phase curve in the plane (k_t, k_{t+1}). The steady state for the given fiscal policy is the fixed point of each curve of the family of curves defined by the tax parameter θ_1 , that is

$$k = E(k, \theta_1)$$

The effect on steady state per capita capital stock of the increase in taxation on the young necessary to balance the increase in public spending depends on the sign of derivative $dk/d\theta_1$. By totally differentiating the steady state condition we can write[10]

$$dk/d\theta_1 = \frac{1 + \partial s/\partial w}{(\partial s/\partial w)kf''(k)} \frac{E'_k(k^*, \theta_1)}{E'_k(k^*, \theta_1) - 1}$$

If s is a normal good and $\partial s/\partial R > 0$, the curve $E(.)$ has positive shape in the phase plane. The steady state is stable, so the second term to the right of equality is negative, and so is the first term. It follows that $dk/\partial\theta_1 < 0$. Graphically, assumptions about the saving function imply that the phase curve in plane (k_t, k_{t+1}) is concave. Thus an increase of θ_1 shifts the phase curve to the right, as shown in Figure 3.9, determining a lower steady state per capita capital k.

Unlike the infinite horizon model with continuous time, where an increase of public spending financed by taxation entirely crowds-out private consumption, in Diamond's model an increase financed by increasing taxation on savers (the young) decreases only per capita capital steady state and increases the natural interest rate.

3.11 Balanced budget policy and lump-sum taxation

We shall consider a policy with a temporary deficit extending over periods t and t + 1. We assume that a deficit policy means a reduction in taxes with unchanged spending and that the government finances the deficit by issuing bonds which in the interval [t, t + 1] will pay the market real interest rate ρ_{t+1}. For the periods up to t − 1 and periods starting from t + 2 on, we assume that taxation and public spending revert to the balanced budget policy. Thus, generations outside the interval [t, t + 1] are not affected by the policy of temporary government debt. Let $x_1 \geq 0$, $x_2 \geq 0$ be respectively current reductions in taxes on the young and the old, so that $x_1 + (x_2/1 + n) = d$, where d is the current per capita deficit. In the period [t, t + 1] per capita deficit d causes per capita public debt $b_{t+1} = R_{t+1}d$. We shall refer to two cases: (a) the older generation in period t does not benefit from a reduction in taxation $x_2 = 0$; (b) the tax cut for the old is positive so that their current subsidy from taxation is $(\theta_2 - x_2)$.

Case a: $x_2 = 0$

In this case the constraints of the representative young are $c_1^t + k_{t+1} = w_t - \theta_1^t + d$; $c_2^{t|1} = R_{t+1}k_{t+1} - \theta_2^{t|1} - R_{t+1}d$. They are the same as the intertemporal constraint

$$c_1^t + (1/R_{t+1})c_2^{t+1} = w_t - \theta_1^t - (1/R_{t+1})\theta_2^{t+1}$$

This is the same as the case of a government balanced budget policy and can be considered as representative of situations where the benefits of reduced taxation are enjoyed by the same people who must eventually repay the debt. Since temporary deficit policy is the same as a balanced budget policy, we obtain the 'Ricardian equivalence' which, however, does not occur when persons who benefit from a deficit are different from those who must pay the subsequent surcharge. We shall verify this in the case (b).

Case b: $x_2 > 0$;

In this case the budget constraint of the old becomes $c_2^t = R_t k_{2t} + x_2 - \theta_2^t$, so that they increase their consumption. The constraints of the young becomes

$$c_1^t + k_{t+1} = w_t - \theta_1^t + x_1$$
$$c_2^{t+1} = R_{t+1}\,k_{t+1} - \theta_2^{t+1} - R_{t+1}d$$

These are the same as the intertemporal budget constraint

$$c_1^t + (1/R_{t+1})c_2^{t+1} = w_t - \theta_1^t - (1/R_{t+1})\theta_2^{t+1} - (d - x_1)$$

which differs from the case of a government balanced budget policy. The difference lies in the amount of disposable resources available to the young. In the aggregate, their resources are reduced by the same amount as the tax reduction currently enjoyed by the old. In this sense a current deficit is a burden for the younger generation. Ricardian equivalence is invalid in case (b) because the government budget deficit redistributes wealth between generations. In general, this occurs when the generation which benefits from the deficit is different from the one which must pay higher taxes.

3.12   Fiscal policy with taxation proportional to income from factors

In this section we set θ_L^t and θ_k^t tax-rates on labour income and capital income. Since by assumption the young possess only their labour and the old possess the entire capital stock, the government budget constraint in per capita terms is

$$\theta_L^t w_t + \theta_k^t \rho_t k_t = g_t$$

The structure of property rights implies that each change in the tax-rate mix is at the same time a change in the burden of taxes on one generation or the other. This means that when taxes are proportional to income factors, there is no Ricardian neutrality. Moreover, the fact that a given level of public expenditure can now be financed by infinite combinations of tax rates on income factors (and on different generations) creates a problem of choosing the optimum distribution of taxes on labour and capital. This complex problem is the object of the optimal taxation field introduced by Ramsey (1927), subsequently considered by Diamond and Mirrlees (1971), and recently studied by Lucas (1990).

Here we shall consider only a stationary fiscal policy, with stationary public spending and tax rates, where the constraints on the young in the two periods are

$$c_1^t + k_{t+1} = (1 - \theta_L)w_t$$
$$c_2^{t+1} = k_{t+1} + (1 - \theta_k)\rho_{t+1}k_{t+1}$$

and the constraint on the old is

$$c_2^t = k_{2t} + (1 - \theta_k)\rho_t k_{2t}$$

With $g_t = g$, the temporary equilibrium condition is

$$c_1^t + c_2^t/(1 + n) + k_{t+1}(1 + n) - k_t + g = f(k_t)$$

By taking into account constraints on agents and the government budget constraint, the equilibrium condition in terms of savings net of taxation $s_t = w_t(1 - \theta_L) - c_1^t$ becomes

$$k_{t+1} = (1/1 + n)s[(1 - \theta_k)\rho_{t+1} + 1, w_t(1 - \theta_L)]$$

To obtain the fundamental dynamic equation we must refer to the implicit condition

$$k_{t+1} - (1/1 + n)s[(1 - \theta_k)f'(k_{t+1}) + 1, w_t + \theta_k f''(k_t)k_t - g] = 0$$

where $w_t + \theta_k f'(k_t)k_t - g = w_t(1 - \theta_L)$ is disposable income y_d. By solving for k_{t+1}, we obtain the non-linear first-order difference equation

$$k_{t+1} = E(k_t, g, \theta_k)$$

For g exogenously given, the resulting phase curve defines a family of curves in plane (k_t, k_{t+1}) defined by tax rate on capital income θ_k. The change of tax-mix is described by the sign of derivative $dk/d\theta_k$ of the function $k(\theta_k)$ which is defined by solving the implicit steady state condition $k - E(k, \theta_k) = 0$. This derivative is

$$dk/d\theta_k = \frac{(\partial s/\partial y_d)kf'(k) - (\partial s/\partial R)f'(k)}{(\partial s/\partial y_d)kf''(k)(1 - \theta_k)} \frac{1}{\frac{E'_k(k,\theta_k)-1}{E'_k(k,\theta_k)} - \frac{2\theta_k}{(1-\theta_k)}\frac{f(k)}{kf''(k)}}$$

where $E'_k(k, \theta_k)$ indicates the same expression reported in note 10, section 3.10. The sign of $dk/d\theta_k$ depends on the sign of $(\partial s/\partial y_d)kf'(k) - (\partial s/\partial R)f'(k)$ which is undetermined even when savings is a normal good and is a non-decreasing function of the interest rate.

However, the effects of a change in the capital tax rate can be examined by approximating $dk/d\theta_k$ as in Aziariadis (1993)

$$dk/d\theta_k \cong \frac{(1 - \theta_k)\alpha}{(1 - \theta_L)(1 - \alpha)} - \frac{\varepsilon_{yd}}{\varepsilon_r}$$

where α is capital's share of output. Now the sign of $dk/d\theta_k$ depends on magnitudes economically significant which are empirically observable, the ratio of factors shares of output and the ratio of elasticity of savings with respect to incomes of factors. This adds to the result of the infinite horizon model a further condition. Indeed, now we can state that an increase in capital tax rate reduces steady state capital stock only if the relative factors share of output and relative elasticity of saving with respect to income factors is less than the unit. On the contrary, a change in the tax burden from labour to capital can even *increase* steady state capital stock if the ratio of income factors and the ratio of corresponding saving

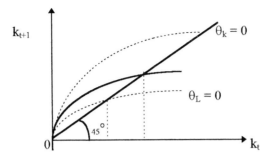

Figure 3.10   Effects of taxation of incomes from factors

elasticities exceed the unit. This is shown in Figure 3.10 and dashed curves indicate the extreme cases, $\theta_L = 0$ when only capital is taxed, or $\theta_k = 0$ when only labour is taxed.

3.13   Effects of social security on capital accumulation

The foregoing analysis of lump-sum taxation can also be used to examine the influence of a social security system on capital accumulation. A social security system pools funds exacted from employed agents to provide income to retired persons. Originally introduced for insurance and income redistribution purposes, social security systems also affect accumulation of capital because rates of contribution and transfers influence agents consumption and saving decisions. The effects, however, differ according to the way a social security system is devised.

There are two forms for hedging transfers. The first is a pay-as-you-go system where the amount of current contributions exacted from the young equals the amount of transfers to the old. The budget of a pay-as-you-go security system is defined as follows. Let z_t be transfers received by a representative old person at t, so that total transfers at t amounts to $z_t L_{t-1}$. Since the young number $L_t = (1+n)L_{t-1}$, a single young person must pay $z_t L_{t-1}/(1+n)L_{t-1} = \theta_t$. Therefore, the budget constraint of the social security system in per capita terms is $z_t/1+n = \theta_t$. A second form of social security system is a fully funded social security system in which transfers equal the principal plus interest earned by funds exacted from the young. The budget constraint of a fully funded social security system in per capita terms is obtained as follows. If θ_t is the rate of contribution of a single young person and R_{t+1} the current interest factor, total transfers at $t+1$ are $R_{t+1}\theta_t L_t$. Since current pensions amount to $z_t L_{t-1,}$, balancing the budget requires $z_t L_{t-1} = R_{t+1}\theta_t L_t$. In per capita terms this becomes $z_t/(1+n) = R_{t+1}\theta_t$.

Let us consider how a single agents constraint changes in a fully funded social security system. In a competitive economy with population growing at constant rate n, with members of the same generation having the same preferences, and with the young possessing only their labour and the old possessing capital stock, the representative agents constraints become

a) for the young

$$c_1^t + k_{t+1} = w_t + \theta_1^t$$
$$c_2^{t+1} = R_{t+1}(k_{t+1} + \theta_1^t)$$

b) for the old

$$c_2^{t+1} = R_t(k_{2t} + \theta_1^{t-1})$$

When a social security system is fully funded, the representative young person is subject to intertemporal budget constraint $c_1^t + (1/R_{t+1})c_2^{t+1} = w_t$. This constraint is the same as in the absence of a social security system. The introduction of a fully funded social security system, therefore, does not modify the individual consumption path and thus has no influence on capital accumulation.

In the aggregate the same conclusion is reached as follows. When the social security system is fully funded, the equilibrium condition is $c_1^t + (1/1+n)c_2^t + k_{t+1}(1+n) - k_t = f(k_t)$. By summing agents budget constraints and by taking into account competitive prices, this condition becomes $k_{t+1}(1+n) = s_t + \theta_1^t - R_t\theta_1^{t+1}/1+n$. Equilibrium still requires equality between desired capital accumulation and savings, but now savings is the sum of both private savings and social security savings. Since from the budget constraint social security savings is null, $\theta_1^t - R_t\theta_1^{t+1}/1+n = 0$, total savings coincides with the private savings of the economy without a social security system.

Let us now consider a pay-as-you-go system. Here agents constraints are

a) for the young

$$c_1^t + k_{t+1} = w_t - \theta_1^t$$
$$c_2^{t+1} = R_{t+1}k_{t+1} + \theta_1^{t+1}(1+n)$$

b) for the old

$$c_2^{t+1} = R_t k_{2t} + \theta_1^t(1+n)$$

The optimal saving function for the young is $s_t = s(R_{t+1}, w_t - \theta_1^t, \theta_1^{t+1}(1+n))$ and the equilibrium condition is

$$k_{t+1}(1+n) = s[1 + f'(k_{t+1}), f(k_t) - k_t f'(k_t) - \theta_1^t, \theta_1^{t+1}(1+n)]$$

In the following, when needed we put $y_1^t = w_t - \theta_1^t$; $y_2^t = \theta_1^{t+1}(1+n)$. Steady state equilibrium is

$$k(1+n) = s[1 + f'(k), f(k) - kf'(k) - \theta_1, \theta_1(1+n)]$$

The effect of changes in the rate of contribution on steady state equilibrium capital stock depends on the sign of the expression

$$dk/d\theta_1 = \frac{(\partial s/\partial y_2)(1+n)/R - \partial s/\partial y_1}{(\partial s/\partial y_1)kf''(k)} \frac{1}{(1+n) - f''(k)(\partial s/\partial R)} + 1$$
$$\frac{}{(\partial s/\partial y_1)kf''(k)}$$

If savings is a normal good and a decreasing function of the interest rate, and steady state is stable, the sign of $dk/d\theta_1$ depends on the sign of $\partial s/\partial y_1 = (\partial s/\partial y_2)(1+n)/R - \partial s/\partial y_1$. In general we can say the effect of an increase in the rate of contribution on savings is no longer a 'one-to-one' relationship as in a fully funded system. In a pay-as-you-go system such an increase is not limited to a pure intertemporal redistribution of resources. Indeed now there are also income effects due to the difference between the discounted value of the disposable income in the retirement period of the young and the amount of current contributions. This difference is caused by a growth in population. A difference between the growth rate of the population and the interest rate can cause a difference between the return of the social security system and the market return. The increase in tomorrows disposable income may make it less impelling for the young to save today and induce them to anticipate today the greater income that a larger population would make possible tomorrow when growth rate is greater than the interest rate. Reduction of current savings then can be greater than the simple amount subtracted for social security contributions. To verify this we must ascertain the sign of $\partial s/\partial \theta_1$. Let us consider the objective of the young in terms of savings $U[y_1^t - s_t, y_2^t + s_t R_{t+1}]$. Necessary first order conditions for optimal savings imply $U'(w_t - \theta_1^t - s_t) = R_{t+1}U'[\theta_1^{t+1}(1+n) + s_t R_{t+1}]$. By differentiating the latter at steady state we get

$$\partial s/\partial \theta_1 = -\frac{(1+n)RU''(c_2) + U''(c_1)}{R^2 U''(c_2) + U''(c_1)}$$

Therefore, $\partial s/\partial \theta_1 < 0$ so that steady state per capita capital stock decreases $dk/d\theta_1 < 0$. A pay-as-you-go security system ultimately has the same effect on capital accumulation as public spending for the elderly financed through a lump-sum tax on the young.

We now have to deduce how much savings is reduced in comparison to social security contributions. By considering the absolute value of the right-hand term of $\partial s/\partial \theta_1$, the numerator is greater, equal or less than the denominator according to $1 + n \geq < R$. Therefore, the reduction of aggregate savings induced by social security contributions in a pay-as-you-go system is greater or less than the resources subtracted from private savings depending upon whether the interest rate is greater or less than the growth rate of the population. This is the criterion for evaluating whether the introduction of a social security system is or is not Pareto-optimal. If at the moment when the social security system is introduced the economy is at a dynamic inefficient steady state, $R < (1 + n)$, the ensuing reduction in over-accumulation is Pareto-improving since inefficiency is reduced or eliminated. On the contrary, if $R > (1 + n)$ the first generation of old people improves its welfare to the detriment of the young welfare. Therefore, according to the Pareto criterion in this case the social security system does not better social welfare.

3.14   Fiscal policies and national debt

We shall now examine the effects on capital accumulation of a permanent deficit policy that generates public debt. The basic framework highlights both the significance and the effects of self-generating public debt. We assume a public debt consisting of one-period government bonds. Currently issued bonds mature in the next period. At time $t + 1$ both debt and accrued interest are refunded. A government policy of self-generating debt consists of refunding the outstanding debt of principal plus interest by issuing new debt. A simple way to model this policy is to hypothesize the absence of both public spending and taxation, so that interest payments are the only government expenditure. We already know that, when both deficit $d_t = R_{t+1}b_t + g_t - \theta_1 - (1/1 + n)\theta_2$ and public debt b_{t+1} are positive, government budget constraint in per capita terms is $(1 + n)b_{t+1} = R_{t+1}b_t + g_t - \theta_1 - (1/1 + n)\theta_2$. By assuming $g_t = \theta_1 = \theta_2 = 0$ we obtain $(1 + n)b_{t+1} = R_{t+1}b_t$. The basic dynamic equations of Diamonds model including servicing the debt by a new debt become

$$(1 + n)(k_{t+1} + b_{t+1}) = s[1 + f'(k_{t+1}), f(k_t) - k_t f'(k_t)]$$
$$(1 + n)b_{t+1} = [1 + f'(k_{t+1})]b_t$$

Before examining the solutions to this system of difference equations it should be pointed out that public debt $b_t > 0$ involves a condition which ensures that public debt is sustainable. In other words, a public debt $b_o > 0$ inherited can be maintained forever, which means $\lim_{t \to \infty} b_t = b_o > 0$.

A condition for sustainable public debt can be provided easily if we assume $R_t = R$, so that public debt evolves over time according to condition $b_t = b_o(R/1 + n)^t$. To be sustainable a public debt $b_o > 0$ requires $R < 1 + n$. Obviously, not every value $b_o > 0$ is admissible even when $R < 1 + n$ since there is a limit to the size of public debt. This limit is the total amount of resources of the economy.

Let us now to examine a steady state of the dynamic system. A steady state is a pair (k, b) that verifies

$$f'(k) = n$$
$$b = \frac{s[1 + f'(k) - kf'(k)] - (1 + n)k}{1 + n}$$

Evidently, the pairs (0, 0) and (0, k_D), where $k_D > 0$ is an economically significant steady state of Diamond's model without public debt, are both steady states. To avoid complications related to multiple equilibria we shall consider only the case where k_D is unique. This occurs when $E'(0) > 1$ and $E'(k_D) < 1$, where $E(k)$ is the phase curve of the model with zero public debt. In the phase plane (k_t, b_t) stationary conditions are the equations of loci $k_{t+1} = k_t$ and $b_{t+1} = b_t$. The equation $k_{t+1} = k_t$ is the familiar golden rule which corresponds to a line in plane (k, b) passing through k* and parallel to the vertical axis, as depicted in Figure 3.11. The direction of motion of points $b_t \neq b$ in the region $k_t \geq k^*$, since $f'(k_t)$ decreases in relation to k_t, is deduced from $b_t \geq b_{t+1}$. If, as we admitted, $b_t \geq 0$, the vector field in the region $k_t \geq k^*$ points in the direction

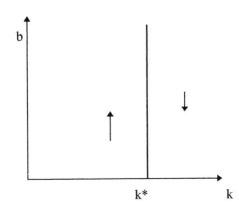

Figure 3.11 Dynamics of capital stock

opposite to the vertical axis, whereas for $k_t < k^*$ the vector field has the same direction of the vertical axis. The locus $b_{t+1} = b_t$ has the following properties:

a) when $k = 0$ it is b= 0 ; when $k = k_D$ it is b = 0
b) for $k \in [\, 0, k_D \,]$ we must have

$$db/dk = [(1 + n) - (\partial s/\partial R)f''][\frac{-(\partial s/\partial w)kf''}{(1 + n) - (\partial s/\partial R)f''} - 1]$$

We already know that $E'(k) = \dfrac{-(\partial s/\partial w)kf''}{(1 + n) - (\partial s/\partial R)f''}$ and, by assumption, $E'(0) > 1$ and $E'(k_D) < 1$. Since $E'(k)$ is continuous, the set $[0, k_D]$ contains k $= k_1$ where $E'(k_1) = 1$. It follows that $db/dk \geq 0$ for $k \in [0, k_1]$ The locus $b_{t+1} = b_t$ has a maximum at $k = k_1$ and it verifies $db/dk < 0$ for $k \in [k_1, k^*]$.

For $b_t \geq 0$ the phase curve $b_{t+1} = b_t$ looks like Figure 3.12. For a given k_t, an increase of b_t implies a lower k_{t+1} since

$$dk_{t+1}/db_t = -\frac{R}{(1 + n) - (\partial s/\partial R)f''} < 0$$

The points above curve $b_{t+1} = b_t$ move in the direction opposite to that of the horizontal axis, whereas points below the curve move in the same direction as the horizontal axis.

The intersection between locuses $k_{t+1} = k_t$ and $b_{t+1} = b_t$ identifies a unique economically meaningful steady state (k^*, b^*). To examine the stability of this solution we consider the system

$$k_{t+1} = F(k_t, b_t)$$
$$b_t = -\frac{\{1 + f''[F(k_t, b_t)]\}b_t}{(1 + n)}$$

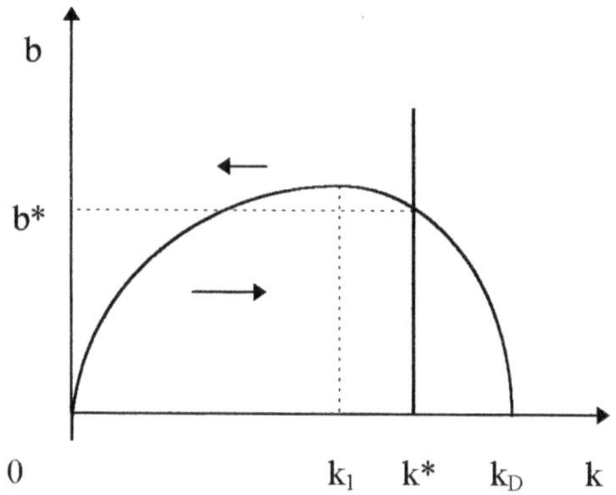

Figure 3.12   Dynamics of public debt and steady state

where $F(k_t, b_t)$ is obtained by solving the equilibrium condition of goods' market for k_{t+1}. Partial derivatives with respect to arguments of $F(.)$ are

$$(\partial F/\partial k_t) = -\frac{[(\partial s/\partial w_t)k_t + b_t]f''(k_t)}{(1+n) - (\partial s/\partial R_{t+1})f''(k_t)}$$

$$(\partial F/\partial b_t) = \frac{1 + f'(k_t)}{(1+n) - (\partial s/\partial R_{t+1})f''(k_t)}$$

Consider a linear approximation in a neighborhood of point (k^*, b^*)

$$k_{t+1} - k^* = -\frac{[\partial s/\partial w)k^* + b^*]f''(k^*)}{(1+n) - (\partial s/\partial R)f''(k^*)}(k_{t+1} - k^*)$$

$$-\frac{1 + f'(k^*)}{(1+n) - (\partial s/\partial R)f''(k^*)}(b_t - b^*)$$

$$b_{t+1} - b^* = -\frac{b^*f''(k^*)}{(1+n)}\frac{[(\partial s/\partial w)k^* + b^*]f''(k^*)}{(1+n) - (\partial s/\partial R)f''(k^*)}(k_t - k^*)$$

$$+ [1 - \frac{f''(k^*)b^*}{(1+n) - (\partial s/\partial R)f''(k^*)}](b_t - b^*)$$

The Jacobian of the system has a determinant and a trace

$$\det J = -\frac{(\partial s/\partial w)kf''}{(1+n) - (\partial s/\partial R)f''} > 0$$

$$\operatorname{Tr} J = [1 - \frac{(\partial s/\partial w)kf''}{(1+n) - (\partial s/\partial R)f''}] - \frac{2bf''}{(1+n) - (\partial s/\partial R)f''} > 0$$

The characteristic equation is

$$\lambda^2 - [1 - \frac{(\partial s/\partial w)kf''(k^*)}{(1+n) - (\partial s/\partial R)f''} - \frac{2bf''}{(1+n) - (\partial s/\partial R)f''}]\lambda$$

$$- \frac{(\partial s/\partial w)kf''(k^*)}{(1+n) - (\partial s/\partial R)f''} = 0$$

We can write $\operatorname{Tr} J = 1 + \det j + C > \det J$, where C is a positive number. The $(\operatorname{Tr} J)^2/4 > \det J$ and the discriminant is positive $\Delta = (\operatorname{Tr} J)^2 - 4\det J > 0$. According to Descartes' rule, the two distinct roots are positive. To check whether both the roots locate on the same side of the unit circle we compute

$$p(1) = \frac{2bf''}{(1+n) - (\partial s/\partial R)f''} < 0$$

so that the greater root, say λ_1, verifies $\lambda_1 > 1$. Therefore, steady state (k^*, b^*) is a saddle point. For a given initial per capita capital stock k_0 there is only one initial public debt b_0 where the starting point (k_0, b_0) locates on the convergent path. Another characteristic of this solution is that the steady state capital stock is the golden rule capital stock. This has implications for the efficiency of the steady state because if $k > k^* = k_g$, the steady state capital stock is dynamically inefficient. Public debt permits the economy to take a path convergent to golden rule capita stock. It eliminates the overaccumulation of capital which can exist in Diamond's model without public debt. This statement can be qualified by modelling fiscal policy and public debt so that public debt is permanently at given $b > 0$.

Given the government budget constraint and the assumption $g_t = \theta_1^t = 0$, a constant public debt policy is reduced to taxing only the old: this yields $(1/1 + n)\theta_2^t = b[R_{t+1} - (1 + n)]$. By substituting these values in the equilibrium condition, the dynamics of per capita capital becomes

$$(1 + n)(k_{t+1} + b) = s[1 + f'(k_{t+1}), f'(k_t) - k_t f'(k_t), (1 + n) \, bf'(k_{t+1}) - n)]$$

The steady state condition is

$$(1 + n)(k + b) = s[1 + f'(k), f(k) - kf'(k), (1 + n)bf'(k) - n)]$$

This equation admits at least one economically significant solution $k > 0$ for predetermined $b > 0$. To evaluate the effects of this policy on capital accumulation we must deduce the sign of dk/db, which is the same as the sign of the expression

$$\frac{(\partial s/\partial \theta_2[R - (1 + n)] - 1}{(\partial s/\partial \theta_2)f''b} G'(k, b)$$

where $G'(k, b) > 0$ is a function that depends on partial derivatives $\partial s/\partial R$, $\partial s/\partial w$, $\partial s/\partial \theta_2$. The ratio has a positive denominator when saving is normal good $-1 < \partial s/\partial \theta_2 < 0$. Moreover if steady state is also dynamically efficient $R \geq 1 + n$, the ratio has a negative numerator. Therefore an increase in the public debt has negative effect on steady state capital stock when $k_g \geq k$. However, sustainable positive public debt requires that $R < 1 + n$. Since this condition is verified, and since $k > k_g$, we must distinguish between two cases:

i) when $|(\partial s/\partial \theta_2)[R - (1 + n)]| < 1$ then dk/db remains negative. On the contrary

ii) when $|(\partial s/\partial \theta_2)[R - (1 + n)]| > 1$ then dk/db becomes positive.

We can give an economic interpretation to these conditions. Normality of saving with respect to taxation can also be stated as $(\partial s/\partial \theta_2) < 1$. Therefore dk/db is negative when $(1 + n) - R > -1$, that is if $f'(k) - f'(k^*) < 1$. From this we can conclude that when the public debt is sustainable and per capita capital k is not too far from golden rule stock, an increase in the public debt determines a reduction in steady state capital stock. However, if k belongs to a sufficiently wide right-neighborhood of golden rule stock k_g, an anomalous situation can occur and capital stock increases when public debt increases. Evidently whether and when one or the other situation prevails is an empirical matter. If we admit that an economy normally follows paths which are not very distant from dynamically efficient paths, or that when there is dynamic inefficiency it does not entail large capital overaccumulation, then it can be maintained that the public debt affects the economy the way a social security system does.

3.15 National debt and capital accumulation in a context of constant deficit policy

In this section we consider the effects of a constant deficit policy. We assume that the deficit is due to public spending on goods and services and that it is financed by interest-bearing debt. We also assume that the government follows a stationary spending policy. Therefore its budget constraint is

$$(1 + n)b_{t+1} = g + R_{t+1}b_t$$

The economy follows the equilibrium paths described by the system of difference equations

$$b_{t+1} = (1/1 + n)g + (1/1 + n)[1 + f'(k_{t+1})]b_t$$
$$k_{t+1} = (1/1 + n)s[1 + f'(k_{t+1}), f(k_t) - k_t f'(k_t)] - (1/1 + n)g$$
$$- (1/1 + n)[1 + f'(k_t)]b_t$$

This system is a family of systems which depend on the parameter g and it is generated by the basic dynamic model with a self-generating debt which is obtained when $g = 0$. Therefore the model with a constant deficit policy can be examined as modifications of the model with $g = 0$ when an arbitrary value $g > 0$ is admitted. Steady state equilibrium of an economy with $g \geq 0$ is a pair (k, b) which satisfies

$$b = \frac{g}{(1 + n) - [1 + f'(k)]}$$
$$k = (1/1 + n)s[1 + f'(k), f(k) - kf'(k)] - (1/1 + n)g - (1/1 + n)[1 + f'(k)]b$$

Examination of properties in the phase plane of the locus of points (k, b) that satisfies a public budget constraint must take into account that the first equation defines a two-fold curve according to condition $1 + f'(k) = R(k) \gtrless (1 + n)$. The slope of the locus therefore corresponds to

$$db/dk = -\frac{gf''}{[(1 + n) - R]^2} > 0 \text{ if } R > 1 + n,$$

$$db/dk = \frac{gf''}{[(1 + n) - R]^2} < 0 \text{ if } R < 1 + n,$$

Moreover $\lim_{R \to 1+n} b = +\infty$; $\lim_{k \to +\infty} b = (1/1 + n)g$, so that line $k = k^*$ is a vertical asymptote to the phase curve whereas line $b = (1/1 + n)g$ is a horizontal asymptote. Finally, when $g \geq 0$ the only region admissible is where $1 + n \geq R$. Based on this information, and by assuming that the relevant branch of the locus satisfying a public budget constraint is convex, a curve $b(k)$ depicting stationary combinations (k, b) satisfying government budget can be drawn as in Figure 3.13.

On the contrary, the locus of the equilibrium for the capital market is the same as in the case where $g = 0$, except that now it has a different location in the plane (k, b), depending on the values of g. It should be noted that changes in g shift both phase curves in plane (k, b) simultaneously. In particular since in the region $g \geq 0$ we have $\partial b/\partial g = 1/(1 + n) - R \geq 0$, increased g in Figure 3.13 shifts the curve $b_1(k)$ upward and to right in the plane. Likewise, since $\partial k/\partial g = -(1/1 + n)$ the phase curve $b_2(k)$ of the equilibrium in the capital market in Figure 3.13 shifts downward in plane. When g increases in the interval $[0, +\infty]$ there must be $g = g+$ so that the two phase curves are tangent, $db_1/dk = db_2/dk$.

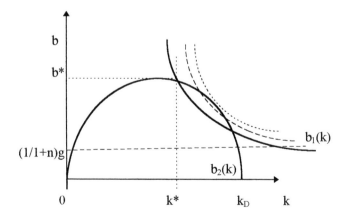

Figure 3.13 A phase diagram for growth with constant public deficit

For $g > g+$ no steady state exists. Therefore $g = g+$ defines the upper limit to feasible public spending. In the feasible set $g \in [0, g+]$ it is easy to deduce the dynamic properties of steady states with positive public debt. For every $g > 0$, the corresponding steady states maintain the stability properties of the model with $g = 0$. We should bear in mind that for $g = 0$ the system admits two steady states: the golden rule (k^*, b^*) and the Diamond solution $(0, k_D)$. The golden rule is a saddle point whereas the Diamond solution is a stable node. By increasing g in the admissible set, except for the limiting value $g = g+$, the shifting curves in plane (k, b) define two steady states, which properties are the same as the steady states for $g = 0$. A dynamic process burdened by a different permanent deficit policy depends on the steady state the economy is close to. Therefore, no general conclusion about the effects of a permanent deficit-spending policy on the dynamics of an economy can be drawn.

Notes

1. From the constraint on the consumption in the second period we obtain $s_t = (1/R_{t+1})(c_{t+1} - e_{t+1})$ which can be substituted into the constraint on consumption in the first period to give
   $$c_t = e_t + (1/R_{t+1})e_{t+1} - (1/R_{t+1})c_{t+1}$$
   This is equivalent to write intertemporal budget constraint
   $$c_t + (1/R_{t+1})c_{t+1} = e_t + (1/R_{t+1})e_{t+1}.$$

2. If savings function is known, constraints on the feasible consumption over the two periods yield
   $$c(R_{t+1}, e_t, e_{t+1}) = e_t - s(R_{t+1}, e_t, e_{t+1});$$
   $$c_1(R_{t+1}, e_t, e_{t+1}) = e_{t+1} + R_{t+1}s(R_{t+1}, e_t, e_{t+1})$$
   Optimality of consumption guarantees that these and the former functions coincide, that is
   $$c(R_{t+1}, e_t, e_{t+1}) = c[R_{t+1}, y(R_{t+1}, e_t, e_{t+1})];$$
   $$c_1(R_{t+1}, e_t, e_{t+1}) = c_1[R_{t+1}, y(R_{t+1}, e_t, e_{t+1})]$$

3. This representation involves a subtle issue in the central planner problem. Indeed, the optimum steady state problem comes from an intertemporal problem in which the central planner takes into account all generations from the start of time to infinity. To be well-defined this problem must admit an asymmetric treatment for the initial generation. Initial generation must be assumed to be old even at moment of birth. In this case a central planner maximizing the life-cycle utility of agents must maximize consumption of the initial generation. But maximum consumption coincides with the total disposable resources of the economy. Therefore, the central planner would devote all of the disposable resources to the old people of the initial generation. To overcome this problem, the solution commonly adopted is to assume initial consumption of the old people as given. But this is the same as admitting that to the central planner welfare function each generation, but one, has the same weight. The general formulation of the central planner

problem with equal weight for each generation and an infinite horizon is

$$\max \sum_{t=1}^{T} \sum_{t=1}^{T} U_h(c_h^t, c_h^{t+1})$$

$$c_h^{t+1} = e_h^t + (1/1+n)e_h^{t+1} - c_h^t \quad (t = 1, ...T)$$

$$c^1 = e^0 > 0; \lim_{T \to \infty} e^T > 0.$$

If we assume that in a steady state the objective of the central planner is the utility of the young, we admit the system has always been in steady state. The old people of yesterday receive the same treatment as those of tomorrow. By going backward in time the central planner would take care of todays old people by maximizing their utility as young people, and so on up to the end of time. This method entails equal treatment for all the old people of history, except obviously for Adam and Eve. We shall examine in detail this type of programming problem when we consider the model with physical capital accumulation.

4. This restriction follows from the assumption that young persons initial endowment is strictly positive and that resources over the entire horizon are limited. This assumption can be relaxed, although it would create formal complexities. Indeed the less restrictive condition of hemicontinuity of the budget constraint correspondence is sufficient to bound the set of economically significant prices. For the conditions required for budget set correspondence see Debreu (1959), Arrow and Hahn (1971),

5. This follows from the bound condition over saving function $s_t(R_{t+1}, w_t)/(1+n) \le w_t/(1+n)$. Since from $k_t = 0$ it follows also that $w_t = 0$ and $s_t(R_{t+1}, 0) = 0$, then $E(0) = 0$.

6. By calculating the derivative of $E'(k_t)$ we find that

$$E''(k_t) = $$
$$- \frac{[\partial^2 Z/\partial k_t^2 + (\partial Z^2/\partial k_t \partial k_{t+1})E'(k_t)]\partial Z/\partial k_{t+1} - [(\partial^2 Z/\partial k_{t+1}^2)E'(k_t) + (\partial Z^2/\partial k_t \partial k_{t+1})]\partial Z/\partial k_t}{(\partial Z/\partial k_t)^2}$$

By taking into account $-\partial Z/\partial k_t = (1/1+n)(\partial s/\partial w_t)k_t f''(k_t)$ and $\partial Z/\partial k_{t+1} = 1 - [(1/(1+n)\partial s/\partial w_t)f''(k_t)]$, and also that their respective second and mixed derivatives are

$$-\partial^2 Z/\partial k_t^2 = (1/1+n)[f''(k_t)\partial^2 s/\partial w_t^2 + f''(k_t)\partial s/\partial w_t + (\partial s/\partial w_t)k_t f'''(k_t)]$$
$$\partial^2 Z/\partial k_{t+1}^2 = -(1/1+n)[f'''(k_{t+1})\partial s/\partial R_{t+1} + f''(k_t)^2 \partial s/\partial R_{t+1}]$$
$$-\partial^2 Z/\partial k_t \partial k_{t+1} = (1/1+n)k_t f''(k_t)[(\partial s/\partial w_t \partial R_{t+1})f''(k_{t+1})]$$

by substituting we get the definitive expression of the second derivative $E''(k_t)$.

7. This follows from the implicit functions theorem. By virtue of this theorem, since $U''(c_2^t) < 0$ there exists a function $c_2^t = c_2(c_1^{t-1})$. The first derivative of this function is obtained by total differential

$$U''(c_1^{t-1})dc_1^{t-1} - U''(c_2^{t+1})(1+n)dc_2^t = 0$$

from which $c_2'(c_1^{t-1}) = U''(c_1^{t-1})/U(c_2^t)(1+n)$.

8. Indeed, it is

$$k^* = (1+n)^{-1}[(f(k^*)) + k^* - c_1^* - (1+n)^{-1}c_2(c_1^*)]$$
$$1 + n = 1 + f'(k^*)$$
$$U'(c_2^*)(1+n) = U'(c_1^*)$$

The first condition, even if only implicitly, is the usual definition of steady state per capita consumption

$$c^* = c_1^* + c_2(c_1^*)(1+n)^{-1} = f(k^*) - nk^*$$

The second condition is the golden rule. The third condition pertains to the intertemporal substitution rate.

9. When the horizon is infinite the central planner's objective is the infinite-sum sequence $\sum_{t=0}^{\infty} U(c_1^t, c_2^{t+1})$ whose terms must be positive because of the instantaneous utility function. The convergence of an infinite-sum sequence is not granted without adding some further restrictions. If it is assumed, as in Ramsey, that there is a 'Bliss' point, or that preferences incorporate a positive rate of temporal preference, or that the central planner discounts utility, it can be demonstrated that the infinite-sum sequence is convergent. A detailed examination of convergence criteria for the case of continuous time can be found in Koopmans (1965).

10. From the total differential taken for $dk_{t+1} = dk_t = dk$, it follows that

$$dk/d\theta_1 = -\frac{1 + \partial s/\partial w}{(1(1+n) - (\partial s/\partial R)f'' + (\partial s/\partial w)kf''}$$

The expression reported in the text is obtained by taking into account that

$$E_k'(k^*, \theta_1) = -\frac{(\partial s/\partial w)kf''}{(1+n) - (\partial s/\partial R)f''}$$

References

Abel, A. (1982) 'Dynamic effects of permanent and temporary tax policies in a q model of Investment', *Journal of Monetary Economics*, 9, pp. 353–73.

Allais, M. (1947) *Economie et Interet* (Paris: Imprimerie National).

Ando, A. and F. Modigliani, (1963) 'The Life Cycle Hypothesis of Saving: Aggregate Implications and Tests', *American Economic Review*, 53, pp. 55–84

Arrow, K. and F. Hahn (1971) *General Competitive Analysis* (San Francisco: Holden-Day).

Arrow, K. and M. Kurz, (1970) *Public Investment, the Rate of Return and Optimal Fiscal Policy* (Baltimore: Johns Hopkins Press).

Auerbach, A. and L. Kotlikoff, (1987) *Dynamic Fiscal Policy* (Cambridge MA: Cambridge University Press).

Azariadis, C. (1981) 'Self-fulfilling Prophecies', *Journal of Economic Theory*, 25, pp. 380–96.

Azariadis, C. (1993) *Intertemporal Macroeconomics* (Oxford: Blackwell).

Balasko, Y. and K. Shell (1980) 'The Overlapping Generations Model I: The Case of Pure Exchange without Money', *Journal of Economic Theory*, 23, pp. 282–306.

Barro R. (1974) 'Are Government Bonds Net Wealth?', *Journal of Political Economy*, 82, pp. 1095–117.

Barro, R. (1989) 'The Neoclassical Approach to Fiscal Policy', in R. Barro (ed.) *Modern Business Cycle Theory* (Cambridge MA:Harvard University Press).

Barro, R. and X. Sala-I- Martin (1995) *Economic Growth* (New York: McGraw-Hill).

Benhabib, J. (ed.) (1992) *Cycles and Chaos in Economic Equilibrium* (Princeton: Princeton University Press).

Benhabib, J. and R. Day (1982) 'A characterization of Erratic Dynamic in the Overlapping Generations Model', *Journal of Economic Dynamic and Controls*, 4, pp. 37–55.

Bertocchi, G. (1990) *Strutture Finanziarie Dinamiche* (Bologna: Il Mulino).

Blanchard, O. and S. Fischer, (1989) *Lectures on Macroeconomics* (Cambridge MA: MIT Press).

Cass, D. (1966) 'Optimum Growth in an Aggregative Model of Capital Accumulation: A Turnpike Theorem', *Econometrica*, 34, pp. 833–50.

Cass, D. (1972) 'On Capital Overaccumulation in the Aggregate Neoclassical Model of Economic Growth: A Complete Characterization', *Journal of Economic Theory*, vol 4, pp. 200–23.

Cass, D. and M. Yaari, (1966) 'A Re-examination of the Pure Consumption-Loans Model', *Journal of Political Economy*, 74, pp. 353–67.

Chamley, C. (1981) 'The Welfare Cost of Capital Income Taxation in Growing Economy', *Journal of Political Economy*, 89, pp. 408–96.

Debreu, G. (1959) *Theory of Value* (New York: Wiley).

Diamond, P. (1965) 'National Debt in a Neoclassical Growth Model', *American Economic Review*, Vol. 55, pp. 1126–150.

Diamond, P. and J. Mirrlees, (1971) 'Optimal Taxation and Public Production', (parts I and II), *American Economic Review*, Vol. 61, pp. 8-27/ pp. 261–78.

Farmer, R. (1986) 'Deficits and Cycles', *Journal of Economic Theory*, 49, pp. 77–88.

Farmer, R. (1993) *The Macroeconomics of Self-fulfilling Prophecies* (Cambridge MA: MIT Press).

Feldstein, M. (1974) 'Social Security, Induced Retirement and Aggregate Capital Accumulation', *Journal of Political Economy*, 82, pp. 905–26

Fisher, I. (1930) *The Theory of Interest* (New York: McMillan).

Gale, D. (1973) 'Pure Exchange Equilibrium of Dynamic Economic Models', *Journal of Economic Theory*, Vol. 6, pp. 12–36.

Galor, O. and H. Ryder, (1989) 'On the Existence of Equilibrium in an Overlapping Generations Model with Productive Capital', *Journal of Economic Theory*, 49, pp. 360–75.

Grandmont, J.M. (1985) 'On Endogenous Business Cycles', *Econometrica*, 53, pp. 995–1045.

Grandmont, J.M. (1986) 'Stabilizing Competitive Business Cycles', *Journal of Economic Theory*, 40, pp. 57–76.

Koopmans, T.C. (1957) *Three Essays on the State of Economic Science* (New York: McGraw-Hill).

Koopmans, T.C. (1965) 'On the Concept of Optimal Economic Growth', in *The Economic Approach to Development Planning* (Amsterdam: North-Holland).

Lucas, R. (1990) 'Supply-side Economics: an Analytical Review', *Oxford Economic papers*, 42, pp. 292–316.

McCandless, G. and N. Wallace, (1991) *Introduction to Dynamic Macroeconomic Theory* (*An Overlapping Generations Approach*) (Cambridge MA: Harvard University Press).

Phelps, E.S (1966) *Golden Rules of Economic Growth* (New York: Norton)

Ramsey, F. (1927) 'A Contribution to the Theory of Taxation', *Economic Journal* , 37, pp. 47–61.

Ramsey, F. (1928) 'A Mathematical Theory of Saving', *Economic Journal*, Vol. 38, 152, pp. 543–59.

Samuelson, P. (1958) 'An Exact Consumption-Loan Model of Interest with or without the Social Contrivance of Money', *Journal of Political Economy*, 66, pp. 467–82.

Samuelson, P. (1968) 'The Two-Part Golden rule Deduced as the Asymptotic Turnpike of Catenary Motions', *Western Economic Journal*, 6, pp. 85–9.

Samuelson, P. (1975) 'Optimum Social Security in a Life-cycle Growth Model', *International Economic Review*, 16, pp. 539–44.

Sargent, T. (1987) *Dynamic Macroeconomic Theory* (Cambridge MA: Harvard University Press).

Shell, K. (1971) 'Notes on the Economics of Infinity', *Journal of Political Economy*, 79, pp. 1002–012.

Stokey, N. and R. Lucas, (1989) *Recursive Methods in Economic Dynamics* (Cambridge MA: Harvard University Press).

Summers, L. (1981) 'Capital Taxation and Accumulation in a Life-Cycle Growth Model', *American Economic Review*, 71, pp. 533–44.

Turnovsky, S. (1995) *Methods of Macroeconomic Dynamics* (Cambridge MA: MIT Press).

4
Intertemporal Monetary Models with Infinite Horizon

4.1 The descriptive monetary growth model as a prototype of intertemporal models of monetary economies

The descriptive monetary growth model of Tobin (1955, 1965), like Solow's model for real economies, is a point of departure for intertemporal monetary models. It is based on the assumption that a money economy has a real sector exactly like that in Solow's model, so that the monetary nature of the model depends on how money is introduced into the model. The characteristics of a monetary economy are:

1. prices are expressed in money;
2. transactions require money;
3. financial wealth can be held in the form of money or financial instruments competing with money.

Point 3 necessitates a portfolio theory. In models like Tobin's, money is 'fiat money', a liability of the public sector and therefore it is not a 'produced' asset but a financial one. However as a depositor of purchasing power money can be held by private agents as an alternative form of wealth to physical capital stock. This enlargement of the set of choices for an owner of wealth as compared to the same set in a barter economy creates a problem of deciding the optimal composition of wealth at every instant.

The distinctive feature of Tobin's model is the assumed portfolio theory, which explains the desired composition of wealth. In real terms aggregate wealth V(t) at every instant t is

$$V(t) = K(t) + [M(t)/P(t)]$$

where P(t) is the price of output. Nominal money stock M(t) is controlled by money authorities. It is assumed that government levies no taxes and purchases no goods, and that its public debt stock is null. In addition the possibility of currently incurring a public debt is excluded. Government outlays at each instant are due only to transfers paid to households and revenues are raised only by the creation of money, that is by seignorage. Let X(t) be the aggregate real transfers to households and d[M(t)/P(t))]/dt the amount of seignorage.

From the former assumptions, the government budget constraint is

$$X(t) = d[M(t)/P(t))]/dt$$

Households disposable income Q_D includes government transfers, so that if Q(t) denotes aggregate output, households disposable income is

$$Q_D = Q(t) + X(t)$$

Let C(t), and $\dot{K}$ be consumption and net investment. The equilibrium condition of the market for goods requires that

$$Q(t) = C(t) + \dot{K}$$

From this, by assuming Keynesian consumption function $C(t) = (1 - s) Q_D$ we obtain the equation for the accumulation of aggregate capital

$$\dot{K} = sQ(t) - (1 - s)d[M(t)/P(t)]/dt$$

Since the assumptions on production function and population growth are the same as those in Solow's model, the equation for capital accumulation can be rewritten in per capita terms. Let L(t) be the instantaneous availability of labour. By dividing both sides of the equation for capital accumulation by L(t), since

$$\dot{K}(t)/L(t) = \dot{k} + nk(t)$$

and

$$\frac{d[M(t)P(t)]/dt}{L(t)} = \frac{d[M(t)/P(t)L(t)]}{dt} + n[M(t)/P(t)L(t)] = \dot{m} + nm(t)$$

if we assume $\dot{M}/M = \vartheta$, we get the following equations of accumulation of per capita physical capital and per capita real stock of money

$$\dot{k} = sf(k(t)) - (1 - s)[\vartheta - \dot{P}/P(t)]m(t) - nk(t)$$
$$\dot{m} = (\vartheta - \dot{P}/P(t) - n)m(t)$$

However, this system does not yet describe the equilibrium dynamics of the economy since it does not take into account for portfolio equilibrium.

Portfolio equilibrium requires that the existing composition of real wealth be equal to desired composition. Desired composition of real wealth is expressed as the desired proportion between real money stock and physical capital stock. On the assumption that this ratio depends on nominal rate of interest $i(t)$, portfolio behaviour in per capita terms can be described as

$$m^d(t) = l(i(t))k(t)$$

where $l(.)$ is a function satisfying $l' < 0$; $l(\infty) = 0$. Nominal rate of interest $i(t)$ is determined, according to Fisher, as the sum of real rate of interest $\rho(t)$ and expected inflation rate $p^e(t) = [\dot{P}/P(t)]^e$. Since the economy is competitive, nominal interest rate at every instant is $i(t) = f'(k(t)) + p^e(t)$. Therefore equilibrium of the money market requires that

$$m(t) = l[f'(k(t) + p^e(t)]k(t)$$

To explain the evolution of the system we must specify how expected inflation is determined. Three significant ways of determining expected inflation have been suggested in the literature (Nagatani 1970; Sidrauski, 1967; Stein, 1970).

a) Exact expectations, or an expected inflation rate equal to steady state inflation rate

$$p^e(t) = \dot{P}/P(t) = \vartheta - n$$

b) Adaptive expectations

$$p^e(t) = \lambda[\dot{P}/P(t) - p^e(t)] \; \lambda > 0$$

c) Perfectly foreseen expectations (rational expectations)

$$p^e(t) = \dot{P}/P(t)$$

We shall examine dynamics and steady states in these settings (a),(b), and (c).

4.1.1 Exact steady state equilibrium expectations

By assuming $p^e(t) = \dot{P}/P(t) = \vartheta - n$, steady state conditions are

$$0 = sf(k) - (-s)nm - nk$$
$$m = l[f'(k) + \vartheta - n]k$$

The first equation implicitly defines a relationship between k and m. If we solve for m, the function we obtain indicates the per capita real money

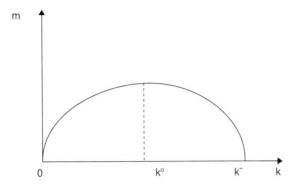

Figure 4.1   Per capita real money stock needed to keep capital stock stationary

stock m_d needed to keep capital stock stationary. Let us indicate this function as $m_d = e\,(k)$ which has the following properties:

1. $e(0) = 0$; $dm_d/dk = e(k) = [sf'(k) - n]/(-s)n$
2. $e(k^\circ) = \max e(k)$, for k° such that $sf'(k^\circ) = n$; $e(k)$ is increasing when $0 < k < k^\circ$; and decreasing when $k^\circ < k < k^\sim$, where $k^\sim$ satisfies $sf(k^\sim) = nk^\sim$.

Graphically in the plane (k, m) the function $e(k)$ corresponds to Figure 4.1
   Let us now consider the second condition as a function $m(k, \vartheta)$ which has the following properties

a) $m(0, \vartheta) = \lim_{k \to 0} l[f'(k) + \vartheta - n]k = 0$

b) $m'_k = [l'f''(k)k + l] > 0$; $m'_\vartheta = l' < 0$.

By assuming $m(.)$ is convex we can draw Figure 4.2.
   Steady state equilibrium (k^*, m^*) corresponds to $m(k, \vartheta) = e(k)$. Graphically this is the intersection of the curves in Figure 4.3
   Figure 4.3 implies the following:

- steady state of a money economy with exact expectations is dynamically efficient;
- an increase in the growth rate of nominal money stock causes a 'Tobin-effect', that is, an increase in steady state physical capital stock. Money, therefore, is not superneutral; and
- an increase in the growth rate of the nominal money stock does not necessarily generate a 'Fisher- effect', that is, an increase in the nominal interest rate.

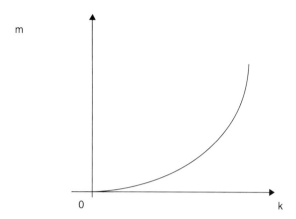

Figure 4.2   Desired real money stock as function of physical capital stock

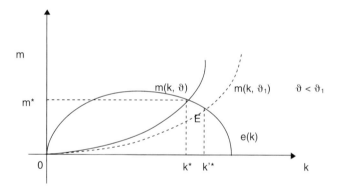

Figure 4.3   Steady state for a monetary economy with exact expectations

These properties can be shown as follows. In regard to dynamic efficiency, we already know that golden rule capital stock k_g is such that $f'(k_g) = n$. Consider now the intersection of the $e(k)$ curve and the horizontal axis located at $k^\sim$. This intersection is such that $f(k)/k = n/s$. Since $0 < s < 1$, then $f(k^\sim)/k^\sim > f'(k_g)$ and $k^\sim < k_g$. Since steady state verifies $0 < k^* < k^\sim$ it also verifies dynamic efficiency condition $k^* < k_g$.

The Tobin effect is the sign of derivative $dk/d\vartheta = -[m'_\vartheta/(m'_k - e'_k)]$. When $sf'(k) - n < 0$, we have $e'_k < 0$. The intersection $m(k, \vartheta) = e(k)$ is located on the decreasing portion of curve $e(k)$. In that portion $dk/d\vartheta$ is positive because $m'_\vartheta < 0$ which implies that when ϑ increases the curve

$m(k, \vartheta)$ shifts to the right in plane (k, m). Therefore the steady state capital stock increases as can be seen at k'^* at intersection E' in Figure 4.3. Finally, the Fisher effect depends on how the steady state nominal interest rate changes when the growth rate of nominal money stock increases. At steady state nominal interest is $i^* = f'(k^*) + \vartheta - n$. Therefore $di^*/d\vartheta = f''(dk^*/d\vartheta) + 1$. A Fisher effect $di^*/d\vartheta > 0$ requires $(1/f'') < dk^*/d\vartheta$. Thus, when $-(1/f'') \geq dk^*/d\vartheta$ there is no Fisher effect.

Now we must consider dynamics. The evolution of the system for a given constant money growth rate is described by the differential equation

$$\dot{k} = sf(k(t)) - (1 - s)nl([f'(k(t)) + \vartheta - n]k(t) - nk(t)$$

Approximating linearly near the steady state, we get

$$\dot{k} = [d\dot{k}/dk(t)]_{k=k^*}(k(t) - k^*) =$$
$$\{sf'(k^*) - n - n[(1 - s)l'(k^*)f''(k^*) + (1 - s)l^*]\}(k(t) - k^*)$$

Stability requires $[d\dot{k}/dk(t)]_{k=k^*} < 0$. Since $n[(1 - s)l'(k^*) f''(k^*) + (1 - s) l^*] > 0$, the sign of $[d\dot{k}/dk(t)]_{k=k^*}$ depends on the difference $sf'(k^*)-n$. Since for $k^{\#}$, $sf'(k^{\#}) = n$ and $d\dot{k}/dk(t) < 0$, the stability condition is verified in the interval $[k^{\#}, k^{\sim}]$ to which steady state capital stock belongs. Therefore the steady state is stable. In Figure 4.4 we can deduce the direction of motion. Since $k < k^*$ implies $\dot{k} > 0$, and $k > k^*$ implies $\dot{k} < 0$, points different from steady state move towards the steady state k^*.

4.1.2 Adaptive expectations

Adaptive expectations are $\dot{p}^e(t) = \lambda[\dot{P}/P(t) - p^e(t)]$ and the dynamic equation of money economy is obtained as follows. By differentiating

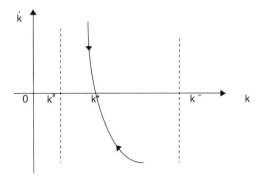

Figure 4.4 A phase diagram for a monetary economy with exact expectations

$m^d(t)$ with respect to time, from the equilibrium condition we obtain

$$\vartheta - \dot{P}/P(t) - n = [\frac{l'f''}{l} + \frac{1}{k}]\dot{k} + \frac{l'}{l}\dot{p}^e = (\frac{\varepsilon}{k})\dot{k} + \frac{l'}{l}\dot{p}^e$$

where $\varepsilon = \dfrac{l'f''k}{l} + 1$. Solving for $\dot{P}/P(t)$, inserting the solution into the equation of adaptive expectations and solving again for $\dot{p}^e$, the dynamic system ultimately reduces to equations

$$\dot{k} = sf(k(t)) - (1 - s)[\vartheta - p^e(t)]m(t) - nk(t)$$

$$\dot{p}^e = [\frac{\lambda}{(1 + \lambda l'/l)}][\vartheta - n - p^e(t) - (\varepsilon\dot{k}/k)]$$

At steady state we have $p^e = \vartheta - n$. The stationary condition for capital stock gives

$$sf(k) - (1 - s)nm - nk = 0$$

which is identical to that of a monetary economy with exact steady state expectations. Similarly, the stationary condition of the money market is the same as that in an economy with exact expectations. Therefore steady states of both the economics coincide.

However the dynamics is different. By approximating linearly in a neighbourhood of steady state (p^{e*}, k^*) we obtain

$$\dot{k} = [sf' - n - (1 - s)nl\varepsilon] (k(t) - k^*) + (1 - s) (m(t) - nl'k^*) (p^e(t) - p^*)$$

$$\dot{p}^e = [\frac{\lambda}{(1 + \lambda l'/l)}](\varepsilon/k^*)(\partial\dot{k}/\partial k)(k(t) - k^*) - [\frac{\lambda}{(1 + \lambda l'/l)}]$$
$$[1 + (\varepsilon/k^*)(\partial\dot{k}/\partial p^e)](p^e(t) - p^*)$$

By imposing stationary condition $\dot{k} = 0$ and $\dot{p}^e = 0$ and by differentiating totally, from the first equation we obtain

$$[\frac{dk}{dp^e}]_{\dot{k} = 0} = -\frac{(1 - s)(m - nl'k^*)}{sf' - n - (1 - s)nl\varepsilon}$$

Similarly, from the second equation we obtain

$$[\frac{dk}{dp^e}]_{\dot{p}e = 0} = -\frac{1 + (\varepsilon/k)(\partial\dot{k}/\partial p^e)}{(\varepsilon/k)(\partial\dot{k}/\partial k)} = -\frac{1}{(\varepsilon/k)(\partial\dot{k}/\partial k)} - \frac{\partial\dot{k}/\partial p^e}{\partial\dot{k}/\partial k}$$

$$= -\frac{1}{(\varepsilon/k)(\partial\dot{k}/\partial k)} + [\frac{dk}{dp^e}]_{\dot{k} = 0}$$

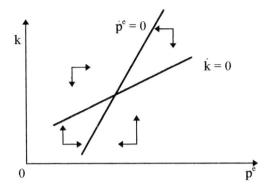

Figure 4.5 The Dynamics of price expectations and capital stock. The stable steady state case for adaptive expectations

If $sf'(k) < n$ the real sector of the economy is stable, both loci slope positively. Moreover since $(\partial \dot{k}/\partial k) < 0$ the $\dot{p}^e = 0$ curve slopes more than the $\dot{k} = 0$ curve. This can be seen in the Figure 4.5.

Figure 4.5 also shows the orientation of points out of the $\dot{k} = 0$ and $\dot{p}^e = 0$ curves. This orientation is deduced by assuming that $\dfrac{\lambda}{(1 + \lambda l'/l)} > 0$. When $p^e(t) - p^* = 0$, if $k > k^*$ it follows $\dot{k} < 0$. Similarly, when $k(t) - k^* = 0$, if $p^e(t) > p^*$ it follows that $\dot{p}^e < 0$. Therefore points above the locus $\dot{k} = 0$ have an orientation opposite to that of the vertical axis, whereas points below have the same orientation as the vertical axis. By the same token, points below locus $\dot{p}^e = 0$ have an orientation opposite to the horizontal axis, whereas points above that locus have the same orientation as the horizontal axis. The field of dynamic forces acting out of steady state is represented by the arrows in Figure 4.5. These forces push the system toward steady state.

This suggests that the steady state is stable. To verify this, let us consider the characteristic equation $\mu^2 - \text{tr}J\,\mu + \det J = 0$ of the linearized system. Since

$$\det\ J == -[\frac{\lambda}{(1 + \lambda l'/l)}]\{[1 + (\varepsilon/k)(\partial \dot{k}/\partial p^e)][sf' - n - (1 - s)nl\varepsilon]$$
$$- [(1 - s)(m - nl'k)(\varepsilon/k)(\partial \dot{k}/\partial k)]\}$$

$$\text{tr}\ J = [sf' - n - (1 - s)nl\varepsilon] - [\frac{\lambda}{(1 + \lambda l'/l)}][1 + (\varepsilon/k)(\partial \dot{k}/\partial p^e)]$$

if $\dfrac{\lambda}{(1 + \lambda l'/l)} > 0$ then $\text{tr}\ J < 0$. Moreover $\det\ J > 0$ requires

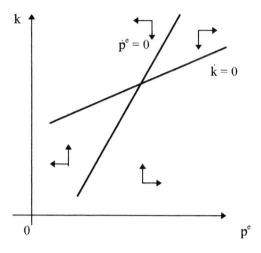

Figure 4.6   The Dynamics of price expectations and capital stock. The saddle-point steady state case for adaptive expectations

$[dk/dp^e]_{pe=0} - [dk/dp^e]_{\dot{k}=0} > 0$ which   is   verified.   However   when $\dfrac{\lambda}{(1 + \lambda l'/l)} < 0$ stability condition is violated.

   We shall investigate this violation of the stability condition later on. At the moment we shall only mention that when $\dfrac{\lambda}{1 + \lambda l'/l)} < 0$ steady state is a saddle point. This is evident in Figure 4.6 where the direction of motion indicates that steady state is stable only for those paths starting from sectors outside $\dot{k} = 0$ and $\dot{p}^e = 0$ loci.

4.1.3   Perfectly foreseen expectations (rational expectations)

With perfect foresight $p^e(t) = p(t) = (\dot{P}/P(t))$ we get the dynamic system of a monetary economy as follows. Given Fisher's rule for the nominal rate of interest, money market equilibrium is

   $m(t) - l[f^{\cdot}(k(t) + p(t)]k(t) = 0$

By differentiating totally and solving for $p(t)$ we get the function

   $p(t) = p(k(t), m(t))$

which has partial derivatives $\partial p/\partial k = -[(l/l')\varepsilon] > 0$ and $\partial p/\partial m = (1/l') < 0$.

By substituting in the equations of motion the differential system becomes

$$\dot{k} = sf(k(t)) - (1 - s)\{\vartheta - p[k(t), m(t)]\}m(t) - nk(t)$$
$$\dot{m} = \{\vartheta - p[k(t), m(t)] - n\}m(t)$$

A steady state solution is such that $p(k,^* m^*) = \vartheta - n$ and $s(f(k^*)) - nk^* = (-s)nm^*$. By approximating linearly in a neighbourhood of $(k,^* m^*)$, the linearized system becomes

$$\dot{k} = [sf'(k^*) - (1 - s)(\partial p/\partial k)m^* - n][k(t) - k^*] + (1 - s)$$
$$[(\partial p/\partial m)m - n][m(t) - m^*]$$
$$\dot{m} = -(\partial p/\partial k)m^*[k(t) - k^*] - (\partial p/\partial m)m^*[m(t)] - m^*]$$

The loci of point $\dot{k} = \dot{m} = 0$ have slopes

$$[dm/dk]_{\dot{k} = 0} = -\frac{sf'(k^*) - n - (1 - s)(\partial p/\partial k)m^*}{(1 - s)\{[\partial p/\partial m)m^*] - n\}}$$

$$[dm/dk]_{\dot{m}-0} = -\frac{\partial p/\partial k}{\partial p/\partial m}$$

The difference between the slopes is

$$[dm/dk]_{\dot{k} = 0} - [dm/dk]_{\dot{m} = 0} =$$
$$\frac{(1 - s)(\partial p/\partial k)[2(\partial p/\partial m)m^* - n] + (\partial p/\partial m)[n - sf'(k^*)]}{(1 - s)(\partial p/\partial m)\{[\partial p/\partial m)m^*] - n\}}$$

By assuming stability in the accumulation of physical capital $n - sf'(k^*) > 0$, the difference between the slopes is negative, so that steady state is unstable. Moreover the same stability condition for physical capital accumulation implies $[dm/dk]_{\dot{k}=0} < 0$ so that in plane (k, m) the $\dot{k} = 0$ locus slopes negatively.

Since the $\dot{m} = 0$ locus slopes positively, the linearized system can be illustrated as in Figure 4.7. The direction of the motion in Figure 4.7 shows the instability of the steady state. Formal proof of instability uses sign of

$$\det J = m^*\{(1 - s)(\partial p/\partial k)[2(\partial p/\partial m)m^* - n] + (\partial p/\partial m)[n - sf'(k^*)]\}$$

Since stability of physical capital accumulation entails $\det J < 0$, steady state is a saddle point. This suggests that since we have assumed accumulation is stable, instability in steady states is caused by the accumulation of money.

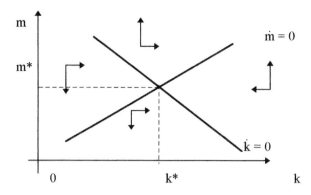

Figure 4.7   The Dynamics of real money stock and physical capital stock for a monetary economy with perfectly foreseen expectations

4.2   A possible source of instability in monetary economies: self-fulfilling anticipation of inflation

The possibility that a monetary economy generates explosive inflationary paths is well-known from Cagan's classical work (1956). We suggest thinking of Cagan's work not as a mere description of money economy, but as an attempt to insulate the pure 'essence' of a monetary economy. After highlighting the tendencies that can be attributed to the 'money-ness' of the economy, we can introduce a real sector and ask whether the interaction and/or feedback caused by the real sector can strengthen or weaken the tendencies caused by the monetary sector. If we keep this in mind and consider Cagan's model, the 'pure' monetary essence of the economy boils down to

1) the agent desire for growth in real money stock, which depends on the expected acceleration of inflation;
2) the monetary authorities desire for seignorage, expressed as rules for changes in the nominal money stock;
3) agents rule for expected inflation. Cagan assumes an adaptive expectations rule.

   Assuming that policy at point (2) is simply a rule for constant growth in nominal money stock, Cagan's model can be formulated as

$$\frac{\dot{m}^d}{m(t)} = -a\dot{p}^e(t)$$

$$\frac{\dot{M}}{M(t)} = \vartheta$$

$$\dot{p}^e(t) = b[p(t) - p^e(t)]$$

where the symbols have the same meaning as before. Dynamic analysis of this 'pure' monetary economy allows us to ask whether the constant nominal-money-stock-growth-rate rule is sufficient to avoid hyperinflation or whether there are conditions that stoke hyperinflation notwithstanding the constant rate monetary policy. We can ask if there is an expected steady rate of inflation $\dot{p}^e(t) = 0$ such that $p^e(t) = \vartheta$. To obtain an answer, let us assume stationary population and let us refer to the above equation for demand for money as the demand for per capita real money. By differentiating the definition of the real money stock in respect to time and by taking account of the constant growth rule for nominal money stock, equilibrium in the money market becomes

$$(\vartheta - p(t))m(t) = -am(t)\dot{p}^e(t)$$

Therefore, the fundamental dynamic equation of this economy is a linear differential equation of expectation of inflation

$$\dot{p}^e + (\frac{b}{1 - ba})p^e = \frac{b\vartheta}{1 - ba}$$

Since $b > 0$, stability condition $b/(1 - ba) > 0$ requires that $ba < 1$. By imposing $\dot{p}^e = 0$ we obtain $p^e = \vartheta$.

This stationary condition for money market equilibrium also implies $p = \vartheta$ so that $p = p^e$.

Deviations near the steady state are

$$\dot{p}^e = -[b/1 - ba](p^e - \vartheta)$$

In phase plane $(p^e, \dot{p}^e)$ this equation corresponds to the straight line depicted in Figure 4.8. The line slopes downwards or upwards, and the dynamics are stable or unstable as in Figure 4.8a or in Figure 4.8b, according to whether $ba < 1$ or $ba > 1$. An alternative representation of dynamics can be obtained by considering the evolution of the expected rate of inflation that is compatible to the equilibrium of the money market. By substituting the expression of the expected inflation rate into the equation for changes in time, we obtain

$$p^e = (\vartheta/ab) + (ba - 1/ba)p$$

In plane $[p, p^e]$ the 45 line is the locus of steady states $p^e = p$, so we can draw Figure 4.9.

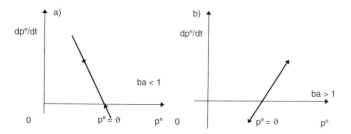

Figure 4.8   A phase diagram of expected inflation in Cagan's model

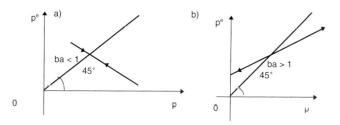

Figure 4.9   Dynamics of inflation in Cagan's model

Clearly, if the instability prevailing when $ba > 1$ is due just to the monetary nature of the economy, it will persist even when the monetary economy is more complex than the 'pure' one, that is even if it also includes a real sector for capital accumulation. Indeed stable accumulation of physical capital *per se* does not remove any possible instability which may have originated in the monetary sector. To demonstrate this let us consider the monetary growth model with adaptive expectation and stationary population in section 4.1.2. Let us now suppose that initial physical per capita capital stock is at its steady state level and the economy works instant by instant to stabilize per capita capital stock to this level. Such an economy has the dynamics described by equations

$$k(t) = k^*$$

$$\dot{p}^e + \frac{\lambda}{1 + (\lambda l'/l)} p^e = \frac{\lambda \vartheta}{1 + (\lambda l'/l)}$$

The stability condition is $\dfrac{\lambda}{1 + (\lambda l'/l)} > 0$, or, since λ is positive, $1 > -(\lambda l'/l)$.

This is exactly the same as Cagan's stability condition with $\lambda = b$; and $-(l'/l) = a$. Consequently when $-(\lambda l'/l) > 1$ the reasons for instability in Cagan's model are the same as they are for instability in the money sector and in general in a monetary economy with adaptive expectations.

4.3 A monetary growth model with consumer optimization on an infinite horizon

The limitation of the descriptive monetary model is that it assumes *ad hoc* behavioural functions, like the saving function which has a constant propensity to save and desired composition of wealth (portfolio preferences) exogenously given. Ramsey-Koopmans model based on optimal choices has also been extended to a monetary economy (Sidrauski, 1967), by reconsidering Patinkin's original static approach (Patinkin, 1965) in an intertemporal setting. In this extension, a monetary economy is characterized by an infinite-lived representative household having an instantaneous utility function which also includes the real money stock. The inclusion of money in the utility function has been justified because of the services money renders as a mean of exchange and because of its purchasing power. Money services consist of avoiding inconveniences caused when desired transactions are postponed or obligations can not be met because of money shortage. More generally money services can be attributed to economizing the resources needed for transactions. The resources needed to transform endowments held into endowments desired for consumption are dictated by a technology of transactions, but this technology is not specified in the money-in-the-utility function approach.

To examine the model, consider an economy with population growing at constant rate n. Using the same arguments as those used for Ramsey's model, a representative households objective is to maximize the functional utility of its representative member. The monetary nature of the economy in the budget constraint of the agent is reflected by the inclusion of the opportunity to accumulate savings in money or in physical capital. On the side of the monetary authorities, we assume as we did in the descriptive model that money is introduced into the system by lump-sum transfers paid to households. Agents disposable income, therefore, includes lump-sum government transfers in addition to labour and capital income. By letting individual real wealth $a(t) = k(t) + m(t)$, the representative agent solves the optimal control problem

$$\max V = \int_0^{+\infty} e^{-\beta t} u[c(t), m(t)] dt$$

$$\dot{a}(t) = w(t) + [\rho(t) - n]k(t) + x(t) - c(t) - (p^e(t) + n)m(t)$$

$$a(t) = k(t) + m(t); \; a(0) = k_0 + m_0; \; \lim_{t \to \infty} a(t) e^{-\int_0^t [\rho(\tau) - n] d\tau} = 0$$

Let $\lambda(t)$ and $\gamma(t)$ be respectively the co-state variable and the Lagrange multiplier. First-order necessary conditions are

$$u_c(c(t), m(t)) - \lambda(t) = 0$$

$$u_m(c(t), m(t)) - \lambda(t)(p^e(t) + n) - \gamma(t) = 0$$

$$[\rho(t) - n]\lambda(t) - \gamma(t) = 0$$

$$\dot{\lambda}(t) = \beta\lambda(t) - \gamma(t)$$

$$\dot{a}(t) = w(t) + [\rho(t) - n]k(t) + x(t) - c(t) - (p^e(t) + n)m(t)$$

These conditions can be proposed as

$$\frac{u_m(c(t), m(t))}{u_c(c(t), m(t))} = \rho(t) + p^e(t)$$

$$\frac{\dot{u}_c(c(t), m(t))}{u_c(c(t), m(t))} = n + \beta - \rho(t)$$

In the latter formulation, the first equality states that the opportunity cost from holding money, or the expected nominal rate of interest $i(t) = \rho(t) + p^e(t)$, must be equal to the marginal rate of substitution of money for consumption. The second equality is the modified golden rule.

In a competitive economy with a constant growth rate of nominal money stock $\dot{M}/M(t) = \vartheta$, the expressions for competitive prices and for growth of real money stock in per capita terms allow us to describe dynamics by the equations

$$u_m(c(t), m(t)) = u_c(c(t), m(t))[f'(k(t)) + p^e(t)]$$

$$\frac{u_{cc}(c(t), m(t))}{u_c(c(t), m(t))}\dot{c} + \frac{u_{cm}(c(t), m(t))}{u_c(c(t), m(t))}\dot{m} = n + \beta - f'(k(t))$$

$$\dot{k} + n\,k(t) + \dot{m} + n\,m(t) = f(k(t)) + x(t) - p^e(t)m(t) - c(t)$$

$$\dot{m} = (\vartheta - n - \dot{P}/P(t))m(t)$$

It is easy to verify that the same equations are derived from the necessary conditions for the central planner optimal control problem of maximizing utility functional of representative agent, that is the control problem

$$\max V = \int_0^{+\infty} e^{-\beta t} u[c(t), m(t)] dt$$

$$\dot{a}(t) = f(k(t)) + x(t) - c(t)$$

to which must be added initial conditions and a transversality condition.

By reworking the first order conditions for optimal control we can trace those conditions back to a normal differential system in the per capita consumption, physical capital and real stock of money.

To this end, let us assume perfect foresight $p^e(t) = p(t) = \dot{P}/P(t)$ and look at the first of the optimal conditions as an implicit function in $(\dot{P}/P(t), c(t), m(t))$. By differentiating totally and solving for the inflation rate we obtain the explicit function

$$\dot{P}/P(t) = p(c(t), m(t), k(t))$$

whose partial first derivatives are

$$\partial p/\partial c = \frac{u_{mc}\, u_c - u_m\, u_{cc}}{u_c^2}$$

$$\partial p/\partial m = \frac{u_{mm}\, u_c - u_m\, u_{cm}}{u_c^2}$$

$$\partial p/\partial k = -f''$$

Here u_i and u_{ij} are first and second partial derivatives with respect to the arguments of the instantaneous utility function. We assume that both per capita consumption and real money stock are normal goods $\partial p/\partial c > 0$; $\partial p/\partial m < 0$. The dynamic system becomes

$$\dot{c} = \frac{u_c}{u_{cc}}[n + \beta - f'(k(t)] - \frac{u_{cm}}{u_{cc}}[\vartheta - n - p(c(t), m(t)]m(t)$$

$$\dot{m} = [\vartheta - n - p(c(t), m(t), k(t)m(t)$$

$$\dot{k} = f(k(t) - nk(t) - c(t)$$

The linearized system in a neighbourhood of steady state is

$$\dot{c} = (\frac{u_{cm}}{u_{cc}}m^* \frac{\partial p}{\partial c})(c(t) - c^*) + (\frac{u_{cm}}{u_{cc}}m^* \frac{\partial p}{\partial m})(m(t) - m^*)$$

$$- [\frac{f''}{u_{cc}}(m^* u_{cm} + u_c)](k(t) - k^*)$$

$$\dot{m} = -(\frac{\partial p}{\partial c}m^*)(c(t) - c^*) - (\frac{\partial p}{\partial m}m^*)(m(t) - m^*) + f'm^*(k(t) - k^*)$$

$$\dot{k} = -(c(t) - c^*) + \beta(k(t) - k^*)$$

The characteristic equation associated with this system is

$$-\mu^3 + \text{tr}\, J\mu^2 - S_2\mu + \det\, J = 0$$

where det J and tr J are determinant and trace of the matrix of the linearized system, while $S_2 = d_{11} + d_{22} + d_{33}$, where d_{ii} (i = 1, 2, 3) are second order principal minors of det J. We have

$$\det J = \frac{u_c f''}{u_{cc}} m^* \frac{\partial p}{\partial m}$$

$$\operatorname{tr} J = m^*[\frac{u_{cm}}{u_{cc}} \frac{\partial p}{\partial c}] - \frac{\partial p}{\partial m} + \beta = m^* \frac{u_{cm}(\partial p/\partial c) - u_{cc}(\partial p/\partial m)}{u_{cc}} + \beta$$

From the first equation it follows det J < 0. To ascertain the sign of tr J we observe that

$$\frac{u_{cm}(\partial p/\partial c) - u_{cc}(\partial p/\partial m)}{u_{cc}} = \frac{1}{u_{cc}} \{u_{cm}[\frac{u_{mc}}{u_c} - \frac{u_m u_{cc}}{u_c^2}]$$

$$+ u_{cc}[\frac{u_m u_{cm}}{u_e^2} - \frac{u_{mm}}{u_c}]\} = (-\frac{1}{u_{cc} u_c})(u_{cc} u_{mm} - u_{cm}^2)$$

This is positive because the instantaneous utility function is strict concave, and this reduces tr J to a sum of positive addends, so that tr J > 0. Since the determinant is negative, det J < 0 the system is unstable. Moreover, a positive tr J entails that at least one root is positive, and this together with det J < 0 entails a negative root. Therefore steady state is a saddle point.

4.4 Issues in the optimizing monetary model: 1. Superneutrality of money

We shall use Sidrauski's model of section 4.3 to consider three controversial issues: the superneutrality of money; the effects of monetary policy on social welfare; and the existence of hyperinflation paths in a monetary economy with perfect foresight and a constant nominal money stock growth policy. We shall begin by considering the superneutrality of money. Steady state $\dot{c} = \dot{k} = \dot{m} = 0$ must verify

$$p(c, m, k) = \vartheta - n$$
$$f'(k) = n + \beta$$
$$c = f(k) - nk$$

that is

$$p(f(k) - nk, m, k) = \vartheta - n$$
$$f'(k) = n + \beta$$

By solving the first equality for m we obtain the function

$$m = \varphi(k, \vartheta)$$

which has partial derivatives

$$\partial m/\partial k = \frac{(\partial p/\partial c)[f'(k) - n] - f''(k)}{\partial p/\partial m}; \text{ and } \partial m/\partial \vartheta = \frac{1}{\partial p/\partial m}$$

From the assumption that both per capita consumption and real money stock are normal goods, in the interval $[0, k_g]$, where k_g is such that $f'(k_g) = n$, it follows that $\partial m/\partial k > 0$. Moreover, it is $\partial m/\partial \vartheta < 0$. In the plane (k, m) by drawing $\varphi(k, \vartheta)$ as in Figure 4.10, steady state graphically locates at the intersection between $\varphi(k, \vartheta)$ and the vertical line $f'(k^*) = n + \beta$.

Since an increase in the growth rate of money shifts the curve $\varphi(k)$ downward in Figure 4.10, the superneutrality of money is easily deduced. Therefore, steady state real money stock is reduced but steady state capital stock k^* remains unchanged. The invariance of per capita capital stock and consequently the invariance of per capita consumption with respect to changes in the growth rate of money stock is not a specific property of optimal monetary growth models. Sidrauski's model is only a prototype of optimizing monetary models, so it is natural to extend it to phenomena that have been ignored until now. Among the various extensions proposed in the literature (Levhari and Patinkin, 1968; Dornbusch and Frenkel, 1973; Siegel, 1983) we shall consider the one which excludes a

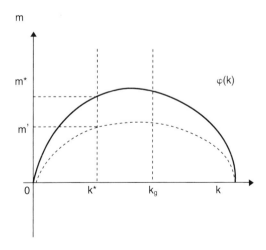

Figure 4.10   Steady state equilbrium of optimizing monetary (Sidrauski's) model

rigid work supply and includes leisure in the individual instantaneous utility function (Brock, 1974). This necessitates a modification of the production function as well.

In fact now output depends on the number of hours worked $N(t)$, so that per capita output is $q(t) = f(k(t), l(t))$, where $l(t) = N(t)/L(t)$. The instantaneous utility function, on the contrary, will include the variable $l(t)$. Available time has been normalized to the unit, so the variable $1 - l(t)$ defines time the agent spent in leisure. Leisure is just another good. Therefore, with respect to leisure the instantaneous utility function has the same properties it has with respect to consumption, that is $u'_{1-l(t)} > 0; u''_{1-l(t)} < 0$. The optimal control problem of the representative individual now becomes

$$\max V = \int_0^{+\infty} e^{-\beta t} u[c(t), 1 - l(t), m(t)] dt$$

$$\dot{a}(t) = w(t)l(t) + [\rho(t) - n] k(t) + x(t) - c(t) - (p^e(t) + n)m(t)$$

$$a(t) = k(t) + m(t); a(0) = k_0 + m_0; \lim_{t \to \infty} a(t) e^{-\int_0^{+\infty} [\rho(\tau) - n] d\tau} = 0$$

First order necessary conditions are

$$u'_c[c(t), 1 - l(t), m(t)] - \lambda(t) = 0$$
$$u'_l[c(t), 1 - l(t), m(t)] + w(t)\lambda(t) = 0$$
$$u'_m[c(t), 1 - l(t), m(t)] - \lambda(t)[p^e(t) + n] - \gamma(t) = 0$$
$$[\rho(t) - n]\lambda(t) - \gamma(t) = 0$$
$$\dot{\lambda}(t) = \beta\lambda(t) - \gamma(t)$$
$$\dot{a}(t) = w(t)l(t) + [\rho(t) - n] k(t) + x(t) - c(t) - (p^e(t) + n) m(t)$$

By taking into account competitive prices, steady state conditions are

$$u'_m[f(k, l) - nk, 1 - l, m] = u'_c[f(k, l) - nk, 1 - l, m][f'_k(k, l) + \vartheta - n]$$
$$u'_l[f(k, l) - nk, 1 - l, m] = u'_c[f(k, l) - nk, 1 - l, m][f'_l(k, l)]$$
$$f'_k(k, l) = n + \beta$$

The first two equations are implicit functions of m and l. By solving for m and l we obtain the respective explicit functions $m(k, \vartheta)$ and $l(k, \vartheta)$, so that the modified golden rule becomes

$$f'_k(k, l(k, \vartheta)) = n + \beta$$

It is now evident that steady state per capita capital stock also depends on the rate of growth of the nominal money stock. Thus, money is no longer superneutral. However, by imposing a further condition on the marginal rate of substitution between consumption and working time it is possible to restore the superneutrality of money even with a flexible labour supply, as for example when the utility function is Cobb-Douglas. But it is also true that conditions which do not greatly restrict the elasticity of marginal utility (in particular of money in relation to consumption) refute the superneutrality of money even in Sidrauski's model with a rigid work supply (Chirichiello, 1992). Practical divergence from superneutrality may even be considered negligible (McCallum, 1990), it is indisputable that from a theoretical point of view superneutrality of money is itself very special result because it is not a general property of intertemporal optimizing monetary models.

4.5   Issues in the optimizing monetary model: 2. Welfare effects of inflation

Friedman (1969) viewed the effects of alternative inflation rates on social welfare as an optimum-quantity-of-money problem in order to support the famous 'Chicago rule' of policy. In reality posing an optimum-quantity-of-money problem is only an indirect way of posing the problem of optimal behaviour of prices, since the real money stock depends on the behaviour of the general price level. Sidrauski's model lends itself to this kind of analysis since superneutrality of money does not exclude steady state real money stock changes as response to changes in growth rate of the nominal money stock. Indeed, effects on social welfare are directly connected to the changes in real money stock due to changes in growth of the nominal money stock. Real money now is one variable in the utility function and the level of real money stock at steady state influences agents welfare. According to Friedman, since monetary policy means changes in the money stock, choice of a policy is a welfare problem which should be evaluated according to the Pareto-optimum criterion.

The point of departure for this argument is that from society's point of view the cost of producing money is null, because real money stock can be modified through changes in the general price level. In order to compare the costs and benefits of changes in real money stock a society must only evaluate the return on money stock compared to the return on other assets. The return on money is the negative of the rate of inflation, that is the deflation rate. Thus it is optimal for a society to have a deflation rate equal to the real interest rate paid on real assets. Brock (1974) has proven this argument in an intertemporal model with money as the only means of accumulating wealth. Brock's proof can be extended to Sidrauski's model where there is physical capital accumulation in addition to money accumulation.

Therefore, let us consider a central planner whose aim is to maximize the welfare function in a monetary economy. We have already seen that this problem is posed as a maximum problem of the functional utility of the representative individual, subject to the constraint of disposable resources. In a monetary economy a monetary policy rule must also be taken into account. Therefore, the optimal control problem of a central planner is

$$\max V = \int_0^{+\infty} e^{-\beta t} u[c(t), m(t)] dt$$

$$\dot{k}(t) + nk(t) + \dot{m} + nm(t) = f(k(t)) + x(t) - c(t)$$

$$\dot{m} + nm(t) = x(t)$$

$$k(0) = k_0; m(0) = m_0; \lim_{t \to \infty} \lambda(t) e^{-\beta t} k(t) = 0$$

In an economy with a stationary population, therefore, we can state the central planner problem

$$\max V = \int_0^{+\infty} e^{-\beta t} u[c(t), m(t)] dt$$

$$\dot{k}(t) = f(k(t)) - c(t)$$

$$k(0) = k_0; m(0) = m_0$$

where we have ignored the transversality condition. First-order conditions for optimal control are

$$u'_c[c(t), m(t)] - \lambda(t) = 0$$

$$u'_m[c(t), m(t)] = 0$$

$$\dot{k}(t) = f(k(t)) - c(t)$$

$$\dot{\lambda}(t) = \beta \lambda(t) - \lambda(t) f'(k(t))$$

Steady state requires

$$u'_c(c^*, m^*) = \lambda^*$$

$$u'_m(c^*, m^*) = 0$$

$$f(k^*) = c^*$$

$$f'(k^*) = \beta$$

Consider now the decentralized monetary economy described in Section 4.3 by assuming a stationary population. Necessary conditions for the optimal control problem of the representative agent show that steady state satisfies

$$u'_c(c^*, m^*) = \lambda^*$$
$$u'_m(c^*, m^*) = \lambda^* p^* + \gamma^*$$
$$f(k^*) = c^*$$
$$f'(k^*) = \beta$$
$$\gamma^* = \lambda^* \beta$$

After substitutions, the second condition becomes

$$u'_m(c*, m^*) = \lambda^*(p^* + \beta)$$

Since $\lambda^* > 0$, the solutions of the decentralized system coincide with those of the central planner when the inflation rate at steady state is such that

$$-p^* = \beta$$

This is Friedman's rule for optimum quantity of money. By virtue of equality $f'(k^*) = \beta$, the same optimum condition can be formulated as

$$u'_m(c^*, m^*) = \lambda^*(p^* + f'(k^*)) = 0$$

which is the same as $i^* = p^* + f'(k^*) = 0$. Therefore, the optimum quantity of money rule is also proposed as the condition that the nominal interest rate at steady state ought to be null.

4.6 Issues in the optimizing monetary model: 3. The possibility of self-generating hyperinflation

The last of issue in optimizing monetary models concerns the admission of hyperinflation phenomena into economies inhabited by rational agents with perfect foresight. To ascertain whether money growth as described by Sidrauski can admit hyperinflation paths we shall adopt a methodology we adopted in the descriptive monetary model. There we described a monetary economy similar to a Cagan-like pure monetary economy 'plunged' into a system which also accumulates physical capital. Consequently, let us suppose that the economy at some instant reaches a state where $\dot{k} = 0$; $\dot{c} = 0$; and $\dot{m} \neq 0$. It then operates by satisfying the conditions $k(t) = k^*$; $c(t) = c^*$. Finally, assume that the instantaneous utility function is separable in consumption and real money stock so that marginal utility of consumption is unchanged when the money stock changes, that is $u'_c(c^*, m(t)) = \lambda^*$.

Under the conditions just described the dynamics of the economy are the following differential equations

$$u'_m(c^*, m(t)) = \lambda^*(p^e(t) + f'(k^*))$$
$$f'(k^*) = n + \beta$$
$$\dot{m} = [\theta - n - p(t)]m(t)$$

Because of perfect foresight, these conditions are the same as

$$u'_m(m(t)) = \lambda^*[p(t) + n + \beta]$$
$$\dot{m} = \{\theta - n - p(t)]m(t)$$

Solving the first equation for $p(t)$ and substituting it into the second we obtain

$$\dot{m} = \{(\theta + \beta) - [u'_m(m(t))/\lambda^*]\}m(t)$$

The dynamic of the real money stock in continous time, therefore, is the same as in Brocks discrete time(1974;1975). Steady state $\dot{m} = 0$ is a real money stock m^* so $u'_m(m^*) = \lambda^*(\theta + \beta)$, that is the same condition as that in the previous section. The stability of this solution can be verified by referring to the linear approximation

$$\dot{m} = -[u'_m m(m(t))/\lambda^*](m(t) - m^*)$$

Since $-[u_{mm}(m(t))/\lambda^*] > 0$, and steady state $m(t) = m^*$ is unstable, we can answer the question of what equilibrium paths $m(t)$ the economy will follow if it starts from a position $m_0 \neq m^*$. In particular are there any feasible paths compatible with hyperinflation phenomena, which prevail when $m(t) \to 0$ as $t \to +\infty$?

As we shall verify, a transversality condition allows us to exclude hyper-deflationary paths for which $m(t) \to +\infty$ because these paths are non-optimal. However the transversality condition is not sufficient to exclude paths for which $m(t) \to 0$. Thus, let $m(t) \to +\infty$ and assume the utility function verifies $u'_m(m(t)) \to 0$ as $m(t) \to +\infty$. Given previous assumptions, each equilibrium path where real money stock diverges belongs to the class of functions $m(t) = (m_0 - m^*)e^{(\theta+\beta)t}$ for $m_0 - m^* > 0$. Such paths verify

$$\dot{m} = (m_0 - m^*)(\theta + \beta)e^{(\theta+\beta)t} = (\theta + \beta)m(t)$$
$$\lim_{m(t)\to+\infty} \dot{m}/m(t) = (\theta + \beta)$$

These solutions, however, do not satisfy the transversality condition since

$$\lim_{t \to +\infty} \lambda^*(m_0 - m^*)e^{(\theta+\beta)t}e^{-\theta t} = \lim_{t \to +\infty} (m_0 - m^*)e^{\beta t} = +\infty$$

On the contrary, let us admit that the utility function also verifies $\lim_{t \to +\infty} u'_m(m(t)) = +\infty$. Paths where $m(t) \to 0$ as $t \to +\infty$ are consistent with transversality condition $\lim_{t \to +\infty} \lambda^* m(t)e^{-\theta t} = 0$. Moreover, by taking into account the equation of dynamic equilibrium, if $\lim_{t \to +\infty} u'_m(m(t))m(t) = 0$ holds, paths where $m(t) \to 0$ as $t \to +\infty$ also verify the steady state condition because $\lim_{t \to +\infty} \dot{m} = 0$. The existence of these paths is proved by observing that

$$\lim_{t \to +\infty} u'_m(m(t))m(t) = \lim_{t \to +\infty} m(t)/[(1/u'_m(m(t))]$$

This is an undetermined form to which Hopital's rule can be applied, so the limit is the same as

$$\lim_{t \to +\infty} \dot{m}/[1/u'_m(m(t))] = \lim_{t \to +\infty} \dot{m}/-(\mu'_m/u'_m)$$

The right-hand side limit is null if the rate of growth of the marginal utility of money is greater than the rate of contraction of the real stock of money. Therefore a competitive economy with perfect foresight admits equilibrium paths with hyperinflation.

Appendix: Alternative Models of Infinite Horizon Monetary Economies

Models of monetary economies which do not incorporate money into the utility function and do not satisfy superneutrality have been proposed by the 'cash-in-advance' and the 'transactions costs' approaches which will be considered in the context of overlapping- generations models. However, to offer a more complete picture this appendix will outline the essential aspects of cash-in-advance and transaction costs in continuous time intertemporal models with infinite horizon.

a)   A Monetary economy with a cash-in-advance constraint

In the cash-in-advance approach money has the distinctive function of medium of exchanges. It has no direct utility and enforces Clower's constraint on expenditure (1967). This constraint can be referred only to consumption (as in Lucas, 1980) or extended to investments (as in Stockman, 1981) or generalized (as in Grandmont and Younès, 1972). Since our aim here is simply to illustrate the basic idea, we assume a constraint only on consumption, so that a representative agent in a Clower-type monetary economy solves the following problem

$$\max V = \int_0^{+\infty} e^{-\beta t} u[c(t)] dt$$

$$\dot{k} + \dot{m} = f(k(t)) + x(t) - c(t) - p^e(t)m(t)$$

$$m(t) \geq c(t)$$

Given $\dot{m} = [\vartheta - p(t)]m(t)$ and an assumption of perfect foresight, necessary first-order conditions are

$$u'_c[c(t)] = \lambda(t) + \gamma(t)$$

$$\gamma(t) = \lambda(t)[\vartheta + f'(k)]$$

$$\dot{\lambda}(t) = \lambda(t)[\beta - f'(k(t))]$$

With $x = \vartheta\, m$, steady state satisfies

$$u'_c(c) = \lambda + \gamma = \lambda[1 + \vartheta + f'(k)]$$

$$f(k) = c$$

$$\beta = f'(k)$$

The third equality is Ramsey's rule, that is, the golden rule for an economy with a stationary population. It states that per capita capital stock at steady state does not depend on the rate of growth of money. Despite this, the superneutrality of money is not valid. Indeed the first equality shows that an increase in the rate of growth of the money stock also determines a decrease in per capita steady state consumption because this involves increase in the marginal utility of steady state consumption.

A simple generalization (Wang and Yip, 1992) of the model considers population growth at constant rate n and incorporates leisure in the utility function. The cash-in-advance constraint is formulated in the manner of Grandmont and Younes but interpreted in the manner of Stockman. The optimal control problem of the representative agent is

$$\max V = \int_0^{+\infty} e^{-\beta t} u[c(t), 1 - l(t),] dt$$

$$\dot{k} + \dot{m} = f(k(t), l(t), +x(t) - nk(t) - c(t) - (p^e(t) + n)m(t)$$

$$m(t) \geq c(t) + \psi \dot{k}$$

The parameter $\psi \epsilon$ [0, 1] expresses the financial constraint or liquidity constraints on the demand for investment in capital goods. Clearly, in these generalized formulations money is not superneutral, especially because leisure is included in the utility function,. Moreover, there are other implications regarding the Tobin-effect (Wang and Yip, 1992). However, these are not clear-cut and consideration of them would require further arguments that will not be deal with here.

b)   Monetary economy with transaction costs technology

This approach admits there are costs the agent incurs in terms of resources to carry out transactions in consumption goods (Benhabib and Bull, 1983; Dornbusch and Frenkel, 1973; Feenstra, 1986; McCallum, 1983; Wang and Yip, 1992; Saving, 1971). A basic assumption is that holding money reduces transaction costs because of the distinctive role of money as the medium of exchange. The concept is that there is a transaction technology which can be described in various ways. However, we assume it is represented by a transaction costs function $T = T(c(t), m(t))$ which is increasing with respect to c and decreasing with respect to m (see Chapter 5, Section 9 for a detailed examination of the properties of the transaction costs function). With a transaction costs technology the optimal control problem of the representative agent is

$$\max V = \int_0^{+\infty} e^{-\beta t} u[c(t)] dt$$

$$\dot{k} + \dot{m} = f(k(t)) + x(t) - c(t) - T(c(t), m(t)) - p^e(t)m(t)$$

Given $\dot{m} = [\vartheta - p(t)]m(t)$ and assuming perfect foresight, necessary first order conditions are

$$u_c'[c(t)] = \lambda(t)(1 + T_c')$$

$$- T_m' = \vartheta + f'(k(t))$$

$$\dot{k} = f(k(t)) + x(t) - c(t) - T(c(t), m(t)) - \vartheta m(t)$$

$$\dot{\lambda}(t) = \lambda(t)[\beta - f'(k(t))]$$

With $x = \vartheta m$ steady state satisfies

$$u'_c(c) = \lambda(1 + T'_c(c, m))$$
$$- T'_m(c, m) = \vartheta + f'(k)$$
$$f(k) - T(c, m) = c$$
$$\beta = f'(k)$$

These conditions are compatible with different conclusions about the super-neutrality of money depending on the characteristics of transaction costs function. In particular, if it assumed that the transaction costs function is separable in c and m, Sidrauski's superneutrality is valid. Indeed, when there is a separable transaction costs function, changes in the nominal money stock growth rate only influence the first-order condition of the real stock of money. On the contrary, steady state consumption is influenced by changes in the rate of growth of the money stock when the transaction costs function is not separable. The optimum quantity of money as intended by Friedman also depends on the nature of the transaction costs function. If the function is separable, the optimum quantity of money in Friedman's sense is verified when $\vartheta = 0$. This condition, however, is not necessary. When the transaction costs function is not separable optimal conditions can be verified with arbitrary $\vartheta > 0$.

References

Benhabib, J. and C Bull. (1983) 'The Optimal Quantity of Money: A Formal Treatment', *International Economic, Review*, 24, pp. 101–11.

Brock, W. (1974) 'Money and Growth: The Case of Long-Run Perfect Foresight, *International Economic Review*', 15, pp. 750–77.

Brock, W. (1975) 'A Simple Perfect Foresight Monetary Model', *Journal of Monetary Economics*, 1, pp. 133–50.

Cagan, P. (1956) 'The Monetary Dynamics of Hyperinflation', in M. Friedman, (ed.) *Studies in the Quantity Theory of Money* (Chicago: University of Chicago Press).

Calvo, G. (1978) 'Optimal Seignorage from Monetary Creation', *Journal of Monetary Economics*, 4, pp. 503–17.

Calvo, G. (1979) 'On Models of Money and Perfect Foresight', *International Economic Review*, 20, pp. 83–103.

Chirichiello, G. (1992) *Ottimizzazione dinamica e Modelli di Teoria Economica (Dynamic Optimization and Economic Models)* (Rome: OCSM, Collana Monografie).

Clower, R. (1967) 'A Reconsideration of the Microeconomic Foundations of Monetary Theory', *Western Economic Journal*, 6, pp. 1–8.

Drazen, A. (1979) 'The Optimal Rate of Inflation Revisited', *Journal of Monetary Economics*, 5, pp. 231–48.

Dornbusch, R. and J. Frenkel. (1973) 'Inflation and Growth: Alternative Approaches', *Journal of Money, Credit and Banking*, 50, pp. 141–56.

Feenstra, R. (1986) 'Functional Equivalence between Liquidity Costs and the Utility of Money', *Journal of Monetary Economics*, 17, pp. 271–91.

Fischer, S. (1979) 'Capital Accumulation on the Transition Path in a Monetary Optimizing Model', *Econometrica*, 47, pp. 1433–9.

Friedman, M. (1969) 'The Optimum Quantity of Money', in M. Friedman, (ed.) *The Optimum Quantity of Money and Other Essays* (Chicago: Aldine).

Grandmont, J.M. and Y. Younès (1972) 'On the Role of Money and the Existence of Monetary Equilibrium', *Review of Economic Studies*, 39 , pp. 355–72.

Levhari, D. and D. Patinkin. (1968) 'The Role of Money in a Simple Growth Model', *American Economic Review*, 58, pp. 713–53.

Lucas, R. (1980) 'Equilibrium in a Pure Currency Economy', in , J. Kareken and N. Wallace. (eds) *Models of Monetary Economies* (Minneapolis: Federal Reserve Bank of Minneapolis).

McCallum, B (1983) 'The Role of Overlapping Generations Model in Monetary Economics', *Carnegie Rochester Conference*, 18, pp. 9–44

McCallum B. (1990) 'Inflation: Theory and Evidence', in , B. Friedman,and F. Hahn . (eds) *Handbook of Monetary Economics*, II, (New York: North-Holland).

Nagatani, K. (1970) 'A Note on Professor Tobin's Money and Economic Growth', *Econometrica*, 38, pp. 171–5.

Obstfeld, M. (1984) 'Multiple Stable Equilibria in an Optimizing Perfect-Foresight Model', *Econometrica*, 52, pp. 221–8.

Obstfeld, M. and K. Rogoff. (1983) 'Speculative Hyperinflations in Maximizing Models: Can We Rule Them Out?', *Journal of Political Economy*, 91, pp. 675–687.

Orphanides, A. and R. Solow. (1990) 'Money, Inflation and Growth, in B. Friedman.and F. Hahn .(eds) *Handbook of Monetary Economics*, Vol II, (New York: North-Holland).

Patinkin, D. (1965) *Money, Interest and Prices*, 2nd edn, (New York: Harper-Row).

Saving, T. (1971) 'Transactions Costs and the Demand for Money', *American Economic Review*, 61, pp. 407–20.

Sidrauski, M. (1967) 'Rational Choice and Patterns of Growth in Monetary Economy', *American Economic Review*, 57, pp. 534–44.

Sidrauski, M. (1967) 'Inflation and Economic Growth', *Journal of Political Economy*, 75, pp. 786–810.

Siegel, J. (1983) 'Technological Change and the Superneutrality of Money', *Journal of Money, Credit and Banking*, 5, pp. 362–67.

Stein, J. (1970) 'Monetary Growth Theory in Perspective', *American Economic Review*, 60, pp. 85-106.

Stein, J. (1971) *Money and Capacity Growth* (New York: Columbia University Press).

Stockman, A. (1981) 'Anticipated Inflation and the Capital Stock in a Cash-in-Advance Economy', *Journal of Monetary Economics*, 8, pp. 534–44.

Tobin, J. (1955) 'A Dynamic Aggregative Model', *Journal of Political Economy*, 63, pp. 103-15.

Tobin, J. (1965) 'Money and Economic Growth', *Econometrica*, 33, pp. 671–84.

Wang, P. and C. K. Yip, (1992) 'Alternative Approaches to Money and Growth', *Journal of Money, Credit and Banking*, 24, pp. 553–62.

5
Alternative Approaches to Monetary Economies of Overlapping-Generations

5.1 Basic monetary model of overlapping-generations: The pure exchange economy

In this chapter we examine the monetary model of overlapping generations and the wide variety of dynamic behaviour it admits. As we have seen, a monetary growth model admitting infinite-lived optimizing agents highlights the role of money, and, in particular, the effects of money on social welfare, the optimality of some types of monetary policy, the admissibility of monetary instability. The question to investigate is whether these are results peculiar to Ramsey-type infinite horizon models or are characteristic of dynamic competitive economies populated by rational agents.

Let us examine a pure exchange economy with a single perishable good. We assume that the individual endowments (e_1^t, e_2^{t+1}) in periods t, t+1 are given and that the young and old are linked through demographic evolution $L_t = (1+n)L_{t+1}$. Money is introduced by supposing that once in a while, in some initial instant, a central bank distributes at no cost to the current old a per capita amount of fiat money M > 0. Moreover, we admit that, from the initial instant on, each generation receiving the constant per capita nominal money stock M believes that money will be exchanged at the expected future price $p_{t+1}^{me} = p_{t+1}^m > 0$. The price of money p_t^m is in terms of goods or it expresses the amount of goods that can be purchased by one unity of money in each period t. If P_t indicates the general price level, then $P_t = 1/p_t^m$. A necessary condition for a monetary economy to exist is that the price of money must be positive. This requirement in turn implies that even an economy with overlapping generations must have an infinite horizon[1]. If money has a positive value, young have an opportunity also to save in money. Thus the maximum problem of the representative young becomes

$$\max U(c_1^t, c_1^{t+1})$$
$$\text{sub } c_1^t + (M_{t+1}/P_{t+1})(P_{t+1}/P_t) = e_1^t$$
$$c_1^{t+1} = e_1^{t+1} + M_{t+1}/P_{t+1}$$

whereas the representative old problem is still to consume the endowment and money stock held at t

$$c_2^t = e_2^t + (M/P_t)$$

According to the definition of the price of money, the deflation rate $(P_t/P_{t+1}) = R_{t+1}^m$ coincides with the real return on money. Indeed, $R_{t+1}^m - 1 = (P_t/P_{t+1}) - 1 = (p_{t+1}^m - p_t^m)/p_t^m$ which is the definition of the rate of return on money. The pure-exchange-pure-consumption-loan model now appears as a model of accumulation of money by virtue of the identity between the individual saving function of the young and their demand for real money. This can be shown as follows. Global consumption of the old is $C_2^t = \sum_{h=1}^{L_{t-1}} c_{2h}^t$. Global consumption of the young is $C_1^t = \sum_{h=1}^{L_t} c_{1h}^t$. Demand for money by the young is $L_t M_{t+1}$. Money stock held by the old is $L_{t-1}M$. Global endowments are $(q_1^t, q_2^t) = (\sum_{h=1}^{L_{t-1}} e_{2h}^{t-1}, \sum_{h=1}^{L_t} e_{1h}^t)$. Equilibrium of the market for goods requires

$$C_1^t + C_2^t = q_1^t + q_2^t$$

Summing over the agent's budget constraint for the current period gives

$$(C_1^t - q_1^t) + (C_2^t - q_2^t) = L_{t-1}(M/P_t) - L_t(M_{t+1}/P_{t+1})(P_{t+1}/P_t)$$

When the market for goods is at equilibrium the money market is also at equilibrium $L_t(M_{t+1}/P_{t+1})(P_{t+1}/P_t) = L_t(M/P_t)$. Since the opposite is also true, by letting $m_t = M/P_t$ and $m_{t+1} = M_{t+1}/P_{t+1}$, equilibrium dynamics of the economy in per capita terms can be described as

$$m_{t+1}(P_t/P_{t+1})\frac{1+n}{(P_t/P_{t+1})} = m_t$$

where the function $m_{t+1}(P_t/P_{t+1})$ indicates the real stock desired for instant $t + 1$ by the young. Steady state requires that $(P_t/P_{t+1}) = R^{m*}$ and $m_{t+1} = m_t$. It follows that $R^{m*} = 1 + n$, which is also the necessary condition for Pareto-optimality of a steady state. Indeed, in the model without accumulation of capital Pareto-optimal intertemporal allocations must verify the golden rule, or the equality between intertemporal substitution rate of present and future consumption and population growth rate. The golden rule is also satisfied in a monetary economy, where optimal allocation of resources is implemented by means of money. Indeed at steady state, necessary conditions for the optimum for the young yield

$$U'(c^y)/U'(c^\circ) = (P_t/P_{t+1}) = R^{m*}$$

This suggests that, while a decentralized economy without money may not be able to reach Pareto-optimum, a decentralized monetary economy does. It also suggests why a society has an incentive to organize its transactions monetarily. Indeed it seems to increase opportunities for exchange and improve social welfare. It is reasonable to question whether this conclusion has general validity. In particular it pays to ask whether organizing an economy as a monetary economy is sufficient to achieving steady state Pareto optimal allocations. This issue is more complex than it appears at first sight so we shall begin by the analysis of dynamic properties of a pure exchange economy and then examine the extension to the more general case including the accumulation of physical capital.

5.2   The dynamics of a pure exchange economy with overlapping generations

The dynamics of the basic monetary model with overlapping generations, as we have seen, is described by the equation

$$m_{t+1}(P_t/P_{t+1})\frac{1+n}{(P_t/P_{t+1})} = m_t$$

Instead of referring to the space $(P_t/P_{t+1}, m_t)$ the dynamics of the economy can be examined in the space (m_t, m_{t+1}). In this space, dynamic analysis make use of a *reflected offer curve* (Cass, Okuno and Zilcha, 1980). This curve describes the evolution over time of per capita real money of the old, given the current desired accumulation of money by the young. To obtain the reflected offer curve we start by observing that in the plane (m_t, m_{t+1}) the relationship

$$m_{t+1} = \frac{P_t/P_{t+1}}{1+n}m_t$$

describes a family of straight lines passing through the origin. Each line has a different slope for different rates of return on money $R_{t+1}^m = (P_t/P_{t+1})$. For each given R_{t+1}^m, the line of the family intersects at a point on the locus constructed by taking $m_{t+1} = m_{t+1}(P_t/P_{t+1})$ as the value of ordinate. This locus is the set of combinations (m_t, m_{t+1}) which associates the stock of money desired by the young to a given current per capita real money stock. Therefore this locus also indicates the future money stock the young will be able to offer when they are old.

In this sense the curve we are describing is a reflected offer curve. Indeed, it 'reflects' the per capita real money stock that will be offered in the future, given the per capita real money stock offered in the present. The equation of the reflected offer curve is obtained as follows. The definition of saving implies the identity $s(P_t/P_{t+1}) = M_{t+1}/P_t$. Therefore the equilibrium dynamics can be described also by the system

$$s(P_t/P_{t+1})(1 + n) = m_{t+1}$$
$$m_{t+1} = \frac{(P_t/P_{t+1})}{1 + n} m_t$$

By inverting the first equation we can write $(P_t/P_{t+1}) = p(m_t)$ because $(1 + n)$ is given. By substituting in the second equation we obtain

$$m_{t+1} = \frac{p(m_t)}{1 + n} m_t$$

which is the reflected offer curve. It has the following properties:

1. $dm_{t+1}/dm_t = p'(m_t)(m_t/1 + n) + p(m_t)/1 + n$
2. $[dm_{t+1}/dm_t]_{m_t=0} = p(0)/(1 + n)$
3. $d^2 m_{t+1}/dm_t^2 = p''(m_t)(m_t/1 + n) + 2p'(m_t)/1 + n$

In plane (m_t, m_{t+1}) the shape of the reflected offer curve depends on the saving function being smooth. In turn, the sign of the second derivative at point 3, which indicates the concavity or convexity of the reflected offer curve, depends on the saving function being concave or convex. By virtue of the properties of the saving function (see Chapter 3, Sections 3.2–3.3) changing shapes is generally admissible and can give rise to multiple steady states, cycles, or chaotic equilibria. Here we shall simply admit a saving function which increases with respect to the interest rate. Consequently, the demand for real money stock, as in Cagan, (see Chapter 4, Section 4.2) is a decreasing function of the inflation rate so that $p'(m_t) > 0$. The reflected offer curve slopes positively. Steady state $m_t = m_{t+1} = m^* > 0$ exists and verifies $p(m^*) = 1 + n$. But $m^* = 0$ is also a steady state. Therefore the dynamics of the system depends on whether the monetary steady state $m^* > 0$ is stable.

Let us approximate linearly in some neighbourhoods $m^* = 0$ and $m^* > 0$. We obtain

$$m_{t+1} = \frac{p(0)}{1+n} m_t$$

$$m_{t+1} - m^* = [\frac{p'(m^*)}{1+n} m^* + 1](m_t - m^*)$$

We can distinguish two cases

1. Let $[p(0)/(1+n)] < 1$

In this case steady state $m^* = 0$ is stable. On the other hand, steady state $m^* > 0$ is unstable. Indeed, from $p'(m_t) > 0$ and $m^* > 0$ it follows that $[p'(m^*)m^*/(1+n)] > 0$ and $p'(m^*)m^*/(1+n)] + 1 > 1$. Paths starting at initial real money stock $m(0) \in [0, m^*]$ converge to non-monetary steady state, as depicted in Figure 5.1 which reproduces a path starting from initial $m(0) < m^*$ for the case $d^2 m_{t+1}/d^2 m_t) > 0$.

2. Let $p(0)/1 + n > 1$

Steady state $m^* = 0$ is unstable. Moreover since $d^2 m_{t+1}/d^2 m_t) > 0$, it is also $dm_{t+1}/dm_t > m_{t+1}/m_t$ so that the existence of monetary steady states $m^* > 0$ is excluded. Instability of steady state $m^* = 0$ implies that paths starting at initial real money stock $m(0)) \subset [0, \, \infty]$ are divergent. Figure 5.2 reproduces these paths.

If we abandon the assumption that saving is an increasing function of the reciprocal of the inflation rate then not necessarily the reflected offer curve is increasing and convex. The curve can alternate increasing and convex parts with decreasing and concave parts, so that multiple equilibria are possible. These equilibria can be stable or unstable, or can

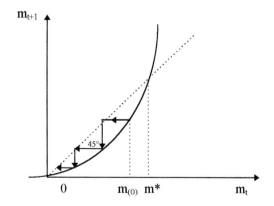

Figure 5.1 The reflected offer curve and the dynamics of a pure exchange monetary economy: convergence to non-monetary steady state

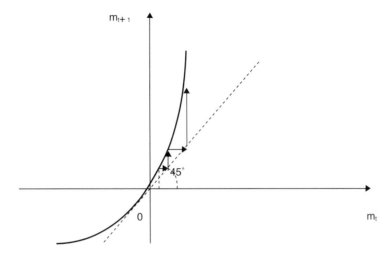

Figure 5.2 The dynamics of a pure exchange monetary economy: divergent paths

be even cycles (see for example. Benhabib and Day 1982; Grandmont, 1985), as shown in Figure 5.3.

5.3. Overlapping-generations monetary model with capital accumulation

If we consider an economy including production and physical capital accumulation we notice that there are other properties of money but this

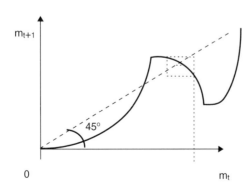

Figure 5.3 The dynamics of a pure exchange monetary economy: multiple equilibria

does not alter the basic framework of the pure exchange economy. Indeed, we can state that the introduction of a stable real sector accumulating physical capital does not alter the potential instability of monetary economies or properties related to multiple equilibria or cycles. Let us start by considering the behaviour of the young. In a context where the young offer one unit of work inelastically at ongoing real wage rate w_t, and accumulate savings in the form of money and physical capital, the constrained intertemporal maximum problem a representative young person faces is

$$\max \quad U(c_1^t, c_1^{t+1})$$
$$\text{sub} \quad c_1^t + k_1^{t+1} + (M_{t+1}/P_{t+1})(P_{t+1}/P_t) = w_t$$
$$c_1^{t+1} = R_{t+1}k_1^{t+1} + (M_{t+1}/P_{t+1})$$

On the contrary, a representative old person strives for maximum consumption which is $c_2^t = R_t k_{2t} + (M_t/P_t)$.

Per capita variables, taking into account the evolution of population $L_t = (1+n)L_{t-1}$, are those normalized with respect to the young workers L_t, that is $(c_2^t/1+n) = C_2^t/L_t$; $c_1^t = C_1^t/L_t$; $k_{t+1}(1+n) = K_{t+1}/L_t$; and $k_t = K_t/L_t = k_{2t}/1+n$. In per capita terms therefore equilibrium of the market for goods is

$$c_1^t + (c_2^t/1+n) + k_{k+1}(1+n) - k_t = f(k_t)$$

This condition, by virtue of agents' budget constraints and the per capita saving definition, can also be written as

$$k_{t+1}(1+n) + m_t = s(R_{t+1}, P_t/P_{t+1}, w_t)$$

In a competitive economy the absence of arbitrage opportunities entails equality of return on assets

$$P_t/P_{t+1} = R_{t+1} = 1 + f'(k_{t+1})$$

Therefore, the dynamics of the economy is described by the difference equations

$$k_{t+1} = (1/1+n)\{s[1 + f'(k_{k+1}), f(k_t) - f'(k_t)k_t] - m_t\}$$
$$m_{t+1} = \frac{1 + f'(k_{t+1})}{(1+n)}m_t$$

We shall now study the existence and stability of a steady state solution. Economically significant steady state $m > 0$ must satisfy

$$k = (1/1 + n)\{s[1 + f'(k), f(k) - f'(k)k] - m\}$$
$$f'(k) = n$$

Condition $f'(k) = n$ is the golden rule. In the plane (k, m) the golden rule is a vertical line passing through the golden rule capital stock k_g. The first necessary condition for steady state solved for m gives a function $m = m(k)$ which has the following properties

a) $m(0) = 0$; $m(k_D) = 0$, with $k_D = (1/1 + n)s[1 + f'(k_D), f(k_D) - f'(k_D)k_D]$
b) for $k \in [0, k_D]$:
b.1) there is k_1 such that $m(k_1) = \max m(k)$; and
b.2) $m'(k) = \dfrac{\partial s}{\partial R} f''(k) - \dfrac{\partial s}{\partial w} kf''(k) - (1 + n) =$

$$[E'(k) - 1][(1 + n) - \dfrac{\partial s}{\partial R} f''(k)]$$

where $E'(k) = -\dfrac{(\partial s/\partial w)kf''(k)}{(1 + n) - (\partial s/\partial R)f''(k)}$

We admit, in addition, that $E''(k) < 0$; $E'(0) > 1$; $E'(k_D) < 1$. From (a) and (b) it follows that $m(k)$ is concave in plane (k, m) passing through the origin. Moreover it is an increasing function for $k \in]0, k_1[$ and a decreasing function for $k \in]k_1, k_D[$. This curve is reproduced in Figure 5.4. Unique monetary steady state with $m^* > 0$ is at the intersection of the line of golden rule capital stock $k = k_g$ and the $m = m(k)$ curve.

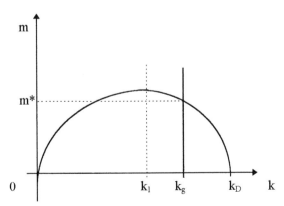

Figure 5.4   Steady state equilibrium of monetary economy with capital accumulation

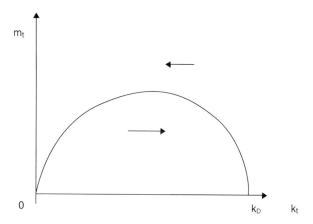

Figure 5.5   The dynamics of capital stock

A phase diagram for a monetary system with capital accumulation is deduced by referring to the difference equations

$$k_{t+1} - k_t = K(k_t, m_t)$$

$$m_{t+1} - m_t = \frac{\{f'[k_t + K(k_t, m_t)] - n\}m_t}{1 + n}$$

where $K(k_t, m_t)] = F(k_t, m_t) - k_t$, and $F(k_t, m_t)$ is the function $k_{t+1} = F(k_t, m_t)$ obtained by solving for k_{t+1} the equilibrium condition of the market for goods. The locus of points $k_{t+1} = k_t$ describes the curve $m_t = m(k_t)$ studied in (b.2). By orientating points outside of $m(k_t)$, we find that points below the curve have a positive orientation and points above have a negative orientation as shown in Figure 5.5.

The locus $m_{t+1} = m_t$ is obtained by the implicit condition $f'[k_t + K(k_t, m_t)] = n$. The slope of the corresponding phase curve $m_1(k_t)$ is positive $m_1'(k_t) = -\dfrac{\partial s}{\partial w} k_t f''(k_t) > 0$. By assuming $m_1''(k_t) < 0$ this curve is also concave. It can be located in the plane (k_t, m_t) by considering the intercept $\bar{k}_t = k$ on the the horizontal axis, which is defined by the condition $f'[\bar{k} + K(\bar{k}, 0)] = n$, or $\bar{k} + K(\bar{k}, 0)] = k_g$. Since $K(\bar{k}, 0)] = k_D$ it follows that k locates to left of the segment $[k_g, k_D]$. Therefore the $m_{t+1} = m_t$ locus looks like the curve AA in Figure 5.6.

Points above the locus $m_{t+1} = m_t$ have a positive orientation with respect to the vertical axis because $E'(k_t) < 1$. The direction of the arrows in

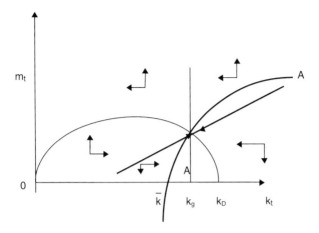

Figure 5.6   Dynamics of monetary economy with capital accumulation

Figure 5.6 suggests that steady state is a saddle point. Proof of this conjecture requires a stability analysis of the system

$$k_{t+1} = F(k_t, m_t)$$

$$m_{t+1} = \frac{1 + f'[F(k_t, m_t)]}{1 + n} m_t$$

The linearized system near steady state is

$$k_{t+1} - k^* = -\frac{(\partial s/\partial w)k^* f''(k^*)}{(1 + n) - (\partial s/\partial R)f''(k^*)}(k_t - k^*) -$$

$$\frac{1}{(1 + n) - (\partial s/\partial R)f''(k^*)}(m_t - m^*)$$

$$m_{t+1} - m^* = -\frac{m^* f''(k^*)}{(1 + n)}\frac{(\partial s/\partial w)k^* f''(k^*)}{(1 + n) - (\partial s/\partial R)f''(k^*)}(k_t - k^*) +$$

$$[1 - \frac{f''(k^*)m^*}{(1 + n)}\frac{1}{(1 + n) - (\partial s/\partial R)f''(k^*)}](m_t - m^*)$$

This system has trace and determinant

$$\text{Tr } J = 1 - \frac{(\partial s/\partial w)k^* f''(k^*)}{(1 + n) - (\partial s/\partial R)f''(k^*)} - \frac{f''(k^*)m^*}{(1 + n)}\frac{1}{(1 + n) - (\partial s/\partial R)f''(k^*)} > 0$$

$$\det J = -\frac{\partial s/\partial w)k^* f''(k^*)}{(1 + n) - (\partial s/\partial R)f''(k^*)} > 0$$

The characteristic equation $\lambda^2 - \text{Tr}J\lambda + \det J$ has two variations in sign of coefficients, so both roots are positive. Moreover

$$p(1) = 1 - \operatorname{Tr} J + \det J = \frac{f'(k^*)m^*}{(1+n)} \frac{1}{(1+n) - (\partial s/\partial R)f''(k^*)} > 0$$

The larger root drops out of the unit interval so that the steady state of a monetary economy with capital accumulation is a saddle point. Steady state of this monetary economy has another peculiarity: it is not necessarily efficient. We already know that with capital accumulation steady states with capital over-accumulation are admissible. This possibility is present even in a monetary economy. Indeed, from Figure 5.6 we can deduce that steady state can be located to the left or to the right of golden rule capital stock k_g.

5.4   A monetary economy with storage. The impossibility of dominance of money in the nominal interest rate of economies with a market for private credit

As we have seen, a basic pure exchange model gives money a role, because it allows the economy to achieve a Pareto-optimal steady state. However this is not necessarily the effect of introducing money. An economy having a productive storage technology offers an example of feasible competitive barter equilibrium which is Pareto optimal and excludes monetary equilibria (Wallace, 1980). Thus, let us assume the monetary economy described also has a storing technology that admits constant returns to scale. The young can now store physical good z_t for a future period. The return on storage σ_{t+1} is positive, if storage activity is treated as a productive investment, or negative if storage results in deterioration of the good. At each instant rate of return $\sigma_{t+1} > -1$ is assumed to be independent from economic forces.

In such an economy the representative young person solves the problem

$$\begin{aligned} \max \quad & U(c_1^t, c_1^{t+1}) \\ \text{sub} \quad & c_1^t + z_1^{t+1} + (M_{t+1}/P_{t+1})(P_{t+1}/P_t) = e_1^t \\ & c_1^{t+1} = e_1^{t+1} + (1 + \sigma_{t+1})z_1^{t+1} + M_{t+1}/P_{t+1} \end{aligned}$$

whereas the old person consumes

$$c_2^t = e_2^t + z_2^t + (M_t/P_t)$$

Total storage and consumption are $C_1^t = \sum\limits_{h=1}^{L_t} c_{1h}^t$, $Z_{t+1} = \sum\limits_{h=1}^{L_t} z_{1h}^{t+1}$, for the young, and $Z_t = \sum\limits_{h=1}^{L_{t-1}} z_{2h}^t$; $C_2^t = \sum\limits_{h=1}^{L_{t-1}} c_{2h}^t$ for the old. Moreover,

$z_{t+1}(1 + n) = Z_{t+1}/L_t$. If we assume the nominal money stock is constant over time, equilibrium conditions in per capita terms become

$$c_1^t + c_2^t(1/1 + n) + z_{t+1}(1 + n) - z_t = e_1^t + e_2^t(1/1 + n)$$

$$m_{t+1}(P_{t+1}/P_t, 1 + \sigma_{t+1})\frac{1 + n}{(P_t/P_{t+1})} = m_t$$

which by taking into account budget constraints and the definition of the aggregate saving function become

$$z_{t+1}(1 + n) + (P_{t+1}/P_t)(1/(1 + n)m_t = s(1 + \sigma_{t+1}, P_t/P_{t+1})$$

$$m_{t+1}(P_{t+1}/P_t, 1 + \sigma_{t+1})\frac{1 + n}{(P_t/P_{t+1})} = m_t$$

We shall now examine conditions under which this economy admits meaningful intertemporal monetary equilibrium. A meaningful monetary equilibrium requires a positive desired money stock and a positive price for money $1/P_t > 0$. In the economy just described there are three classes of equilibria (a) pure monetary equilibrium, where money is the only means desired for savings; (b) non-monetary equilibrium, where goods are the only means desired for savings; (c) mixed equilibrium, where both goods and money are used, even separately, as means desired for savings.

Separating the set of equilibria into classes (a), (b) and (c), is done as follows. If we solve the second period constraint of the young for z_1^{t+1} and substitute this into the first period constraint, the young must respect the budget constraint in the entire horizon

$$c_1^t + c_1^{t+1}(1/1 + \sigma_{t+1}) + m_{t+1}[(P_{t+1}/P_t)][1 - \frac{P_t/P_{t+1}}{1 + \sigma_{t+1}}] = e_1^t + e_1^{t+1}(1/1 + \sigma_{t+1})$$

This intertemporal budget constraint emphasizes that to have meaningful monetary equilibrium $m_{t+1} > 0$ in the classes (a) and (c), we must have $1 + \sigma_{t+1} \leq P_t/P_{t+1}$. This follows directly from the exclusion of arbitrage opportunities implied by competitive equilibria. Indeed at a given instant whenever $1 + \sigma_{t+1} > P_t/P_{t+1}$ each young person storing a positive stock of money would benefit from transforming it into physical goods because stored physical goods yield a greater return than money. With similar reasoning we can deduce that an equilibrium with a positive store of physical goods, belonging to classes (b) and (c) requires that $P_t/P_{t+1} \leq 1 + \sigma_{t+1}$. The intersection of the two classes gives $P_t/P_{t+1} = 1 + \sigma_{t+1}$. These results have implications for the dynamic efficiency of steady states. If monetary equilibrium is efficient

$(P_t/P_{t+1}) = R^m = 1 + n$ and barter equilibrium is inefficient $1 + \sigma < 1 + n$, then a money economy clearly improves allocation of resources by increasing social welfare. On the contrary, if $R^m < 1 + \sigma = 1 + n$ there can be no monetary equilibrium since nobody wants to hold money. In such an economy the introduction of money does not improve the welfare since condition $1 + \sigma = 1 + n$ means that the barter equilibrium is dynamically efficient.

It can be shown that a monetary economy with overlapping-generations generally does not allow the coexistence of money and financial assets yielding a positive nominal rate of interest because dominance of money in nominal interest rate can be excluded. To show dominance of money in the nominal rate of interest is excluded we need only to re-elaborate the former model. Let us admit a market for private loans to substitute for storage of goods and let us explicitly exclude that money pays interest, so that money yields a nominal interest rate zero. Now in addition to outside money the model also admits *inside* money that comes from agents' borrowing and lending. Let X_1^{t+1} be the amount of nominal loans exchanged by the young at t, and let $i_{t+1} > -1$ be the nominal interest rate on loans. Constraints of the young for each period now become

$$c_1^t + (X_1^{t+1}/P_{t+1})(P_{t+1}/P_t) + (M_{t+1}/P_{t+1})(P_{t+1}/P_t) = e_1^t$$
$$c_1^{t+1} = e_1^{t+1} + (1 + i_{t+1})(X_1^{t+1}/P_{t+1}) + M_{t+1}/P_{t+1}$$

From these we get the intertemporal budget constraint

$$c_1^t + c_1^{t+1}(1/1 + i_{t+1})(P_{t+1}/P_t) + m_{t+1}[(P_{t+1}/P_t)]$$
$$[1 - \frac{1}{1 + i_{t+1}}] = e_1^t + e_1^{t+1}(1/1 + i_{t+1})(P_{t+1}/P_t)$$

The magnitude $(1/1+i_{t+1})$ (P_{t+1}/P_t) indicates a real discount factor that is the inverse of the real interest factor, so that the budget constraint is similar to that of the case when goods can be stored. At steady state with $M_t > 0$ and $1/P_t > 0$ at each t we must have

$$\frac{P_t(1 + i_{t+1})}{P_{t+1}} = \frac{P_t}{P_{t+1}} \quad \text{from which it follows that } i_{t+1} = 0.$$

Thus, the nominal interest rate on loans can not be positive, or it can not dominate the nominal rate of interest on money.

5.5 Constant growth rate of money policy and inefficiency of seignorage

If we abandon the constant nominal stock of money hypothesis by assuming that monetary authorities follow a constant growth rate of money policy, we can consider two ways to inject money into an economy: (a) direct transfers to individuals and (b) monetary financing of government purchases for a given level of per capita public expenditure (*seignorage*).

In the case (a), by assuming that transfers are directed solely to the old, two possible forms are: (1) lump-sum transfers and (2) transfers proportional to the money stock. In case (1) each old person receives money transfers independent of past decisions about money accumulation. By indicating ϑ a constant growth rate of aggregate nominal money stock A_t, the nominal money increase after transfers is $A_{t+1} - A_t = \vartheta A_t$, or in per capita terms $M_{t+1} - M_t(1/1+n) = (\vartheta/1+n)M_t$. The young do not hold money but they can rely on real transfers equal to h_{t+1} when they grow old. The representative young person solves the problem

$$\begin{aligned} \max \quad & U(c_1^t, c_1^{t+1}) \\ \text{sub} \quad & c_1^t + (M_{t+1}/P_{t+1})(P_{t+1}/P_t) = e_1^t \\ & c_1^{t+1} = e_1^{t+1} + (M_{t+1}/P_{t+1}) + h_{t+1} \end{aligned}$$

The old possess the current stock of money. Therefore the consumption of the representative old person is

$$c_2^t = e_2^t + (M_t/P_t) + h_t$$

Equilibrium in per capita terms is

$$m_{t+1}(h_{t+1}, P_t/P_{t+1}) \frac{1+n}{(1+\vartheta)(P_t/P_{t+1})} = m_t$$

Steady state requires that $m_{t+1}(\vartheta/1+n, P_{t+1}/P_t) = m_t$, which is verified when $(1+\vartheta)(P_t/P_{t+1}) = 1+n$. By enforcing efficiency condition $(P_t/P_{t+1}) = 1+n$, we deduce that a monetary steady state with positive growth of money $\vartheta > 0$ is inefficient, so that to maximize a welfare society it is preferable to have a monetary policy with $\vartheta = 0$.

Let us now consider the second way to inject money or transfers proportional to money stock. In this case the representative young problem is

$$\max \quad U(c_1^t, c_1^{t+1})$$
$$\text{sub} \quad c_1^t + (M_{t+1}/P_{t+1})(P_{t+1}/P_t) = e_1^t$$
$$c_1^{t+1} = e_1^{t+1} + (M_{t+1}/P_{t+1})(1 + \vartheta)$$

whereas representative old consumption is

$$c_2^t = e_2^t + (M_t/P_t)(1 + \vartheta)$$

Transfers proportional to money stock look like interest paid by monetary authorities on the money stock at the implicit real interest rate $(1 + \vartheta)(P_t/P_{t+1})$. Indeed constraint for the young in the second period can be written as $c_1^{t+1} = e_1^{t+1} + (M_{t+1}/P_t)(1 + \vartheta)(P_t/P_{t+1})$which is the same as when money pays interest at the real interest rate $(1 + \vartheta)(P_t/P_{t+1})$. Equilibrium in per capita terms is now

$$m_{t+1}[(1 + \vartheta)(P_t/P_{t+1})]\frac{1+n}{(1+\vartheta)(P_t/P_{t+1})} = m_t$$

Steady state requires that $(1 + \vartheta)(P_t/P_{t+1}) = 1 + n$, that is $(P_{t+1}/P_t) = (1 + \vartheta)/(1 + n)$. The latter way of writing the steady state condition emphasizes that, since growth rate of population does not vary with respect to the growth rate of nominal money stock, changes in the growth rate of money translate into changes in the inflation rate in exactly the same proportion. Money, therefore, is superneutral since a change in growth rate of money leaves the real interest rate and consequently even intertemporal allocation of resources unchanged.

Let us now consider case (b), that is government expenditure financed with seignorage revenues. The assumption is that monetary authorities wish to monetize the public deficit entirely by expanding money at rate $\vartheta > 0$. By assuming constant per capita public spending g, the nominal government budget constraint in per capita terms becomes

$$M_{t+1} - M_t = (1 - \frac{1}{1+\vartheta})M_t = P_t g.$$

We assume that public spending does not influence agents' preferences. Therefore the single agent problem remains unchanged with respect to the basic pure-exchange monetary model. The steady state condition also is similar to the case of lump-sum transfers and at steady state the real rate of return on money $R^m = P_t/P_{t+1}$ must satisfy the condition $R^m = (1 + n)/(1 + \vartheta)$. The two most significant aspects of seignorage policy are (1) rate of return on money at steady state appears 'distorted' with respect to the Pareto-optimal golden rule; (2) seignorage is similar to a tax on the money stock held by agents. The tax rate is the ratio between the growth rate of population and the growth rate of the money stock.

Point (1) is true, since steady state satisfies the golden rule when $\vartheta = 0$. Thus, each $\vartheta > 0$ defines an inefficient steady state. Point (b) is true if we consider that in the case of a tax rate paid by the old on saving they accumulated in their youth, the steady state government budget constraint is $g = \alpha s[(1 + n)/(1 + \vartheta)]$. Since savings coincide with the real money stock, we can write $g = \alpha(M_t/P_t)$. If we compare this government budget with the budget when revenue is raised only with seignorage, the two budget constraints coincide if $\alpha = 1 - (1/1 + \vartheta) = \vartheta/(1 + \vartheta)$, that is if the tax rate is the same as the seignorage rate. By substituting the latter expression into the government budget constraint with taxation on savings, we also obtain seignorage as a function of the growth rate of nominal money stock, that is

$$g(\vartheta) = (\vartheta/1 + \vartheta) \, s[(1 + n)/(1 + \vartheta)]$$

Since a government has the legal power to issue money, it acts as a monopolist in the 'production' of it. Indeed, government can try to maximize seignorage. The growth rate of money that maximizes seignorage solves the first order necessary condition

$$g'(\vartheta) = \frac{s}{(1 + \vartheta)^2} - \frac{s'\vartheta}{(1 + \vartheta)} \frac{1 + n}{(1 + \vartheta)^2} = \frac{s}{(1 + \vartheta)^2}[1 - \frac{s'}{s}\frac{1 + n}{(1 + \vartheta)}\vartheta] = 0$$

The first derivative $g'(\vartheta)$ is null when the term in square brackets is null. Defining the elasticity of saving to steady state interest rate ε_{S,R^*} as

$$\varepsilon_{S,R^*} = \frac{s'}{s}\frac{1 + n}{1 + \vartheta}$$

we obtain a condition very similar to that of a monopolist producer of a good, that is $\vartheta = 1/\varepsilon_{S,R^*}$. The growth rate of money stock maximizing seignorage also measures the degree of government monopoly in the production of money, which depends on the elasticity of the saving function in relation to the interest rate.

5.6   The optimum quantity of money and money in the utility function

In Sidrauski-type infinite horizon model Friedman's optimal money rule is valid if some conditions are met. To attain maximum social welfare monetary authorities should offer nominal money stock which locates the real money stock of the economy at the satiety level. This is the famous Chicago rule which is tied to the notion of 'satiety', hence to the notion of utility of money. A similar, but theoretically more neutral view regards the optimum-quantity-of-money rule in a manner more suitable to a money economy where there are also other financial assets. To this view an optimal monetary policy means offering a nominal quantity of money that makes nominal interest rate zero (see Chapter 4, Section 4.5; also Woodford, 1990).

In a competitive overlapping-generations monetary model admitting at least one other financial asset, the nominal interest rate is null at equilibrium, so the equivalent version of the Chicago rule seems to be valid. This claim, however, is based only on appearances. Indeed Friedman's optimum quantity of money *also* requires that the growth rate of the nominal stock of money be null. In the overlapping-generations model with financial assets alternative to fiat money, particularly inside money, this additional condition is not necessarily satisfied because the nominal rate of interest is null even when the nominal money stock grows at any positive rate. The validity of the optimum-quantity-of-money claim in a model with overlapping-generations, therefore, can not be based simply on the ascertaining that nominal rate of interest is null. A more direct account for 'satiety' invoked by Friedman is required.

However, this account of satiety must be based on the notion of marginal utility of money. Hence, even in the model with overlapping-generations we must assume (as in Patinkin and Sidrauski) that the utility function also includes real money. This solution adopted by Weiss (1980) has reopened the debate on the validity of the Chicago rule for the model with overlapping-generations. The idea that transaction opportunities must be described by means of transactions technology exposes the money-in-utility-function approach to the criticism of being merely an analytical device, an easy short cut to avoid more complex representations of transaction technology (Kareken and Wallace, 1980). It is indisputable, however, that such a device allows to overcome a weakness of conventional model with overlapping-generations where money as a means of intergenerational transactions is only a reserve of value. The money-in-the-utility approach recognizes, even only implicitly, the role of money as means of exchange, so we can give a precise definition to the notion of 'satiety'. With this in mind, let us consider a pure-exchange overlapping-generations model with a representative agent for each generation and a constant growth of population n > 0. A monetary economy has only outside money whose stock grows according to the rule

$A_{t+1} = A_t(1 + \vartheta)$. Money enters the economy through real transfers h_t to the old. Preferences of the young are described by the utility function $U(c_1^t, c_1^{t+1}, m_{t+1})$ which is assumed to be increasing, concave and also, for the sake of uniformity with Weiss (1980), additively separable in its arguments. If we assume a discount factor $0 < \beta < 1$, the problem of the representative young person is

$$\max U(c_1^t) + \beta U(c_1^{t+1}) + L(m_{t+1})$$
$$\text{sub } c_1^t + m_{t+1}(P_{t+1}/P_t) = e_1^t$$
$$c_1^{t+1} = e_1^{t+1} + m_{t+1} + h_{t+1}$$

At steady state $h_t = h = m(\vartheta/1 + n)$ and the above problem becomes

$$\max \quad U(c_1) + \beta U(c_2) + L(m)$$
$$\text{sub} \quad c_1 + c_2 = e_1 + e_2 + m(P_{t+1}/P_t)[(1 + \vartheta/1 + n)(P_t/P_{t-1}) - 1]$$

First order conditions give

$$\frac{U'(c_1)}{U'(c_2)} = \beta; \quad \frac{L'(m)}{U'(c_2)} = \beta(P_{t+1}/P_t)[1 - (1 + \vartheta/1 + n)(P_t/P_{t+1})]$$

We are already in a position to see implications for the optimum-quantity-of-money thesis. Since $L'(m) > 0$, at equilibrium, when money growth rate is null $\vartheta = 0$, the rate of return on money can be less than that at the golden rule and the demand for money can be positive. Indeed, now competitive monetary equilibria with $1 - (1 + \vartheta/1 + n)$ $(P_t/P_{t+1}) > 0$ are admissible, so that the Chicago rule does not appear necessary for these equilibria. It is important to verify explicitly whether competitive equilibria not verifying the Chicago rule are Pareto-suboptimal. Therefore, let us deduce Pareto-optimal conditions. Consider the choices of a central planner who can fix the terms of exchange for money between the young and old. The central planners objective is to allocate consumption and a real money stock so that the utility of the representative young is maximised. For fixed P_t/P_{t+1}, the central planner solves the problem

$$\max \quad U(c_1) + \beta U(c_2) + L(m)$$
$$\text{sub} \quad c_1 + c_2 - m(P_{t+1}/P_t)[(1 + \vartheta/1 + n)(P_t/P_{t-1}) - 1] = E$$

where E indicates disposable aggregate resources. The first-order condition for monetary Pareto-optimum is

$$L'(m) = \beta U'(c_2)(P_{t+1}/P_t)[1 - (1 + \theta/1 + n)(P_t/P_{t-1})]$$

This is exactly the same as the condition of competitive equilibrium and does not require the Chicago rule. On the other hand, if the central planner follows the Chicago rule and chooses m by keeping $(P_t/P_{t-1}) = \beta$, he/she must also keep the condition

$$\frac{L'(m)}{U'(c_2)} = 1 - \frac{1+\vartheta}{(1+n)} = \beta$$

In this case, since $[L'(m)/U'(c_2)] > 0$ and $L'(m) > 0$, the efficiency condition dictated by golden rule is violated. Indeed if a central planner for given ϑ acts according to the Chicago rule, the real rate of return $(1+\vartheta) < 1+n$, less than demographic factor growth. Even with $\vartheta = 0$ Chicago's rule in this context violates efficiency condition.

5.7   Money in the utility function and implications for open market monetary policy

The inclusion of money in the utility function of the young is a substantial improvement to the basic monetary model with overlapping-generations because it clarifies the nature and role of money. But monetary policy is understood exclusively as changes in nominal money stock or its growth rate. Moreover money is injected into the economy through government transfers or payment of interest on the money stock. These are not recognizable neither in the present policy practice nor in the current debates on conventional macroeconomics. In both practice and conventional theory, money is introduced through loans from the central bank to commercial banks or by open market purchases of bonds by the central bank. The latter is particularly difficult to fit into the basic monetary model with overlapping-generations because it excludes the coexistence of money and bonds. Since money is no longer dominated in the nominal interest rate it is impossible to ascertain any link between monetary policy and nominal rate of interest. However, we should bear in mind that increase in the nominal rate of interest as a response to restrictive monetary policy has been one of the most controversial subjects in conventional macroeconomics. The inclusion of money in the utility function implies that dominance of money in the rate of interest is also admissible. This allows open market operations and the effects of monetary policy on nominal interest rate to be considered.

   In order to study this, let us add to the private pure-exchange economy with constant population a public sector consisting of the government and the central bank whose tasks are respectively to decide on public spending and to decide on the quantity of money to put into the economy. We assume this occurs in a context of perfect co-ordination, so that the public sector budget constraint is defined as a single consolidated budget which indicates how the primary deficit and expiring public debt are financed. The expiring public debt is made up of bonds issued the previous period and the interest due on principal. We shall consider bonds that mature after one period and pay the nominal value and the interest in money. If $r_{t+1} = 1 + i_{t+1}$ is the nominal interest factor, the nominal government budget constraint in per capita terms is

$$B_{t+1} + M_{t+1} - M_t = B_t r_{t+1} + P_t d_{t+1}$$

where d_{t+1} is the real per capita primary deficit. We shall further simplify our analysis by assuming that the policy followed by the authorities is to maintain a null primary deficit $d_{t+1} = 0$ and a constant ratio $\alpha = \alpha_t = (B_{t+1}/M_{t+1})$ of bonds to money. When $d_{t+1} = 0$ the government's real budget constraint becomes

$$a_{t+1} = b_{t+1} + m_{t+1} = (P_t/P_{t+1})m_t + (P_t/P_{t+1})b_t r_{t+1}$$

Given the utility function of the representative young and the assumption that the money stock is held entirely by the old, the problem of the representative young is

$$
\begin{aligned}
\text{max} \quad & U(c_1^t) + \beta U(c_1^{t+1}) + L(m_{t+1}) \\
\text{sub} \quad & c_1^t + m_{t+1}(P_{t+1}/P_t) + b_{t+1}(P_{t+1}/P_t) = e_1^t \\
& c_1^{t+1} = e_1^{t+1} + m_{t+1} + b_{t+1}r_{t+1}
\end{aligned}
$$

From first-order conditions we obtain

$$\frac{U'(c_1^t)}{U'(c_1^{t+1})} = \beta \frac{P_t r_{t+1}}{P_{t+1}}; \quad \frac{L'(m_{t+1})}{U'(c_1^{t+1})} = (\beta/r_{t+1})[r_{t+1} - 1]$$

Since $L'(m_{t+1}) > 0$, we deduce the dominance of money in the nominal rate of interest at competitive equilibrium, $r_{t+1} > 1$. For the entire economy the function for the desired per capita financial assets in real terms is

$$a_{t+1}\left(\frac{P_t r_{t+1}}{P_{t+1}}, r_{t+1}\right) = b_{t+1}\left(\frac{P_t r_{t+1}}{P_{t+1}}, r_{t+1}\right) + m_{t+1}\left(\frac{P_t r_{t+1}}{P_{t+1}}, r_{t+1}\right)$$

Given financial assets stock $a_{t+1} = (1 + \alpha)m_{t+1}$, equilibrium conditions, which require money market equilibrium and equality between the composition of desired financial assets and the existing stocks, are

$$m_{t+1}(\frac{P_t r_{t+1}}{P_{t+1}}, r_{t+1}) = m_{t+1}$$

$$m_{t+1}(\frac{P_t r_{t+1}}{P_{t+1}}, r_{t+1})\{[b_{t+1}(\frac{P_t r_{t+1}}{P_{t+1}}, r_{t+1})/m_{t+1}\frac{(P_t r_{t+1}}{P_{t+1}}, r_{t+1})] + 1\} = (1+\alpha)m_{t+1}$$

Let us indicate the composition of desired financial assets

$$[b_{t+1}(\frac{P_t r_{t+1}}{P_{t+1}}, r_{t+1})/m_{t+1}(\frac{P_t r_{t+1}}{P_{t+1}}, r_{t+1})] = \alpha^d[(P_t r_{t+1}/P_{t+1}), r_{t+1})]$$

Since the public budget constraint can also be written as $(1+\alpha)m_{t+1} = (1+\alpha r_{t+1})(P_t/P_{t+1})m_t$, by solving the latter for (P_t/P_{t+1}) and by substituting it into equilibrium conditions, we deduce that steady state requires

$$\alpha^d[\frac{(1+\alpha)r}{1+\alpha r}, r) = \alpha$$

Arguments r and d of the function $\alpha^d[\,.\,]$ are respectively a variable and a parameter. Taking this into account, if we think of the steady state condition as a parametric form we obtain a simple graph. Let us also take the liberty of indicating α^d the images of function $\alpha^d[\,.\,]$. Since the left hand term of the former equality ultimately defines the function $\alpha^d = \alpha^d(r, \alpha)$, its inverse $r = r(\alpha^d, \alpha)$ describes a family of curves parametrized with respect to α in the plane (α^d, r). With this interpretation, steady state equilibrium requires

$$r = r(\alpha^d, \alpha)$$

$$\alpha^d = \alpha$$

We can examine the properties of this system in the plane (α^d, r). For given α, the second condition is a straight line parallel to the r axis with an intercept at α. To study the first condition, we admit that both desired per capita real wealth a(.) and per capita desired real money stock m(.) are:

i) normal goods with respect to changes in the real rate of return $[(1+\alpha)r/(1+\alpha r)]$; and

ii) substitutes with respect to changes in the nominal interest rate r.

As a consequence of (i) and (ii) we have the following signs of partial derivatives of $\alpha^d(.)$:

$$\frac{\partial \alpha^d}{\partial[(1+\alpha)r/1+\alpha r]}\frac{\partial[(1+\alpha)r/1+\alpha r)]}{\partial r} + \frac{\partial \alpha^d}{\partial r} > 0;$$

$$\frac{\partial \alpha^d}{\partial[(1+\alpha)r/1+\alpha r]}\frac{\partial[(1+\alpha)r/1+\alpha r]}{\partial \alpha} < 0$$

By virtue of the inverse function theorem we deduce

$$\frac{\partial r}{\partial \alpha^d} = \frac{1}{\dfrac{\partial \alpha^d}{\partial[(1+\alpha)r/1+\alpha r]}\,\dfrac{\partial[(1+\alpha)r/1+\alpha r)]}{\partial r} + \dfrac{\partial \alpha^d}{\partial r}} > 0;$$

$$\frac{\partial r}{\partial \alpha} = -\frac{\dfrac{\partial \alpha^d}{\partial[(1+\alpha)r/1+\alpha r]}\,\dfrac{\partial[(1+\alpha)r/1+\alpha r]}{\partial \alpha}}{\dfrac{\partial \alpha^d}{\partial[(1+\alpha)r/1+\alpha r]}\,\dfrac{\partial[(1+\alpha)r/1+\alpha r)]}{\partial r} + \dfrac{\partial \alpha^d}{\partial r}} > 0$$

Therefore, in plane (α^d, r) the family of curves is formed by positively sloped curves each shifting to the left and upward in the plane as a response to an increase in parameter α. To place a single curve for given α exactly we should look further into the properties of function $r = r(\alpha^d)$. When $r = 1$ we must have $\alpha^d = 0$, because with null nominal rate of interest nobody wants to hold bonds. Therefore, when $\alpha^d = 0$ the curve $r(\alpha^d)$ has an intercept on the vertical axis at $r = 1$. Moreover when the nominal interest rate stretches to infinite, $r \to \infty$, we must have $\alpha^d(r, \alpha) \to \infty$. Under these circumstances the financial assets consist only of bonds, since nobody will hold money. Combining all the information about $r = r(\alpha^d, \alpha)$ we obtain Figure 5.7, which shows that in the set of steady state equilibria with a positive nominal interest rate a restrictive monetary policy rises the steady state nominal interest rate.

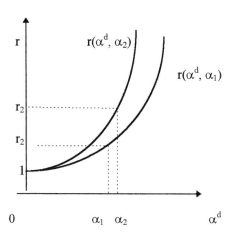

Figure 5.7 Effects of a restrictive monetary policy

5.8 Alternative models of an overlapping-generations monetary economy: (a) Cash-in-advance approach

Another way to fathom the role of money as a medium of exchange is to assume that a monetary economy is defined by the 'exchange relation' (Benassy, 1975). In the abstract set of goods the exchange relation establishes that 'money buys good, goods buy money but goods do not buy goods' (Clower, 1967). The exchange relation implies a peculiar transactions set-up which excludes financing current purchases by current selling. To make desired purchases agents must already hold the money required. Mathematically this is enforced by adding a liquidity or a cash-in-advance constraint to the usual budget constraint. This approach has been adopted in an intertemporal context with infinite horizon by Lucas (1980) and Stockmann (1981). Models with overlapping generations and a cash-in-advance constraint have been proposed by Wallace (1987) and Woodford (1987).

In an economy with overlapping- generations by assumption the young hold no money. This would preclude participation of the young in transactions. Enabling the young to transact would require assuming some special market set-up. Here we assume a credit market which closes before the goods market opens and where the young can obtain the necessary money for purchases. Since the life cycle of an agent is finite, it is also necessary to specify how agents will settle debts and credits at the final instant. To simplify we assume that each agent closes his/her life-cycle without debts and credits.

By virtue of the assumptions introduced so far, this life cycle of an agent has three periods. Each of the first two periods are divided into two sub-periods. The first sub-period is devoted to transactions on the credit market. The second to transactions on the goods market. The third period, unlike the other two, is really composed of only a sub-period, since by assumption there are no transactions on the goods market and the period is devoted to settling debts and credits. We assume a stationary population and exogenous endowments of a young person (e_1^t, e_1^{t+1}). By taking into account the whole set of constraints, the representative young person solves the problem

$$\text{max} \quad U(c_1^t, c_1^{t+1})$$
$$\text{sub} \quad M_1^t = -B_1^t$$
$$P_t c_1^t \leq M_1^t$$
$$\overline{M}_1^{t+1} = M_1^t - P_t c_1^t + P_t e_1^t$$

$$M_1^{t+1} = \overline{M}_1^{t+1} + r_{t+1}B_1^t - B_1^{t+1}$$
$$P_{t1}c_1^{t+1} \leq M_1^{t+1}$$
$$\overline{M}_1^{t+2} = M_1^{t+1} - P_{t+1}c_1^{t+1} + P_{t+1}e_1^{t+1}$$
$$\overline{M}_1^{t+3} = \overline{M}_1^{t+2} + r_{t+2}B_1^{t+1} = 0$$

This problem has the following first-order conditions:

$$c_1^t \quad : \quad U'(c_1^t) = P_t(\lambda_2 + \lambda_3)$$
$$c_1^{t+1} \quad : \quad U'(c_1^{t+1}) = P_{t+1}(\lambda_5 + \lambda_6)$$
$$B_1^t \quad : \quad -\lambda_1 + r_{t+1}\lambda_4 = 0$$
$$B_1^{t+1} \quad : \quad -\lambda_4 + r_{t+2}\lambda_7 = 0$$
$$M_1^t \quad : \quad -\lambda_1 + \lambda_2 + \lambda_3 = 0$$
$$M_1^{t+1} \quad : \quad -\lambda_4 + \lambda_5 + \lambda_6 = 0$$
$$\overline{M}_1^{t+1} \quad : \quad -\lambda_3 + \lambda_4 = 0$$
$$\overline{M}_1^{t+2} \quad : \quad -\lambda_6 + \lambda_7 = 0$$

where $\lambda_i (i = 1, ..., 7)$ is the Lagrange multiplier referring to i-th constraints. There the constraints are in the sequence $i = 1, ..., 7$ written in the maximum problem above. First-order conditions are written so that all the constraints are satisfied as equality. As matter of fact, the third and the fifth constraint of the maximum problem are formulated as weak inequalities so that conditions pertinent to magnitudes c_1^t, c_1^{t+1}, M_1^t, M_1^{t+1} must, more rigorously, be rewritten as weak inequalities $\leq$. These also require the slackness conditions $[M_1^t - P_t c_1^t]\lambda_2 = 0$ and $[M_1^{t+1} - P_{t+1}c_1^{t+1}]\lambda_5 = 0$ which are important in verifying the admissibility of equilibria having a dominance of money in the nominal interest rate.

Indeed by eliminating the Langrage multipliers, first-order conditions imply

$$\frac{U'(c_1^t)}{U'(c_1^{t+1})} = \frac{P_t r_{t+1}}{P_{t+1}}; \lambda_2 = \frac{U'(c_1^{t+1})}{P_{t+1}}[r_{t+1} - 1]; \lambda_5 = \frac{U'(c_1^{t+1})}{P_{t+1}r_{t+1}}[r_{t+2} - 1]$$

Solutions for which the second and fifth constraint of the maximum problem are satisfied as equalities require $\lambda_2 > 0$ and $\lambda_5 > 0$ so that $r_{t+1} - 1 > 0$ and $r_{t+2} - 1 > 0$, that is dominance of money in nominal interest rate at each t. More generally, we can say that $r_{t+1} \geq 1$ is a requirement for a competitive equilibrium. A private agent demand function for net real borrowing (net demand of *inside* money) from monetary authorities follows from the first order conditions, which appear as

$$a_1^{t+1}\left(\frac{P_t r_{t+1}}{P_{t+1}}, r_{t+1}, r_{t+2}\right) = -[m_1^{dt+1}\left(\frac{P_t r_{t+1}}{P_{t+1}}, r_{t+1}, r_{t+2}\right)$$

$$+ \frac{P_t}{P_{t+1}} b_1^t\left(\frac{P_t r_{t+1}}{P_{t+1}}, r_{t+1}, r_{t+2}\right)]$$

$$a_2^{t+1}\left(\frac{P_1 r_{t+1}}{P_{t+1}}, r_{t+1}, r_{t+2}\right) = -[m_2^{dt+1}\left(\frac{P_t r_{t+1}}{P_{t+1}}, r_{t+1}, r_{t+2}\right)$$

$$+ \frac{P_t}{P_{t+1}} b_2^t\left(\frac{P_t r_{t+1}}{P_{t+1}}, r_{t+1}, r_{t+2}\right)]$$

Having proved that equilibria with a positive nominal interest rate are admissible, we can now examine the effects of monetary policies carried out through open market operations. In considering pure open market operations, let F_{t+1} be the total current loans of the monetary authorities and let F_t be the expired loans currently refunded with interest by agents. The budget constraint of monetary authorities in per capita nominal terms is

$$M_{t+1} - M_t = F_{t+1} - r_{t+1} F_t$$

General equilibrium is the simultaneous equilibrium of the credit and money markets. In nominal per capita terms these equilibrium conditions are

$$F_{t+1} + B_2^{t+1} + B_1^t \geq 0$$
$$\overline{M}_1^{t+1} + \overline{M}_2^{t+1} = M_{t+1}$$

In per capita real terms for $r_{t+1} > 1$, the equilibrium conditions are

$$f_{t+1} = -[b_2^{t+1}\left(\frac{P_t r_{t+1}}{P_t}, r_{t+1}, r_{t+2}\right) + \frac{P_t}{P_{t+1}} b_1^t\left(\frac{P_t r_{t+1}}{P_t}, r_{t+1}, r_{t+2}\right)$$

$$m_{t+1} = m_2^{dt+1}\left(\frac{P_t r_{t+1}}{P_t}, r_{t+1}, r_{t+2}\right) + m_1^{dt+1}\left(\frac{P_t r_{t+1}}{P_t}, r_{t+1}, r_{t+2}\right)$$

When the former conditions are verified so must be

$$f_{t+1} - m_{t+1} = -[m_2^{dt+1}\left(\frac{P_t r_{t+1}}{P_t}, r_{t+1}, r_{t+2}\right) + b_2^{t+1}\left(\frac{P_t r_{t+1}}{P_t}, r_{t+1}, r_{t+2}\right)]$$

$$- [m_1^{dt+1}\left(\frac{P_t r^{t+1}}{P_t}, r_{t+1}, r_{t+2}\right) + \frac{P_t}{P_{t+1}} b_1^t\left(\frac{P_t r_{t+1}}{P_t}, r_{t+1}, r_{t+2}\right)]$$

that is

$$a_{t+1} = a_{t+1}^d\left(\frac{P_t r_{t+1}}{P_{t+1}}, r_{t+1}, r_{t+2}\right)$$

where $a_{t+1} = f_{t+1} - m_{t+1}$; $a_{t+1}^d(.) = a_2^{t+1}(.) + a_1^{t+1}(.)$. By solving the public budget constraints in real terms for P_t/P_{t+1} we get

$$\frac{P_t}{P_{t+1}} = \frac{f_{t+1} - m_{t+1}}{r_{t+1}f_t - m_t} = \frac{a_{t+1}}{a_t + (r_{t+1} - 1)f_t}$$

so that necessary conditions for equilibrium reduce to

$$a_{t+1} = a_{t+1}^d[\frac{(a_{t+1}/a_t,\,)r_{t+1}}{1 + (r_{t+1} - 1)(f_t/a_t)}, r_{t+1}, r_{t+2}]$$

We assume that monetary authorities follow a constant rate net credit policy $a_{t+1} = \gamma a_t$ in addition to a constant desired portfolio composition policy $f_t/a_t = \delta$. A steady state equilibrium with $r_{t+1} = r_{t+2} = r$ is such that

$$\gamma = \gamma^d[\frac{\gamma r}{1 + (r - 1)\delta}, r)$$

If a_{t+1}^d (.) is a normal good and a gross substitute, then

$$\partial\gamma^d/\partial[\frac{\gamma r}{1 + (r - 1)\delta}] > 0;$$

$$d\gamma^d/dr = \partial\gamma^d/\partial[\frac{\gamma r}{1 + (r - 1)\delta})\partial[\frac{\gamma r}{1 + (r - 1)\delta}]/\partial r + \partial\gamma^d/\partial r > 0$$

Given these assumptions, if we consider the inverse function γ^d and write equilibrium in parametric form we obtain

$$r = r(\gamma^d, \gamma, \delta)$$
$$\gamma^d = \gamma$$

By virtue of the inverse function theorem it follows that

$$\partial r/\partial\gamma^d = 1/(d\gamma^d/dr) > 0;\ \partial r/\partial\gamma = -[(\partial\gamma^d/\partial\gamma)/(d\gamma^d/dr)] < 0;\ \partial r/\partial\delta = -[(\partial\gamma^d/\partial\delta)/(d\gamma^d/dr)] < 0$$

A picture in the plane (γ^d, r) similar to the one of the money-in-the-utility-function model looks like Figure 5.8 which shows that, for a given growth rate of inside money γ, a change in monetary policy mix towards more credit $\delta_2 > \delta_1$ reduces the nominal interest rate. An increase $\gamma_2 > \gamma_1$ in the growth rate of inside money that does not change the composition of monetary liabilities of the authorities has the same effect on the nominal interest rate, as shown in Figure 5.9.

5.9   Alternative models of an overlapping-generations monetary economy: (b) Transaction costs approach

Another way to model a monetary economy is based on the transaction costs function. This model is a generalization of the Baumol-Tobin

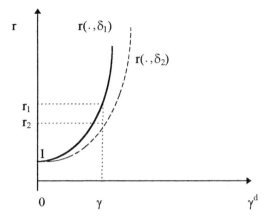

Figure 5.8   Effects of a looser credit policy

classical transaction costs approach (Baumol, 1952; Tobin, 1956). The transaction costs approach (Saving, 1971; Feenstra, 1986) allows alternative modelling of a monetary economy both in an intertemporal context (with discrete time and infinite horizon (Kimbrough, 1986) and in continuos time (Benhabib and Bull, 1983; Wang and Yip, 1992)) and in overlapping-generations context with a finite horizon (Michaelis, 1993). Here we shall limit ourselves to pure-exchange economies with overlapping generations and a stationary population in order to evaluate the results with respect to the other approaches examined.[2] A basic

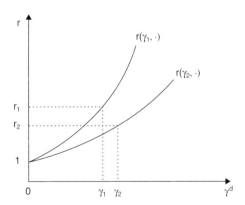

Figure 5.9   Effects of an increase in the growth rate of inside money

assumption of the transaction costs approach is that the transaction process absorbs real resources. Money is a way to economize the costs incurred in carrying out transactions. It is assumed that total per capita resources absorbed by transactions are described by a function $T_t = T(c_t, m_t)$ which depends on per capita consumption and on real per capita money stock. Transaction technology T(.) is assumed to be continuous, differentiable at least two times and satisfies the following properties:

a) $T'_c > 0$; $T'_m < 0$; $T''_{cc} > 0$; $T''_{mm} > 0$;
b) $T_{cm} \le 0$; $T(0, m) = 0$;
c) $\lim_{m \to 0} T'_m = -\infty$; there exists $m^* < \infty$ such that $T'_m (c, m^*) = 0$; $T(c, m^*) = 0$

Properties (a) describe a transaction technology which uses increasing resources as consumption increases and decreasing resources as money stock increases. Technology is convex so money reduces costs at an increasing rate. Properties (b) indicate that a greater money stock does not change or reduce the marginal cost of consumption and there are no benefits of money when there are no transactions in consumer goods. The first property of (c) guarantees the efficacy of money in reducing costs, while the second postulates the existence of a finite satiety money stock beyond which agents accrue no advantages neither absolute nor incremental from holding money. The characteristics of a monetary economy with overlapping-generations and a transaction technology depend on how transaction technology is conceived.

In one view, we can attribute the economizing on costs to the *initial* money stock held by agents. Assume that money comes into the economy from a central bank that follows a policy of constant growth rate for the per capita money stock $M_{t+1} = (1 + \vartheta)M_t$. The current money stock is held by the old. Hence to allow the young to economize transaction costs as well we assume newly created money is distributed through transfers to the young. Therefore, they benefit from real money transfers $h_t = \vartheta m_t$ and the problem solved by the representative young is

$$\max \quad U(c_1^t, c_1^{t+1})$$
$$\text{sub} \quad c_1^t + T(c_1^t, h_t) + (P_{t+1}/P_t)m_{t+1} = e_1^t + h_t$$
$$c_1^{t+1} + T(c_1^{t+1}, m_{t+1}) = e_1^{t+1} + m_{t+1}$$

On the other hand, the old maximize consumption subject to constraint $c_2^t + T(c_2^t, m_t) = e_2^t + m_t$.

First-order necessary conditions for the maximum of the young are

$$\frac{U_1'(c_1^t, c_1^{t+1})}{U_2'(c_1^t, c_1^{t+1})} = \frac{1 + T_{c_{1t}}'}{1 + T_{c_{1,t+1}}'} \frac{P_t}{P_{t+1}}$$

$$(\frac{P_{t+1}}{P_t} T_{m_{t+1}}')\lambda = 0$$

The first condition is the equality between the marginal rate of substitution of current to future consumption and the marginal rate of transformation of current consumption to future consumption indirectly via money. The second condition, where the Lagrange multiplier is positive $\lambda > 0$, is an optimality condition for the desired money stock. Because of it, the only admissible dynamic competitive equilibrium is the one satisfying a satiety condition for the real money stock $m_{t+1} = m_t = m^*$. Moreover the only policy supporting the satiety condition is the constant money stock policy. Indeed, competitive steady states satisfy $(P_{t+1}/P_t) = (1 + \vartheta)$. In the set of these equilibria, efficient equilibria equalize the marginal rate of substitution and the marginal rate of transformation between present and future consumption. Therefore, the efficiency condition is

$$\frac{U_1'(c_1^t, c_1^{t+1})}{U_2'(c_1^t, c_1^{t+1})} = \frac{1 + T_{c_{1,t}}'}{1 + T_{c_{1,t+1}}'}$$

which implies $(P_{t+1}/P_t) = 1$, and thus $\vartheta = 0$. Friedman's rule, understood as the joint nullity of the nominal rate of interest and the zero rate in growth of money, is a necessary condition for the optimality. The economics underlying the mathematics is easy to understand. If money reduces the quantity of resources wasted in an exchange process and it is a public good produced at zero cost, then it is optimal for the society to have *at each instant* a real money stock which nullifies the quantity of resources absorbed in an exchange activity. Moreover, such a system has no dynamics of money stock, since each deviation from the satiety level is a disequilibrium state.

Another formulation consistent with solutions admitting equilibrium dynamics assumes that the transaction costs function does not depend on the money stock held at the beginning of period but on the *desired* money stock at the start of the succeeding period (Michaelis, 1993). It has been demonstrated (Feenstra, 1986) that this assumption is only consistent with the inclusion of a transaction costs function in agents' budget constraint on the basis of Whalen's (1966) precautionary motive. In this view T(.) measures a penalty that an agent must pay in terms of real resources after having accumulated money for the next period if he wishes to take advantage of using money in the current period to reduce transaction costs. In this context the old, even though they no longer have a future, are motivated to accumulate money since they benefit from a reduction in current transaction costs. The behaviour of agents is described as follows. The young solve the constrained maximum problem

$$\max \quad U(c_1^t, c_1^{t+1})$$
$$c_1^t + T(c_1^t, m_{t+1}) + (P_{t+1}/P_t)m_{t+1} = e_1^t + h_t$$
$$c_1^{t+1} + T(c_1^{t+1}, m_{t+2}) + m_{t+2} = e_1^{t+1} + m_{t+1}$$

First-order conditions are now

$$\frac{U_1'(c_1^t, c_1^{t+1})}{U_2'(c_1^t, c_1^{t+1})} = (\frac{1 + T_{c_{1,t}}'}{1 + T_{c_{1,t+1}}'})(\frac{1}{T_{m_{t+1}'}' + (P_{t+1}/P_t)})$$
$$T_{m,t+2}' = -1$$

The second condition excludes that a satiety monetary policy can be optimal for the old because the old must accumulate money to benefit from a reduction in transaction costs. Therefore they must renounce consumption in order to finance the accumulation of money. This allows monetary authorities to follow a policy of satiety only if that satiety is *different* for the young and the old. From the equality of the marginal rate of substitution and the marginal rate of transformation between current and future consumption we have

$$\frac{U_1'(c_1^t, c_1^{t+1})}{U_2'(c_1^t, c_1^{t+1})} = (\frac{1 + T_{c_{1,t}}'}{1 + T_{c_{1,t+1}}'})$$

Optimality requires

$$T_{m't+1} + (P_{t+1}/P_t) = 1$$

The latter condition implies $(P_{t+1}/P_t) = 1 - T_{m_{t+1}'}'$ which admits $P_{t+1}/P_t = 1$ only if $T_{m_{t+1}'}' = 0$ is compatible with $T_{m_{t+2}'}' = -1$. It remains to be verified whether such a policy is workable under the conditions admitted by the model. The problem of agent's choice has been formulated so that at the end of a period the old generation dies and can leave a positive money stock. A way to avoid wasting the money stock is to assume (Michaelis, 1993) that money stock held by the old is appropriated by authorities in the form of tax. In this case the government budget constraint becomes $h_t - m_2^{t+1} = \vartheta m_t$.

The ongoing supply of money now consists of three components. The first component is the emission of new money. The second is the money stock accumulated in previous period, and the third is the money reintroduced into circulation. The latter component is the same for both demand and supply, so that the dynamic equilibrium condition is

$$m_2^{t+1} + \vartheta m_t = (P_{t+1}/P_t)m_{t+1}$$

In steady state where $m_2^{t+1} = m_t = m_{t+1}$, we must have

$$(P_{t+1}/P_t) = (1 + \vartheta)$$

A satiety policy, with $(P_{t+1}/P_t) = 1$, is admissible and requires $\vartheta = 0$. However even policies implying a positive rate of inflation are optimal so that, strictly speaking, Friedman rule is not necessary. Evidently, the transaction costs approach depends on both the formalization of costs and a mix of fiscal and monetary policies to keep the model consistent. We can now verify that, since Friedman's rule is not necessary, a transaction costs approach with transaction technology depending on a desired money stock admits a competitive equilibrium with the dominance of money in the nominal interest rate on bonds and once again, assume perfect co-ordination between the central bank and the Treasury department. Fiscal and transfer policies remain those already admitted, so that the government budget constraint in per capita real terms is

$$h_t - m_2^{t+1} + i_{t+1}b_{t+1} = (P_{t+1}/P_t)b_{t+1} + (P_{t+1}/P_t)m_{t+1} - m_t$$

With a primary-deficit-null-policy such that $h_t - m_2^{t+1} = 0$, the government budget constraint becomes

$$i_{t+1}b_{t+1} + m_t = (P_{t+1}/P_t)(b_{t+1} + m_{t+1})$$

We can now verify that competitive equilibrium with a positive nominal interest rate exists.[3] Since public bonds are an alternative to money in savings, the problem of choice for the representative young is

$$\max U(c_1^t, c_2^{t+1})$$
$$c_1^t + T(c_1^t, m_{t+1}) + (P_{t+1}/P_t)m_{t+1} + (P_{t+1}/P_t)b_{t+1} = e_1^t + h_t$$
$$c_1^{t+1} + T(c_1^{t+1}, m_{t+2}) + m_{t+2} = e_1^{t+1} + m_{t+1} + r_{t+1}b_{t+1}$$

From necessary first-order conditions

$$\frac{U_1'(c_1^t, c_1^{t+1})}{U_2'(c_1^t, c_1^{t+1})} = \left(\frac{1 + T_{c_{1,t}}'}{1 + T_{c_{1,t+1}}'}\right)\frac{P_t}{P_{t+1}}r_{t+1}$$

$$T'_{m,t+2} = -1$$

$$r_{t+1} = \frac{P_{t+1}/P_t}{T'_{m_{t+1}} + (P_{t+1}/P_t)}$$

Since $T'_{m_{t+1}} < 0$ it follows that $r_{t+1} > 1$; that is bonds dominate money in the nominal interest rate.

5.10 Alternative models of an overlapping-generations monetary economy: (c) Legal restrictions approach

All the previous representations of a monetary economy are based on a common denominator: the search for the distinctive character of a monetary economy. However, from another point of view they can be simply seen as analytical devices to guarantee a positive demand for and a positive price of money at equilibrium. In this section we shall examine models of legal restrictions on financial intermediaries (Bryant and Wallace, 1979, 1984; Freeman, 1987; Sargent and Wallace, 1982; Sargent and Smith, 1987; Smith,1991; Wallace, 1983,1987a,b;). In a sense they can also be interpreted as a way to guarantee a positive price for money.

However, the regulation of financial intermediaries is not intended as a useful gimmick. It is, instead, a useful governmental *instrument* for raising revenue when money has a positive price. This revenue is the maximum seignorage or the reduction of the burden of interest on the public debt. The most important restriction on financial intermediaries is certainly a compulsory reserve for bank deposits, which is common in most banking systems. If we view bank deposits as private securities competing with government bonds, a compulsory reserve becomes a kind of taxation on privately issued securities. More exactly it is a legal obligation on the part of the issuer of that security named 'deposit' to buy a barren public security named 'currency' at face value. Another important restriction (Sargent and Wallace,1983; Sargent and Smith, 1987) is forbidding banking intermediaries to issue banknotes competing with the currency issued by the central bank. This restriction, together with a restriction on minimum size for bonds has proved useful in modelling monetary economies admitting steady state equilibria with the dominance of money in the nominal interest rate.

We will examine a monetary economy with a reserve requirement and then one with a minimum-size-for-bonds restriction. The simplest model with a reserve requirement is that of a pure-exchange economy populated by overlapping-generations and having no taxation or public spending. If central bank and banking intermediaries are not explicitly included, it can be assumed that (1) new money enters the economy through transfers to private agents; and (2) reserve requirements apply to loans of a single creditor. Because there are no public assets, only private assets are exchanged in the credit market. The current young generation is divided into two groups of unchanging proportions, that is:

a) type 1 agents, savers with life–cycle endowments $(e_{11}^t, 0)$ and $c_{11}^t - e_{11}^t < 0$;
b) type 2 agents, non-savers with life–cycle endowments (h_{t+1}, e_{12}^{t+1}) and $c_{12}^t - h_{t+1} > 0$, where h_{t+1} is the real money received as current transfers from the government.

When the credit market is open, group 1 agents participate as lenders and group 2 agents participate as borrowers. Credit contracts are 'pure consumption-loan' contracts. Finally, we assume that only group 2 agents benefit from government transfers of money.

We start by considering group 1 agents (savers). Since savers are potential lenders, they are the agents for whom a compulsory reserve restriction can be binding. Let $0 < \kappa < 1$ be a coefficient for compulsory reserve and let $r_{t|1} = 1 + i_{t|1}$ be the nominal interest rate. The effective return $r_{t|1}^L$ obtained from a unit of nominal saving when savers act as lenders is a weighted average of rate of interest on loan and the compulsory reserve coefficient, that is

$$r_{t+1}^L = \kappa + (1 - \kappa)r_{t+1}$$

From definitions $R_{t+1}^L = (P_t/P_{t+1})\, r_{t+1}^L;\ R_{t+1} = (P_t/P_{t+1})\, r_{t+1}$, the real rate of return for lenders is

$$R_{t+1}^L = \kappa(P_t/P_{t+1}) + (1 - \kappa)R_{t+1}$$

In examining the conditions under which the constraint of compulsory reserve is binding, we see that from a general point of view to a saver a compulsory reserve as a legal restriction looks like a lower bound to real money stock holding. If b_{t+1} is the amount of private loans, $b_{t+1}^+ = \max(0, b_{t+1})$. Given a compulsory reserve coefficient, for a saver the lower bound to holding money is κb_{t+1}^+. Therefore the representative saver solves the following problem

$$\max U_1(c_{11}^t, c_{11}^{t+1})$$
$$c_{11}^t + (P_{t+1}/P_t)m_{t+1} + b_{t+1} = e_{11}^t$$
$$c_{11}^{t+1} = m_{t+1} + R_{t+1}\, b_{t+1}$$
$$m_{t+1} \geq \kappa b_{t+1}^+$$

By reducing constraints to only one intertemporal constraint, the former problem is the same as

$$\max U_1(c_{11}^t, c_{11}^{t+1})$$
$$c_{11}^t + c_{11}^{t+1}(1/R_{t+1}) = c_{11}^t - m_{t+1}[((P_{t+1}/P_t) - (1/R_{t+1})$$
$$m_{t+1} \geq \kappa b_{t+1}^+$$

Let $\lambda_i(i = 1, 2)$ be Lagrange multipliers. By virtue of Kuhn-Tucker and slackness conditions we can reduce the first-order necessary conditions to

$$\frac{U'_{11}(c_1^t, c_1^{t+1})}{U'_{21}(c_1^t, c_1^{t+1})} = R_{t+1}; \quad \frac{\lambda_2}{\lambda_1} = (P_{t+1}/P_t) - (1/R_{t+1});$$
$$(\lambda_2/\lambda_1)(m_{t+1} - \kappa b_{t+1}^+) = 0; \quad \lambda_2 \geq 0; \quad m_{t+1} - \kappa b_{t+1}^+ \geq 0;$$

Since $\lambda_1 > 0$, we can put

$$R_{t+1} \geq (P_t/P_{t+1}); \quad [R_{t+1} - (P_t/P_{t+1})](m_{t+1} - \kappa b^+) = 0;$$

Two cases can be distinguished

a) when $R_{t+1} = (P_t/P_{t+1})$ savers are indifferent to money or loans. The compulsory reserve constraint is not binding and the money stock desired by savers is greater than the lower bound. To be more exact, the desired optimal money stock is simply greater than zero and coincides with savings if the saver chooses to have zero loans. On the contrary, it is greater than the compulsory reserve if the saver chooses positive loans;

b) when $R_{t+1} > (P_t/P_{t+1})$, the compulsory reserve constraint is binding. The saver wants to hold all savings as a loan, but since he must also hold money he will hold the minimum amount required as a reserve. In this case since $b_{t+1}^+ = b_{t+1} > 0$, the money stock held is $m_{t+1} = \kappa b_{t+1}$.

The problem of choice is simpler for the representative agent of non-savers group 2. Since the agent does not want to hold money, the reserve constraint does not concern the agent. For the representative saver of group 2 the problem is

$$\max U_2(c_{12}^t, c_{12}^{t+1})$$
$$c_{12}^t = b_{t+1}^s + h_{t+1}$$
$$c_{12}^{t+1} = e_{12}^{t+1} - R_{t+1} b_{t+1}^s$$

We are now able to describe equilibrium in per capita terms. The economy is composed of three markets: goods; money; and private loans. General equilibrium requires the simultaneous equilibrium of all three markets. Walras law allows us to ignore any one of the markets. We shall consider only the markets for goods and money. We assume a policy of constant growth in money stock. Current real transfers are $h_{t+1} = m_t$, so the current supply of real money is $(1 + \vartheta)m_t$. By taking into account agent's budget constraints, equilibrium in the goods market is equivalent to equality between savings and the supply of financial assets. The latter are the borrowings of group 2 agents. Therefore equilibrium is

$$s_1(R_{t+1}, P_t/P_{t+1}) + s_2(R_{t+1}, h_{t+1}) = (1 + \vartheta)m_t$$

$$\frac{m_{t+1}(R_{t+1}, P_t/P_{t+1})}{P_t/P_{t+1}} = (1 + \vartheta)m_t$$

For a given ϑ, steady state with $m_t = m_{t+1}$, $h_t = h_{t+1}$, is the pair $(R, P_t/P_{t+1})$ so $R \geq (P_t/P_{t+1})$ and $(P_t/P_{t+1}) = (1/1 + \vartheta)$. Steady state with a binding compulsory reserve constraint occurs when $R > (P_t/P_{t+1})$.

Therefore this equilibrium admits gross nominal interest rate $r > 1$, that is it admits dominance of money in the nominal interest rate. Note that if the economy is at this kind of equilibria, an appropriate change in the money stock by the monetary authorities can render the compulsory reserve constraint not binding. For example, consider a steady state with constant money stock $m > 0$, that is $\vartheta = 0$. Steady state with a binding compulsory reserve constraint satisfies $R > 1$. Monetary authorities can fix $\vartheta^* < 0$ so that $(P_t/P_{t+1})^* = 1/1 + \vartheta^* > 1$, and particularly so that $(P_t/P_{t+1})^* = R$. This is a shrinking rate of money stock corresponding to the optimal deflation rate required by Friedman's rule. This policy permits equality between substitution rates required for Pareto-optimum in intertemporal context, but it does not satisfy dynamic efficiency condition $(P_t/P_{t+1})^* > 1$. On the other hand if we consider any kind of fiscal policy feasible, some policy can be designed to be compatible with constant money stock, which leads steady state real return R toward the level $R = 1 = (P_t/P_{t+1})$, making it unnecessary to adopt monetary policy *à la* Friedman to reach efficient steady state. A refinement of partition of the set of agents of previous model permits to assume, instead of reserve requirements, a minimum size denomination of private bonds.

Following Sargent-Wallace (1982) and Sargent-Smith (1987) let us assume that endowments and preferences are such that it is meaningful to further distinguish savers into (a) small savers, that is 'poor' savers whose temporal endowments profile, although allows positive saving, determines an amount of saving insufficient to subscribe minimum size loan contracts; and (b) large savers, or 'rich' savers whose temporal endowments profile allows them to subscribe loan contracts that respect the minimum size constraint. As before, money enters the economy through transfers only to borrowers. The choices of borrowers are further constrained by the minimum amount of borrowing $b^s_{t+1} \geq b^*$, so that the representative borrower problem is

$$\max U_2(c^t_{12}, c^{t+1}_{12})$$
$$c^t_{12} = b^s_{t+1} + h_{h+1}$$
$$c^{t+1}_{12} = e^{t+1}_{12} - R_{t+1}\, b^s_{t+1}$$
$$b^s_{t+1} \geq b^* \text{ or } b^s_{t+1} = 0$$

First-order conditions are

$$\frac{U'_{12}(c^t_1, c^{t+1}_1)}{U'_{22}(c^t_1, c^{t+1}_1)} \leq R_{t+1}$$

where the strict inequality sign < applies when the minimum-size constraint for bonds is binding.

The representative poor savers endowment is $e^t_{1p} < b^*$. For this type of saver the maximum problem is

$$\max U_p(c^t_{1p}, c^{t+1}_{1p})$$
$$c^t_{1p} + (P_{t+1}/P_t)m_{t+1} = e^t_{1p}$$
$$c^{t+1}_{1p} = m_{t+1}$$
$$m_{t+1} > 0$$

First order conditions are

$$\frac{U'_{1p}(c^t_1, c^{t+1}_1)}{U'_{2p}(c^t_1, c^{t+1}_1)} = P_t/P_{t+1}$$

The rich representative savers endowment is $e^t_{1r} - c^t_1 > b^*$. For this type of saver the maximum problem is

$$\max U_r(c^t_{1r}, c^{t+1}_{1r})$$
$$c^t_{1r} + (P_{t+1}/P_t)m_{t+1} + b_{t+1} = e^t_{1r}$$
$$c^{t+1}_{1r} = m_{t+1} + R_{t+1}\, b_{t+1}$$
$$b_{t+1} \geq 0; m_{t+1} \geq 0; \text{ with at least one inequality verified as a strict}$$
equality.

First-order necessary conditions reduce to

$$\frac{U'_{11}(c^t_1, c^{t+1}_1)}{U'_{12}(c^t_1, c^{t+1}_1)} = R_{t+1}; R_{t+1} \geq P_t/P_{t+1}$$

On the basis of these conditions we can distinguish two cases

1. when $R_{t+1} = P_t/P_{t+1}$ the rich representative saver is indifferent to the composition of savings;
2. when $R_{t+1} > P_t/P_{t+1}$ the real return on loans is greater than the real return on money.

The saver in case 2. chooses $m_{t+1} = 0$, so that savings is entirely in the form of loans.

General equilibrium in per capita terms can be reduced to the following equations

$$s_p(P_t/P_{t+1}) + s_r(R_{t+1}, P_t/P_{t+1}) + s_b(R_{t+1}, h_{t+1}) = (1 + \vartheta)m_t$$
$$\frac{m_{t+1}(R_{t+1}, P_t/P_{t+1})}{P_t/P_{t+1}} = (1 + \vartheta)m_t$$

Even in the case we are considering, for given ϑ, a steady state equilibrium, with $m_t = m_{t+1}$, $h_t = h_{t+1}$, is a pair $(R, P_t/P_{t+1})$ such that $R \geq (P_t/P_{t+1})$ and $(P_t/P_{t+1}) = (1/1 + \vartheta)$. A steady state equilibrium where $R > (P_t/P_{t+1})$ implies $r > 1$, that is steady state admits dominance of money in the nominal interest rate. Moreover, at this equilibrium

a) money stock is entirely held by poor savers
$$s_p(P_t/P_{t+1}) = \frac{m_{t+1}(R_{t+1}, P_t/P_{t+1})}{P_t/P_{t+1}} = (1 + \vartheta)m_t$$
b) loans desired by borrowers respect the minimum size constraint and are entirely held by rich savers
$$s_r(R_{t+1}, P_t/P_{t+1}) + s_b(R_{t+1}, h_{t+1}) = 0$$
$$0 > -b^* \geq s_b(R_{t+1}, h_{t+1})$$

We are now interested in examining the effects of monetary policies implemented through open market operations. Let us depart from the assumption that money enters the economy through government transfers. As we have already seen, allowing monetary authorities to implement open market operations is equivalent to assuming that monetary authorities are constrained by budget constraint $M_{t+1} - M_t = F_{t+1} - r_{t+1}F_t$, or by $(P_{t+1}/P_t)m_{t+1} - m_t = (P_{t+1}/P_t)\ b^g_{t+1}$ $-r_{t+1}b_{gt}$. If we take into account the supply of public bonds, equilibrium conditions become

$$s_p(P_t/P_{t+1}) + s_r(R_{t+1}, P_t/P_{t+1} + s_b(R_{t+1}) = m_t + b_{gt}$$
$$m_{r+1}(R_{t+1}, P_t/P_{t+1}) = m_t$$

Given ϑ, steady state with $m_t = m_{t+1}$, is a pair $(R, P_t/P_{t+1})$ in which $R \geq (P_t/P_{t+1})$ and $(P_t/P_{t+1}) = (1/1 + \vartheta)$. Steady state with $R > (P_t/P_{t+1})$ has nominal interest factor $r > 1$, that is dominance of money in the nominal interest rate. Moreover, this equilibrium has the same (a) and (b) properties as before, that is money stock is held entirely by poor savers, borrowings satisfy the minimum size constraint and all loans are made by rich savers. It is also interesting to examine open-market monetary policies. In this view a steady state is the quadruple of values $(m, b_g, R, P_t/P_{t+1})$ that verifies

$$s_p(P_t/P_{t+1}) + s_r(R, P_t/P_{t+1}) + s_b(R) = m + b_g$$
$$m(R, P_t/P_{t+1}) = m$$

With constant money stock at equilibrium we must have $P_t/P_{t+1} = 1$ and $R \geq 1$.

Let us examine these two situations separately:

1. when $R > 1$, equilibrium is such that
$$s_p(1) = m$$
$$s_r(R, 1) + s_b(R) = b_g$$
$$b_g \geq 0$$

By virtue of the public budget constraint, each steady state where

$$s_p(P_t/P_{t+1}) = m, \text{ and}$$
$$s_r(R, P_t/P_{t+1}) + s_b(R) = b_g$$

must also satisfy the condition

$$[1 - (P_t/P_{t+1})]s_p(P_t/P_{t+1}) + (1 - R)[s_r(R, P_t/P_{t+1}) + s_b(R)] = 0$$

From this it follows that $s_r(R, 1) + s_b(R) = 0$, that is $b_g = 0$. Therefore, at steady state with $R > 1$ monetary authorities play no role on the bond market;

2. when $R = P_t/P_{t+1} = 1$, assuming $s_p(1) + s_r(1) + s_b(1) > 0$, since $s_r(1) + s_b(1) < 0$ the steady state

$$s_p(1) + s_r(1) + s_b(1) = m + b_g$$
$$s_r(1) + s_b(1) = b_g$$

is admissible if $m + b_g > 0$, $b_g < 0$. In this case monetary authorities must perform the role of lender and they must offer credit by purchasing bonds on the market.

Notes

1. Otherwise, assume the economy has terminal instant T. Knowing that at T + 1 fiat money is worthless, the young at T would not accept money in exchanges. But the old at T are in turn the young at T − 1. Knowing that at T fiat money is worthless because it is not accepted in exchanges, the T − 1 fiat money is also worthless. By the same token, fiat money would be worthless at T − 2, and by induction even from the start money would never have a positive value. However, even when the horizon is infinite it is necessary that at least the initial young will expect the future value of money to be positive. Otherwise they would not accept money in exchanges, which, therefore, would always have zero value.
2. The reader can also refer to the Appendix to Chapter 4.
3. This reformulation also allows us to examine the effects of open market operations on the nominal interest rate.

References

Abel, A. (1987) 'Optimal Monetary Growth', *Journal of Monetary Economics*, 19, pp. 417–50.
Baumol, W. (1952) 'The Transaction Demand for Cash: An Inventory Theoretic Approach', *Quarterly Journal of Economics*, 66, pp. 545–56.
Benassy, J. P. (1975) 'Disequilibrium Exchange in Barter and Money Economies', *Economic Inquiry*, 13, pp. 131–156
Benhabib, J. and C. Bull (1983) 'The Optimal Quantity of Money: A Formal Treatment', *International Economic Review*, 24, pp. 101–11.
Benhabib, J. and R. Day, (1982) 'A Characterization of Erratic Dynamics in the Overlapping Generations Model', *Journal of Economic Dynamic and Control*, 4, pp. 37–55.
Boldrin, M. and M. Woodford (1990) 'Equilibrium Models Displaying Endogenous Fluctuations and Chaos: A Survey', *Journal of Monetary Economics*, 25, pp. 189–222.
Bose, A. (1993) 'Pareto Optimality and Productive Efficiency in the Overlapping Generations Model' in K. Basu, M. Majamdar, and T. Mitra (eds) *Capital, Investment and Development: Essays in Memory of Sukhamoy Chakravarty* (Cambridge MA: Basil Blackwell).
Brock, W. and J. Scheinkman (1980) 'Some Remarks on Monetary Policy in an Overlapping Generations Model', in J. Kareken and, N. Wallace (eds.) *Models of Monetary Economies* (Minneapolis: Federal Reserve Bank of Minneapolis).
Bryant, J. and N. Wallace (1979) 'The Inefficiency of Interest-Bearing National Debt', *Journal of Political Economy*, 87, pp. 363–81.
Bryant, J. and N. Wallace, (1984) 'A Price Discrimination Analysis of Monetary Policy', *Review of Economic Studies*, 51, pp. 279–88.
Cass, D., M. Okuno, and I. Zilcha (1980) 'The Role of Money in Supporting the Pareto Optimality of Competitive Equilibrium in Consumption Loan Type Models', in J. Kareken and N. Wallace (eds) *Models of Monetary Economies* (Minneapolis: Federal Reserve Bank of Minneapolis).
Clower, R. (1967) 'A Reconsideration of the Microeconomic Foundations of Monetary Theory', *Western Economic Journal*, 6, pp. 1–8.

Feenstra, R. (1986) 'Functional Equivalence between Liquidity Costs and the Utility of Money', *Journal of Monetary Economics*, 17, pp. 271–91.

Freeman, S. (1987) 'Reserve Requirements and Optimal Seignorage', *Journal of Monetary Economics*, 19, pp. 307–14.

Freeman, S. and Haslag, J. (1996) 'On the Optimality of Interest-Bearing Reserves in Economies of Overlapping Generations', *Economic Theory*, 7, pp. 557–65.

Friedman, M. (1969) *The Optimum Quantity of Money and Other Essays* (Chicago: Aldine).

Grandmont, J.M. (1985) 'On Endogenous Competitive Business Cycles', *Econometrica*, 53, pp. 995-1046.

Helpman, E. and E. Sadka (1979) 'Optimal Financing of the Governments Budget: Taxes, Bonds, or Money?', *American Economic Review*, 69, pp. 152–60.

Jovanovic, B. (1982) 'Inflation and Welfare in the Steady State', *Journal of Political Economy*, 90, pp. 561–77.

Kareken, J. and N. Wallace (1980) 'Introduction', in J. Kareken and N. Wallace (eds) *Models of Monetary Economies* (Minneapolis: Federal Reserve Bank of Minneapolis).

Kimbrough, K. (1986) 'Inflation, Employment, and Welfare in the Presence of Transactions Costs', *Journal of Money, Credit and Banking*, 18, pp. 127–40.

Lucas, R. (1980) 'Equilibrium in a Pure Currency Economy', in J. Kareken and N. Wallace (eds) *Models of Monetary Economies* (Minneapolis: Federal Reserve Bank of Minneapolis).

McCallum, B. (1983) 'The Role of Overlapping-Generations Models in Monetary Economics', *Carnegie-Rochester Conference Series on Public Policy*, 18, pp. 9–44.

McCallum, B. (1987) 'The Optimal Inflation Rate in a Overlapping-Generations Economy with Land', in W. Barrett, and K. Singleton, (eds) *New Approaches in Monetary Economics* (Cambridge: Cambridge University Press).

Michaelis, J. (1993) 'On the Superneutrality of Money', *Jarhrbücher für National-ökonomie und Statistik*, 212, pp. 257–69.

Mourmouras, A. and S. Russell (1992) 'Bank Regulation as an Antidote to Price Level Instability', *Journal of Monetary Economics*, 29, pp. 125–50.

Patinkin, D. (1966) *Money, Interest and Prices*, 2nd edn, (New York: Harper-Row).

Raut, L. and T. Srinivasan, (1993) 'Theories of Long-Run Growth: Old and New' in K. Basu, and M. Majamdar, and T. Mitra, (eds) *Capital, Investment and Development: Essays in Memory of Sukhamoy Chakravarty* (Cambridge MA: Basil Blackell).

Romer, D. (1985) 'Financial Intermediation, Reserve Requirements, and Inside Money', *Journal of Monetary Economics*, 16, pp. 175–94.

Sargent, T. and B. Smith (1987) 'Irrelevance of Open Market Operations in Some Economies with Government Currency Being Dominate in Rate of Return', *American Economic Review*, 77, pp. 78–92.

Sargent, T. and N. Wallace, (1982) 'The Real-Bills Doctrine versus the Quantity Theory: A Reconsideration', *Journal of Political Economy*, 90, pp. 1212–136.

Saving, T. (1971) 'Transactions Costs and the Demand for Money', *American Economic Review*, 61, pp. 407–20.

Smith, B. (1988) 'Legal Restriction, "Sunspots" and the Peels Bank Act: The Real Bills Doctrine versus the Quantity Theory Reconsidered', *Journal of Political Economy*, 96, pp. 3–19.

Smith, B. (1991) 'Interest on Reserves and Sunspot Equilibria: Friedman's Proposal Reconsidered', *Review of Economic Studies*, 58, 93–105.

Stockmann, A. (1981) 'Anticipated Inflation and the Capital Stock in a Cash-In-Advance Economy', *Journal of Monetary Economics*, 8, pp. 387–93.

Tirole, J. (1985) 'Asset Bubbles and Overlapping Generations', *Econometrica*, 53, pp. 1071–100.

Tobin, J. (1956) 'The Interest-elasticity of Transactions Demand for Cash', *Review of Economic Studies*, 38, pp. 241–7.

Waldo, D. (1985) 'Open Market Operations in an Overlapping Generations Model', *Journal of Political Economy*, 93, pp. 1242–57.

Wallace, N. (1980) 'The Overlapping Generations Model of Fiat Money', in J. Kareken, and N. Wallace, (eds.) *Models of Monetary Economies* (Minneapolis: Federal Reserve Bank of Minneapolis).

Wallace, N. (1983) 'A Legal Restrictions Theory of the Demand for "Money" and the Role of Monetary Policy', *Federal reserve bank of Minneapolis Quarterly Review*, 7, pp. 1–7.

Wallace, N. (1987a) 'Some Alternative Monetary Models and Their Implications for the Role of Open-Market Policy' in R. Barro (ed.) *Modern Business Cycle Theory* (Cambridge : Cambridge University Press).

Wallace, N. (1987b) 'Some Unsolved Problems for Monetary Theory', in W. Barrett and Singleton K. (eds.) *New Approaches in Monetary Economics* (Cambridge: Cambridge University Press).

Wang, P. and C.K. Yip, (1992) 'Alternative Approaches to Money and Growth', *Journal of Money, Credit and Banking*, 24, pp. 553–62.

Whalen, E. (1966) 'A Rationalization of the Precautionary Demand for Cash', *Quarterly Journal of Economics*, 80, pp. 314–24.

Weiss, L. (1980) 'The Effects of Money Supply on Economic Welfare in the Steady State', *Econometrica*, 48, pp. 565–76.

Woodford, M. (1987) 'Credit Policy and the Price Level in a Cash-In-Advance Economy', in W. Barrett, and K. Singleton, (eds) *New Approaches in Monetary Economics* (Cambridge: Cambridge University Press).

Woodford, M. (1990) 'The Optimum Quantity of Money', in B. Friedman, and F. Hahn, (eds) *Handbook of Monetary Economics*, Vol. II (New York: North-Holland).

6
Models of Endogenous Growth with Infinite Horizon

6.1 Introduction

In this chapter we introduce endogenous growth models with infinite horizon. However, it would be futile to look for a leitmotif in the various proposals advanced in the literature. We describe the class of aggregate models by distinguishing between competitive and non-competitive models and among the latter we limit ourselves only to the model of Romer (1987). For our purposes, the common feature of competitive and non-competitive model is the departure from the constant-returns-to-scale assumption. The initial reason for departing from this assumption (Romer, 1986) is the incompatibility of neoclassical growth models with a production–function technology (in Solow's model and in optimal growth models) and some stylized facts. In particular, long run sustained growth of per capita real income is highlighted by time series. For example, in the period 1870–1990 the eight most developed countries in the OECD area had a growth rate of per capita real income (not less or) greater than 1.5 per cent (Barro and Sala-I-Martin, 1995).

In conventional growth models for closed economies, if we exclude population growth this kind of sustained growth can be attributed only to technological progress, which, however, is exogenous. Models of endogenous growth can also reproduce sustained growth of per capita variables shown by the data. This chapter is organized as follows. Section 6.2 offers a basic scheme for endogenous growth by combining the assumption of a constant returns-to-scale (Rebelo, 1991) with the presence of human capital accumulation (Lucas, 1988). Section 6.3 considers the role of externalities (Lucas, 1988) and the increasing returns-to-scale (Romer, 1986). Section 6.4 describes a model of growth with non-competitive markets, where non-competitiveness is due to the firms' specialization (Romer, 1987). Section 6.5 uses the schemes of section 6.2 to discuss the effects on growth of taxation in the presence of constant-returns-to-scale and human capital. Section 6.6 deals with the effects of public spending on growth and discusses a Rebelo-type model that includes human capital (Barro, 1990; Lin, 1994). Section 6.7 extends models of endogenous growth to a monetary economy with constant-returns-of-scale and human capital.

A monetary economy is characterized by money-in-the-utility-function. Sections 6.8 and 6.9 consider the same endogenous growth scheme for monetary economies with a cash-in-advance constraint and a transaction costs technology. For the sake of brevity, we will ignore possible extensions of the various models to include a household's choice between leisure (labour) time and consumption, and questions concerning transitional dynamics (see Benhabib and Perli, 1994a; 1994b; Boldrin, 1992; Bond, Wang, and Yip, 1996; Caballè and Santos, 1993; King and Rebelo, 1993; Lucas, 1990; Chamley, 1993; Mulligan and Sala-I-Martin, 1993)

6.2 A basic framework for endogenous growth: (a) Models with constant-returns-to-scale technology and human capital

Rebelo's 'Ak' model (1991) clearly shows how departing from the neoclassical production function makes endogenous growth possible. Here we shall consider a descriptive version of that model which starts from Solow's model with a constant population and no technological progress. Solow's model can be reduced to two equations in per capita terms

$$q(t) = f(k(t))$$
$$\dot{k} = sf(k(t))$$

Among others properties, the per capita production function $f(k(t))$ is assumed to have decreasing returns on per capita capital, $f''(k) < 0$. Suppose, on the contrary, that $f(k(t))$ is homogeneous of degree one in k, and, therefore, admits constant-returns-to-scale in $k(t)$. This assumption permits us to write

$$q(t) = f(1)k(t) = Ak(t)$$

Since $A > 0$, the constant-returns-to-scale technology behaves as if it were linear in per capita capital. This technology implies a uniform growth rate of both per capita output and capital stock

$$\dot{q}/q(t) = A\dot{k}/Ak(t) = \dot{k}/k(t)$$

Moreover, there is positive constant growth in per capita variables since homogeneity of degree one of per capita output function yields

$$\dot{k}/k(t) = [s\,f(k(t))]/k(t) = sA > 0$$

These properties in the literature are traditionally demonstrated by assuming a Cobb-Douglas technology (for example Sala-I-Martin, 1990). With constant population $L(t) = L$ and no technological progress $A(t) = A$, and with a Cobb-Douglas production function Solow's model becomes

$$Q(t) = AK^a(t)L^{1-a}$$
$$\dot{K}(t) = sAK^a(t)L^{1-a}$$

In per capita terms these relationships are

$$q(t) = Ak^a(t)$$
$$\dot{k} = sAk^a(t)$$

Homogeneity of degree one of the per capita production function means $a = 1$ so that

$$\dot{q}/q(t) = \dot{k}/k(t) = sA > 0$$

There is a positive growth rate of per capita output even when the economy is populated by infinitely-lived agents making optimal inter-temporal saving choices. Indeed, let us model the economy as an infinitely-lived representative agent. With linear technology in per capita capital, the representative agent's optimal control problem is

$$\max V = \int_0^\infty e^{-\beta t}u(c(t))dt$$
$$\dot{k} = Ak(t) - c(t)$$
$$k(0) = k_0;\ \lim_{t\to\infty} e^{-\beta t}u'(c(t))k(t) = 0$$

Assuming the transversality condition is verified, first-order necessary conditions for optimal control are

$$e^{-\beta t}u'(c(t)) = \lambda(t)$$
$$\dot{k} = Ak(t) - c(t)$$
$$\dot{\lambda}(t) = -\lambda(t)A$$

Letting $-[u''(c(t))/u'(c(t))](t) = cost = \sigma$, the first and the third conditions give

$$\dot{c}/c = (A - \beta)/\sigma$$

On the other hand, technology implies the following growth rate of per capita capital

$$\dot{k}/k = A - [c(t)/k(t)]$$

This rate evolves over time according to

$$\frac{d(\dot{k}/k)}{dt} = \frac{c}{k}\left(\frac{\dot{k}}{k} - \frac{\dot{c}}{c}\right)$$

If stationary conditions are imposed

$$\dot{k}/k = \dot{c}/c = (A - \beta)/\sigma$$

There is a positive growth rate when $A > \beta$. On the contrary, a negative rate can occur when $A < \beta$. Compared to the models of exogenous growth in per capita variables, the following non-trivial deductions are (trivially) evident:

a) uniform growth rate of the per capita output and capital stock depends on parameters endogenous to the model, parameter A (technology) and parameters β and σ (preferences);
b) because of constant-returns-to-scale technology thrift and productivity play a role in determining living standards of individuals. Greater or lesser growth of per capita real income depends on these characteristics. For instance, greater 'impatience' (a lesser propensity to save which is reflected in a greater β) implies a lower growth rate of per capita real income. The opposite occurs when there is a lower propensity to substitute future consumption for present consumption, expressed by a smaller σ, or as a consequence of greater global productivity A[1].

The limit of Rebelo's 'AK' model is that apparently it assigns no role at all to labour as input for production. Indeed, with a constant-returns-to-scale technology, the real wages of a competitive system are $w(t) = f(k(t)) - k(t)f'k) = f(k(t)) - Ak(t) = 0$. With a Cobb-Douglas technology, if $a = 1$, labour's share on output is $1 - a = 0$. To give economic meaning to this, it has been suggested that work participates in production not as 'rough' work but as skilled work, that is human capital. With this interpretation the symbol $k(t)$ in production technology must be intended as capital in general, including human capital. Consequently, the assumption $a = 1$ means that constant-returns-to-scale refer to all the inputs that can be accumulated to constitute the community's capital stock. The argument that human capital plays a primary role in determining endogenous growth has been developed by Lucas (1988) and by Rebelo (1991). Skilled work, as human capital, is assumed to give a greater contribution to production than simple work.

Moreover, the enhancement of a worker's qualifications depends on the accumulation of more skill. Let us adopt Lucas' original description of the process of accumulating qualifications and regard disposable time exclusively as a productive input. Therefore, a single agent can use time either for production or for acquiring qualification. If we normalize disposable time to the unit and let $z(t)$ be the fraction of time spent in production, labour input in terms of effective units becomes $L_e(t) = z(t)h(t)L$. The per capita production function becomes $q(t) = f[k(t), z(t)h(t)]$, so that with a Cobb-Douglas technology we have:

$$q(t) = Ak^a(t)[z(t)h(t)]^{1-a}$$

In addition to what it produces, skilled work contributes also to the global productivity of the system. This contribution is expressed by external effect $h_a^\gamma(t)$ caused by the mean qualification $h_a(t)$ in the economy. Initially we exclude external effects by putting $\gamma = 0$.

Moreover we shall admit that the technology of accumulation of human capital is linear

$$\dot{h} = \delta[1 - z(t)]h(t)$$

The coefficient $\delta[1 - z(t)]$ depends on the time spent in working. It ranges from $\delta[1 - z(t)] = 0$, when $z(t) = 1$, to $\delta[1 - z(t)] = \delta$ when $z(t) = 0$. By assuming the constant elasticity of marginal utility function $u(c(t) = \dfrac{c(t)^{1-\sigma} - 1}{1 - \sigma}$, the optimal control problem of the representative agent in the absence of external effects is

$$\max V \int_0^\infty \frac{c(t)^{1-\sigma} - 1}{1 - \sigma} e^{-\beta t} dt,$$
$$\dot{k} = Ak^a(t)[z(t)h(t)]^{(1-a)} - c(t)$$
$$\dot{h} = \delta[1 - z(t)]h(t)$$

where initial conditions and transversality conditions referring to both types of capital are taken for granted.

First-order necessary conditions for the optimal control are

$$e^{-\beta t}c(t)^{-\sigma} = \lambda_1(t)$$
$$\lambda_1(t)(1 - a)z^{-a}(t)h^{1-a}(t) = \lambda_2(t)\delta h(t)$$

$$\dot{\lambda}_1 = -\lambda_1(t)aAk^{a-1}(t)[z(t)h(t)]^{(1-a)}$$

$$\dot{\lambda}_2 = -\lambda_1(t)(1-a)Ak^a(t)z^{1-a}(t)h^{-a}(t) - \lambda_2(t)\delta[1-z(t)]$$

From the first and fourth conditions we get

$$[\beta + \sigma(\dot{c}/c)] = aAk^{a-1}(t)[z(t)h(t)]^{(1-a)}$$

From this and the growth rate of per capita capital deduced from the equation for accumulation of physical capital we obtain

$$\dot{k}/k = (1/a)[\beta + \sigma(\dot{c}/c)] - (c(t)/k(t))$$

Over time the growth rate of per capita capital evolves according to

$$\frac{d(\dot{k}/k)}{dt} = \frac{\sigma}{a}\frac{d(\dot{c}/c)}{dt} - \frac{c(t)}{k(t)}\left(\frac{\dot{k}}{k} - \frac{\dot{c}}{c}\right)$$

where

$$\frac{\sigma}{a}\frac{d(\dot{c}/c)}{dt} = A(a-1)k^{a-1}[z(t)h(t)]^{(1-a)}[\dot{k}/k - \dot{z}/z - \dot{h}/h]$$

Consider steady state in rates. By taking into account that time spent in working $z(t)$ is bounded, $0 \leq z(t) \leq 1$, so that $\dot{z} = 0$, steady state in rates requires that

$$\dot{c}/c = \dot{k}/k = \dot{h}/h$$

The steady state growth rate of the economy coincides with growth rate $\dot{h}/h$ of human capital, which can be obtained as follows. By differentiating with respect to time the necessary condition for the optimal control for $z(t)$ and by making substitutions, we obtain

$$(\dot{\lambda}_1/\lambda_1) = (\dot{\lambda}_2/\lambda_2).$$

Since $(\dot{\lambda}_2/\lambda_2) = -\delta$; $(\dot{\lambda}_1/\lambda_1) = -[\beta + \sigma(\dot{c}/c)]$, the uniformity condition $(\dot{c}/c) = (\dot{k}/k) = (\dot{h}/h)$ yields

$$\dot{h}/h = (\delta - \beta)/\sigma$$

The steady state growth rate is positive when human capital accumulation is sufficiently productive, or more than compensates the impatience for future consumption $\delta > \beta$.

6.3 A basic framework for endogenous growth: (b) Models with externalities

The condition $\gamma = 0$ in the formerly 'AK' model extended to human capital allows us to maintain the constant-returns-to-scale assumption and also to preserve the 'Ak' structure. When human capital causes external effects, conditions for endogenous growth change. Production technology becomes $Ak^a(t)[z(t)h(t)]^{(1-a)}h_a^\gamma(t)$ and, by taking into account that at equilibrium $h_a(t) = h(t)$, from the necessary conditions for optimal control we get

$$[\beta + \sigma(\dot{c}/c)] = aAk^{a-1}(t)z(t)^{(1-a)}h(t)^{(1+\gamma-a)}$$

$$\frac{\sigma}{a}\frac{[d(\dot{c}/c)]}{dt} = (1-a)Ak^{a-1}(t)z(t)^{(1-a)}h(t)^{(1+\gamma-a)}[-(\dot{k}/k) + (1-a)(\dot{z}/z) +$$
$$(1+\gamma-a)(\dot{h}/h)$$

The stationary rates condition and $\dot{z} = 0$ yield

$$(\dot{k}/k) = \frac{(1+\gamma-a)}{(1-a)}(\dot{h}/h)$$

The expression for human capital stationary rate $(\dot{h}/h)$ is obtained as before, by differentiating with respect to time the optimality condition for $z(t)$ and by making the necessary substitutions. Thus we obtain

$$(\dot{\lambda}_2/\lambda_2) = (\dot{\lambda}_1/\lambda_1) + (\dot{k}/k)a + (\dot{h}/h)(\delta - a)$$

Since $(\dot{\lambda}_2/\lambda_2) = -\delta$,

$$\delta = \beta + \left[\frac{(\sigma-a)(1+\gamma-a)}{(1-a)} - (\gamma-a)\right](\dot{h}/h)$$

from which

$$(\dot{h}/h) = \frac{(\delta-\beta)(1-a)}{\sigma(1+\gamma-a)-(\gamma-a)}$$

whereas

$$(\dot{c}/c) = (\dot{k}/k) = \frac{(\delta-\beta)(1+\gamma-a)}{\sigma(1+\gamma-a)-(\gamma-a)}$$

When human capital generates a positive externality, $\gamma > 0$, per capita consumption and physical capital have growth rates greater than human capital. The fact that increasing-returns-to-scale due to external effects stimulate growth is a fundamental contribution of Romer (1986; 1987; 1990). He questioned the realism of the constant-returns-to-scale assumption by maintaining that property of a replication of production processes implicitly excludes the presence of non-rival inputs in production. Non-rivalry of inputs is defined like non-rivalry of public goods. It indicates that non-rival inputs can be used by two or more producers without reducing the productivity of the inputs. If $Q = F(K, L, A)$ is a production function, which, in addition to capital and labour, also admits a non-rival input A, it is not necessary to increase non-rival input A to replicate the scale of production. Therefore, it follows that $\alpha Q = F(\alpha K, \alpha L, A)$ for each $\alpha > 0$. Consequently, the production function is no longer concave since $F(\alpha K, \alpha L, \alpha A) > F(\alpha K, \alpha L, A)$ and it admits increasing returns of scale because $F(\alpha K, \alpha L, \alpha A) > \alpha Q$.

A simple way to incorporate increasing returns-to-scale is to admit external effects for physical capital accumulation, as Lucas does for human capital accumulation. In the following we refer to a model with only physical capital. Let F be the number of identical firms in the economy. Let k_j be the physical capital stock owned by j-th firm so that the aggregate capital is $K = \sum_{j=1}^{F} k_j$. Because of the spreading of new knowledge, capital K allows a single j-th firm to improve its production possibilities, so that production technology looks like $f(k_j, K)$. In an economy where the number of firms is equal to the number of consumers $F = L$, capital employed by a single firm coincides with per capita capital. Therefore, by assuming a Cobb-Douglas technology, the aggregate production function in per capita terms is

$$q(t) = k(t)^a K(t)^\eta$$

Evidently, with $a \leq 1$, to have increasing returns of scale it suffices that externality originated by aggregate capital be positive, that is $\eta > 0$. Dynamic equilibrium of economy with increasing returns-to-scale can be described by modelling the economy as a representative agent. With stationary population and constant elasticity of the marginal utility function, optimal control problem becomes

$$\max V = \int_0^\infty \frac{c(t)^{1-\sigma} - 1}{1 - \sigma} e^{-\beta t} dt,$$
$$\dot{k} = k(t)^a K(t)^\eta - c(t)$$
$$k(0) = k_0; \lim_{t \to \infty} e^{-\beta t} c^{-\sigma}(t) k(t) = 0$$

Necessary first-order conditions are

$$\dot{\lambda}_1 = -\beta c(t)^{-\sigma} [\beta + \sigma(\dot{c}/c(t))]$$
$$\dot{\lambda}_1 = -c(t)^{-\sigma} a k(t)^{a-1} K(t)^\eta$$

At equilibrium we have $K(t) = Fk(t)$. Since $F = L$, the growth rate steady state condition yields

$$\frac{\dot{c}}{c} = \frac{ak(t)^{a+\eta-1}L^{\eta} - \beta}{\sigma}$$

for the rate of growth of the economy.

To obtain endogenous growth it is not sufficient to admit positive externality $\eta > 0$. External effects must be large enough to satisfy $\eta + a \geq 1$. If this condition is verified as equality $a + \eta = 1$, technology can generate endogenous growth if $aL^{\eta} > \beta$. Notwithstanding that a single firm is subject to decreasing returns, in this technology the externality of aggregate capital offsets the tendency to stop growth caused by decreasing returns-to-scale at the microeconomic level. External effects generated by physical capital, therefore, offer an alternative to Rebelo's interpretation. Indeed, in this case Rebelo's interpretation is obtained by putting $A = aL^{\eta}$. The existence of externalities also allows us to verify that the competitive equilibrium with external effects is Pareto-suboptimal, one of the classic results of general competitive equilibrium. We shall limit ourselves to the proof for Lucas' model, where the externality is generated by human capital. Let us consider the central planner problem. In selecting an optimal consumption path, the central planner takes into account external effects. Given production technology $Ak^{a}(t)z(t)^{(1-a)}h(t)^{(1+\gamma-a)}$, after the central planner optimal control problem has been solved, the optimality condition for the shadow price of human capital appears as

$$\dot{\lambda}_2 = -\lambda_1(t)(1-a)Ak^{a}(t)z^{1-a}(t)h^{-a}(t) - \lambda_2(t)\delta[1 - z(t)]$$

If we derive the expressions $\dot{\lambda}_2/\lambda_2$ by the same procedure that was used in Section 6.2, we obtain the following conditions

$$(\dot{\lambda}_2/\lambda_2) = \left[\delta + \gamma\frac{(\dot{h}/h) - \delta}{1 - a}\right]$$

$$(\dot{\lambda}_2/\lambda_2) = -\left[\beta + (\sigma - a)\frac{(1 + \gamma - a)}{(1 - a)} - (\gamma - a)\right](\dot{h}/h)$$

Equalizing and solving for $(\dot{h}/h)$ we obtain

$$(\dot{h}/h) = \frac{1}{\sigma}\left[\delta - \frac{\beta(1 - a)}{(1 + \gamma - a)}\right]$$

The restriction $\delta \geq (\dot{h}/h)$ must be valid and strict inequality occurs when $\gamma > 0$. Therefore the growth rate of human capital in a centralized economy, and consequently the growth rate of the economy, is greater than the growth rate of a competitive economy. The latter, therefore, is sub-optimal.

6.4 A Basic framework for endogenous growth: (c) A non-competitive economy

Romer (1987) also proposed a model of endogenous growth which may be considered an example of growth based on imperfect competition among producers and an example of R&D directed specifically toward new products and/or new capital goods. Still the basic idea is that the production of a single firm generates externalities. These externalities, however, are now due to a firm's specialized production and new products after new firms enter the market. Unlike as in Marshall (1920) and Young (1928), Romer firm's specialization does not refer to final products but to intermediate goods. For simplicity it is assumed that each of these goods is produced by a single firm and enters as input into the production of final goods. The aggregate output function becomes

$$Q(t) = F[L(t), \mathbf{x(t)}]$$

where output $Q(t)$ depends on labour $L(t)$ and on a list of intermediate inputs $\mathbf{x} = \{x_i\}_{i=0}^{\infty}$ that potentially is infinitely long. It is useful to consider the intermediate inputs as part of the set of non-negative real numbers. In this case $x(i)$ is a function, defined over the interval $[0, \infty]$, which indicates the interval drawn from the set of real numbers to list intermediate goods of i-th variety. The production function is

$$Q(t) = L(t)^{(1-a)} \int_0^F x^a(j, t)dj = L(t)^{(1-a)}X(t)$$

where magnitude $X(t)$ can be interpreted as the list of intermediate inputs entering the production of the final good. This formulation indicates that productivity of an economic system increases with specialization.

The aggregate quantity of intermediate goods

$$X(t) = \int_0^F x^a(j, t)dj$$

is obtained from a kind of technology

$$X(t) = A(t)^{(1-a)}K(t) = [A(t)K(t)]^{(1-a)}K(t)^a$$

which indeed is a reduced form of the equilibrium of the industry producing intermediate goods. By assuming that production of intermediate goods uses as capital K resources not used for consumption, global productivity A at equilibrium in the productive sector depends on the number of active firms. Because of specialization, this is the same as saying that A depends on the number of intermediate goods produced. As a consequence, even aggregate production of final good depends positively on the number of intermediate goods produced. The equilibrium condition in the industrial sector excludes the entry of new firms and requires profit be null. Whatever the number of firms at equilibrium is, for a given productivity of the system A(t), the resources required for producing one unit of intermediate good by a single firm are 1/A(t). Therefore, if the amount of resources K(t) available for the production of intermediate goods is given, the number of firms F(t) must satisfy

$$F(t)(1/A(t)) = K(t)$$

By substituting, it follows that

$$X(t) = F(t)^{(1-a)}K(t)^a = \int_0^F [K(t)/F(t)]^a dj == \int_0^F (x^a(j, t)dj$$

It is possible to determine an explicit expression for the demand function $x(j, t)$ for intermediate goods j of firms producing the final good. Indeed, given the amount X(t) (measured in terms of final good) of intermediate goods used in producing the final good, the inverse demand is proportional to the first derivative of the integrand function in the expression of X(t), so that we can write

$$p(j, t) = x(j, t)^{a-1}$$

where $p(j, t)$ is the price of the j-th intermediate good in terms of final good. The j-th firm is the only producer of that good, so that it maximizes profit by assuming the demand for its production is given. Since the firm faces decreasing demand, the market is one of monopolistic competition. In a context like this, specialization and variety of intermediate goods becomes consistent because there are fixed production costs.

As a consequence of these costs there is a limit to the number of firms in the sector and, therefore, there is a finite number of intermediate goods introduced into the economy. A fixed cost of production x(j) means that firms supplying these goods must use their market power to survive competition by pricing more than marginal cost in order to cover fixed costs. This can be ascertained as follows. Assume costs of production, measured in terms of produced good, are linear function $c(j, t) = c_f + c_m x(j, t)$. Profit of the j-th firm is

$$\pi(j, t) = x(j, t)^a - c_f - c_m x(j, t)$$

The first-order condition for maximum profit gives the price charged by the firm

$$p(j, t) = (c_m/a)$$

Competition at equilibrium nullifies profit $[p(j, t) - c_m]x(j, t) - c_f = 0$. Therefore output of the j-th firm is

$$x(j, t) = (c_f/c_m)\,[a/(1 - a)]$$

It is clear that monopoly's price $p(j, t)$ is simply a mark-up $(1/a)$ on marginal cost c_m, and the mark-up coefficient depends on the elasticity of demand for the intermediate good. On the contrary, if we know the amount of production of each firm at every t, the aggregate production of intermediate goods measured in terms of a final good is

$$X(t) = \int_0^F p(j, t)x(j, t)dj = \int_0^F x^a(j, t)dj$$

With this view of a decentralized production sector it might be possible to formulate a dynamic model of monopolistic competition by combining the behaviour of firms and the behaviour of households. However it is easier to represent an economic system as a representative agent. By assuming an isoelastic instantaneous utility function and a stationary population, a representative household solves the optimal control problem

$$\max V = \int_0^\infty \frac{c(t)^{1-\sigma} - 1}{1 - \sigma} e^{-\beta t}dt$$
$$\dot{k} = [A(t)K(t)]^{(1-a)}k(t)^a - c(t)$$
$$k(0) = k_0; \ \lim_{t \to \infty} e^{-\beta t}c(t)^{-\sigma}k(t) = 0$$

where $k(t)$ now is per capita capital and $[A(t)K(t)]^{(1-a)}$ is assumed to be given exogenously for the household. First-order conditions for optimal control can be reduced to

$$\dot{\lambda}_1 = -e^{-\beta t}c(t)^{-\sigma}[\beta + \sigma(\dot{c}/c(t))]$$
$$\dot{\lambda}_1 = -e^{-\beta t}c(t)^{-\sigma}a[A(t)K(t)]^{(1-a)}k(t)^{a-1}$$

from which the steady state growth rate of the economy is

$$\frac{\dot{c}}{c} = \frac{a[A(t)K(t)]^{(1-a)}k(t)^{a-1} - \beta}{\sigma}$$

At equilibrium $A(t) = (F(t)/L)k(t)$, so that by letting $(F(t)/L) = N(t)$ the growth rate becomes

$$\frac{\dot{c}}{c} = \frac{aN(t)^{(1-a)} - \beta}{\sigma}$$

This economy, therefore, allows endogenous growth if $aN(t)^{(1-a)} > \beta$ and the rate of return on capital (the productivity of capital) changes when the variety of intermediate goods changes. The term $[A(t)K(t)]^{(1-a)}$ behaves as if it were a positive externality caused by specialization of firms.

The central planner problem differs from the representative household's problem. The central planner must account for the externality in solving the planning problem. Therefore the optimal control problem of the central planner is

$$\max V = \int_0^\infty \frac{c(t)^{1-\sigma} - 1}{1 - \sigma} e^{-\beta t} dt$$
$$\dot{k} = A(t)^{(1-a)}k(t) - c(t)$$
$$k(0) = k_0; \lim_{t\to\infty} e^{-\beta t} c(t)^{-\sigma} k(t) = 0$$

whose first-order conditions are

$$\dot{\lambda}_1 = -e^{-\beta t}c(t)^{-\sigma}[\beta + \sigma(\dot{c}/c(t))]$$
$$\dot{\lambda}_1 = -e^{-\beta t}c(t)^{-\sigma}A(t)^{(1-a)}$$

which give the endogenous rate of growth at steady state

$$\frac{\dot{c}}{c} = \frac{A(t)^{(1-a)} - \beta}{\sigma}$$

On the contrary, the growth rate of a decentralized economy can be written as

$$\frac{\dot{c}}{c} = \frac{aA(t)^{(1-a)} - \beta}{\sigma}$$

Since $a < 1$ we immediately deduce that the rate of growth of a decentralized economy is suboptimal. Romer's contribution (1987), extended to include human capital (1990), can be seen once more as a pioneering contribution. There can be another interpretation for fixed costs. They can be considered a firm's instantaneous settlement cost as a result of technological innovation or product innovation. Market power would be the consequence and expression of these processes. In this context a monopoly's profit over time would be justified as the repayment for innovation and research in a typically Schumpeterian vein (1934; 1942). This will not considered in this book (see Aghion and Howitt, 1992; Barro and Sala-I-Martin, 1995; Grossman and Helpman, 1991).

6.5   Taxation in the model with constant returns-to-scale and human capital

The basic model of endogenous growth with constant-returns-to-scale and human capital described in Section 6.2 is also useful in examining the effects of fiscal policy on growth. From the analytical point of view it is convenient to separate the effects of taxation from those of public spending. Therefore we shall make assumptions similar to those in Chapter 6.2, Section 2.7:

(a) public budget is balanced;
(b) taxation is proportional to income or consumption, and the tax rate is non-progressive.

Assuming taxation proportional to income, the public budget constraint in per capita terms is $g(t) + x(t) = \theta(t)q(t)$, where $x(t)$ and $\theta(t)$ are respectively per capita transfers and tax rate. We shall assume a pure transfers policy with $g(t) = 0$. Consider a competitive system. When production technology admits constant-returns-to-scale on per capita capital, the capital stock is the only source of an agent's income to which public transfers are added. Let $\rho(t)$ be the real rate of return on capital net of tax. The budget constraint of a single agent is

$$\dot{k} + c(t) = \rho(t)k(t) + x(t)$$

The agent's objective is to maximize the utility function. By admitting the isoelastic instantaneous utility function $u(c(t)) = \dfrac{c(t)^{1-\sigma} - 1}{1 - \sigma}$, the optimal control problem of the agent is

$$\max V = \int_0^\infty \frac{c(t)^{1-\sigma} - 1}{1 - \sigma} e^{-\beta t} dt$$
$$\dot{k} = \rho(t)k(t) + x(t) - c(t)$$
$$k(0) = k_0; \lim_{t\to\infty} e^{-\beta t} c(t)^{-\sigma} k(t) = 0$$

From first-order necessary conditions we can deduce the optimal growth rate of consumption

$$\frac{\dot{c}}{c} = [\rho(t) - \beta]/\sigma$$

With reference to firms, if we assume identical constant-returns-to-scale technology for all of them and let $p_k(t)$ be the price of services for one unit of capital. The individual firm's instantaneous profit is

$$\pi(t) = [Ak_f(t) - p_k(t)k_f(t)]L_f$$

The necessary condition for maximum profit is

$$A = p_k(t)$$

Given tax rate $\theta(t)$, the relationship between the real return on capital net of taxes and the market remuneration for capital is

$$\rho(t) = [1 - \theta(t)]p_k(t) = [1 - \theta(t)]A$$

In a competitive system populated by identical firms and consumers, equilibrium conditions are derived from the optimum conditions for the agents. By assuming constant tax rate $\theta(t) = \theta$, the uniform growth rate of per capita consumption and capital is

$$\dot{c}/c = \dot{k}/k = [A(1 - \theta) - \beta]/\sigma$$

Equilibrium conditions for a decentralized competitive economy differ from those of a central planner economy. Indeed, the central planner solves the optimal control problem

$$\max V = \int_0^\infty \frac{c(t)^{1-\sigma} - 1}{1 - \sigma} e^{-\beta t}dt$$
$$\dot{k} = [1 - \theta(t)]Ak(t) + x(t) - c(t)$$
$$x(t) = \theta(t)Ak(t)$$
$$k(0) = k_0; \lim_{t \to \infty} e^{-\beta t}c(t)^{-\sigma}k(t) = 0$$

If we take into account the balanced budget condition, the first-order necessary conditions give the following expression for the growth rate of consumption and per capita capital

$$\dot{c}/c = \dot{k}/k = [A - \beta]/\sigma$$

This is the same as the expression for a competitive system without taxation. Thus, in a decentralized economy, taxation proportional to income entails a reduction in productivity of capital and this leads to a growth rate less than that in a planned economy. This is due to distortive nature of taxation. Indeed let us assume a tax rate proportional to consumption rather than proportional to income. The government budget constraint becomes $g(t) = \theta_c c(t)$ and the path of capital accumulation is described by equation

$$\dot{k} = Ak(t) - (1 + \theta_c)c(t)$$

Using this to solve the optimal control problem of a representative agent in a competitive system, the per capita consumption growth rate is, as before,

$$\dot{c}/c = [A - \beta]/\sigma$$

Thus taxation on consumption does not have distortive effects on the growth rate. Intuitively the result stems from the fact that taxation on consumption acts like a consumption transaction cost and reduces consumption level but does not distort intertemporal saving decisions. Indeed, the return of capital does not change due to taxation on consumption. The inclusion of human capital in the 'Ak' model also allows us to consider the case of taxation with different tax rates on physical capital and human capital. This extension is not only a refinement, but leads to different results even when government budget policy remains unchanged. These results are particularly sensitive to the way technology and accumulation of human capital are conceived. For a decentralized economy with a stationary population, let us now admit a taxation structure consisting of different non-progressive tax rates on income from physical capital and human capital $\theta_k(t)$ and $\theta_h(t)$. Taxes on human capital are levied by taxing labour income. The real wage per simple working hour is $w(t)$ and the price of services for one unit of physical capital is $\rho_k(t)$. The optimal control problem of a representative agent in this new context is

$$\max V = \int_0^\infty \frac{c(t)^{1-\sigma} - 1}{1 - \sigma} e^{-\beta t} dt$$
$$\dot{k} = (1 - \theta_k)\rho_k(t)k(t) + (1 - \theta_L)w(t)z(t)h(t) + x(t) - c(t)$$
$$\dot{h} = \delta[1 - z(t)]h(t)$$
$$0 \leq z(t) \leq 1; \ k(0) = k_0; \ h(0) = h_0;$$
$$\lim_{t \to \infty} e^{-\beta t}c(t)^{-\sigma}k(t) = 0; \ \lim_{t \to \infty} e^{-\beta t}c(t)^{-\sigma}z(t)^{-a}h(t)^{1-a} = 0$$

The representative firm solves

$$\max \pi(t) = [q_f(t) - \rho_k(t)k_f(t) - w(t)z_f(t)h(t)]L_f$$

If marginal productivities of physical and human capital are q'_{fk} and $q'_{fh} = q'_{f(hz)}z$, the relationships for return net of taxation and price of services are

$$[1 - \theta_k(t)]\rho_k(t) = [1 - \theta_k(t)]q'_k$$
$$[1 - \theta_L(t)]w(t) = [1 - \theta_L(t)]q'_{(hz)}$$

On the other hand first-order conditions for consumer optimum control yields

$$\beta + \sigma(\dot{c}/c) = [1 - \theta_k(t)]\rho_k(t)$$
$$\dot{\lambda}_1/\lambda_1 = -[1 - \theta_k(t)]\rho_k(t)$$
$$\dot{\lambda}_2/\lambda_2 = -\delta$$

and by virtue of a stationary condition on rates we must also have $\dot{\lambda}_1/\lambda_1 = \dot{\lambda}_2/\lambda_2$. Therefore, the equilibrium growth rate of the economy, which is the growth rate of consumption $\dot{c}/c = (\delta - \beta)/\sigma$, is the same as that without taxation. In this context, the most taxation policy can do is to influence the composition of capital at large, that is the levels of physical and human capital, but it can not influence their growth. The absence of Rebelo-type distortive effects is due to the different nature of the growth process. Technology for the accumulation of human capital implies that the true engine of growth is the productivity of the marginal hour devoted to qualification. This productivity is independent of both taxation structure and physical capital productivity.

However, this independence is no longer true in a different formulation of human capital accumulation. Following Rebelo (1991), let us assume that human capital accumulation is the result of a purposeful production process which uses both physical and human capital. Moreover, let us suppose that both production activities have Cobb-Douglas technology

$$q(t) = A[v(t)k(t)]^a[z(t)h(t)]^{(1-a)}$$
$$\dot{h}/h = B\{[1 - v(t)]k(t)\}^b\{[1 - z(t)]h(t)\}^{(1-b)}$$

where $0 \le v(t) \le 1$ is the fraction of physical capital used in the production of goods. As before, we assume production of goods is decentralized in firms competing with each other, whereas human capital accumulation is realized by households. In order to accumulate qualification, households employ their time and a fraction of their accumulated physical capital. The budget constraint of a single household is

$$\dot{k} + c = [1 - \theta_k(t)]\rho_k(t)v(t)k(t) + [1 - \theta_L(t)]w(t)z(t)h(t) + x(t)$$

The problem of the household is to select paths $\{c(t), v(t), z(t), h(t), k(t)\}$ which solve the optimal control problem

$$\max V = \int_0^\infty \frac{c(t)^{1-\sigma} - 1}{1 - \sigma} e^{-\beta t} dt$$

$$\dot{k} = [1 - \theta_k(t)]\rho_k(t)v(t)k(t) + [1 - \theta_L(t)]w(t)z(t)h(t) + x(t) - c(t)$$

$$\dot{h} = B\{[1 - v(t)]k(t)\}^b\{[1 - z(t)]h(t)\}^{(1-b)}$$

to which must be added initial conditions on capital stocks and the appropriate transversality conditions.

First-order necessary conditions are

$$\beta + \sigma(\dot{c}/c) = [1 - \theta_k(t)]\rho_k(t)$$

$$\dot{\lambda}_1/\lambda_1 = -[1 - \theta_k(t)]\rho_k(t)$$

$$\dot{\lambda}_2/\lambda_2 = -(1 - b)B\{[1 - v(t)]k(t)\}^b\{[1 - z(t)]h(t)\}^{-b}$$

Since steady state on rates also implies $\dot{\lambda}_1/\lambda_1 = \dot{\lambda}_2/\lambda_2$, the equality between rate of return on physical capital and its marginal productivity in the production of good implies

$$(1 - b)B\{[1 - v(t)]k(t)\}^b\{[1 - z(t)]h(t)\}^{-b}$$

$$= (1 - \theta_k)aA[v(t)k(t)]^{a-1}[z(t)h(t)]^{(1-a)}$$

This is an equation in the unknown k/h, the relative intensity of the two types of capital used by the two sectors. By solving for k/h we get

$$(k/h) = [(1 - v)/(1 - z)]^{-(b/1+b-a)} (v/z)^{-(1-a)/1+b-a}$$

$$[a/(1 - b)]^{(1/1+b-a)}(1 - \theta_k)^{(1/1+b-a)}(A/B)^{(1/1+b-a)}$$

Letting $(b/1 + b - a) = \mu$, by substituting the solution k/h into the left-hand term of previous equality and letting $\varphi = (1 - b)(a/1 - b)^\mu$ $[(1 - v)/(1 - z)]^{b(1-\mu)}(v/z)^{-(1-a)\mu}$ we obtain the expression for the equilibrium rate of return on physical capital net of taxation

$$(1 - \theta_k)\rho_k = \varphi(1 - \theta_k)^\mu A^\mu B^{1-\mu}$$

Therefore the rate of growth of the economy is

$$\dot{k}/k = \dot{c}/c = \frac{\varphi(1 - \theta_k)^\mu A^\mu B^{1-\mu} - \beta}{\sigma}$$

When $B = \delta$ and $b = 0$, since $\mu = 0$ and $\varphi = 1$, we find the same result in Lucas' model without externalities, that is the growth rate is independent of taxation policy. This model can be considered the decentralized version of a centralized economy whose central planner solves the following planning problem

$$\max V = \int_0^\infty \frac{c(t)^{1-\sigma} - 1}{1 - \sigma} e^{-\beta t} dt$$

$$\dot{k} = A[v(t)k(t)]^a [z(t)h(t)]^{(1-a)} - c(t)$$

$$\dot{h}/h = B\{[1 - v(t)]k(t)\}^b \{[1 - z(t)]h(t)\}^{(1-b)}$$

$$0 \le z(t) \le 1; 0 \le v(t) \le 1$$

First-order necessary conditions for this problem yield

$$\beta + \sigma(\dot{c}/c) = aA\{[v(t)/z(t))(k(t)/h(t))]^{a-1}$$

$$\dot{\lambda}_1/\lambda_1 = -aA\{[(v(t)/z(t))(k(t)/h(t))]^{a-1}$$

$$\dot{\lambda}_2/\lambda_2 = -(1 - b)B\{[(1 - v(t)/1 - z(t))](k(t)/h(t))]^b$$

At steady state we must have $\dot{\lambda}_1/\lambda_1 = \dot{\lambda}_2/\lambda_2$. Taking into account the expression (k/h), the growth rate of a centralized economy is

$$\dot{k}/k = \dot{c}/c = \frac{\varphi A^\mu B^{1-\mu} - \beta}{\sigma}$$

By comparing this expression to the growth rate of a decentralized economy we see that taxation on physical capital income influences growth negatively, whereas taxation on labour, even if it reduces net return on human capital has no influence on the growth rate.

Suppose the aim of taxation policy is to achieve the maximum growth rate. Since the growth rate decreases with an increase in tax rate on physical capital, the objective of maximum growth would require tax rate $\theta_k = 0$ for the feasible interval $0 \le \theta_k \le 1$ in a decentralized economy. However, this is based only on intuition and ignores trade-offs authorities face when they shift the tax burden entirely to labour. It also ignores possible feedback effects on growth caused by authorities' response to those trade-offs. A rigorous proof of this would require reconsidering the issue in a context of optimal taxation policy (for a discussion see Chamley, 1986, 1993; Lucas, 1990; Jones and Manuelli, and Rossi 1993; Pecorino, 1993; Stokey and Rebelo 1995). We can state that taxation on physical capital discourages accumulation of this form of capital. If this disincentive can not be removed by reducing the tax rate, the only way to remove it is to adopt a policy of subsidies. Another approach looks at human capital accumulation as a market activity (Pecorino, 1993; Stokey and Rebelo, 1995). Production of human capital is made by firms that maximize profit. Production of human capital distributes income which then becomes a component of taxable income. This changes the view of the effects of taxation.

To examine them, let us assume the production sector of a competitive economy is made of two kinds of firms, one producing a final good available for consumption and the accumulation of physical capital, and the other producing human capital. Let q_h be the per capita output of human capital and p_h be the relative price of human capital in terms of the good. The economy now has a combined per capita output of $q + p_h q_h$. As before, the technology in each sector it is assumed that is Cobb-Douglas

$$q = A[v(t)k(t)]^a [z(t)h(t)]^{(1-a)}$$
$$q_h = B\{[1 - v(t)]k(t)\}^b \{[1 - z(t)]h(t)\}^{(1-b)}$$

For households, the fact that desired accumulation of human capital stock can now be achieved at market prices entails the following budget constraint

$$c(t) + I_k(t) + p_h(t)I_h(t) = [1 - \theta_k(t)]\rho_k(t)k(t) + [1 - \theta_L(t)]w(t)p_h(t)h(t) + x(t)$$

where I_k and I_h are the desired variations of stocks of physical and human capital.

The household optimal control problem now is

$$\max V = \int_0^\infty \frac{c(t)^{1-\sigma} - 1}{1 \quad \sigma} e^{-\beta t} dt$$
$$\text{sub } c(t) + I_k + p_h I_h = [1 - \theta_k(t)]\rho_k(t)k(t) + [1 - \theta_L(t)]w(t)p_h(t)h(t) + x(t)$$
$$\dot{k} = I_k$$
$$\dot{h} = I_h$$

to which must be added initial conditions on stocks and transversality conditions.

First-order conditions are

$$\beta + \sigma(\dot{c}/c) = (1 - \theta_k(t))\rho_k(t)$$
$$\dot{\lambda}_1/\lambda_1 = -(1 - \theta_k(t))\rho_k(t)$$
$$\dot{\lambda}_2/\lambda_2 = -(1 - \theta_L(t))w(t)$$

Steady state on rates implies $\dot{\lambda}_1/\lambda_1 = \dot{\lambda}_2/\lambda_2$ from which it follows that the returns of human and physical capital net of taxation must be the same. Therefore, competition between firms in the inputs market sets off a mechanism which transmits the distortion induced by taxation on physical capital to human capital. This is another reason why a tax rate on human capital, that is taxation on labour, influences the growth rate of the economy. Indeed we now have

$$(1 - \theta_L)(1 - b)B[(1 - v/1 - z)(k/h)]^b = a(1 - \theta_k)A[(v/z)(k/h)]^{a-1}$$

from which, after solving for k/h it follows that

$$(k/h) = [(1-v)/(1-z)]^{-(b/1+b-a)}(v/z)^{(a-1/1+b-a)}[a/(1-b]^{1/1+b-a)}$$
$$(1-\theta_k)^{1/1+b-a}A^{(1/1+b-a)}(1-\theta_L)^{-(1/1+b-a)}B^{-(1/1+b-a)}$$

Let $(b/1+b-a) = \mu$ and $\varphi = (1-b)(a/1-b)^\mu[(1-v)/(1-z)]^{b(1-\mu)}$
$(v/z)^{-(1-a)\mu}$. The expression for the rate of return on the physical capital net of taxation

$$(1-\theta_k)\rho_k = \varphi(1-\theta_k)^\mu A^\mu (1-\theta_L)^{1-\mu}B^{1-\mu}$$

Therefore growth rate of the economy is

$$\dot{k}/k = \dot{c}/c = \frac{\varphi(1-\theta_k)^\mu A^\mu (1-\theta_L)^{1-\mu}B^{1-\mu} - \beta}{\sigma}$$

In this approach an increase in the tax rate on human capital also determines reductions in growth. However, the quantitative significance of these effects is controversial. Quantitative results from calibrations of the models examined so far differ greatly, depending on the parameters of technology and preferences. The reasons for the difference in quantitative results are at the center of a current debate (cf. Stokey and Rebelo, 1995).

6.6 Public spending in the model with constant returns-to-scale and human capital

Separating the effects of taxation from those of public spending distract us from paying attention to the effects on consumption and production of goods supplied by the public sector. In this section we shall continue to ignore external effects related to the nature of public goods. To simplify we shall also continue to assume separability of the effects of public spending in the utility function of households and, following Barro (1990), we shall interpret public spending as influencing only output.

The assumption is that public goods are inputs to private production (for instance spending on infrastructure). Therefore, the aggregate production function appears as $Q(t) = F(K(t), L(t), G(t))$. We assume the production function can be defined in per capita terms $q(t) = f[k(t), g(t)]$ and that the per capita function is homogeneous of degree one in k and g. Therefore, technology admits decreasing marginal returns for capital k and spending g considered separately, but admits constant-returns-to-scale globally. The corresponding Cobb-Douglas production function in per capita terms is $q(t) = Ak(t)^{1-a}g(t)^a$. Government policy is assumed to keep a balanced budget constraint in per capita terms $g(t) = \theta(t)q(t)$. To simplify further we refer to a representative agent economy with a constant population and preferences represented by an isoelastic instantaneous utility function. With a Cobb-Douglas technology, equilibrium paths of consumption, production and capital accumulation are the solutions to the following optimal control problem

$$\max V = \int_0^\infty \frac{c(t)^{1-\sigma} - 1}{1 - \sigma} e^{-\beta t} dt$$
$$\dot{k} = Ak(t)^{1-a}g(t)^a - c(t) - g(t)$$
$$g(t) = \theta(t)Ak(t)^{1-a}g(t)^a$$
$$k(0) = k_0; \lim_{t\to\infty} e^{-\beta t}c(t)^{-\sigma}k(t) = 0$$

The representative agent assumes paths of g(t) and θ(t) as given, so that from the first-order conditions we obtain the following consumption growth rate

$$\dot{c}/c(t) = \{(1 - \theta(t))A(1 - a)[g(t)/k(t)]^a - \beta\}/\sigma$$

From the government budget constraint we obtain

$$g(t)/k(t) - [\theta(t)A]^{(1/1-a)}$$

The steady state growth rate is

$$\dot{k}/k = \dot{c}/c = \{[(1 - a)A^{1/(1-a)}(1 - \theta)\theta^{(a/1-a)})] - \beta\}/\sigma$$

The effect of fiscal policy on growth now depends on two conflicting forces. An increase of θ depresses the growth rate, but a simultaneous increase of the ratio g/k increases it. This is indicated by the sign of

$$\frac{d(\dot{c}/c)}{d\theta} = \frac{1}{\sigma}A^{1/(1-a)}\theta^{(a/1-a)}[(a - \theta)/\theta]$$

Evidently when θ increases the growth rate decreases (or remains unchanged, or increases) if $(a/\theta) < 1$; $(or(a/\theta) = 1$; or $(a/\theta) > 1)$. The competitive solution differs from that of a centralized economy. Given Cobb-Douglas technology, from the government budget constraint we get $g^a = \theta^{(a/1-a)}A^{(a/1-a)}k^a$. The central planner problem is

$$\max V = \int_0^\infty \frac{c(t)^{1-\sigma} - 1}{1 - \sigma} e^{-\beta t} dt$$
$$\dot{k} = (1 - \theta)A^{1/1-a}k(t)\theta^{a/1-a} - c(t)$$
$$k(0) = k_0; \lim_{t\to\infty} e^{-\beta t}c(t)^{-\sigma}k(t) = 0$$

Solving, we obtain the following growth rate

$$\dot{k}/k = \dot{c}/c = \frac{A^{(1/1-a)}(1-\theta)\theta^{(a/1-a)} - \beta}{\sigma}$$

Since $a < 1$, by comparing this expression to that for the competitive economy, we deduce that the competitive rate is sub-optimal. Barro's model admits a straightforward extension to an economy where capital consists of physical and human capital (Lin, 1994).

Here we shall consider an extension only for a Rebelo-type growth model. When public spending is an input of production and the economy accumulates human capital, the technology for accumulating human capital includes public goods and services as inputs. By assuming a Cobb-Douglas function in both sectors we have

$$q(t) = A[v(t)k(t)]^a[z(t)h(t)]^{(1-a)}[(1-\phi)g]\Phi$$
$$\dot{h} = B\{[1-v(t)]k(t)\}^b\{[1-z(t)]h(t)\}^{(1-b)}(\phi g)\epsilon$$
$$0 \le z(t) \le 1; 0 \le v(t) \le 1; 0 < \phi < 1$$

The magnitude Φ indicates the fraction of public spending for services to the human capital sector, whereas parameters Φ and ϵ define respective elasticities of public spending in the production of goods and accumulation of human capital. The government budget always balances. The assumption on how public spending enters both productive sectors renders Barro's taxation proportional to income an assumption incompatible with a constant growth rate of the economy. To exclude explosive growth we assume, as in Lin (1994), that public spending is financed with lump-sum taxation.[2] In this case the public budget constraint is $g(t) = \tau(t)$. In a competitive economy, the household's budget constraint is

$$\dot{k} + c(t) - \tau(t) = \rho_k(t)v(t)k(t) + w(t)z(t)h(t)$$

and the objective of a single household is to select paths $\{c(t), v(t), z(t), h(t), k(t)\}$ as solutions to the problem

$$\max V = \int_0^\infty \frac{c(t)^{1-\sigma} - 1}{1-\sigma} e^{-\beta t} dt$$
$$\dot{k} = \rho_k(t)v(t)k(t) + w(t)z(t)h(t) - c(t) - \tau(t)$$
$$\dot{h} = B\{[1-v(t)]k(t)\}^b\{[1-z(t)]h(t)\}^{(1-b)}[\phi\tau(t)]^\epsilon$$
$$0 \le z(t) \le 1; 0 \le v(t) \le 1$$

First-order necessary conditions are

$$\beta + \sigma(\dot{c}/c) = \rho_k(t)$$
$$\dot{\lambda}_1/\lambda_1 = -\rho_k(t)$$
$$\dot{\lambda}_2/\lambda_2 = -(1-b)B\{[1-v(t)]k(t)\}^b\{[1-z(t)]h(t)\}^{-b}[\phi\tau(t)]^\epsilon$$

Steady state in growth rates implies that $\dot{\lambda}_1/\lambda_1 = \dot{\lambda}_2/\lambda_2$ whereas competition implies the rate of return and marginal productivity of physical capital in the production of good are equal. Therefore

$$(1-b)B\{[1-v(t)]k(t)\}^b\{[1-z(t)]h(t)\}^{-b}[\phi\tau(t)]^\epsilon$$
$$= aA[v(t)k(t)]^{a-1}[z(t)h(t)]^{(1-a)}[(1-\phi)\tau(t)]^\Phi$$

This equation for relative intensity k/h is similar to that of Rebelo's model. By solving, we have

$$(k/h) = [(1-v)/(1-z)]^{-(b/1+b-a)}(v/z)^{-(1-a)/1+b-a}[a/(1-b)]^{(1/1+b-a)}$$
$$\phi^{-(\epsilon/1+b-a)}(1-\phi)^{(\Phi/1+b-a)}(A/B)^{(1/1+b-a)}\tau^{(\Phi-\epsilon)/1+b-a)}$$

When $(b/1 + b - a) = \mu$, by substituting the solution of k/h in the previous equality, and by letting

$$\varphi = (1-b)(a/1-b)^\mu[(1-v)/(1-z)]^{b(1-\mu)}(v/z)^{-(1-a)\mu}$$

we obtain the expression for the equilibrium rate of return on physical capital

$$\rho_k = \varphi A^\mu B^{1-\mu}\left[\phi^{\epsilon(1-\mu)}(1-\phi)^{\Phi\mu}\tau^{[\Phi+\epsilon(1-\mu)]}\right]$$

so that the growth rate of the economy is

$$\dot{k}/k = \dot{c}/c = \frac{\varphi A^\mu B^{1-\mu}[\phi^{\epsilon(1-\mu)}(1-\phi)^{\Phi\mu}\tau^{[\Phi+\epsilon(1-\mu)]}] - \beta}{\sigma}$$

The effects of fiscal policy now depend on both the levels of taxes and public expenditure, and on the composition of public expenditure. For a given composition, the effect on the growth rate of an increase in taxes and therefore in public spending, depends on the sign of $[\Phi + \epsilon(1-\mu)]$. Since this term is positive, it follows that the growth rate increases as taxation increases. Intuitively, when public spending is productive and supplies services to capital, its increase has two effects: on the one hand it subtracts resources from consumption, and consequently there is a reallocation of present and future consumption; on the other hand it stimulates physical capital accumulation. However, for a given taxation a change in the composition of public spending can also influence the growth rate. In particular, an increase in the quota of public spending for the services increasing human capital accumulation has an effect on growth rate described by the sign of derivative

$$d(\dot{c}/c)/d\phi = [(\dot{c}/c) + \beta/\sigma][\epsilon(1-\mu)\phi^{-1} - \Phi\mu(1-\phi)^{-1}]$$

This is positive, null or negative depending on whether

$$\frac{\epsilon(1-\mu)}{\epsilon(1-\mu) + \Phi\mu} \geq < \phi$$

This confirms that changing public spending to favour human capital accumulation affects growth according to the initial allocation of public spending (Lin, 1994). If initially the quota of public spending for services to increase education and training is sufficiently low, an increase in this quota increases the growth rate of the economy. However, beyond a certain ratio the opposite happens[3].

6.7   Endogenous growth in monetary economies: a premise

Models of endogenous growth also offer new prospects for studying the relationship between money and growth. In particular, they allow us to reconsider the relationship between money, inflation and growth, in terms of the relationship between the growth rate of money and the growth rate of the economy. Although there have not been many contributions to this subject (De Gregorio, 1993; Gomme, 1993; Jones and Manuelli, 1995; Roubini and Sala-I-Martin,1992), even limiting the topic to the endogenous growth models examined here, would require a study apart. Indeed, think of how many models could be made by combining the endogenous growth models considered so far and the alternative ways of characterizing a monetary economy described in the former chapters. For this reason we shall limit ourselves to the various monetary versions of the 'AK' model and the Lucas' extension including human capital.

6.8   A monetary economy with 'AK' technology and money in the utility function

The monetary economy we shall describe in this section assumes a representative household's instantaneous utility function u(c(t), m(t)) which has real money as its argument. In the class of constant elasticity utility functions we shall consider the function   u(c(t), m(t)) =

$\{[c(t)^\sigma m(t)^{1-\sigma}]^{1-\sigma} - 1\}/(1 - \sigma)$, which is compatible with endogenous growth. We assume a stationary population, the absence of depreciation of physical capital and a money stock controlled by authorities. To simplify, we admit that the authorities have only seignorage as a source of revenue. We also assume that revenue is re-introduced into the economy through lump-sum transfers x(t) to agents. The monetary policy consists of an increase in the nominal money stock at given constant rate $\vartheta > 0$. The instantaneous government budget constraint in per capita real terms is $x(t) = \vartheta m(t)$. The wealth of a single agent at each instant consists of physical capital and money, $a(t) = k(t) + m(t)$. The budget constraint of a single agent supplying a unit of work is

$$\dot{a}(t) = w(t) + \rho(t)k(t) + x(t) - c(t) - p^e(t)m(t)$$

The optimal control problem of the representative agent in the monetary economy described here is

$$\max V = \int_0^\infty \frac{\{[c(t)^\gamma m(t)^{1-\gamma}]^{1-\sigma} - 1\}}{1 - \sigma} e^{-\beta t} dt$$
$$\dot{a}(t) = w(t) + \rho(t)k(t) + x(t) - c(t) - p^e(t)m(t)$$
$$a(t) = k(t) + m(t)$$

to which must be added initial and transversality conditions for wealth. First-order conditions become

$$e^{-\beta t}\gamma[c(t)^{[\gamma(1-\sigma)]-1}][m(t)^{(1-\gamma)(1-\sigma)}] = \lambda(t)$$
$$e^{-\beta t}(1 - \gamma)[c(t)^{\gamma(1-\sigma)}][m(t)^{(1-\gamma)(1-\sigma)-1}] = \lambda(t)[\rho(t) + p^e(t)]$$
$$\dot{\lambda}(t) = -\lambda(t)\rho(t)$$

We assume that $p^e(t)] = p(t)$. If we differentiate the first equation with respect to time and compare it to the last equation, the growth rate of consumption is

$$\beta + (\dot{c}/c(t)) = \rho(t) + \gamma(\dot{c}/c(t)) + (1 - \gamma)(\dot{m}/m(t))$$

By dividing side by side the first and the second equations we can deduce the optimal real money stock

$$m(t) = [(1 - \gamma)/\gamma(\rho(t) + p(t)]c(t)$$

If we differentiate this expression with respect to time and impose a stationary condition on nominal interest rate $d[\rho(t) + p(t)]/dt = 0$, we obtain $\dot{m}/m = \dot{c}/c$. By substituting this into the expression for the rate of growth of consumption, it follows that

$$\beta + \sigma(\dot{c}/c(t)) = \rho(t)$$

With linear production technology $q(t) = Ak(t)$, in a competitive system $\rho(t) = A$. Therefore the rate of growth of this monetary economy is

$$(\dot{c}/c) = (A - \beta)/\sigma$$

The superneutrality of money, therefore, is also confirmed in a money-in-the-utility-function monetary economy with linear technology 'AK' and endogenous growth. In the present context, however, steady state growth of the real stock of money is *endogenous*. The growth rate of the real money stock is the same as that of the economy. In the practical field of policy, an endogenous real money stock means that when authorities assume a policy of constant growth in the nominal money stock and the economy has positive growth, they must accept a permanent rate of inflation $p(t) = \vartheta - (A - \beta)/\sigma$. On the contrary, if they follow an inflation-targeting policy, the monetary authorities must give up discretionality in establishing the money growth rate, since for each fixed inflation target there is only one optimal growth for the nominal money stock, $p(t) + (A - \beta)/\sigma = \vartheta$.

6.9   A monetary economy with 'AK' technology and a cash-in-advance constraint

Assume now that a monetary economy is characterized by Clower's cash-in-advance constraint. Suppose at the start that this constraint refers only to consumption, so that the representative agent in this economy solves the problem

$$\max V = \int_0^\infty \frac{c(t)^{1-\sigma} - 1}{1 - \sigma} e^{-\beta t} dt$$
$$\dot{a} = w(t) + \rho(t)k(t) + x(t) - c(t) - p^e(t)m(t)$$
$$m(t) \geq c(t)$$
$$a(t) = k(t) + m(t)$$

With perfect foresight and the cash-in-advance constraint as equality, and with a Hamiltonian current value, we obtain first-order necessary conditions which can be reduced to

$$c(t)^{-\sigma} = \lambda_1(t)[1 + p(t) + \rho(t)]$$
$$\lambda_3(t)/\lambda_1(t) = p(t) + \rho(t)]$$
$$\dot{\lambda}_1(t) = \lambda_1(t)[\beta - \rho(t)]$$

By imposing a stationary condition on the nominal interest rate, from the first and the last equations, consumption growth rate becomes

$$\dot{c}/c = [\rho - \beta]/\sigma$$

With a linear production technology $q(t) = Ak(t)$, in a competitive system $\rho(t) = A$. Therefore the growth rate of monetary economy with a cash-in-advance constraint on consumption is the same as that of a monetary economy with money-in-the-utility-function

$$\dot{c}/c = (A - \beta)/\sigma$$

Thus the superneutrality of money and the effects of monetary policy are confirmed. Let us now interpret a cash-in-advance constraint according to Grandmont-Younes and Stockman, by including a financial (or liquidity) constraint on investments. With this constraint the optimal control problem of a representative agent becomes

$$\max V = \int_0^\infty \frac{c(t)^{1-\sigma} - 1}{1 - \sigma} e^{-\beta t} dt$$
$$m - w(t) + p(t)k(t) + \pi(t) \quad c(t) - p^e(t)m(t) - I(t)$$
$$m(t) \geq c(t) + \psi I(t)$$
$$\dot{k} = I(t)$$

Letting μ be the Lagrange's multiplier of the cash-in-advance constraint and taking this constraint as equality, first-order conditions become

$$e^{-\beta t}c(t)^{-\sigma} = \mu(t) + \lambda_1(t)$$
$$\lambda_1(t) = \lambda_2(t) - \psi\mu(t)$$
$$\dot{\lambda}_1 = \lambda_1(t)p(t) - \mu(t)$$
$$\dot{\lambda}_2 = -\lambda_1(t)\rho(t)$$

By differentiating the first condition with respect to time and by imposing a stationary condition on the Lagrange multiplier and on nominal interest rate $\dot{\mu}(t) = 0$, $d[\rho(t) + p(t)]/dt = 0$, and by taking into account that $\dot{\lambda}_1 = \dot{\lambda}_2$, we obtain consumption growth rate

$$\dot{c}/c = [\rho/(1 + \rho + p)] - \beta/\sigma$$

With linear production technology $q(t) = Ak(t)$, in a competitive system $\rho(t) = A$, so that

$$\dot{c}/c = \left[A/(1 + A + p)\right] - \beta)/\sigma$$

In a steady state with $A + p > 0$, the consumption growth rate when there is a liquidity constraint is less than the consumption growth rate when there is no such constraint. Moreover, money is no longer superneutral since the inflation rate influences the growth rate of the economy negatively. Monetary model with a liquidity constraint on investments, therefore, can account for the negative correlation between inflation and growth found in various empirical studies (Kormendi and Meguire, 1985; De Gregorio, 1993: Levine and Renelt, 1992; Roubini and Sala-I-Martin, 1992). Finally, we must note that a Friedman optimal money policy, with $A + p = 0$, enables the economy to overcome liquidity constraint and restores superneutrality of money.

6.10 A monetary economy with 'AK' technology and transaction costs

To complete the analysis we shall consider a monetary model of endogenous growth characterized by transaction costs technology. The transaction costs function $T = T(c(t), m(t))$ is assumed to depend on per capita consumption $c(t)$ and real money stock $m(t)$. This technology is the same as that described in the previous chapter. It commands resources to implement transactions. Costs are expressed in terms of consumption. The costs function $T(:)$ is continuous and convex, and increases with consumption and decreases with real money stock. Money reduces costs, but there is a positive satiety level of real money beyond which no benefit, either absolute or marginal, comes to agents from holding it. There is no benefit from money with no transactions for consumption. Mathematically:

a) $T(.)$ is continuous and differentiable at least two times;
b) $T'_c > 0$; $T'_m < 0$; $T''_{cc} > 0$; $T''_{mm} > 0$;
c) $T_{cm} \leq 0$; $T(0, m) = 0$;
d) $\lim_{m \to 0} T'_m = -\infty$; there is $m^* < \infty$ such that $T'_m(c, m^*) = 0$; $T(c, m^*) = 0$

The optimal control problem of the representative agent in the presence of transaction costs is

$$\max V = \int_0^\infty \frac{c(t)^{1-\sigma} - 1}{1 - \sigma} e^{-\beta t} dt$$
$$\dot{a} = w(t) + \rho(t)k(t) + x(t) - c(t) - T(c(t), m(t)) - p^e(t)m(t)$$
$$a(t) = k(t) + m(t)$$

First-order conditions are

$$e^{-\beta t}c(t)^{-\sigma} = \lambda(t)(1 + T'_c)$$
$$\mu(t) = \lambda(t)\rho(t)$$
$$\mu(t) = -\lambda(t)[p(t) + T'_m]$$
$$\dot{\lambda} = -\mu(t)$$

Even if it is more plausible to admit that there are increasing returns-to-scale with transaction technology, in order to obtain a steady state solution we assume that T(.) is homogeneous of degree one. Therefore partial derivatives T'_c and T'_m are homogeneous of degree zero, so that steady state condition $\dot{c}/c = \dot{m}/m$ implies $T'_c = 0$. By differentiating the first necessary condition with respect to time, and by taking into account the aforesaid steady state condition, it follows that

$$\beta + \sigma(\dot{c}/c(t)) = -\dot{\lambda}/\lambda = \rho$$

Since from necessary conditions it also follows that $\dot{\lambda}/\lambda = p + T'_m$, along a steady state path

$$\rho = -(p + T'_m), \quad \text{that is} \quad -T'_m = \rho + p$$

The second equality emphasizes that return on money, represented by the nominal rate of interest, must be equal to the marginal productivity of money in the transaction process. With linear production technology $q(t) = Ak(t)$, in a competitive system $\rho = A$ and the growth rate of a monetary economy is identical to that of an economy without any restriction on transaction technology

$$\dot{c}/c(t) = [A - \beta]/\sigma$$

In this context too we find the superneutrality of money. An increase in the rate of growth of the money stock causes higher inflation, which determines a lower demand for real money. A reduction of the latter reduces the marginal transactions cost and therefore increases the marginal productivity of money in the transaction process. Marginal productivity of money increases just enough to compensate for the greater cost for holding money due to greater inflation. The final result is that return on physical capital is not influenced by changes in the growth rate of money. It is determined solely by the marginal productivity of capital in the production of goods. Transaction technology can be reformulated to include transactions for investment goods. With this assumption, transaction technology becomes $T = T(c, I, m)$, where $I = \dot{k}$, and the optimal control problem of representative agent becomes

$$\max V = \int_0^\infty \frac{c(t)^{1-\sigma} - 1}{1 - \sigma} e^{-\beta t} dt$$

$$\dot{m} = w(t) + \rho(t)k(t) + x(t) - c(t) - p^e(t)m(t) - I(t) - T(c(t), I(t), m(t))$$

$$\dot{k} = I(t)$$

First-order necessary conditions are

$$e^{-\beta t} c(t)^{-\sigma} = \lambda_1(t)(1 + T_c')$$

$$\lambda_2(t) = \lambda_1(t)(1 + T_I')$$

$$\dot{\lambda}_1 = \lambda_1(t)[p(t) + T_m']$$

$$\dot{\lambda}_2 = -\lambda_1(t)(\rho(t))$$

At steady state, given homogeneity of degree one of transactions technology $T(.)$, we must have

$$\beta + \sigma(\dot{c}/c(t)) = -\dot{\lambda}_1/\lambda_1$$

$$\dot{\lambda}_1/\lambda_1 = -\rho/(1 + T_I')$$

Moreover

$$\dot{\lambda}_2/\lambda_1 = (\dot{\lambda}_1/\lambda_1)(1 + T_I')$$

so that

$$\rho/(1 + T_I') + p = -T_m'$$

The cost for holding money at steady state no longer coincides with nominal interest in the Fisher sense, since its marginal productivity in transactions at equilibrium is equal to the inflation rate plus real rate of interest weighted by a coefficient $1 + T_I'$. The ratio $\rho/(1 + T_I')$ is the effective rate of return on capital. Indeed it can be seen as the transformation rate of one unit of real income subtracted from consumption in order to accumulate capital. Since in a competitive system $\rho = A$, the steady state growth rate of the economy is

$$(\dot{c}/c(t)) = [A/(1 + T_I')] - \beta/\sigma$$

An increase in the growth rate of money decreases the demand for real money, and this implies a lower ratio c/m and a lower effective return on capital $A/(1 + T_I')$. Money, therefore, is no longer superneutral. Consequently, in an economy there is a negative relationship between the inflation rate and the growth rate.

6.11   Endogenous growth of monetary economies with human capital

In the monetary economy we shall examine, human capital accumulation uses inputs of both physical capital and human capital. Goods are produced by competitive firms, while human capital is accumulated by households. In this economy, therefore, at every instant a single agent's wealth has two different components. One is tangible wealth, consisting of physical capital and money, $a(t) = k(t) + m(t)$. This form of wealth is accumulated through saving. Another component is intangible wealth, which consists of professional skill. This form of wealth is accumulated through a purposeful process of production.

We shall assume, as previously, that both technologies for goods and capital accumulation are Cobb-Douglas, that is

$$q(t) = A[v(t)k(t)]^a[z(t)h(t)]^{(1-a)}$$
$$\dot{h}/h = B\{[1 - v(t)]k(t)\}^b\{[1 - z(t)]h(t)\}^{(1-b)}$$

where $0 \leq v(t) \leq 1$ is the fraction of physical capital employed in the production of goods, and $0 \leq z(t) \leq 1$ is the fraction of time employed in the same production.

Let us first consider a money-in-the-utility-function economy. The instantaneous utility function is $u = \dfrac{\{[c(t)^\gamma m(t)^{1-\gamma}]^{1-\sigma} - 1\}}{1 - \sigma}$ and the budget constraint of a single agent is $\dot{a}(t) = \rho_k(t)v(t)k(t) + w(t)z(t)h(t) + x(t) - c(t) - p^e(t)m(t)$

Assuming perfect foresight $p(t) = p^e(t)$, the optimal control problem of a representative agent in this monetary economy is

$$\max V = \int_0^\infty \frac{\{[c(t)^\gamma m(t)^{1-\gamma}]^{1-\sigma} - 1\}}{1 - \sigma} e^{-\beta t} dt$$
$$\dot{a}(t) = \rho_k(t)v(t)k(t) + w(t)z(t)h(t) + x(t) - c(t) - p(t)m(t)$$
$$a(t) = k(t) + m(t)$$
$$\dot{h} = B\{[1 - v(t)]k(t)\}^b\{[1 - z(t)]h(t)\}^{(1-b)}$$
$$0 \leq z(t) \leq 1; 0 \leq v(t) \leq 1$$

to which must be added the usual initial conditions for capital stocks and the appropriate transversality conditions. First-order necessary conditions are

$$e^{-\beta t}\gamma[c(t)^{[\gamma(1-\sigma)]-1}][m(t)^{(1-\gamma)(1-\sigma)}] = \lambda_1(t)$$
$$m(t) = [(1 - \gamma)/\gamma(p(t) + \rho_k(t))]c(t)$$

$$\dot{\lambda}_1/\lambda_1 = -\rho_k(t)$$

$$\dot{\lambda}_2/\lambda_2 = -(1-b)B\{[1-v(t)]k(t)\}^b[1-z(t)]^{-b}h(t)^{-b}$$

By differentiating the first condition with respect to time, we obtain

$$\beta + [\gamma(1-\sigma)-1](\dot{c}/c) + (1-\gamma)(1-\sigma)(\dot{m}/m) = -(\dot{\lambda}_1/\lambda_1)$$

By differentiating the second condition with respect to time and by enforcing a stationary condition on the nominal interest rate it follows $\dot{m}/m = \dot{c}/c$. Therefore steady state requires

$$\beta + \sigma(\dot{c}/c) = \rho_k(t)$$

On the other hand the same stationary conditions imply $\dot{\lambda}_1/\lambda_1 = \dot{\lambda}_2/\lambda_2$. Since competition implies $\rho_k(t) = Aav(t)^a k(t)]^{a-1} z(t)h(t)]^{(1-a)}$, at steady state in growth rate we must have $(1-b)B\{[1-v(t)]k(t)\}^b[1-z(t)]^{-b}h(t)^{-b}$ $= Aav(t)^a k(t)]^{a-1} z(t)h(t)]^{(1-a)}$.

This is an equation for the unknown k/h, the relative intensity of the two kinds of capital in the two sectors of the economy. By solving for k/h we obtain the expression for the rate on return of physical capital $\rho_k = \varphi A^\mu B^{1-\mu}$. Here, as in Rebelo's model, we set $(b/1+b-a) = \mu$ and $\varphi = (1-b)(a/1-b)^\mu[(1-v)/(1-z)]^{b(1-\mu)}(v/z)^{-(1-a)\mu}$

It follows that the growth rate is

$$\dot{k}/k = \dot{c}/c = \frac{\varphi A^\mu B^{1-\mu} - \beta}{\sigma}$$

Thus, superneutrality of money is confirmed even when human capital accumulation is admitted. When a monetary economy is represented through transaction costs technology $T(c(t), m(t))$, the optimum control problem of the representative agent becomes

$$\max V = \int_0^\infty \frac{c(t)^{1-\sigma} - 1}{1-\sigma} e^{-\beta t} dt$$

$$\dot{m} = \rho_k(t)v(t)k(t) + w(t)z(t)h(t)x(t) - c(t) -$$

$$T(c(t), m(t)) - p^e(t)m(t) - I(t)$$

$$\dot{k}(t) = I(t)$$

$$\dot{h} = B\{[1-v(t)]k(t)\}^b\{[1-z(t)]h(t)\}^{(1-b)}$$

$$0 \le z(t) \le 1; 0 \le v(t) \le 1$$

First-order necessary conditions are

$$e^{-\beta t}c(t)^{-\sigma} = \lambda_1(t)(1 + T'_c)$$

$$\lambda_1(t) = \lambda_2(t)$$

$$\lambda_1(t)\rho_k(t)k(t) = \lambda_3(t)Bb[1 - v(t)]^{b-1}k(t)^b\{[1 - z(t)]h(t)\}^{(1-b)}$$
$$\lambda_1(t)w(t)h(t) = \lambda_3(t)B(1 - b)[1 - v(t)]^b k(t)^b [1 - z(t)]^{-b}h(t)^{(1-b)}$$
$$\dot{\lambda}_1(t) = \lambda_1(t)(p + T'_m)$$
$$\dot{\lambda}_2(t) = \lambda_1(t)\rho_k(t)v(t) - \lambda_3(t)Bb[1 - v(t)]^b k(t)^{b-1}\{[1 - z(t)]h(t)\}^{(1-b)}$$
$$\dot{\lambda}_3(t) = -\lambda_1(t)w(t)z(t) - \lambda_3(t)B(1 - b)[1 - v(t)]^b k(t)^b [1 - z(t)]^{(1-b)} \; h(t)^{-b}$$

which become

$$e^{-\beta t}c(t)^{-\sigma} = \lambda_1(t)(1 + T'_c)$$
$$\lambda_1(t) = \lambda_2(t)$$
$$\dot{\lambda}_1(t)/\lambda_1(t) = T'_m + p$$
$$\dot{\lambda}_2(t)/\lambda_2(t) = -\rho_k(t)$$
$$\dot{\lambda}_3(t)/\lambda_3(t) = -B(1 - b)[1 - v(t)]^b k(t)^b [1 - z(t)]^{-b}h(t)^{-b}$$

Steady state requires that

$$\beta + \sigma(\dot{c}/c) = \rho_k$$
$$\rho_k - -(T'_m + p)$$
$$\rho_k = B(1 \quad b)[1 - v(t)]^b k(t)^b [1 - z(t)]^{-b}h(t)^{-b}$$

Even in the present context the second condition implicitly requires that at equilibrium the return on money, represented by nominal interest rate, must be equal to the marginal productivity of money in the transaction process. Competition implies $\rho_k = Aav(t)^a k(t)^{a-1}z(t)h(t)]^{(1-a)}$, so that the last necessary condition becomes

$$(1 - b)B\{[1 - v(t)]k(t)\}^b[1 - z(t)]^{-b}h(t)^{-b} = Aav(t)^a k(t)^{a-1}[z(t)h(t)]^{(1-a)}$$

This solved for k/h, the relative intensity of the two kinds of capitals in the two sectors of the economy, gives the expression for the rate of return on physical capital $\rho_k = \varphi A^\mu B^{1-\mu}$, where $(b/1 + b - a) = \mu$ and $\varphi = (1 - b)(a/1 - b)^\mu[(1 - v)/(1 - z)]^{b(1-\mu)}(v/z)^{-(1-a)\mu}$

From this it follows that the growth rate is

$$\dot{k}/k = \dot{c}/c = \frac{\varphi A^\mu B^{1-\mu} - \beta}{1 - \sigma}$$

This rate is identical to that in the money-in-the-utility-function model. Money, therefore, is superneutral even when there is an accumulation of human capital and a transaction costs technology $T(c(t), m(t))$. On the contrary, when transaction technology also admits costs for transactions on physical capital $T(c(t), I(t), m(t))$, the first-order conditions of the representative agent's optimum control problem become

$$e^{-\beta t}c(t)^{-\sigma} = \lambda_1(t)(1 + T'_c)$$
$$\lambda_2(t) = \lambda_1(t)(1 + T'_I)$$
$$\dot{\lambda}_1(t)/\lambda_1(t) = T'_m + p$$
$$\dot{\lambda}_2(t)/\lambda_2(t) = -\rho_k(t)/(1 + T'_I)$$
$$\dot{\lambda}_3(t)/\lambda_3(t) = -B(1 - b)[1 - v(t)]^b k(t)^b [1 - z(t)]^{-b} h(t)^{-b}$$

Steady state growth now requires

$$\beta + \sigma(\dot{c}/c) = \rho_k/(1 + T'_I)$$
$$\rho_k/(1 + T'_I) = -(T'_m + p)$$
$$\rho_k/(1 + T'_I) = B(1 - b)[1 - v(t)]^b k(t)^b [1 - z(t)]^{-b} h(t)^{-b}$$

Therefore by taking into account competition, the growth rate of the economy becomes

$$\dot{k}/k = \dot{c}/c = \frac{[1/(1 + T'_I)]^\mu \varphi A^\mu B^{1-\mu} - \beta}{\sigma}$$

Once again (in a model without human capital) money is no longer superneutral. Consequently, there is a negative relationship between inflation rate and the growth rate of the economy.

To complete the analysis, let us eventually consider a monetary model with a cash-in-advance constraint imposed both on consumption and capital goods. Optimum control problem of the representative agent in this case is

$$\max V = \int_0^\infty \frac{c(t)^{1-\sigma} - 1}{1 - \sigma} e^{-\beta t} dt$$
$$\dot{m} = \rho_k(t)v(t)k(t) + w(t)z(t)h(t) + x(t) - c(t) - p^e(t)m(t) - I(t)$$
$$m(t) \geq c(t) + \psi I(t)$$
$$\dot{k}(t) = I(t)$$
$$\dot{h} = B\{[1 - v(t)]k(t)\}^b \{[1 - z(t)]h(t)\}^{(1-b)}$$
$$0 \leq z(t) \leq 1; 0 \leq v(t) \leq 1$$

First-order conditions are

$$e^{-\beta t}c(t)^{-\sigma} = \mu(t) + \lambda_1(t)$$
$$\lambda_1(t) = \lambda_2(t) - \psi\mu(t)$$

$$\lambda_1(t)\rho_k(t)k(t) = \lambda_3(t)Bb[1 - v(t)]^{b-1}k(t)^b\{[1 - z(t)]h(t)\}^{(1-b)}$$
$$\lambda_1(t)w(t)h(t) = \lambda_3(t)B(1 - b)[1 - v(t)]^b k(t)^b[1 - z(t)]^{-b}h(t)^{(1-b)}$$
$$\dot{\lambda}_1 = \lambda_1(t)p(t) - \mu(t)$$
$$\dot{\lambda}_2(t) = \lambda_1(t)\rho_k(t)v(t) - \lambda_3(t)Bb[1 - v(t)]^b k(t)^{b-1}\{[1 - z(t)]h(t)\}^{(1-b)}$$
$$\dot{\lambda}_3(t) = -\lambda_1(t)w(t)z(t) - \lambda_3(t)B(1 - b)[1 - v(t)]^b k(t)^b[1 - z(t)]^{(1-b)}h(t)^{-b}$$

They can be reduced to

$$e^{-\beta t}c(t)^{-\sigma} = \mu(t) + \lambda_1(t)$$
$$\lambda_1(t) = \lambda_2(t) - \psi\mu(t)$$
$$\dot{\lambda}_1 = \lambda_1(t)p(t) - \mu(t)$$
$$\dot{\lambda}_2(t) = -\lambda_1(t)\rho_k(t)$$
$$\dot{\lambda}_3(t)/\lambda_3(t) = -B(1 - b)[1 - v(t)]^b k(t)^b[1 - z(t)]^{-b}h(t)^{-b}$$

By differentiating the first condition with respect to time and by imposing a stationary condition on the Lagrange multiplier $\dot{\mu}(t) = 0$ and on the nominal rate of interest $d[\rho_k(t) + p(t)]]/dt = 0$, it follows that

$$\beta + \sigma(\dot{c}/c) = -(\dot{\lambda}_1/\lambda_1) = \rho_k(t)$$

Since at steady state

$$\dot{\lambda}_1/\lambda_1 = \dot{\lambda}_3/\lambda_3 = B(1 - b)[1 - v(t)]^b k(t)^b[1 - z(t)]^{-b} h(t)^{-b}$$

by virtue of competition

$$Aav(t)^a k(t)^{a-1}[z(t)h(t)]^{(1-a)} = B(1 - b)[1 - v(t)]^b k(t)^b[1 - z(t)]^{-b}h(t)^{-b}$$

As a consequence of $\lambda_1(t) = \lambda_2(t)/[1 + \psi(\rho_k(t) + p(t)]$, from the expression for the rate of return on physical capital $\rho_k = \varphi A^\mu B^{1-\mu}$ (where $(b/1 + b - a) = \mu$ and $\varphi = (1 - b)(a/1 - b)^\mu [(1 - v)/(1 - z)]^{b(1-\mu)} (v/z)^{-(1-a)\mu}$) we obtain

$$\dot{k}/k = \dot{c}/c = \frac{\varphi A^\mu B^{1-\mu}/[1 + \psi(p + \varphi^\mu A^\mu B^{1-\mu})] - \beta}{\sigma}$$

which is the growth rate of the economy. Money is not superneutral, and monetary policy can influence the growth rate negatively.

Notes

1. A direct relation between saving behaviour and endogenous growth rate is obtained by defining the ex-post propensity to save $s = (S/L)(L/Q)$ and observing that at steady state $s = \dot{k}/q = (\dot{k}/k)(k/q) = [(A - \beta)/\sigma](1/A)$.

2. This assumption could easily be abandoned in favour of taxation proportional to the income of the inputs.
3. The model admits some straightforward extensions. In addition to taxation proportional to the income of inputs, it can be considered that a part of services from public spending enters into utility function of agents as consumption (Barro, 1990), or can be considered a congestion phenomenon (Barro and Sala-I-Martin, 1990; 1995). However, we shall not examine these possible extensions further.

References

Aghion, P. and P. Howitt, (1992) 'A model of Growth Trough Creative Destruction', *Econometrica*, 60, 2, pp. 323-51.

Arrow, K. (1962) 'The Economic Implications of Learning by Doing', *Review of Economic Studies*, 29, pp. 155–73.

Barro, R. (1990) 'Government Spending in a Simple Model of Endogenous Growth', *Journal of Political Economy*, 98, 5, pp. S103–25.

Barro, R. and X. Sala-I-Martin (1995) *Economic Growth* (New York: McGraw-Hill).

Benhabib, J. and R. Perli (1994a) 'Uniqueness and Indeterminacy: On the Dynamics of Endogenous Growth', *Journal of Economic Theory*, 63, pp. 113–42.

Benhabib, J. and R. Perli (1994b) 'Monopolistic Competition, Indeterminacy and Growth', *Ricerche Economiche*, 48, pp. 270–98.

Boldrin, M. (1992) 'Dynamic Externalities, Multiple Equilibria and Growth', *Journal of Economic Theory*, 58, 2, pp. 198–218.

Bond, E. and P. Wang and C. Yip (1996) 'A General Two-Sector Model of Endogenous Growth with Human and Physical Capital: Balanced Growth and Transitional Dynamics', *Journal of Economic Theory*, 68, 149–73

Caballè, J. and M. Santos (1993) 'On Endogenous Growth with Physical and Human Capital', *Journal of Political Economy*, 101, 61, pp. 1042-67.

Cashin, P. (1995) 'Government Spending, Taxes, and Economic Growth', *IMF Staff Papers*, 42, 2, pp. 237–69

Chamley, C. (1986) 'Optimal Taxation of Capital Income in General Equilibrium with Infinite Lives', *Econometrica*, 54, pp. 607–22.

Chamley, C. (1993) 'Externalities and Dynamics in Models of "Learning or Doing" ', *International Economic Review*, 34, 3, pp. 583–609.

De Gregorio, J. (1993) 'Inflation, Taxation and Long-run Growth', *Journal of Monetary Economics*, 31, pp. 271–98

Devereux, M. and D. Love (1995) 'The Dynamic Effects of Government Spending Policies in a Two-Sector Endogenous Growth Model', *Journal of Money, Credit and Banking*, 27, 1, pp. 232–56

Gomme, P. (1993) 'Money and Growth Revised–Measuring the Costs of Inflation in an Endogenous Growth Model', *Journal of Monetary Economics*, 32, pp. 51–77.

Grandmont, J.M. and Y. Younès (1972) 'On the Role of Money and the Existence of Monetary Equilibrium', *Review of Economic Studies*, 39, pp. 355–72

Grossman, G. and E. Helpman (1991) *Innovation and Growth in the Global Economy* (Cambridge, MA: MIT Press).

Helpman, E. (1992) 'Endogenous Macroeconomic Growth Theory', *European Economic Review*, 36, pp. 237–67

Jones, L. and R. Manuelli and P. Rossi (1993) 'Optimal Taxation in Models of Endogenous Growth', *Journal of Political Economy*, 101, 3, pp. 485–517

Jones, L. and R. Manuelli (1995) 'Growth and the Effects of Inflation' *Journal of Economic Dynamics and Control*, 19, pp. 1405–28

Jones, L. and R. Manuelli (1997) 'Endogenous Growth Theory: An Introduction', *Journal of Economic Dynamics and Control*, 21, pp. 1–22.

King, R. and S. Rebelo (1990) 'Public Policy and Economic Growth: Developing New-Classical Implications', *Journal of Political Economy*, 98, pp. S126–50.

King, R. and S. Rebelo (1993) 'Transitional Dynamics and Economic Growth in the Neoclassical Model', *American Economic Review*, 83,4, pp. 908–31.

Kormendi, R. and P. Meguire (1985) 'Macroeconomic Determinants of Growth: Cross-country Evidence', *Journal of Monetary Economics*, 16, pp. 141–63

Levine, R. and D. Renelt (1992) 'A Sensitivity Analysis of Cross-country Growth Regressions', *American Economic Review*, 82, pp. 942-63.

Lin, S. (1994) 'Allocation of Government Spending and Economic Growth', *Economic Notes*, 23, 1, pp. 130–41

Lucas, R. (1988) 'On the Mechanics of Economic Development', *Journal of Monetary Economics*, 22, pp. 3–42.

Lucas, R. (1990) 'Supply-Side Economics: An Analytical Review', *Oxford Economic Papers*, 42, pp. 293-316

Lucas, R. (1993) 'Making a Miracle', *Econometrica*, 61, 2, pp. 251–72.

Marshall, A. (1920) *Principles of Economics* (London: Macmillan).

Mulligan, C. and X. Sala-I-Martin (1993) 'Transitional Dynamics in Two-Sector Models of Endogenous Growth', *Quarterly Journal of Economics*, 108, 3, pp. 739–74.

Pecorino, P. (1993) 'Tax Structure and Growth in a Model with Human Capital', *Journal of Public Economics*, 52, pp. 251–71.

Rebelo, S. (1991) 'Long Run Policy Analysis and the Long-Run Growth', *Journal of Political Economy*, 99, pp. 500-21.

Romer, P. (1986) 'Increasing Returns and Long-Run Growth', *Journal of Political Economy*, 94, pp. 1002–36.

Romer, P. (1987) 'Growth Based on Increasing Returns Due to Specialization', *American Economic Review Papers and Proceedings*, 77, pp. 56–62.

Romer, P. (1989) 'Capital Accumulation in the Theory of Long-Run Growth', in R. Barro (ed.) *Modern Business Cycle Theory* (Oxford: Basil Blackwell).

Romer, P. (1990) 'Endogenous Technological Change', *Journal of Political Economy*, 98, pp. S71–102

Romer, P. (1993) 'The Origins of Endogenous Growth', *Journal of Economic Perspective*, 8, 1, pp. 3–22.

Roubini, N. and X. Sala-I-Martin (1992) 'Financial Repression and Economic Growth', *Journal of Development Economics*, 39, pp. 5–30.

Sala-I-Martin, X. (1990) 'Lecture Notes On Economic Growth', I & II, *Working Papers NBER,*

Schumpeter, A. (1934) *The Theory of Economic Development* (Cambridge MA: Harvard University Press).

Schumpeter, A. (1942) *Capitalism, Socialism and Democracy* (New York: Harper).

Stockman, A. (1981) 'Anticipated Inflation and the Capital Stock in a Cash-in-Advance Economy', *Journal of Monetary Economics*, 8, pp. 534–44

Stokey, N. and Rebelo, S. (1995) 'Growth Effects of Flat-Rate Taxes', *Journal of Political Economy*, 103, 1, pp. 519–50.

Young, A. (1928) 'Increasing Returns and Economic Progress', *Economic Journal*, 38, pp. 527–42.

Mathematical Appendixes

Foreword

Mathematical Appendixes A, B and C review the essential concepts of differential equations, difference equations and the theory of optimal control. Theorems and propositions are stated without proof. Interested readers will find rigorous proofs and more systematic treatment of these subjects in books listed in the references, at the end of each appendix. For ease of reference, we also reproduce here the table of contents of each appendixes A, B, C.

Appendix A: Differential equations and systems of differential equations

Appendix B: Difference equations and systems of difference equations

APPENDIX C: Calculus of variations and optimal control theory (Pontryagin's maximum principle)

Appendix A: Differential equations and systems of differential equations

A.1 Differential equations: General theory, existence and properties of solutions

An equation

$$F(t, x, x', .., x^{(n)}) = 0$$

which involves an independent variable t, an unknown function x(t) and its derivatives up to n-th order x', $x^{(2)}$,...,$x^{(n)}$ is an ordinary differential equation of order n. The order of the differential equation is the highest order of the derivatives involved. The word ordinary indicates that the unknown function x(t) is a function of one variable. In the following we shall consider only unknown functions of one variable, so the word ordinary with reference to differential equations will be taken for granted, except when this might cause confusion.

If the relationship F(.) can be solved for the highest derivative, we can write

$$x^{(n)} = f(t, x, x', ..., x^{(n-1)})$$

in which case the ordinary differential equation of order n is in the normal form. A relationship $g(t, x, c_1, ..., c_n) = 0$ where $c_1, ..., c_n$ are constants, is the general integral or the general solution of the n-th order differential equation if, by looking at x as function of t, and by repeating total differentiation n times, and consequently eliminating the constants $c_1, ..., c_n$ from g(.), it is possible to find the equation F(.) = 0. This procedure highlights how difficult it is, from both the existence and the analytical points of view, to find the general solution of the n-th order differential equation. Geometrical considerations make it useful to refer to the normal form of the equation and then to verify if there exists a function x(t), which solves a differential equation of order n and satisfies the following additional conditions

$$x(t_0) = x_0; x'(t_0) = x'_0; \ldots; x^{(n-1)}(t_0) = x_0^{(n-1)}$$

Here $x_0; x'_0; ...; x_0^{(n-1)}$ are constants called initial conditions. The problem formulated in this way is called Cauchy's problem or the initial conditions problem. For this problem the following theorem is

Theorem A.1

Let $f(t, x, x', .., x^{(n-1)})$ be a continuous function with continuous partial derivatives, except perhaps for x, on the rectangle

$$D = \{t_0 - a \leq t \leq t_0 + a; x_0 - b \leq x \leq x_0 + b; x'_0 - b \leq x' \leq x'_0 + b; \ldots;$$
$$x_0^{(n-1)} - b \leq x^{(n-1)} \leq x_0^{(n-1)} + b\}$$

There exists $\varepsilon > 0$ such that in the closed interval $t_0 - \varepsilon \leq t \leq t_0 + \varepsilon$ there is a unique function continuous x(t) with continuous derivatives up to order n that satisfies the equation $x^{(n)} = f(t, x, x', ..., x^{(n-1)})$ and the initial conditions $x(t_0) = x_0; x'(t_0) = x'_0; ...; x^{(n-1)}(t_0) = x_0^{(n-1)}$.

These concepts can be applied to the special case of n = 1. Differential equation in this case corresponds to a first-order ordinary differential equation. It has the form

$F(t, x, x') = 0$. A relationship $g(t, x, c) = 0$ is the general solution or the general integral of $F(.) = 0$ if, by considering x as function of t and by differentiating totally, it is possible, if we eliminate the constant c from $g(.)$, to get the equation $F(.) = 0$. In the normal form the first-order differential equation is $x' = f(t, x)$. Cauchy's problem for this equation is to find a solution $x(t)$ which also satisfies the initial condition $x(t_0) = x_0$, where x_0 is a constant. Theorem A.1 of the existence and uniqueness of the solution to Cauchy's problem can be expressed as follows

Theorem A.2

Let $f(t, x)$ be a continuous function with a continuous first partial derivative $\partial f / \partial x$ on the rectangular neighbourhood $D = \{t_0 - a \leq t \leq t_0 + a; x_0 - b \leq x \leq x_0 + b\}$. There exists $\varepsilon > 0$ such that in the closed interval $t_0 - \varepsilon \leq t \leq t_0 + \varepsilon$ there is a unique continuous function $x(t)$ with a continuous first derivative that satisfies the equation $x' = f(t, x(t))$ and the initial condition $x(t_0) = x_0$.

The condition for derivatives of the function $f(.)$ is sometimes inaccurate. For this reason in more general statements of the theorem for the existence and uniqueness of the solutions to Cauchy's problem the requirement of *Lipschitz's condition* is preferred. Lipschitz's condition for the n-th order differential equation in normal form can be proposed as follows. Let D^n be a rectangular dominion in the space R^n. A function $f(t, x, x',.., x^{(n-1)})$ defined on D^n satisfies Lipschitz's condition if there exists a constant $h > 0$ such that for every $(t, x_1, x_1',..., x_1^{(n-1)})$ and $(t, x_2, x_2',..., x_2^{(n-1)})$ in D^n

$$|f(t, x_1, x_1', .., x_1^{(n-1)}) - f(t, x_2, x_2', .., x_2^{(n-1)})| \leq h|(x_1, x_1', .., x_1^{(n-1)}) - (x_2, x_2', .., x_2^{(n-1)})|$$

for some appropriate norm in the vector space of the elements $(x, x', .., x^{(n-1)})$. Evidently, in the case of the first-order differential equation Lipschitz's condition becomes

$$|f(t, x_1(t)) - f(t, x_2(t))| \leq h|x_1 - x_2|$$

where $|.|$ is the absolute value of a real number.

A.2   Linear differential equations: General theory and properties of solutions

An ordinary differential equation of order n is linear if, given $n + 2$ continuous real-valued functions $b_0(t)$, $b_1(t),..$, $b_n(t)$, $g(t)$ on some real interval $t_a \leq t \leq t_b$, it is the linear combination of the unknown function $x(t)$ and its derivatives up to n-th order x', $x^{(2)}$, .., $x^{(n)}$, that is

$$b_0(t)x^{(n)} + b_1(t)x^{n-1} + \ldots + b_{n-1}(t)x' + b_n(t)x = g(t)$$

Letting be $b_0(t) \neq 0$ and putting $g(t)/b_0(t) = y(t)$; $b_1(t)/b_0(t) = a_1(t); ...; b_n(t)/b_0(t) = a_n(t)$ the linear differential equation of order n in normal form is

$$x^{(n)} + a_1(t)x^{n-1} + \ldots + a_{n-1}(t)x' + a_n(t)x = y(t)$$

The equation is called homogeneous if $y(t) = 0$, otherwise it is called non-homogeneous and the function $y(t)$ is called the driving term or forcing term. To examine the solutions it is convenient to introduce the notation $P(D^n)x(t) = y(t)$ where $P(D^n)$ is a polynomial for the differential operator D. The operator D^n indicates the derivative operation applied to function $x(t)$ up to order n, with the convention $Dx^0 = x(t)$. The differential operator is linear, which means (1) if $f_1(t)$ and $f_2(t)$ are two continuous functions of class C^n, then $D[f_1(t) + f_2(t)] = Df_1(t) + Df_2(t)$ and (2) if c is arbitrary constant $D(cf(t)) = cDf(t)$. From (1) and (2) it follows that, given n functions $f_1(t), f_2(t),..., f_n(t)$ and n constants $c_1, c_2,..., c_n$ it is true that $D[\Sigma c_i f_i(t)] = \Sigma c_i Df_i(t)$.

These properties of operator D permit us to state

Proposition A.1

If $x_1(t), x_2(t),..., x_m(t)$ are m solutions to the linear homogeneous differential equation of order n $P(D^n)x(t) = 0$ and $c_1, c_2,..., c_m$ are m arbitrary constants, then the function $c_1x_1(t) + c_2x_2(t) + . + c_mx_m(t)$ is also a solution to the homogeneous equation $P(D^n)x(t) = 0$.

Another important property of solutions to the non-homogeneous linear equation is stated by

Proposition A.2

If $x_0(t)$ is a solution to the linear non-homogeneous differential equation and $z(t)$ is a solution to the complementary homogeneous equation obtained when the forcing term $y(t) = 0$, then $x_0(t) + z(t)$ is also a solution to the linear non-homogeneous differential equation. On the contrary, each solution to non-homogeneous linear equation is obtained by adding the solution to the homogeneous equation to a given solution to the non-homogeneous equation.

Proposition A.1 can be qualified further if we introduce the Wronskian definition. Consider a set of solutions $x_1(t), x_2(t),..., x_n(t)$ to the homogeneous differential equation $P(D^n)x(t) = 0$ consisting of a number of functions equal to the order of the differential equation. It is possible to form an nxn matrix of rows which are, in order, the solutions and the respective derivatives up to order n − 1. The determinant of this matrix is the Wronskian of the set of n solutions. In symbols

$$W(t) = \det \begin{bmatrix} x_1(t) & x_2(t) & .....x_n(t) \\ x_1' & x_2'(t) & ....x_n'(t) \\ .... \\ x_1(t)^{(n-1)} & x_2(t)^{(n-1)} & .....x_n(t)^{(n-1)} \end{bmatrix}$$

The set of solutions $x_1(t), x_2(t),..., x_n(t)$ of the homogeneous differential equation $P(D^n)x(t) = 0$ constitutes a fundamental set or fundamental system of solutions if $W(t) \neq 0$. Given a fundamental set of solutions, the general solution to the homogeneous differential equation $P(D^n)x(t) = 0$ is obtained as a linear combination of this set, that is given n solutions forming a fundamental system $x_1(t), x_2(t),..., x_n(t)$, and $c_1, c_2,..., c_n$ arbitrary constants, the general solution to the differential equation $P(D^n)x(t) = 0$ is

$$z(t) = c_1x_1(t) + c_2x_2(t) + ... + c_nx_n(t)$$

Therefore, if $x_0(t)$ is a solution to the non-homogeneous linear equation of order n, then the general solution to the equation is

$$x(t) = x_0(t) + z(t) = x_0(t) + c_1x_1(t) + c_2x_2(t) + ... + c_nx_n(t)$$

A.3   Specific cases: Solutions to first- and second-order linear differential equations

The first-order non-homogeneous linear equation is

$$x'(t) = a(t)x(t) + y(t)$$

The complementary homogeneous equation is $x'(t) - a(t)x(t) = 0$. The general solution to this equation can be obtained by rewriting it in the form $x'(t)e^{-\int a(t)dt} - a(t)x(t)e^{-\int a(t)dt} = 0$. The term to the left is the derivative with respect to time of the function $x(t)e^{-\int a(t)dt}$. Therefore by integrating we obtain $x(t)e^{-\int a(t)dt} = c$, where c is an arbitrary constant. By setting $c = x(t_0)$, the solution to the homogeneous linear equation is $z(t) = x(t_0)e^{\int a(t)dt}$. By direct proof, function $x_0(t) = \int y(t)e^{-a(t)dt}dt + c$ is a particular solution of the non-homogeneous equation. Indeed by differentiating with respect to time, $e^{-a(t)dt}[x_0'(t) - a(t)x_0(t)] = y(t)e^{-a(t)dt}$, or $x_0'(t) = a(t)x_0(t) + y(t)$. Therefore the general solution to the first-order non-homogeneous linear equation can be written as

$$x(t) = x_0(t) + z(t) = e^{\int a(t)dt}[x(t_0) + y(t)e^{-\int a(t)dt}dt]$$

The second-order non-homogeneous linear equation is the second degree differential polynomial $P(D^2)x(t) = y(t)$, that is

$$x''(t) = a_1(t)x'(t) + a_2(t)x(t) + y(t)$$

Let us consider the complementary homogeneous equation $x''(t) = a_1(t)x'(t) + a_2(t)x(t)$. We already know that if $x_1(t)$, $x_2(t)$ is a fundamental system of solutions to the homogeneous equation its general solution is $z(t) = c_1 x_1(t) + c_2 x_2(t)$. Once we know a fundamental system $x_1(t)$, $x_2(t)$ of the homogeneous equation, to obtain the general solution of the non-homogeneous equation $P(D^2)x(t) = y(t)$ it is sufficient to find a particular solution to the non-homogeneous equation. This particular solution can be found by applying Lagrange's method, which is also referred to as the variation of arbitrary constants method. In practice one seeks to find a particular solution with the form $x_0(t) = v_1(t) x_1(t) + v_2(t) x_2(t)$, where the linear combination of $x_1(t)$, $x_2(t)$ has the unknown functions $v_1(t)$, $v_2(t)$ instead of the arbitrary constants c_1, c_2. Among functions $v_1(t)$, $v_2(t)$, we can choose those which simultaneously satisfy

$$v_1'(t)x_1(t) + v_2'(t)x_2(t) = 0$$
$$v_1'(t)x_1'(t) + v_2'(t)x_2'(t) = y(t)$$

The determinant of this system coincides with the Wronskian $W[x_1(t), x_2(t)]$ of the fundamental set of solutions to the homogeneous equation $P(D^2)x(t) = 0$. It must be different from zero. By solving for $v_1'(t)$ and $v_2'(t)$ we obtain

$$v_1'(t) = -\frac{y(t)x_2(t)}{W[x_1(t), x_2(t)]}; v_2'(t) = \frac{y(t)x_1(t)}{W[x_1(t), x_2(t)]}$$

By integrating, it follows that

$$v_1(t) = -\int \{[y(t)x_2(t)]/W[x_1(t), x_2(t)]\}dt \quad \text{and}$$

$$v_2(t) = \int \{[y(t)x_1(t)]/W[x_1(t), x_2(t)]\}dt$$

Therefore the general solution to the second-order non-homogeneous equation is

$$x(t) = x_0(t) + z(t) = [\int \{[y(t)x_2(t)]/W[x_1(t), x_2(t)]\}dt + c_1]x_1(t) +$$

$$[\int \{[y(t)x_1(t)]/W[x_1(t), x_2(t)]\}dt + c_2]x_2(t)$$

A.4 Linear differential equations with constant coefficients: General theory and solution to n-order equations

In many applications linear differential equations are linear differential equations with constant coefficients. The normal form of this equation of order n is

$$x^{(n)} + a_1 x^{n-1} + \ldots + a_{n-1}x' + a_n x = y(t)$$

where $a_1, \ldots, a_{n-1}, a_n$ are n real constants. It is convenient to distinguish between autonomous equations and non-autonomous equations. Autonomous linear equations have a forcing term independent of time, that is, y(t) is also a constant, $y(t) = b$. To find the solution, the general properties of the solutions of linear equations are used.

First the set of fundamental solutions to the complementary homogeneous equation is found, then a particular solution of the non-homogeneous equation is found. The general solution to the non-homogeneous equation is obtained by adding the general solution to the homogeneous equation to the particular solution to the non-homogeneous equation. Therefore, let us consider the equation $P(D^n)x(t) = 0$. We shall see that $x(t) = e^{\lambda t}$ (where λ is a constant to be determined) verifies $P(D^n)e^{\lambda t} = 0$, that is, functions of type $x(t) = e^{\lambda t}$ are integrals of homogeneous linear equation with constant coefficients $P(D^n)x(t) = 0$. Indeed, by substituting the exponential function $e^{\lambda t}$ for x(t) in $P(D^n)x(t) = 0$ we obtain

$$e^{\lambda t}[\lambda^n + a_1\lambda^{n-1} + \ldots + a_{n-1}\lambda + a_n] = 0$$

For $e^{\lambda t}$ to verify $P(D^n)(e^{\lambda t}) = 0$ it is necessary and sufficient that the constant be selected so that it verifies the algebraic equation $P(\lambda^n) = 0$. Three cases must be distinguished:

a) the algebraic equation $P(\lambda^n) = 0$ admits n real roots $\lambda_1, \lambda_2, \ldots, \lambda_n$. In this case the homogeneous linear equation with constant coefficients has n distinct integrals $(e_1^{\lambda t}, e_2^{\lambda t}, \ldots, e_n^{\lambda t})$ for which the Wronskian is $W(e_1^{\lambda}{}^t, e_2^{\lambda}{}^t, \ldots, e_n^{\lambda}{}^t) \neq 0$. Therefore, the integrals $(e_1^{\lambda}{}^t, e_2^{\lambda}{}^t, \ldots, e_n^{\lambda}{}^t)$ constitute a fundamental system of solutions, and by virtue of the general theory we can say the general solution to the homogeneous linear equation is a linear combination of those integrals, that is

$$z(t) = c_1 e^{\lambda_1 t} + c_2 e^{\lambda_2 t} + \ldots + c_n e^{\lambda_n t}$$

b) the algebraic equation $P(\lambda^n) = 0$ admits multiple roots. Counting the repeated roots only once, let $\lambda_1, \lambda_2, \ldots, \lambda_s$ be the resulting distinct roots, so that $s < n$. Let $r_1, r_2, \ldots, r_s$ be the multiplicity of each distinct roots of s, so that $r_1 + r_2 + \ldots + r_s = n$. If λ_i is a root with multiplicity r_i the equation $P(D^n)(e^{\lambda_i t}) = 0$ admits the $r_i - 1$ integrals $(te^{\lambda_i t}, t^2 e^{\lambda_i t}, \ldots, t r_i e^{\lambda_i t})$ in addition to the integral $e^{\lambda_i t}$. The general solution to the homogeneous equation $P(D^n)x(t) = 0$ therefore is a linear combination of the type

$$z(t) = c_1 [e^{\lambda_1 t} + \sum_{j=1}^{r_1-1} b_{1j} t^j e^{\lambda_1 t}] + c_2 [e^{\lambda_2 t} + \sum_{j=1}^{r_2-1} b_{2j} t^j e^{\lambda_2 t}] + \ldots$$

$$+ c_s [e^{\lambda_s t} + \sum_{j=1}^{r_s-1} b_{sj} t^j e^{\lambda_2 t}]$$

c) the algebraic equation $P(\lambda^n) = 0$ among the n's roots $\lambda_1, \lambda_2,..., \lambda_n$ admits some complex roots. This is possible even if the coefficients $a_1 ,.., a_n$ are all real. Complex roots occur in complex conjugate pairs $a \pm i\theta$. Therefore, if a root $\lambda = a + i\theta$ has multiplicity r, the equation $P(\lambda^n) = 0$ also admits the root $a - i\theta$ with the same multiplicity. In addition to solution $e^{(a+i\theta)t}$, the equation $P(D^n)x(t) = 0$ admits $2r - 1$ integrals $[e^{(a-i\theta)t}, t\,e^{(a+i\theta)t}, t^2 e^{(a+i\theta)t}, \ldots, t^{r-1} e^{(a+i\theta)t}]$. Moreover the combinations $[(1/2)t^q e^{(a+i\theta)t} + (1/2)t^q e^{(a-i\theta)t};$ $(1/2)t^q\,e^{(a+i\theta)t} - (1/2)t^q\,e^{(a-i\theta)t}](q = 0, 1, \ldots, r - 1)$ are integrals of the equation $P(D^n)x(t) = 0$. By virtue of Euler's formulas for complex numbers these combinations can be rewritten in the trigonometric form $[t^q e^{at} \cos\theta t ; t^q e^{at} \sin\theta t]$. As a consequence of b) and c) we can state the following

Proposition A.3

The general solution to the equation $P(D^n)x(t) = 0$ is a linear combination with arbitrary constant coefficients of real solutions of the kind

1. $(te^{\lambda t}, t^2 e^{\lambda t},\ldots, t^{r-1}e^{\lambda t})$ *for each real root of the equation $P(\lambda^n) = 0$ with multiplicity $r - 1$;*
2. $(e^{at} \cos\theta t; te^{at} \cos\theta t,\ldots, t^{r-1}e^{at} \cos\theta t; e^{at} \sin\theta t, te^{at} \sin\theta t,\ldots, t^{r-1}e^{at} \sin\theta t)$ *for each complex conjugate pair of roots $\pm ti\theta$ of the equation $P(\lambda^n) = 0$ with multiplicity r.*

The complete solution to the equation $P(D^n)x(t) = y(t)$ is obtained by finding a particular solution $x_0(t)$ to be added to the general solution to the homogeneous equation $P(D^n)x(t) = 0$. To find $x_0(t)$ we can apply Cauchy's method (see references) or the method of undetermined coefficients. The latter exploits a principle that seeks as a particular solution some function similar to y(t), with the coefficients determined by substituting $x_0(t)$ and its derivative into $P(D^n)x(t) = 0$. The unknown coefficients are solved by equating equal powers of x.

A.5   Specific cases: Solutions to first- and second-order linear differential equations with constant coefficients

The autonomous first-order non-homogeneous linear differential equation with constant coefficients is

$$x'(t) = ax(t) + b$$

where $a \neq 0$ is a constant. The complementary homogeneous equation is $x'(t) - ax = 0$. According to the general theory, the function $e^{\lambda t}$ is an integral of the homogeneous equation if $e^{\lambda t}(\lambda - a) = 0$. This is true for $\lambda = a$, so that $z(t) = ce^{at}$, where c is arbitrary constant. This is the general solution to the homogeneous first-order linear differential equation with constant coefficients. A particular solution to the non-homogeneous equation can be found by enforcing stationary condition $x'(t) = 0$. The particular solution becomes $x = -(b/a)$ and the general solution to the non-homogeneous equation is

$$x(t) = x_0(t) + z(t) = -(b/a) + ce^{at}$$

A unique solution is obtained by enforcing an initial condition $x_0 = -(b/a) + c$, with x_0 given, and by finding the constant c. The autonomous second-order non-homogeneous linear differential equation with constant coefficients is

$$x''(t) = a_1 x'(t) + a_2 x(t) + b$$

The complementary homogeneous equation is $x''(t) - a_1 x'(t) - a_2 x(t) = 0$ which has solutions like $e^{\lambda t}$ if λ solves the algebraic equation $\lambda^2 - a_1 \lambda - a_2 = 0$. Letting λ_1 and λ_2 be the roots of this algebraic equation, the general solution to the homogeneous differential equation is

$$z(t) = c_1 e^{\lambda_1 t} + c_1 e^{\lambda_2 t}$$

Since $\lambda_{1,2} = (1/2) \pm \sqrt{[a_1(a_1^2 + 4a_2)]}$ three cases are possible:

1. $a_1^2 + 4\,a_2 > 0$. The algebraic equation has two real roots;
2. $a_1^2 + 4\,a_2 = 0$. The algebraic equation has only one real root with a multiplicity of order two, so that in addition to solution $e^{\lambda t}$ the homogeneous differential equation also admits the solution $te^{\lambda t}$. In this case the general solution to the homogeneous differential equation is $z(t) = e^{\lambda t}(c_1 + c_1 t)$;
3. $a_1^2 + 4a_2 < 0$. The algebraic equation has complex conjugate roots. By letting $a = (1/2)a_1$ and $\theta = [(a_1^2/4) + a_2]^{1/2}$ we have $\lambda = a \pm i\theta$ so that the solution to the homogeneous differential equation is $z(t) = e^{at}(c_1 e^{i\theta t} + c_2 e^{-i\theta t})$, that is $z(t) = e^{at}$ $(a_1 \cos\theta t + a_2 \,\text{sen}\,\theta t)$
   where a_1 and a_2 are two arbitrary constants.

A particular solution to the non-homogeneous equation can be found by using the stationary condition $x''(t) = x'(t) = 0$, from which it follows that $x_0(t) = -(b/a)$ and the general solution to the autonomous second-order non-homogeneous linear differential equation with constant coefficients becomes

$$x(t) = x_0(t) + z(t) = -(b/a) + e^{at}(a_1 \cos\theta t + a_2 \,\text{sen}\,\theta t)$$

where a_1, a_2 are constants to be determined by assigning the initial conditions $x(t_0) = x_0$; $x'(t_0) = x'_0$.

A.6 Linear systems of first-order differential equations with constant coefficients

In this section we shall consider linear systems of first-order differential equations but we shall limit our examination only to autonomous systems with constant coefficients. A linear first-order differential equation of n unknown functions $x_1(t)$, $x_2(t),..., x_n(t)$ with constant coefficients has the form

$$\dot{x}_1(t) = a_{11}x_1(t) + a_{12}x_2(t) + ... + a_{1n}x_n(t) + b_1$$
$$\dot{x}_2(t) = a_{21}x_1(t) + a_{22}x_2(t) + ... + a_{2n}x_n(t) + b_2$$
$$. ....$$
$$\dot{x}_n(t) = a_{n1}x_1(t) + a_{n2}x_2(t) + ... + a_{nn}x_n(t) + b_n$$

where a_{ij} and $b_i (i, j = 1, \ldots, n)$ are given coefficients. We can also apply the general theory of solutions to linear equations also for finding the solution to this system. Indeed, first we have to find the set of fundamental solutions to the complementary homogeneous system obtained for $b_1 = b_2 = \ldots = b_n = 0$. Then we must find a particular solution to the non-homogeneous system, so that the sum of the fundamental solutions to the homogeneous system and the particular solution to the non-homogeneous system gives the general solution to the non-homogeneous system.

Let us consider the homogeneous differential system

$$\dot{x}_1(t) = a_{11}x_1(t) + a_{12}x_2(t) + \ldots + a_{1n}x_n(t)$$
$$\dot{x}_2(t) = a_{21}x_1(t) + a_{22}x_2(t) + \ldots + a_{2n}x_n(t)$$

$$\dot{x}_n(t) = a_{n1}x_1(t) + a_{n2}x_2(t) + \ldots + a_{nn}x_n(t)$$

The n functions of type $x_1(t) = v_1 e^{\lambda t}$; $x_2(t) = v_2 e^{\lambda t}$; ...; $x_n(t) = v_n e^{\lambda t}$, where λ is undetermined and $v_1, v_2, \ldots, v_n$ are parameters to be determined, are a solution to the homogeneous differential system if, when we substitute in order the $x_i(t) = v_i e^{\lambda t} (i = 1, \ldots, n)$ in the respective equations, the following are verified

$$\lambda v_1 = a_{11}v_1 + a_{12}v_2 + \ldots + a_{1n}v_n$$
$$\lambda v_2 = a_{21}v_1 + a_{22}v_2 + \ldots + a_{2n}v_n$$

$$\lambda v_n = a_{n1}v_1 + a_{n2}v_2 + \ldots + a_{nn} v_n$$

that is

$$(\lambda - a_{11}) v_1 - a_{12} v_2 - \ldots \ldots \ldots \ldots - a_{1n}v_n = 0$$
$$-a_{21} v_2 + (\lambda - a_{22}) v_2 - \ldots \ldots \ldots \ldots - a_{2n}v_n = 0$$

$$-a_{n1}v_1 - a_{n2}v_2 - \ldots - a_{n,n-1} - v_{n-1} + (\lambda - a_{nn})v_n = 0$$

For a given λ, this system is a homogeneous system of linear algebraic equations for the unknown scalars $v_1, v_2, \ldots, v_n$. It has non-trivial solutions only if the determinant of the system is null, that is only if

$$\det(\lambda I - A) = \det \begin{bmatrix} (\lambda - a_{11}) & -a_{12} \ldots \ldots \ldots \ldots & -a_{1n} \\ -a_{21} & (\lambda - a_{22}) \ldots \ldots \ldots \ldots & -a_{2n} \\ \ldots \ldots \ldots \ldots \ldots \ldots \ldots \ldots \ldots \ldots \ldots \ldots \\ -a_{n1} & -a_{n2} \ldots \ldots \ldots \ldots \ldots (\lambda - a_{nn}) \end{bmatrix} = 0$$

This condition gives the characteristic equation for a homogeneous linear differential system with constant coefficients. The set of values for which λ nullifies the determinant is the set of eigenvalues for the characteristic matrix $(\lambda I - A)$. For each given eigenvalue λ_i the solutions $v_1, v_2, \ldots, v_n$ of the corresponding linear homogeneous system are called eigensolutions or eigenvectors of the system. To find the set of eigenvalues we expand the determinant of the characteristic equation and obtain an n-th order polynomial $P_A(\lambda^n)$ for the variable λ. Therefore when the determinant of the characteristic equation is null, we obtain the algebraic equation

$$P_A(\lambda^n) = \lambda^n + \alpha_1 \lambda^{n-1} + \alpha_2 \lambda^{n-2} + \ldots + \alpha_n = 0$$

where the coefficients α_1, α_2, .., α_n depend on the elements of matrix A (in particular, when $\lambda = 0$ we have det A $= \alpha_n$). The properties of the solutions to the characteristic equation $P_A(\lambda^n) = 0$ allow us, by analogy to the case of the n-order linear differential equation, to propose the following:

1. If the n roots $\lambda_1,..., \lambda_n$ of the characteristic equation $P_A(\lambda^n) = 0$ are real and distinct, the associated eigensolutions $(v_{11}, v_{21}..,v_{n1})$; $(v_{12}, v_{22}..,v_{n2})$; ... ...; $(v_{1n}, v_{2n}..,v_{nn})$ are linearly independent. Therefore, the general solution to the homogeneous linear differential system with constant coefficients is made up of n functions $[z_1(t), z_2(t),.., z_n(t)]$ each of which is a linear combination of the solutions

   $(v_{11} e^{\lambda_1 t}, v_{12} e^{\lambda_2 t} ,... v_{1n} e^{\lambda_n t})$; $(v_{21} e^{\lambda_1 t}, v_{22} e^{\lambda_2 t} ,... v_{2n} e^{\lambda_n t})$;.................;
   $v_{n1} e^{\lambda_1 t}, v_{n2} e^{\lambda_2 t} ,... v_{nn} e^{\lambda_n t})$.

   Note that the eigensolutions, or eigenvectors solving each system, are determined up to an arbitrary multiplicative constant. This means that each homogeneous system for each eigenvalue gives only $n - 1$ values of the unknowns, whereas one unknown for each eigensolution can be assigned arbitrarily. In the applications it is convenient to choose $v_{11} = v_{22} = v_{nn} = 1$, so that the resulting linear combinations give the following general solution to the homogeneous differential system

   $$z_1(t) = c_1 e^{\lambda_1 t} + c_2 v_{12} e^{\lambda_2 t} + \ldots + c_n v_{1n} e^{\lambda_n t}$$
   $$z_2(t) = c_1 v_{21} e^{\lambda_1 t} + c_2 e^{\lambda_2 t} + \ldots + c_n v_{2n} e^{\lambda_n t}$$
   $$\ldots\ldots\ldots\ldots\ldots\ldots\ldots\ldots\ldots\ldots\ldots\ldots\ldots\ldots\ldots\ldots\ldots$$
   $$z_n(t) = c_1 v_{n1} e^{\lambda_1 t} + c_2 v_{n2} e^{\lambda_2 t} + \ldots + c_n e^{\lambda_n t}$$

2. If the n roots of the characteristic equation $P_A(\lambda^n) = 0$ are real but $s < n$ are repeated, by letting $r_1,...,r_s$ be the multiplicity of each distinct root, so that $r_1 + \ldots + r_s = n$, then in addition to s integrals like $(e^{\lambda_1 t},..., e^{\lambda_s t})$ the homogeneous system also admits $r_i - 1$ integrals (i = 1,..., s) of the kind (t $e^{\lambda_1 t}$, t^2 $e^{\lambda_1 t},...,t^{r_1 - 1}$ $e^{\lambda_1 t}),...,$ (t $e^{\lambda_n t}$, t^2 $e^{\lambda_n t},...,t^{r_n - 1}$ $e^{\lambda_n t}$). It follows that, by letting $p_j(t_i^{r-1})$ $= c_{1j} t_i^{r-1} + c_{2j} t_i^{r-2} + \ldots + c_{ri-1,j} t + c_{nij}$ (i = 1,..., s; j = 1,...,s) the general solution to the homogeneous system with repeated roots is

   $$z_1(t) = p_{11}(t^{r_1-1}) e^{\lambda_1 t} + p_{12}(t^{r_2-1}) e^{\lambda_2 t} + \ldots p_{1s}(t^{r_s-1}) e^{\lambda_s t}$$
   $$z_2(t) = p_{21}(t^{r_1-1}) e^{\lambda_1 t} + p_{22}(t^{r_2-1}) e^{\lambda_2 t} + \ldots p_{2s}(t^{r_s-1}) e^{\lambda_s t}$$
   $$\ldots\ldots\ldots\ldots\ldots\ldots\ldots\ldots\ldots\ldots\ldots\ldots\ldots\ldots\ldots\ldots\ldots$$
   $$z_n(t) = p_{n1}(t^{r_1-1}) e^{\lambda_1 t} + p_{n2}(t^{r_2-1}) e^{\lambda_2 t} + \ldots p_{ns}(t^{r_s-1}) e^{\lambda_s t}$$

3. If some roots of the characteristic equation $P_A(\lambda^n) = 0$ are complex, the complex roots are conjugate complex numbers, a $\pm$ iθ because the matrix A of the homogeneous system has real coefficients. Therefore if a root λ = a+ iθ has a multiplicity of order r, the equation $P_A(\lambda^n) = 0$ also admits the root a – iθ with the same multiplicity. To be more specific, let q be the number of pairs of complex conjugate roots, each of multiplicity s_q so that if $r_1,...r_s$ is the multiplicity of remaining real roots and $r_1 + \ldots + r_s + 2s_1 + \ldots + 2s_q = n$, then the general solution of the homogeneous system is

$$z_1(t) = \sum_{i=1}^{s} p_{1i}(t^{r_i-1})e^{\lambda_i t} + \sum_{j=1}^{q} Q_{1j}(t^{s_j-1})e^{a_j t}\cos\theta_j t + \sum_{j=1}^{q} R_{1j}(t^{s_j-1})e^{a_j t}\sin\theta_j t$$

$$z_2(t) = \sum_{i=1}^{s} p_{2i}(t^{r_i-1})e^{\lambda_i t} + \sum_{j=1}^{q} Q_{2j}(t^{s_j-1})e^{a_j t}\cos\theta_j t + \sum_{j=1}^{q} R_{2j}(t^{s_j-1})e^{a_j t}\sin\theta_j t$$

....

$$z_n(t) = \sum_{i=1}^{s} p_{ni}(t^{r_i-1})e^{\lambda_i t} + \sum_{j=1}^{q} Q_{nj}(t^{s_j-1})e^{a_j t}\cos\theta_j t + \sum_{j=1}^{q} R_{nj}(t^{s_j-1})e^{a_s t}\sin\theta_j t$$

where $p_{hi}(t^{r_i})$; $Q_{hj}(t^{s_j})$; $R_{hj}(t^{s_j})$ (h= 1,...,n) are polynomials respectively of degree $r_i - 1$ (i = 1,...s); $s_j - 1$ (j = 1,...q); and $s_j - 1$ (j = 1,...q).

To conclude, it can be said for the general solution to the non-homogeneous differential system that the general principle of seeking a particular solution by taking n functions similar to forcing terms $y_1(t),...,y_n(t)$ with unknown coefficients, in the case of autonomous systems means to look for a particular solution that satisfies the stationary conditions

$$\dot{x}_1(t) = \dot{x}_2(t) = .. = \dot{x}_n(t) = 0.$$

A.7   Linear systems of two first order differential equations and phase plane analysis

In this section we shall consider the particular case of first-order linear systems of two equations in the unknown functions $x_1(t)$, $x_2(t)$. This case is the starting point for the analysis of the phase plane, extensively used in the main text. To simplify, here we change the notations and refer to the autonomous system of two differential equations as

$$\dot{x} = f(x, y)$$
$$\dot{y} = g(x, y)$$

The functions x(t), y(t) which solve the system can be considered the coordinates of points in the plane (x, y). The fact that these coordinates form a system means that in the plane (x, y) they are tied by a functional relationship. To detect this relationship we note that the ratio $\dot{y}/\dot{x}$ is equivalent to

$$dy/dx = g(x, y)/f(x, y)$$

The latter is a differential equation. Its general solution in the phase plane (x, y), is a family of curves called characteristic curves. A phase plane is characterised by the property that at most only one curve whose coordinates are components of the solution to the dynamic system $(\dot{x}, \dot{y})$ pass through each of its points. However, there are points where phase curves can intersect. These are singular points, where the theorem of uniqueness of solution fails, as well as stationary points where f(x, y) = 0 and g(x, y) = 0. To simplify, let us admit that there is a unique stationary point which without loss of generality can be assumed to be the origin of the phase plane (0, 0). The phase curves of the differential equation can be considered as solutions to a first-order linear system with constant coefficients. Indeed, approximating by Taylor's expansion of the first degree around the stationary point, we get

$$f(x, y) = [\partial f/\partial x](0, 0)x + [\partial f/\partial y](0, 0)y$$
$$g(x, y) = [\partial g/\partial x](0, 0)x + [\partial g/\partial y](0, 0)y$$

With a trivial change of notation $[\partial f/\partial x](0, 0) = a$; $[\partial f/\partial y](0, 0) = b$; $[\partial g/\partial x](0, 0) = c$; $[\partial g/\partial x](0, 0) = d$, Taylor's approximation is equivalent to the linear system

$$f(x, y) = ax + by$$
$$g(x, y) = cx + dy$$

Let A be the matrix of this system. By expanding the characteristic determinant condition $\det(\lambda I - A) = 0$ we obtain the following second order equation for λ

$$\lambda^2 - (\operatorname{tr} A)\lambda + \det A = 0$$

where $\operatorname{tr} A = a + d$ is the trace of det A, that is the sum of the elements on the principal diagonal of det A. Uniqueness of the stationary solution (0, 0) is guaranteed when $\det A \neq 0$.

The solutions to the second-order equation in λ allow us to classify singular points according to the following scheme:

1. If the discriminant of the characteristic equation is positive $\Delta = (\operatorname{tr} A)^2 - 4 \det A > 0$, the roots λ_1, λ_2 are real and distinct. The general solution to the system is

$$x(t) = c_1 v_{11} e^{\lambda_1 t} + c_2 v_{12} e^{\lambda_2 t}$$
$$y(t) = c_1 v_{21} e^{\lambda_1 t} + c_2 v_{22} e^{\lambda_2 t}$$

where c_1 and c_2 are arbitrary constants and $v_{11}v_{22} - v_{12}v_{21} \neq 0$
We can distinguish three sub-cases
1. a) Let $\lambda_1 < \lambda_2 < 0$. If $c_1 = c_2 = 0$, the solution to the system coincides with the origin of the phase plane. If $c_1 = 0$; $c_2 \neq 0$ the equation of the phase curve is

$$y/x = v_{22}/v_{21} \text{ that is } y = (v_{22}/v_{21})x$$

This is the equation for a line passing through the origin. Deprived of the origin, the equation describes two half-lines located to the right and left of the origin. By noting that both $x(t) \to 0$ and $y(t) \to 0$ as $t \to \infty$, it follows that the path along half-lines approaches the origin. Similarly, when $c_2 = 0$ the equation of the phase curve is $y = (v_{21}/v_{11})x$ which, deprived of the origin, describes two half-lines to the right and to the left of the origin. Location in the plane of the line containing these two half-lines depends on $(v_{21}/v_{11}) \gtrless (v_{22}/v_{12})$. Since as $t \to \infty$ both $x(t) \to 0$ and $y(t) \to 0$, the path along these half lines also approach the origin. In general, the equation for the phase curve is

$$y(t)/x(t) = \frac{c_1 v_{21} e^{\lambda_1 t} + c_2 v_{22} e^{\lambda_2 t}}{c_1 v_{11} e^{\lambda_1 t} + c_2 v_{12} e^{\lambda_2 t}}$$

As $t \to \infty$, for $c_1 \neq 0$ and $c_2 \neq 0$ the limit can be reduced to

$$\lim_{t \to \infty} [y(t)/x(t)] = \lim_{t \to \infty} \frac{[(c_1/c_2)v_{21}e^{(\lambda_1 t; -\lambda_2 t)} + 1]v_{22}}{[(c_1/c_2)v_{11}e^{(\lambda_1 t; -\lambda_2 t)} + 1]v_{12}} = \frac{v_{22}}{v_{12}}$$

Therefore all the characteristic curves approach the origin along a path similar to those followed by the two half-lines dividing the line $y = (v_{22}/v_{12})x$. At the origin the line is tangent to the characteristic curves so that graphical representation of trajectories in the phase plan looks like Figure A.1

The origin in Figure A.1 is called a *stable node*.

1. b) Let be $0 < \lambda_1 < \lambda_2$. In this case the trajectories are exactly the same as those in case (i), but the direction of the phase curve is symmetrically opposite, so that the origin is an *unstable node*.

1. c) Let be $\lambda_1 < 0 < \lambda_2$. If $c_1 = 0$ and $c_2 \neq 0$ again we obtain the equation for line y $= (v_{22}/v_{12})x$ deprived of the origin, but now $y(t) \to \pm \infty$ as $t \to \infty$ is verified. Therefore, the motion along the line $y = (v_{22}/v_{12})x$ leads away from the origin. On the contrary if $c_2 = 0$ and $c_1 \neq 0$ the motion along the line $y = (v_{21}/v_{11})x$ leads toward the origin. Since these lines are asymptotes of the characteristic curve, the phase curve looks like Figure A.2. The origin in this case is a *saddle point*. If $\lambda_2 < 0 < \lambda_1$, the figure is exactly the same but the orientation of the phase curve is opposite to that in Figure A.2

2. If the discriminant of the characteristic equation is null $\Delta = (tr\, A)^2 - 4\, det A = 0$, the roots λ_1, λ_2 are real and equal. Here we can distinguish two sub-cases.

2. a) If the matrix $[\lambda I - A]$ has rang zero, the general solution to the system is

$$x(t) = (c_1 v_{11} + c_2 v_{12})e^{\lambda t}$$
$$y(t) = (c_1 v_{21} + c_2 v_{22})e^{\lambda t}$$

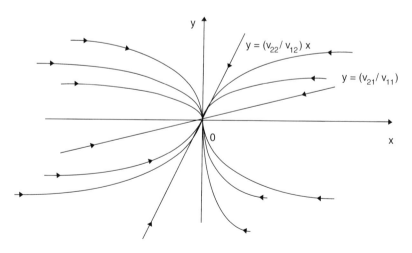

Figure A.1   Stable node

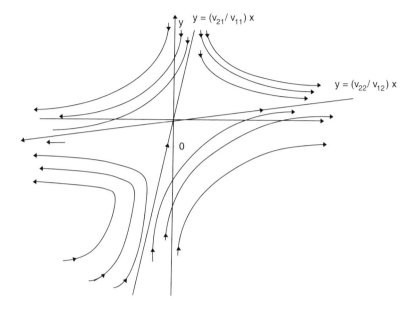

$y = (v_{21}/v_{11})\,x$

$y = (v_{22}/v_{12})\,x$

0

Figure A.2   Saddle point

The equation of the phase curves is

$$y(t)/x(t) = \frac{(c_1 v_{11} + c_2 v_{12})}{(c_1 v_{11} + c_2 v_{12})} = d$$

Thus, the curves have the form $y = dx$ which defines a line passing through the origin. If $\lambda_1 = \lambda_2 = \lambda < 0$, the direction of the motion is towards the origin in Figure A.3. In this case the origin is a stable proper node.

In the case where $\lambda > 0$, the direction of motion is reversed and the proper node is unstable.

2. b) If matrix $[\lambda I\text{-}A]$ has rang 1, the general solution to the system is

$$x(t) = (c_1 v_{11} t + c_2 v_{12})e^{\lambda t}$$
$$y(t) = (c_1 v_{21} t + c_2 v_{22})e^{\lambda t}$$

If $c_1 = 0$ and $c_2 \neq 0$ the line deprived of the origin is $y = (v_{22}/v_{12})x$. If $c_2 = 0$ and $c_1 \neq 0$ the line deprived of the origin is $y = (v_{21}/v_{11})x$. For any characteristic curve with $c_1 \neq 0$ and $c_2 \neq 0$ the equation is

$$y(t)/x(t) = \frac{c_1 v_{21} + c_2 v_{22}/t}{c_1 v_{11} + c_2 v_{12}/t}$$

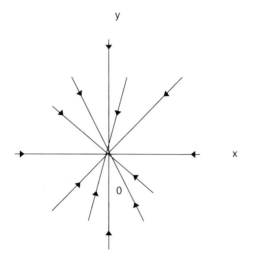

Figure A.3   A proper stable node

As $t \to \infty$, $\lim [y(t)/x(t)] = v_{21}/v_{11}$. If $\lambda_1 = \lambda_2 = \lambda < 0$, the origin is a stable *improper node*. Its graph is the same as Figure A.1. If $\lambda_1 = \lambda_2 = \lambda > 0$, the improper node is unstable.

3. If the discriminant of the characteristic equation is negative $\Delta = (\text{tr } A)^2 - 4 \det A < 0$, the roots λ_1, λ_2 are complex conjugate $\lambda_{1,2} = a \pm i\theta$. Here we can distinguish two sub-cases.

    3. a) If the real part of the roots is null $a = 0$, the general solution to the system is

    $$x(t) = c_1 v_{11} \cos \theta t + c_2 v_{12} \sin \theta t$$
    $$y(t) = c_1 v_{21} \cos \theta t + c_2 v_{22} \sin \theta t$$

    It can be demonstrated that these are the parametric equations of an elipse centred at $(0, 0)$. The direction of the motion along the elipse depends on the coefficient of the term cx in the equation $y(t)$ of the initial linear dynamic system. If $c > 0$, the motion is counterclockwise, as in Figure A.4. If $c < 0$, the motion is clockwise, opposite to that in Figure A.4.

    The origin in case (3) is called a centre.

    3. b) If the real part of the roots is not null $a \neq 0$, the general solution to the system is

    $$x(t) = e^{at}[c_1 v_{11} \cos \theta t + c_2 v_{12} \sin \theta t]$$
    $$y(t) = e^{at}[c_1 v_{21} \cos \theta t + c_2 v_{22} \sin \theta t]$$

    These are the parametric equations of a logarithmic spiral, which spirals towards the origin if $a < 0$, and spirals away from the origin if $a > 0$. The direction of the motion depends on the sign of parameter c, as represented in Figure A.5.

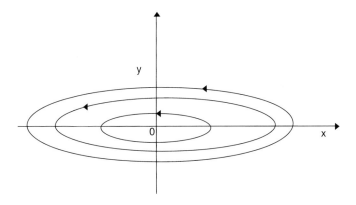

Figure A.4 Centre

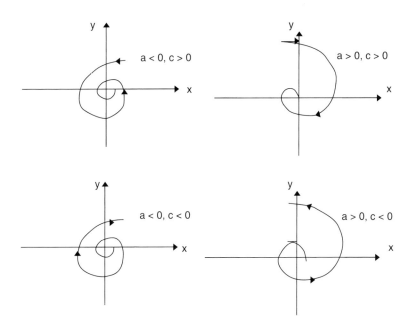

Figure A.5 Spirals

The classification of stationary points can also be made according to two parameters of the system, trace TrA and the determinant detA. The condition $\Delta = 0$ gives $detA = (TrA/2)^2$. This equation in plane (TrA, detA) corresponds to a parabola with its minimum at the origin (0, 0). Therefore it is possible to produce Figure A.6 which shows all the possible cases previously considered.

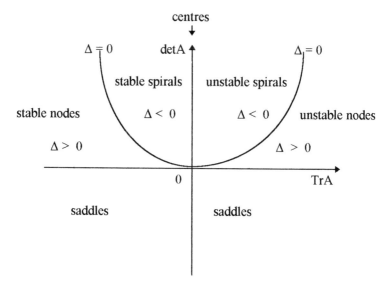

Figure A.6 A diagrammatic classification of stationary points for the linear differential system

A.8 Steady states and stability conditions for linear systems of first-order differential equations with constant coefficients

In this section we refer to a dynamic first-order autonomous system with the notation

$$\dot{x} = f(x(t))$$

with $f : R^n \to R^n$ a vector of functions. We start by defining a stationary solution or steady state.

Definition A.1

A point $x^\star \in R^n$ is a stationary solution or steady state of the system $\dot{x} = f(x(t))$ if it is a zero of the vector of functions $f(x)$, that is if it verifies $f(x^\star) = 0$.

A stationary solution is such that $x(t) = x^\star$ for each t. We are interested in the behaviour of trajectories different from steady state and want to compare their tendency to the steady state as $t \to +\infty$. Two concepts of stability are particularly relevant. Let us introduce the notation $x(t, t_0, x_0)$ to indicate the solution of a dynamic system for an arbitrary initial condition (t_0, x_0). We say that a steady state $x^\star$ is *stable* (or even stable *in Liapunovs sense*) if any solution near steady state remains near steady state. Similarly, we say that a steady state $x^\star$ is *asymptotically stable* (or even locally stable) if any solution near steady state converges to steady state. Let the symbol ‖ x ‖ be a norm of the generic vector x. These definitions of stability are formally equivalent to

Definition A.2 (Stability)

The steady state x^* is stable for the dynamic system $\dot{x} = f(x(t))$ if for any $\varepsilon > 0$ there is a $\delta > 0$ such that for $\| x_0 - x^* \| < \delta$ it is $\| x(t, t_0, x_0) - x^* \| < \varepsilon$.

Definition A.3 (Asymptotic stability)

The steady state x^* is asymptotically stable for the dynamic system $\dot{x} = f(x(t))$ if it is stable for the dynamic system and the constant $\delta > 0$ can be chosen so that if $\| x_0 - x^* \| < \delta$ then $\lim_{t \to +\infty} \| x(t, t_0, x_0) - x^* \| = 0$.

A basin of attraction or region of asymptotic stability is defined as the largest neighbourhood from which any solution entering into a neighbourhood with a radius lesser than the radius of the basin of attraction converges to steady state. When the region of asymptotic stability coincides with the entire dominion of $f(\cdot)$ in R^n, the steady state is said to be globally stable. Formally therefore we have

Definition A.4 (Global stability)

The steady state x^* is globally stable for the dynamic system $\dot{x} = f(x(t))$ if $\lim_{t \to +\infty} \| x (t, t_0, x_0) - x^* \| = 0$ for every $x(t, t_0, x_0) \in R^n$ solution of $\dot{x} = f(x(t))$.

A classical result for the solutions of a homogeneous linear system with constant coefficients $\dot{x} = Ax(t)$, where $x \in R^n$ and A is a matrix (n x n), is contained in

Theorem A.3

Let $x(t, 0) = 0$ be a steady state of the linear system with constant coefficients $\dot{x} = Ax(t)$. (i) The solution $x (t, 0) = 0$ is globally stable if, and only if, the real parts of the eigenvalues of A are all negative; (ii) The solution $x(t, 0) = 0$ is stable (in Liapunov sense) if all the real parts of the eigenvalues of A are non-positive and the eigenvalues with real part zero are not repeated.

Stability conditions contemplated by Theorem A.3 for the homogeneous systems can be easily extended to the non-homogeneous systems $\dot{x} = Ax(t) + b$. Indeed, since A is non-singular, it is possible to define $y = x + A^{-1}b$, so that the non-homogeneous system becomes $\dot{y} = Ax(t) + A^{-1}Ab = A(x(t) + A^{-1}b) = Ay$.

The following theorems are true:

Theorem A.4

The real parts of the eigenvalues of matrix A are negative if, and only if,
i) Matrix A is symmetric and negative definite
ii) Matrix $B = (A + A')/2$, where A' is the transposed matrix of A, is negative definite
iii) When all the elements of matrix A are nonnegative, $a_{ij} \geq 0$ for $i \neq j$ and the leading principal minors alternate in sign, starting from minus.

Theorem A.5

The real parts of eigenvalues of matrix A are negative if matrix A has negative diagonal dominance: if $a_{ii} < 0$ and $| a_{ii} | > \sum\limits_{\substack{i=1 \\ j \neq i}}^{n} | a_{ij} |$ or $| a_{ii} | > \sum\limits_{\substack{j=1 \\ i \neq j}}^{n} | a_{ij} |$

Theorem A.6

If the real parts of the eigenvalues of matrix A are negative then the following must be true
i) tr $A = \sum\limits_{i=1}^{n} a_{ij} < 0$
ii) sign det $A = (-1)^n$

The conditions of Theorem A.6 are those reproduced in Section A.7 Figure A.6 for the differential system 2×2. Since the characteristic equation for the 2×2 system is $\lambda^2 - (\text{tr A})\lambda + \det A = 0$, $\text{tr A} = \lambda_1 + \lambda_2$ and $\det A = \lambda_1\lambda_2$, we deduce the following

i)   if the system is stable, then $\det A > 0$ and $\text{tr A} < 0$; and
ii) if $\det A < 0$, the roots must have the opposite sign.

Therefore in case ii, the system is unstable, and steady state x^* is a saddle point.

A.9 Saddle point instability and stability of dynamics in economics

In the former classification of steady state a saddle point is an unstable steady state. Nevertheless many economic models with saddle point steady states are said to have 'stable' saddle point. To clarify this, let us refer to the homogeneous linear $n \times n$ system

$$\dot{x}_1(t) = a_{11}x_1(t) + a_{12}x_2(t) + \ldots + a_{1n}x_n(t)$$
$$\dot{x}_2(t) = a_{21}x_1(t) + a_{22}x_2(t) + \ldots + a_{2n}x_n(t)$$
$$\ldots\ldots\ldots\ldots\ldots\ldots\ldots\ldots\ldots\ldots\ldots\ldots\ldots\ldots\ldots\ldots\ldots\ldots\ldots$$
$$\dot{x}_n(t) = a_{n1}x_1(t) + a_{n2}x_2(t) + \ldots + a_{nn}x_n(t)$$

Assume that the n eigenvalues of the characteristic polynomial $\lambda_1, \ldots, \lambda_n$, are distinct so that the general solution to the differential system is

$$x_1(t) = c_1 e^{\lambda_1 t} + c_2 v_{12} e^{\lambda_2 t} + \ldots + c_n v_{1n} e^{\lambda_n t}$$
$$x_2(t) = c_1 v_{21} e^{\lambda_1 t} + c_2 e^{\lambda_2 t} + \ldots + c_n v_{2n} e^{\lambda_n t}$$
$$\ldots\ldots\ldots\ldots\ldots\ldots\ldots\ldots\ldots\ldots\ldots\ldots\ldots\ldots\ldots\ldots\ldots\ldots\ldots$$
$$x_n(t) = c_1 v_{n1} e^{\lambda_1 t} + c_2 v_{n2} e^{\lambda_2 t} + \ldots + c_n e^{\lambda_n t}$$

If steady state is a saddle point, some eigenvalues are positive and the remaining are negative. With appropriate changes in the indexes, it is always possible to arrange the eigenvalues so that $\lambda_1 < 0, \ldots \lambda_k < 0$ and $\lambda_{k+1} > 0, \ldots \lambda_n > 0$. The system has a unique solution for the Cauchy's problem with n initial conditions $x_1(t_0) = x_{01}; \ldots; x_n(t_0) = x_{0n}$. Except for one particular case, this solution determines trajectories that diverge from steady state.

Now let us assume that initial conditions are $x_1(t_0) = x_{01}; \ldots; x_k(t_0) = x_{0k}; x_{k+1}(t_0) =$ whatever;$\ldots; x_n(t_0) =$ whatever. In this case the initial conditions are less than the number of functions to be determined, and in general the Cauchy's problem admits infinite solutions, depending on the n-k initial arbitrary conditions. To establish an appropriate terminology, it is useful to separate the solutions to this dynamic system into two groups. We call those variables whose initial conditions in the Cauchy's problem are given *predetermined variables*, and call those variables whose initial conditions in the Cauchy's problem are free *non-predetermined variables*. On this basis we can formulate

Proposition A.4

Consider a homogeneous linear differential system with constant coefficients $\dot{x} = Ax$, where $x \in R^n$. Assume the n eigenvalues of the associated characteristic system are distinct, and such that $\lambda_1 < 0, \ldots \lambda_k < 0; \lambda_{k+1} > 0, \ldots \lambda_n > 0$. If the system admits predetermined variables *in the same number k of negative eigenvalues, it is always possible to determine a set of initial conditions for the non-predetermined variables so that Cauchy's problem has a unique solution. This unique solution is stable.*

Proof: It is sufficient to reformulate Cauchy's problem with the initial conditions

$x_1(t_0) = x_{01}$

....

$x_k(t_0) = x_{0k}$;
$x_{k+1}(t_0) = c_1 v_{11} + c_2 v_{12} + \ldots + c_k v_{1k}$

....

$x_n(t_0) = c_1 v_{n1} + c_2 v_{n2} + \ldots + c_k v_{nk}$

In the conditions stated, the unique solution is

$x_1(t) = c_1 v_{11} e^{\lambda_1 t} + c_2 v_{12} e^{\lambda_2 t} + \ldots + c_k v_{1k} e^{\lambda_k t}$
$x_2(t) = c_1 v_{21} e^{\lambda_1 t} + c_2 v_{22} e^{\lambda_2 t} + \ldots + c_k v_{2k} e^{\lambda_k t}$

....

$x_n(t) = c_1 v_{n1} e^{\lambda_1 t} + c_2 v_{n2} e^{\lambda_2 t} + \ldots + c_k v_{nk} e^{\lambda_k t}$

Since $\lambda_1 < 0, \ldots \lambda_k < 0$, the solution is stable because as $t \to \infty$ it converges to steady state $(0, \ldots, 0)$.

References

Arnold, V. (1973) *Ordinary Differential Equations* (Cambridge MA: MIT Press).

Aziariadis, C. (1993) *Intertemporal Macroeconomics* (Cambridge MA: Blackwell)

Buiter, W. (1984) 'Saddle Point Problems in Continuos Time Rational Expectations Models: A General Method and Some Macroeconomic Example', *Economica, 52, 3*, pp. 665–80.

Black, F. (1974) 'Uniqueness of the Price Level in Monetary Growth Models with Rational Expectations', *Journal of Economic Theory, 7*, pp. 53–65.

Blanchard, O.J. and C.M. Kahn (1980) 'The Solution of Linear Difference Models under Rational Expectations', *Econometrica, 48, 5*, pp. 1305–11.

Brock, W.A. and A.G. Malliaris (1989) *Differential Equations, Stability and Chaos in Dynamic Economics* (Amsterdam: Elsevier).

Burmeister, E. (1980), 'On Some Conceptual Issues in Rational Expectations Modelling', *Journal of Money, Credit and Banking, 12, 4, Part 2*, pp. 800–16.

Chirichiello, G. (1993) *Equazioni e Sistemi Lineari differenziali e alcuni Modelli Dinamici Macroeconomici (Differential Linear Equations and Systems, and Some Dynamic Macroeconomic Models)* (Rome: OCSM).

Gandolfo, G. (1996) *Economic Dynamics* (Berlin: Springer-Verlag).

Ghizetti, A. and F. Rosati (1993) *Analisi Matematica (Mathematical Analysis)*, Vol. II, (Milan: Masson).

Jordan, D. W. and P. Smith (1992) *Nonlinear Ordinary Differential Equations* (Oxford: Oxford University Press).

Sargent T. and N. Wallace (1973) 'The Stability of Models of Money and Growth With Perfect Foresight', *Econometrica, 41, 6*, pp. 1043–48.

Sargent, T. and N. Wallace, (1973) 'Rational Expectations and The Dynamics of Hyperinflation', *International Economic Review*, 14, 2, pp. 328–50.
Stanpacchia, G. (1973) *Lezioni di Analisi Matematica (Lectures on Mathematical Analysis)*, Vol. II (Neaples: Liguori).

Appendix B: Difference equations and systems of difference equations

B.1 Difference equations: General theory and existence of solutions. Linear difference equations

The equation

$$F(t, x_t, x_{t+1}, \ldots, x_{t+n}) = 0$$

involving an independent variable t which takes integer values, and the terms x_t, $x_{t+1}, \ldots, x_{t+n}$, of an unknown sequence $\{x_t\}$, is an ordinary difference equation of order n. The order of the equation is the difference between the greatest integer t+n and the initial integer t. The term 'ordinary' indicates that the unknown sequence is defined over a set of integer numbers. If the relationship $F(\cdot)$ can be solved for the term indexed with highest integer, we can write

$$x_{t+n} = f(t, x_t, x_{t+1}, \ldots, x_{t+n-1})$$

in which case the ordinary difference equation of order n is in the normal form.
 A solution to the ordinary difference equation of order n is a sequence $\{x_t\}$ whose n terms are spaced at unit time intervals and satisfy the relationship $x_{t+n} = f(t, \cdot)$. If there are n initial conditions, $x_0, \ldots, x_{n-1}$, the solution to the difference equation can be constructed by reiterating the function $f(\cdot)$ n times. The following theorem is valid

Theorem B.1

Let $f(t, x_t, x_{t+1}, \ldots, x_{t+n-1})$ be a real valued function defined on the set of the integer numbers $\{t, t+, t+2, \ldots\}$. For any assigned n-tple of initial conditions $x_0, \ldots, x_{n-1}$ there exists a unique sequence $\{x_t\}$ that satisfies the equation $x_{t+n} = f(t, x_t, x_{t+1}, \ldots, x_{t+n-1})$ for each $t \in N$.

These concepts can be applied to the special case n =1, which corresponds to a first-order ordinary difference equation $F(t, x_t, x_{t+1}) = 0$. If the relationship $F(\cdot)$ can be solved for the term with the highest index, we can write $x_{t+1} = f(t, x_t)$ so that the ordinary difference equation of order 1 is in the normal form. If an initial value x_0 is given, a sequence $\{x_t\}$ is a solution to the equation $x_{t+1} = f(t, x_t)$ when the infinite terms of the sequence $\{x_t\}$ are obtained by reiterating the function $f(\cdot)$ infinite times. The Theorem B.1 of the existence and uniqueness of solution also can be applied to the first-order difference equation. An ordinary difference equation of order n is linear if, given n+2 real valued functions $b_0(t)$, $b_1(t), \ldots, b_n(t)$, $g(t)$, defined on the set of integers t, it can be written as

$$b_0(t), x_{t+n} + b_1(t)x_{t+n-1} + \ldots + b_{n-1}(t)x_{t+1} + b_n(t)x_t = g(t)$$

By assuming $b_0(t) \neq 0$ and defining $g(t)/b_0(t) = y(t)$; $b_1(t)/b_0(t) = a_1(t); \ldots$; $b_n(t)/b_0(t) = a_n(t)$ we obtain the first-order linear difference equation in normal form

$$x_{t+n} + a_1(t)x_{t+n-1} + \ldots + a_{n-1}(t)x_{t+1} + a_n(t)x_t = y(t)$$

The equation is homogeneous if y(t) = 0, otherwise it is non-homogeneous and the function y(t) on the set of indexes t is referred to as a forcing term or moving term. A property of solutions is stated in

Proposition B.1

If ({x_{1t}}, {x_{2t}}..., {x_{mt}}) are m solutions to the linear homogeneous difference equation of order n and $c_1, c_2, \ldots, c_m$ are m arbitrary constants, then the sequence {$c_1x_{1t} + c_2x_{2t}+\ldots +c_m x_{mt}$} is also a solution to the homogeneous difference equation of order n.

Another important property of solutions to the non-homogeneous linear equation is stated in

Proposition B.2

If {x_{0t}} is a solution to the linear non-homogeneous differential equation and {z_t} is a solution to the complementary homogeneous linear equation obtained when the forcing term is y(t) = 0, then the sum sequence {$x_{0t} + z_t$} is also a solution to the linear non-homogeneous differential equation. On the contrary, all solutions to non-homogeneous linear equation can be obtained by adding the solution to the homogeneous equation to a given solution to the non-homogeneous equation.

Proposition B.1 can be further qualified if we introduce the concept of a fundamental set of solutions. Consider a set of solutions {z_{1t}}, {z_{2t}}..., {z_{nt}} to the homogeneous difference equation consisting of the same number of sequences as the order of the difference equation. By virtue of Theorem B.1 for the existence and uniqueness of a solution, each solution is associated with a given set of n initial conditions. It is possible to construct a particular set of n distinct solutions {z^*_{1t}}, {z^*_{2t}}..., {z^*_{nt}} each of which corresponds to appropriate n initial conditions. Indeed, the i-th solution {z^*_{it}} can be defined for the initial conditions $x_{i0} = 1$; $x_{i1} = 0;\ldots$; $x_{in} = 0$. The set of n solutions obtained is called the fundamental set of solutions which are linearly independent, in the sense that the linear combination $c_1z^*_{1t}+c_2 z^*_{2t} + c_nz^*_{nt}$ is null only when $c_1= c_2=\ldots= c_n= 0$. This set of solutions can be used to construct the general solution to the n-order linear homogeneous difference equation according to

Theorem B.2

Consider the n-order linear homogeneous difference equation

$$x_{t+n} + a_1(t)x_{t+n-1} + \ldots + a_{n-1}(t)x_{t+1} + a_n(t)x_t = 0$$

If {z_t} is a solution, then it can be expressed as a linear combination of n fundamental solutions

$$z_t = c_1z^*_{1t} + c_2z^*_{2t} + \ldots + c_nz^*_{nt}$$

where $c_1, c_{2,\ldots,} c_n$ are arbitrary constants

It follows that if x_{0t} is a particular solution to the n-order non-homogeneous linear difference equation, the general solution to the non-homogeneous equation is

$$x_t = x_{0t} + z_t = x_{0t} + c_1 z_{1t}^* + c_2 z_{2t}^* + \ldots + c_n z_{nt}^*$$

Theorem B.2 can be extended to include

Proposition B.3

Every set of n linearly independent solutions $\{z_{1t}\}, \{z_{2t}\}\ldots,\{z_{nt}\}$ to the n-order linear homogeneous difference equation is a fundamental system of solutions.

As a corollary to proposition B.3 the general solution to the n-order homogeneous difference equation can be expressed as a linear combination of a linearly independent system of n solutions

$$z_t = c_1 z_{1t} + c_2 z_{2t} + \ldots + c_n z_{nt}$$

where $c_1, c_{2,\ldots,} c_n$ are arbitrary constants.

B.2   Linear difference equations with constant coefficients: General theory and properties of solutions

A n-order linear difference equation with constant coefficients in normal form is

$$x_{t+n} + a_1 x_{t+n-1} + \ldots + a_{n-1} x_{t+1} + a_n x_t = y_t$$

When $y_t = y$ is a constant for each t, the equation is called autonomous. To find a solution, we shall use the general properties of solutions to linear equations. Indeed, first the set of fundamental solutions to the complementary homogeneous equation is studied. Then a particular solution to the non-homogeneous equation is found. Finally, the general solution to the non-homogeneous equation is obtained as the sum of the general solution to the homogeneous equation and the particular solution to the non-homogeneous equation. Let us consider the equation $x_{t+n} + a_1 x_{t+n-1} + \ldots + a_{n-1} x_{t+1} + a_n x_t = 0$. The sequence $\{x_t\} = \{\lambda^t\}$ with λ constant to be determined verifies this equation. To simplify, in the following the generic term x_t also indicates the sequence $\{x_t\}$. If we substitute λ^t for x_t in the homogeneous equation we get

$$\lambda^t [\lambda^n + a_1 \lambda^{n-1} + \ldots + a_{n-1}\lambda + a_n] = 0$$

In order for an λ^t to verify this condition, the constant λ must be a solution to the algebraic equation $P(\lambda^n) = 0$. From this point on, the solution to the n-order homogeneous difference equation can be discussed in the same way as the n-order differential equation. Indeed, we can distinguish three cases:

a) the algebraic equation $P(\lambda^n) = 0$ admits n real roots $\lambda_1, \lambda_2, \ldots, \lambda_n$. In this case the homogeneous linear equation with constant coefficients admits n distinct geometric sequences $(\lambda_1^t, \lambda_2^t, \ldots, \lambda_n^t)$ which constitute a fundamental set of solutions. Therefore, in the light of the general theory we can say the general solution to the homogeneous linear equation is a linear combination of sequences

$$z(t) = c_1 e^{\lambda_1 t} + c_2 e^{\lambda_2 t} + \ldots + c_n e^{\lambda_n t}$$

where $c_1, c_2, \ldots, c_n$ are arbitrary constants. In the initial-condition problem, these n constants depend on the assigned n initial conditions;

b) the algebraic equation $P(\lambda^n) = 0$ admits multiple roots. By counting the repeated roots only once, let $\lambda_1, \lambda_2,\ldots, \lambda_s$ be the resulting distinct roots, so that $s < n$. Let $r_1, r_2,\ldots, r_s$ be the multiplicity of the distinct roots of s, so that $r_1 + r_2 +\ldots+ r_s = n$. If λ_i is a root with multiplicity r_i, the algebraic equation in addition to the sequence λ^t admits the $r-1$ sequences $(t\,\lambda^t, t^2\,\lambda^t,\ldots, t^{r-1}\lambda^t)$. The general solution to the homogeneous difference equation, therefore, is a linear combination

$$z(t) = c_1[\lambda_1^t + \sum_{j=1}^{r_1-1} b_{1j}t^j\lambda_1^t] + c_2[\lambda_2^t + \sum_{j=1}^{r_2-1} b_{2j}t^j\lambda_2^t] + \ldots + c_s[\lambda_s^t + \sum_{j=1}^{r_s-1} b_{sj}t^j\lambda_s^t]$$

c) the algebraic equation $P(\lambda^n) = 0$ among the n roots $\lambda_1, \lambda_2,\ldots, \lambda_n$ admits some complex roots even if all the coefficients $a_1,\ldots, a_n$ are real. Complex roots occur in complex conjugate pairs $a \pm i\theta$. Therefore, in addition to the solution $(a + i\theta)^t$, the homogeneous difference equation admits the $2r - 1$ sequences

$$[(a - i\theta)^t, t(a \pm i\theta)^t, t^2(a \pm i\theta)^t,\ldots, t^{r-1}(a \pm i\theta)^t]$$

By transforming complex numbers into polar coordinates $(a \pm i\theta) =$ $m (\cos \alpha \pm i \operatorname{sen} \alpha)$ (where $m = \sqrt{(a^2 + \theta^2)}$ is the modulus of the complex number) and by applying de Moivres formula (which implies $(\cos \alpha \pm i \operatorname{sen} \alpha)^t = \cos \alpha t \pm i \operatorname{sen} \alpha t$) the $2r - 1$ solutions associated with the complex solution $m^t (\cos \alpha t + i \operatorname{sen} \alpha t)$ are $[m^t (\cos \alpha t - i \operatorname{sen} \alpha t); tm^t(\cos \alpha t \pm i \operatorname{sen} \alpha t);\ldots; t^{r-1}m^t (\cos \alpha t \pm i \operatorname{sen} \alpha t)]$.
As a consequence of (b) and (c) we can state

Proposition B.4
The general solution to the normal n-order linear homogeneous difference equation with constant coefficients is a linear combination with arbitrary constant coefficients of the solutions

1. $(t\lambda^t, t^2\lambda^t,\ldots, t^{r-1}\lambda^t)$ *for each real root λ of the equation $P(\lambda^n) = 0$ with multiplicity $r - 1$;*
2. $(m^t \cos \alpha t ; tm^t\cos \alpha t,\ldots t^{r-1}m^t \cos \alpha t; m^t \sin \alpha\, t, t^t\, m^t \sin \alpha\, t,\ldots, t^{r-1}m^t \sin \alpha t)$ *for each complex conjugate pair of roots $a \pm i\theta$ of the equation $P(\lambda^n) = 0$ with multiplicity r.*

The complete solution to the non-homogeneous equation with the forcing term $y(t) \neq 0$ is obtained by finding a particular solution x_{0t} to be added to the general solution to the homogeneous equation. In the applications we choose a sequence whose terms are obtained from a function with the same form of $y(t)$ that has undetermined coefficients.

B. 3   Specific cases: Solutions to first and second-order linear difference equations with constant coefficients

The autonomous first-order linear difference equation with constant coefficients is

$$x_{t+1} = ax_t + b$$

where $a \neq 0$ is a constant. The complementary homogeneous equation is $x_{t+1} - ax_t = 0$. According to the general theory, the sequence λ^t is a solution to the homogeneous equation if it verifies $\lambda^t(\lambda - a) = 0$. This condition is verified for $\lambda = a$, so that $z_t = ca^t$ with c an arbitrary constant, is the general solution to the homogeneous first-order linear difference equation with constant coefficients. A particular solution to the autonomous non-homogeneous equation can be found by enforcing stationary conditions $x_{t+1} = x_t = x^\#$. The solution that satisfies this condition is $x^\# = [b/1 - a]$. Therefore the general solution to the non-homogeneous autonomous first-order linear difference equation with constant coefficients is

$$x_t = x^\# + z_t = (b/1 - a) + c\,a^t$$

The constant c can be found by enforcing a given initial condition $x_0 = (b/1 - a) + c$, from which $c = x_0 - (b/1 - a)$. Thus the unique dynamic path starting from x_0 is defined by the equation

$$x_t = (b/1 - a) + [x_0 - (b/1 - a)]a^t$$

The autonomous second-order linear difference equation with constant coefficients is

$$x_{t+2} = a_1 x_{t+1} + a_2 x_t + b$$

The complementary homogeneous equation is $x_{t+2} - a_1 x_{t+1} - a_2 x_t = 0$ which admits the sequence λ^t as a solution if λ solves the algebraic equation $\lambda^2 - a_1\lambda - a_2 = 0$. If λ_1 and λ_2 are the roots of this equation, the general solution to the second-order homogeneous differential equation is

$$z_t = c_1\lambda_1^t + c_2\lambda_2^t$$

Since $\lambda_{1,2} = (1/2)\,[a_1 \pm \sqrt{(a_1^2 + 4\,a_2)}]$, three cases are possible:

1. $a_1^2 + 4a_2 > 0$. The algebraic equation has two real roots;
2. $a_1^2 + 4a_2 = 0$. The algebraic equation has one real root with multiplicity of order two, so that in addition to solution λ^t the homogeneous differential equation admits $t\lambda^t$. Therefore, the general solution to the homogeneous differential equation is $z_t = \lambda^t(c_1 + c_2 t)$;
3. $a_1^2 + 4\,a_2 < 0$. The algebraic equation has complex conjugate roots. If $a = (1/2)a_1$ and $\theta = [(a_1^2/4) + a_2]^{1/2}$ then $\lambda = a \pm i\theta$. After applying the transformations $m \cos\alpha = (1/2)\,a_1$ and $m \sin\alpha = (1/2)\,\sqrt{(a_1^2 + 4\,a_2)}$, by using de Moivre's formula the solution to the homogeneous difference equation is

$$z_t = m^t(c_1 \cos t\alpha + c_2 \sin t\alpha)$$

where c_1 and c_2 are arbitrary constants.

A particular solution to the non-homogeneous difference equation can be obtained by enforcing a stationary condition $x_{t+2} = x_{t+1} = x_t = x^\#$.

A non-autonomous difference equation like $x_{t+1} = ax_t + b_t$ where the forcing term is an autonomous 'impulse' b_t from period to period, has frequent applications in economics. The fact that the forcing term is mobile over time prevents us from considering steady state to find a particular solution to the non-homogeneous equation. Two relevant particular solutions are those referred to in the literature as a *forward-looking* solution and a *backward-looking* solution. For forward-looking solution we mean the sequence obtained by solving iteratively for the future value

x_{t+1} (the significance here is the same as in Azariadis, 1993). Running subsequent substitutions for *n periods* we have

$$x_{t+1} = ax_t + b_t = a(ax_{t-1} + b_{t-1}) + b_t = a^2 x_{t-2} + (ab_{t-1} + b_t)$$
$$= a^2(ax_{t-3} + b_{t-3}) + (ab_{t-1} + b_t) = a^3 x_{t-3} + (a^2 b_{t-2} + ab_{t-1} + b_t)$$
$$= \ldots = a^{n-1}(ax_{t-n} + b_{t-n})(a^{n-1}b_{t-1} + a^{n-2}b_{t-2} + \ldots + a^2 b_{t-2} +$$

$$ab_{t-1} + a^0 b_t) = a^n x_{t-n} + \sum_{i=0}^{n-1} a^i b_{t-i}$$

We distinguish two cases for unique solution. The first case is the familiar Cauchy's problem with given initial conditions. The second case is a problem with some boundary conditions. Enforcing initial condition $x_{t=0} = x_0$ is equivalent to admitting terminal time t = n, so that a particular solution is $x_{t+1} = x_0 a^t + \sum_{i=0}^{t-1} a^i b_{t-i}$ and the general solution of the non-homogeneous difference equation having the forward-looking solution as a particular solution becomes

$$x_t = ca^t + \sum_{i=0}^{t-1} a^i b_{t-i}$$

Frequently, however, in the application there is no initial condition and time stretches to infinity $n \to \infty$. In this case a particular solution is

$$x_{t+1} = \lim_{n\to\infty} (a^n x_{t-n}) + \sum_{i=0}^{\infty} a^i b_{t-i}$$

In order for this expression to be definite, the limit of the first term to the right of equality must exist and be finite, and the series of the second term must be convergent. The first condition is verified when $|a| < 1$. The second is verified also when it is $|b_t| < L$, where L is a real positive finite number. By assuming both the conditions are true and by keeping in mind that if $|a| < 1$ then $\lim_{n\to\infty} (a^n x_{t-n}) = 0$, we can conclude that the general solution to the non-homogeneous difference equation admitting the forward-looking solution as a particular solution is

$$x_t = ca^t + \sum_{i=0}^{\infty} a^i b_{t-i}$$

where c is an arbitrary constant.

The backward-looking solution is obtained by solving iteratively for x_t and by assuming x_{t+n} is a terminal value. By letting $x_t = (1/a)x_{t+1} - (1/a)b_t$ and running subsequent substitutions for n periods we have

$$x_t = (1/a)^n x_{t+n} - (1/a) \sum_{i=0}^{n-1} (1/a)^i b_{t+i}$$

For a given terminal value x_{t+n} the expression just obtained for t = 1, . . . n, describes a sequence from current period t up to period t + n. As $n \to \infty$, the sequence x_t extends to an infinite future and its expression becomes

$$x_t = \lim_{n\to\infty} [(1/a)^n x_{t+n}] - (1/a) \sum_{i=0}^{\infty} (1/a)^i b_{t+i}$$

To be definite this expression must admit a finite limit for the first term to the right of equality and the series of the second term must be convergent. The first condition is verified when $|(1/a)| < 1$. The second also requires $|b_t| < L$, where L is a finite real positive number. Assume both these conditions are verified. If $|(1/a)| < 1$ then $\lim_{n \to \infty} (1/a)^n x_{t-n} = 0$, so that we can conclude that the general solution to the the difference equation admitting the backward-looking solution as a particular solution is

$$x_t = ca^t - (1/a) \sum_{i=0}^{\infty} (1/a)^i b_{t+i}$$

where c is an arbitrary constant.

B.4 Linear systems of first-order difference equations with constant coefficients

In this section we consider only the autonomous system of first-order difference equations with constant coefficients. A system of first-order difference equations with constant coefficients in the n unknown sequences $x(1)_t, x(2)_t, \ldots, x(n)_t$ has the form

$$x(1)_{t+1} = a_{11}x(1)_t + a_{12}x(2)_t + \ldots + a_{1n}x(n)_t + b_1$$
$$x(2)_{t+1} = a_{21}x(1)_t + a_{22}x(2)_t + \ldots + a_{2n}x(n)_t + b_2$$
$$\ldots\ldots\ldots\ldots\ldots\ldots\ldots\ldots\ldots\ldots\ldots\ldots\ldots\ldots\ldots$$
$$x(n)_{t+1} = a_{n1}x(1)_t + a_{n2}x(2)_t + \ldots + a_{nn}x(n)_t + b_n$$

A solution to this system is found by applying the general theory of the solutions to linear difference equations. Indeed, we first seek a set of fundamental solutions to the complementary homogeneous system obtained for $b_1 = b_2 = \ldots = b_n = 0$. Then we seek a particular solution to the non-homogeneous system, so that the general solution to the non-homogeneous system is obtained as the sum of the fundamental solutions to the homogeneous system and the particular solution to the non-homogeneous system.

Let us consider the homogeneous difference system

$$x(1)_{t+1} = a_{11}x(1)_t + a_{12}x(2)_t + \ldots + a_{1n}x(n)_t$$
$$x(2)_{t+1} = a_{21}x(1)_t + a_{22}x(2)_t + \ldots + a_{2n}x(n)_t$$
$$\ldots\ldots\ldots\ldots\ldots\ldots\ldots\ldots\ldots\ldots\ldots\ldots\ldots\ldots\ldots$$
$$x(n)_{t+1} = a_{n1}x(1)_t + a_{n2}x(2)_t + \ldots + a_{nn}x(n)_t$$

The n sequences $x(1)_t = v_1\lambda^t$; $x(2)_t = v_2\lambda^t; \ldots$; $x(n)_t = v_n\lambda^t$, where λ is undetermined and $v_1, v_2, \ldots, v_n$ are parameters to be determined, constitute a solution to the homogeneous system of difference equations when by substituting in order the $x(i)_t = v_i \lambda^t$ ($i = 1, \ldots, n$) in the respective equations, the following are verified

$$\lambda v_1 = a_{11}v_1 + a_{12}v_2 + \ldots + a_{1n}v_n$$
$$\lambda v_2 = a_{21}v_1 + a_{22}v_2 + \ldots + a_{2n}v_n$$
$$\ldots\ldots\ldots\ldots\ldots\ldots\ldots\ldots\ldots\ldots\ldots\ldots\ldots\ldots\ldots$$
$$\lambda v_n = a_{n1}v_1 + a_{n2}v_2 + \ldots + a_{nn}v_n$$

The discussion of solutions now follows the same line as the differential systems. Indeed by rewriting

$$(\lambda - a_{11})v_1 - a_{12}v_2 - \dotsb - a_{1n}v_n = 0$$
$$- a_{21}v_2 + (\lambda - a_{22})v_2 - \dotsb - a_{2n}v_n = 0$$
$$\dotsb$$
$$- a_{n1}v_1 - a_{n2}v_2 - \dots - a_{n,n-1}v_{n-1} + (-a_{nn})v_n = 0$$

for given λ we have a homogeneous system of linear algebraic equations for the unknown scalars v_1, v_2,..., v_n. The system has non-trivial solutions only if the determinant of the system is null, that is only if

$$\det(\lambda I - A) = \det \begin{bmatrix} (\lambda - a_{11}) & -a_{12}\dotsb & -a_{1n} \\ -a_{21} & (\lambda - a_{22})\dotsb & -a_{2n} \\ -a_{n1} & -a_{n2}\dotsb & (\lambda - a_{nn}) \end{bmatrix} = 0$$

The set of values for λ for which $\det(\lambda I - A) = 0$ is the set of eigenvalues for the characteristic matrix $(\lambda I - A)$. For each eigenvalue λ_i the solutions v_1, v_2,..., v_n of the homogeneous system are called eigensolutions or eigenvectors. The set of eigenvalues are the roots of the n-th order polynomial $P_A(\lambda^n)$ for the undetermined λ, that is the roots of the algebraic equation

$$P_A(\lambda^n) = \lambda^n + \alpha_1\lambda^{n-1} + \alpha_2\lambda^{n-2} + \dots + \alpha_n = 0$$

where the coefficients α_1, α_2, ... , α_n depend on the elements of matrix A (in particular if $\lambda = 0$ we have $\det A = \alpha_n$). Three cases can be distinguished

1. If the n roots λ_1,..., λ_n of the characteristic equation $P_A(\lambda^n) = 0$ are real and distinct, the associated eigensolutions $(v_{11}, v_{21}\dots ,v_{n1})$; $(v_{12}, v_{22}\dots ,v_{n2})$;......; and $(v_{1n}, v_{2n}\dots, v_{nn})$ are linearly independent. Therefore, the general solution to the homogeneous system of linear difference equations with constant coefficients is made up of n sequences $[z(1)_t, z(2)_t,..., z(n)_t]$ each of which is a linear combination of the solutions $(v_{11}\lambda_1^t, v_{12}\lambda_2^t,..., v_{1n}\lambda_n^t)$; $(v_{21}\lambda_1^t, v_{22}\lambda_2^t,...,v_{2n}\lambda_n^t)$;... and $(v_{n1}\lambda_1^t, v_{n2}\lambda_2^t,... v_{nn}\lambda_n^t)$;

2. If the n roots of the characteristic equation $P_A(\lambda^n) = 0$ are real but $s < n$ are repeated, by letting r_1,...,r_s be the multiplicity of each root, where $r_1 + \dots + r_s = n$, then, in addition to s sequences $(\lambda_1^t,..., \lambda_s^t)$, the homogeneous system admits $r_i - 1$ sequences (i = 1,..., s) of the kind $(t\,\lambda_1^t, t^2\,\lambda_1^t,...,t^{r_1-1}\lambda_1^t),...,(t\lambda_n^t, t^2\lambda_n^t,...,t^{r_n-1}\lambda_n^t)$. If we set $p_j(t^{r_i-1}) = c_{1j}\,t^{r_i-1} + c_{2j}\,t^{r_i-2} + \dots + c_{r_i-1,j}t + c_{nij}$ (i = 1,..., s; j = 1,...,s), the general solution to the homogeneous system is

$$z(1)_t = p_{11}(t^{r_1-1})\lambda_1^{t_i} + p_{12}(t^{r_2-1})\lambda_2^t + \dots + p_{1s}(t^{r_s-1})\lambda_s^t$$
$$z(2)_t = p_{21}(t^{r_1-1})\lambda_1^{t_i} + p_{22}(t^{r_2-1})\lambda_2^t + \dots + p_{2s}(t^{r_s-1})\lambda_s^t$$
$$\dotsb$$
$$z(n)_t = p_{n1}(t^{r_1-1})\lambda_1^{t_i} + p_{n2}(t^{r_2-1})\lambda_2^t + \dots + p_{ss}(t^{r_s-1})\lambda_n^t$$

3. If some roots of the characteristic equation $P_A(\lambda^n) = 0$ are complex these complex roots must be conjugate numbers, $a \pm i\,\theta$, since the matrix A of the homogeneous system has real coefficients. Therefore, in addition to the solution $(a + i\theta)^t$, the homogeneous difference equation admits also the $2r - 1$ sequences

$[(a - i\theta)^t, t(a \pm i\theta)^t, t^2(a \pm i\theta)^t, \ldots, t^{r-1}(a \pm i\theta)^t]$. Let us set $(a \pm i\theta) = m (\cos \alpha \pm i \text{ sen } \alpha)$, where $m = \sqrt{(a^2 + \theta^2)}$ is the modulus of the complex number, and suppose that q is the number of pairs of complex conjugate roots, each of multiplicity s_q. Let $r_1, \ldots r_s$ be the multiplicity of the remaining real roots so that $r_1 + \ldots + r_s + 2s_1 + \ldots + 2s_q = n$. By applying de Moivre's formula, the general solution to the homogeneous system is

$$z_1(t) = \sum_{i=1}^{s} P_{1i}(t^{r_i - 1})\lambda_i^{t_i} + \sum_{j=1}^{q} Q_{1j}(t^{s_j - 1})m_j^t \cos \alpha_j t + \sum_{j=1}^{q} R_{1j}(t^{s_j - 1})m_j^t \sin \alpha_j t$$

$$z_2(t) = \sum_{i=1}^{s} P_{2i}(t^{r_i - 1})\lambda_i^{t_i} + \sum_{j=1}^{q} Q_{2j}(t^{s_j - 1})m_j^t \cos \alpha_j t + \sum_{j=1}^{q} R_{2j}(t^{s_j - 1})m_j^t \sin \alpha_j t$$

$$z_n(t) = \sum_{i=1}^{s} P_{ni}(t^{r_i - 1})\lambda_i^{t_i} + \sum_{j=1}^{q} Q_{nj}(t^{s_j - 1})m_j^t \cos \alpha_j t + \sum_{j=1}^{q} R_{nj}(t^{s_j - 1})m_j^t \sin_j t$$

where $p_{hi}(t^{r_i})$; $Q_{hj}(t^{s_j})$; $R_{hj}(t^{s_j})$ (h = 1,…,n) are respectively polynomials of degree $r_i - 1$ (i = 1,…s); $s_j - 1$ (j = 1,…q); $s_j - 1$ (j = 1,…q).

To conclude, it can be said for the general solution to the non-homogeneous differential system that the general principle of finding the particular solution by taking a sequence similar to forcing terms in the case of autonomous systems means considering the stationary solution the particular solution. It is obtained by enforcing the conditions $x(1)_t = x(1)^*$; $x(2)_t = x(2)^*$; …; $x(n)_t = x(n)^*$.

B.5 Phase plane analysis for the first-order difference equation and for systems of two first-order difference equations

In this section to extend the phase plane analysis to difference equations we consider the particular case of the linear difference equation and systems of first-order linear difference equations. It is useful to begin by studying the first order linear equation, since the information obtained is useful in constructing the phase diagram of the 2x2's system of first-order difference equations. Although the following analysis is limited to linear equations with constant coefficients, it is valid locally for the non-linear equations in a neighbourhood of steady state. Indeed a steady state for a first-order non linear difference equation of the $x_{t+1} = f(x_t)$ is fix-point $x^* = f(x^*)$. By assuming $f(\cdot)$ is continuously differentiable, Taylors first-degree approximation in a neighbourhood of steady state gives the linear equation

$$x_{t+1} = ax_t + b$$

where $a = f'(x^*) = x^*$ and $b = [1 - f'(x^*)]x^*$.

Let us consider the homogeneous linear difference equation $x_{t+1} = ax_t$. The phase plane of this equation is the plane (x_t, x_{t+1}) where the homogeneous difference equation represents a line passing through the origin. The equation $x_{t+1} = x_t$ describes the diagonal of the plane (x_t, x_{t+1}) and translates x_{t+1} on the horizontal axis. This makes it possible to compare the trajectory of x_t with the unique stationary solution (0, 0). Let us consider Figure B.1. Given the initial condition x_0, the value x_1 for t = 1 is determined by the relationship $x_1 = ax_0$. This is also the initial value at instant t = 1. To read this value on the horizontal axis it is sufficient

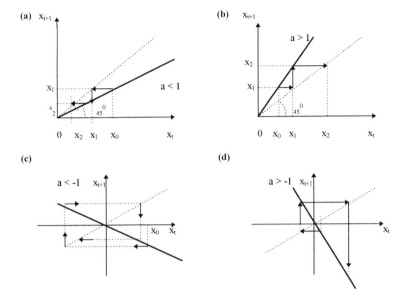

Figure B.1   Phase diagrams for the first-order linear difference equation

to use the diagonal and translate the point from the vertical axis to the horizontal axis. Given x_1 when $t = 1$, we obtain $x_2 = ax_1$ on the phase line. This point translated to the horizontal axis indicates the initial point x_2 at $t = 2$, and so on. By examining Figures B.1. (a) to B.1. (d) we can conclude:

1. if $0 < a < 1$ then $x_t \to 0$ as $t \to \infty$ (Figure B.1. (a); on the contrary if $a > 1$, then $x_t \to \infty$ as $t \to \infty$ (Figure B.1. (b);
2. if $a < -1$ then $x_t \to 0$ as $t \to \infty$, but convergence to steady state alternates positive values and negative values in x_t; if $a > -1$ then $x_t \to \infty$ as $t \to \infty$, so that x_t diverges from the steady state and alternates positive and negative values.

Now we consider the system of first order difference equations

$$x_{t+1} = f_1(x_t, y_t)$$
$$y_{t+1} = f_2(x_t, y_t)$$

and the locus of points $x_{t+1} = x_t$ and $y_{t+1} = y_t$. Let us use the condition $x_{t+1} = x_t$ and admit that the conditions of the implicit function theorem are verified, so that we can solve the relationship $x_t - f_1(x_t, y_t) = 0$ obtained from the first equation for y_t. The explicit function $y_t = g_1(x_t)$ in the phase plane (x_t, y_t) describes a curve which indicates the sequence of values of y_t satisfying the first difference equation of the system when x_t follows a steady state path. In a similar way, if we use the condition $y_{t+1} = y_t$ and solve the implicit condition $y_t - f_2(x_t, y_t) = 0$ for y_t we obtain a curve $y_t = g_2(x_t)$ which indicates the x_t required when y_t follows a steady state path. There is a steady state (x^*, y^*) of the system at the intersection $y^* = g_1(x^*) = g_2(x^*)$ of the two curves. The direction of the motion is deduced by comparing the state at every instant of variables (x_t, y_t) to the phase curves. However the graph of the motion of the system alone is not sufficient to classify the nature of the steady state or any other singular point. To do this we need to use analytical methods similar to those used for the differential equations.

Therefore, let us consider the linear system

$$x_{t+1} = a_{11}x_t + a_{12}y_t$$
$$y_{t+1} = a_{21}x_t + a_{22}y_t$$

which can also be considered the linear approximation of a non-linear system in a neighbourhood of steady state. Let A be the matrix of this system. The characteristic equation for the system obtained from the condition $\det(\lambda I - A) = 0$ is

$$\lambda^2 - (\text{tr}A)\lambda + \det A = 0$$

where $\text{tr}A = a_{11} + a_{22}$. Uniqueness of steady state $(0, 0)$ is guaranteed by assuming $\det(I - A) \neq 0$. The solutions to the algebraic equation allow us to classify the origin and singular points of the system according to the following scheme:

1. If the discriminant of the characteristic equation is positive $\Delta = (\text{tr } A)^2 - 4 \det A > 0$, the roots λ_1, λ_2 are real and distinct. The general solution to the linear difference system is

$$x_t = c_1v_{11}\lambda_1^{t_i} + c_2v_{12}\lambda_2^t$$
$$y_t = c_1v_{21}\lambda_1^{t_i} + c_2v_{22}\lambda_2^t$$

where c_1 and c_2 are arbitrary constants and $v_{11} v_{22} - v_{12} v_{21} \neq 0$
We can distinguish three sub-cases
1.a) Suppose $0 < \lambda_1 < 1$ and $0 < \lambda_2 < 1$. If $c_1 = c_2 = 0$, the solution coincides with the origin of the phase plane. If $c_1 = 0$; $c_2 \neq 0$ the evolution of the system is described by $x_t = c_2 v_{12} \lambda_2^t$; $y_t = c_2 v_{22}\lambda_2^t$. As $t \to \infty$ both $x_t \to 0$ and $y_t \to 0$. This is also so when $c_2 = 0$. In general, when $c_1 \neq 0$ and $c_2 \neq 0$, as $t \to \infty$ the limit of solutions is the sum of the two particular cases just examined. Therefore as $t \to \infty$ it follows that $x_t \to 0$ and $y_t \to 0$. The origin in this case is a *stable node*. Let us now suppose $-1 < \lambda_1 < 0$ and $-1 < \lambda_2 < 0$. If we change notations and let $\mu_1 = -\lambda_1$; $\mu_2 = -\lambda_2$, we can rewrite the solutions as

$$x_t = c_1v_{11}(-1)^t\mu_1^{t_i} + c_2v_{12}(-1)^t\mu_2^t$$
$$y_t = c_1v_{21}(-1)^t\mu_1^t + c_2v_{22}(-1)^t\mu_2^t$$

Since $\mu_1 < 1$ and $\mu_2 < 1$, as $t \to \infty$, once more it follows that $x_t \to 0$ and $y_t \to 0$; but now the convergence occurs by alternating positive values and negative values. However, even in this case the nature of the origin is unchanged. We can say the origin is a *stable* node if both the roots of the characteristic equation verifiy $|\lambda_1| < 1$; $|\lambda_2| < 1$, that is if both fall inside the circle with unit ray;
1. b) If $\lambda_1 > 1$; $\lambda_2 > 1$, by reasoning as in point (1.a) we conclude that $x_t \to \infty$ and $y_t \to \infty$ when $t \to \infty$. Therefore the origin is *unstable node*. If $\lambda_1 < -1$ and $\lambda_2 < -1$, when $c_1 = 0$; $c_2 \neq 0$, once again we obtain the solutions $x_t = c_2 v_{12} \lambda_2^t$; $y_t = c_2$

$v_{22}\lambda_2^t$, but now, if we set $\mu_1 = -\lambda_1$ and $\mu_2 = -\lambda_2$ we have $x_t = c_2 v_{12}(-1)^t \mu_2^t$ and $y_t = c_2 v_{22}(-1)^t \mu_2^t$. As $t \to \infty$ both x_t and y_t diverge and assume negative values when t is odd and positive values when t is even. The origin, therefore, is *unstable* if both roots of the characteristic equation verify $|\lambda_1| > 1$ and $|\lambda_2| > 1$, that is if both roots fall outside the circle with unit ray;

1.c) Suppose $\lambda_1 > 1$ and $\lambda_2 < 1$. If $c_2 \neq 0$ and $c_1 = 0$, the origin is stable, whereas if $c_1 \neq 0$ and $c_2 = 0$ the origin is unstable. In the latter case the origin is a *saddle point*. The nature of the origin does not change if $\lambda_1 > -1$ and $\lambda_2 < -1$, nor does it change if in the former inequalities we change the roles of λ_1 and λ_2. Therefore, the origin is a *saddle point* if only one of the characteristic roots falls inside the circle with unit ray.

2. If the discriminant of the characteristic equation is zero $\Delta = (\text{tr } A)^2 - 4 \det A = 0$, the roots λ_1, λ_2 are real and coincident. Here we can distinguish two sub-cases.
2.a) If the characteristic matrix $[\lambda I - A]$ has null rang, the general solution to the difference system is

$$x_t = (c_1 v_{11} + c_2 v_{12})\lambda^t$$
$$y(t) = (c_1 v_{21} + c_2 v_{22})\lambda^t$$

If $|\lambda| < 1$, the direction of motion leads toward the origin which classifies as an *improper stable node*. In the case when $|\lambda| > 1$ the direction of motion is reversed and the origin is *improper unstable node*.
2. b) If the characteristic matrix $[\lambda I-A]$ has rang 1, the general solution to the difference system is

$$x_t = (c_1 v_{11} t + c_2 v_{12})\lambda^t$$
$$y_t = (c_1 v_{21} t + c_2 v_{22})\lambda^t$$

If $c_1 = 0$ and $c_2 \neq 0$ we obtain solutions similar to (2.a). If $c_2 = 0$ and $c_1 \neq 0$ we obtain an improper unstable node. In general, when both $c_1 \neq 0$ and $c_2 \neq 0$ as $t \to \infty$, the limit is an undetermined form when $|\lambda| < 1$ due to $t\lambda^t$. However if we let $\lambda = 1/\mu$, this component goes to zero and, therefore, the entire expression has the same tendency of the component λ^t. We can conclude when $\Delta = 0$ the origin is an *improper node*;

3. If the discriminant of the characteristic equation is negative $\Delta = (\text{tr } A)^2 - 4 \det A < 0$, the roots λ_1, λ_2 are complex conjugate $\lambda_{1,2} = a \pm i\theta$. Here we can distinguish two sub-cases.
3. a) If the real part of the root is null $a = 0$, the general solution to the difference system is

$$x_t = c_1 v_{11}\cos \alpha t + c_2 v_{12}\sin \alpha t$$
$$y_t = c_1 v_{21}\cos \alpha t + c_2 v_{22}\sin \alpha t$$

These equations are the parametric representation of an elipse with centre $(0, 0)$. The direction of motion along the elipse depends on the sign of the coefficient a_{21} in the equation for y_t in the original dynamic system. If $a_{21} > 0$ the motion is counterclockwise; if $a_{21} < 0$ the motion is clockwise. The origin in the case we are considering is a *centre or focus*.
3. b) If the real part of the root is not null $a \neq 0$, the general solution to the difference system is

$$x(t) = m^t[c_1v_{11}\cos \alpha t + c_2v_{12}\sin \alpha t]$$
$$y(t) = m^t[c_1v_{21}\cos \alpha t + c_2v_{22}\sin \alpha t]$$

As in the case of differential equations, it can be demonstrated that these equations are the parametric representation of a logarithmic *spiral*. This spiral points toward the origin, and therefore is stable, if the modulus m of the root is inside the circle with unitary ray, that is if $| m | < 1$, and is unstable if $| m | > 1$.

B.6   Steady states and stability conditions for linear systems of first-order difference equations with constant coefficients

In this section we shall refer to autonomous systems of first-order difference equations with the notation

$$x_{t+1} = f(x_t)$$

where f: $R^n \to R^n$ is a vector of functions. A steady state is a fixpoint of the system which verifies $x^* = f(x^*)$. For this point the following concepts of Section A.8 remain unchanged

a) *stability (in the sense of Liapunov)* if every solution near steady state remains near steady state;
b) *asymptotic stability* (or even local stability) if every solution near the steady state converges to the steady state;
c) *global stability* if the region of asymptotic stability coincides with the dominion of f(·) in R^n.

For the solutions to the homogeneous systems $x_{t+1} = Ax_t$, where $x \in R^n$ and A is matrix (n x n), it is possible to state the following classical theorem

Theorem B.3

Let $x_t = 0$ be the stationary solution of the system of linear difference equations with constant coefficients $x_{t+1} = Ax_t$:

i) *The solution $x_t = 0$ is globally stable if, and only if, the eigenvalues of A, real or complex, have moduli that are less than one;*
ii) *The solution $x_t = 0$ is stable (in the sense of Liapunov) if the eigenvalues of A, real or complex, have moduli not greater than one and if the eigenvalues with moduli equal to one are not repeated.*

Conditions for stability contemplated by Theorem B.3 for the homogeneous systems are trivially true also for the non-homogeneous systems $x_{t+1} = Ax_t + b$.
Some relevant conclusions are contained in the following theorems

Theorem B.4

The eigenvalues of n × n matrix A have moduli less than one if the sum of all the moduli of the elements in the column are less than unit, that is if $\sum_{i=1}^{n} | a_{ij} | < 1$ (j = 1,...,n)

Theorem B.5

If the eigenvalues of the nxn matrix A have moduli less than one

i) $\mid trA \mid = \sum_{i=1}^{n} \mid a_{ij} \mid < n$

ii) $\mid det A \mid < 1$

Theorem B.6

If the n × n matrix is non negative A ≥ 0, its eigenvalues have moduli less than one if, and only if, the matrix I − A verifies Hawkins-Simon conditions, that is if, and only if, all leading principal minors are positive.

With reference to the 2×2 difference system, conditions of the Theorem B.5 permit the following deductions. If we bear in mind that the characteristic equation for the 2×2 system is the algebraic equation $\lambda^2 - (tr\ A)\lambda + detA = 0$ and that $trA = \lambda_1 + \lambda_2$ and $det\ A = \lambda_1\lambda_2$, we can deduce that the system is stable if $\mid detA \mid < 1$ and $\mid trA \mid < 2$. The previous discussion regarding the classification of steady states can be summarized in terms of the two parameters TrA and detA which characterize the system. However to produce a graph similar to Figure A.6 for the systems of two difference equations, we must include other conditions. Condition $\Delta = 0$ gives the equation $detA = (TrA/2)^2$. This represents a parabola with a minimum at the origin $(0, 0)$ in the plane of coordinates (TrA, detA). To delimit the region where roots of the characteristic equation have moduli less than one we can proceed as follows. To have roots $\lambda_1 = \lambda_2 = 1$ or $\lambda_1 = \lambda_2 = -1$, the conditions $detA = TrA -1$ or $detA = -(TrA+1)$ must be satisfied. The former describes a line with a positive slope passing through points $(0, -1)$ and $(1, 0)$, the latter describes a line with a negative slope passing through points $(-1, 0)$ and $(0, -1)$. The classification of stationary points therefore corresponds to the regions of Figure B.2.

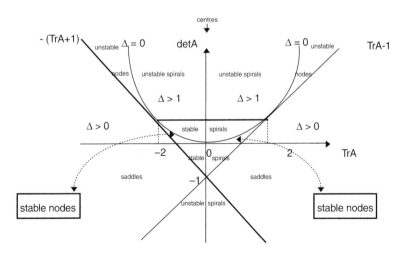

Figure B.2 General diagrammatic classification of stationary points for the linear difference system

References

Aziariadis, C. (1993) *Intertemporal Macroeconomics* (Cambridge MA: Blackwell).
Baumol, W. (1970) *Economic Dynamics* (New York: Macmillan).
Bellman, R. and K. Cooke (1963) *Differential-Difference Equations* (New York: Academic Press).
Boole, G. (1960) *A Treatise on the Calculus of Finite Differences* (New York: Dover).
Chiang, A. (1974) *Fundamental Methods of Mathematical Economics* (New York: McGraw-Hill).
Gandolfo, G. (1996) *Economic Dynamics* (Berlin: Springer-Verlag).
Goldberg, S. (1986) *Introduction to Difference Equations* (Dover: New York).
Jordan, C. (1979) *Calculus of Finite Differences* (New York: Chelsea).
Luenberger, D. (1979) *Introduction to Dynamic Systems* (New York: Wiley).
Miller, R. (1968) *Linear Difference Equations* (Reading MA: Benjamin).
Takayama, A. (1974) *Mathematical Economics* (Hinsdale: Dryden Press)

Appendix C: Calculus of variations and optimal control theory (Pontryagin's maximum principle)

C.1   Calculus of variations: Concepts and definitions

In this appendix we examine the problem of maximizing (or minimizing) a functional which depends on state variables $x(t)$ and input variables (or control variables) $y(t)$. The objects of choice are the inputs variables which also determine the dynamics of a system, described by the equations of motion for the state variables. The optimal control problem can be formulated as the problem of finding an extremal function for a functional. Since it can be solved by classical calculus of variations, it is useful to start from this by recalling the exact meaning of functional

Definition C.1 (Functional)

Let M be a class of real-valued functions $x(t)$. A functional is a map $F: M \to R$.

We shall indicate this map by $J = F[x(t)]$. The definition of functional can be extended to spaces M^n of vectors of functions. By limiting ourselves at the moment to one-dimensional spaces of functions, we see that functionals can be handled in the same way as the elementary functions of one variable. However, some preliminary remarks about topological concepts are necessary. Given a functional $J = F[x(t)]$, the increment, or the variation of its argument $\partial x(t)$, is the difference between the functions $x(t)$, $x_0(t) \in M$, that is $\partial x(t) = x(t) - x_0(t)$. When $x(t) \in C^k$, or $x(t)$ is k-times differentiable, for every $x(t)$, $x_0(t) \in C^k$ the k-th difference is defined as $\partial x(t)^k = x(t)^k - x_0(t)^k$ where $x(t)^k$ is the k-th derivative of $x(t)$.

Based on this definition of difference between functions, a neighbourhood of order k-th for k integer 0, 1,..., k, can also be defined. The functions $x(t)$ and $x_0(t)$ defined in the interval [a, b] are said to be near by proximity of order zero if for $\varepsilon > 0$, $|\partial x(t)| < \varepsilon$. Similarly $x(t)$ and $x_0(t)$ are near by proximity of first-order if for $\varepsilon > 0$ $|\delta x(t)| < \varepsilon$ and $|\partial x(t)^1| < \varepsilon$. In general, $x(t)$ and $x_0(t)$ are near by proximity of order k if for $\varepsilon > 0$ $|\partial x(t)^k| < \varepsilon$ for all the indexes 0, 1,..., k. Let us introduce the notion of distance of order zero and order k into the space of functions, that is

$$d_0(x(t), x_0(t)) = \max_{a \leq x(t) \leq b} \mid x(t) - x_0(t)$$

$$d_k(x(t), x_0(t)) = \max_{a \leq x(t) \leq b} \sum_k \mid x(t)^k - x_0(t)^k \mid$$

For $\varepsilon > 0$ we define a neighbourhood of order zero as the set $I_\varepsilon (x(t), x_0(t))^0 = \{x (t) \in C^0:$ $d(x(t), x_0(t)) < \varepsilon\}$, and, in the same way, a neighbourhood of order k as the set $I_\varepsilon(x(t), x_0(t))^k = \{x (t) \in C^k: d_k(x(t), x_0(t)) < \varepsilon\}$. Having the concept of ε-neighbourhood of order k, it is quite natural to extend the notion of continuity to functionals. A functional $F[x(t)]$ defined on M is said continuous at $x_0(t)$ in the sense of proximity of order zero if, for $\varepsilon > 0$, there is $\eta > 0$ such that when $\mid x(t) - x_0(t) \mid < \eta$ we have $\mid F[x(t)] - F[x_0(t)] \mid < \varepsilon$, or such that $d_0(x(t), x_0(t)) < \eta$ implies $\mid F[x(t)] - F[x_0(t)] \mid < \varepsilon$.

When the argument changes from $x_0(t)$ to $x(t) = x_0(t) + \partial x(t)$, the functional change is $\Delta J = F[x_0(t) + \partial x(t)] - F[x_0(t)]$. Then continuity in the sense of proximity of order zero can also be expressed as follows: for a given $\varepsilon > 0$ it is possible to determine $\eta > 0$ so that variation $\mid \partial x(t) \mid < \eta$ implies $\mid \Delta J \mid < \varepsilon$. Let $x(t) = x_0(t) + \alpha w(t)$, where $\alpha \in R$ and $w(t) \in M$. Since $x_0(t) + \alpha w(t) \to x_0(t)$ as $\alpha \to 0$, the notion of continuity in the sense of proximity of order zero can also be stated by saying that $F[x(t)]$ is continuous at $x_0(t)$ if

$$\lim_{\alpha \to 0} F[x_0(t) + \alpha w(t)] = F[x_0(t)]$$

The approximation $\Delta J = F[\partial x(t)] + \beta[x_0(t), \partial x(t)]$ of an increment in a functional $F(\cdot)$ is obtained by admitting $F(\cdot)$ linear in $\partial x(t)$. The functional $\beta[x_0(t), \partial x(t)]$ measures the error made due to this approximation. This error is assumed negligible, in the sense $\beta[x_0(t), \partial x(t)] \to 0$ as $\mid \partial x(t) \mid \to 0$.
We use the following

Definition C.2 (Variation of a functional)

A variation at $x_0(t)$ of a functional $F(x(t))$ is the limit

$$\partial J = \lim_{|\partial x(t)| \to 0} F[\partial x(t)] + \beta[x_0(t), \partial x(t)]$$

This is the principal part of the increment in $F(\cdot)$ in respect to $\partial x(t)$.

If $x(t) = x_0(t) + \alpha \, \partial x(t)$ it can be demonstrated that $\partial J = [\partial F[x_0(t) + \alpha \, \partial x(t)/\partial \alpha]_{\alpha = 0}$. We can also introduce the following definitions

Definition C.3 (Extremal function)

A function $x(t)^* \in M$ is an extremal for a functional $J = F[x(t)]$ if $x(t)^*$ is a minimum or a maximum for $F[x(t)]$.

Definition C.4 (Maxima or minima of a functional)

A Functional $J = F[x(t)]$ reaches a maximum (a minimum) at $x(t)^*$ if for every $x(t) \in I_\varepsilon$ $(x(t), x(t)^*)^0$, $\partial J \leq 0$ $(\partial J \geq 0)$. The function $x(t)^*$ is a proper maximum (a proper minimum) when $\partial J = 0$ is true only for $x(t) = x(t)^*$.

C.2 Euler's equation

The most classical control problem solved by the calculus of variations is illustrated as follows. Let $F[t, x(t), \dot{x}(t)]$ be a continuous function having continuous derivatives at least up to the second order with respect to all of the arguments. Let $J = \int_{t_0}^{t_1} F[\, t, x(t), \dot{x}(t)]\, dt$ be the functional defined in the set M, where $M \subset C^1$ is a subset of the class of continuous functions having a first derivative continuous, with boundary conditions $x(t_0) = x_0$; $x(t_1) = x_1$ and x_0, x_1 given. A necessary condition for $x^*(t) \in M$ to be a solution to the problem

$$\max J = \int_{t_0}^{t_1} F[t, x(t), \dot{x}(t)] dt$$

$$x(t) \in M; x(t_0) = x_0; x(t_1) = x_1$$

is that the function $x^*(t) \in M$ satisfies Euler's equation

$$\frac{\partial F}{\partial x} - \frac{d}{dt}(\partial F/\partial \dot{x}) = 0$$

Written in the expanded form, Euler's equation is a linear second-order ordinary differential equation with variable coefficients

$$\ddot{x}(\partial^2 F/\partial \dot{x}^2) + \dot{x}(\partial^2 F/\partial x \partial \dot{x}) - (\partial F/\partial x) = 0$$

which, because of boundary conditions $x(t_0) = x_0$; $x(t_1) = x_1$, admits a unique solution.

The proof that Euler's equation is a necessary condition for a maximum can be obtained as follows

At an extremal point we must have

$$\partial J = [\partial F[x * (t) + \alpha w(t), \dot{x} * (t) + \alpha \dot{w}(t)]/\partial \alpha]_{\alpha=0} = 0$$

From Leibinitz's rule of derivatives we get

$$\partial J\,|_{\alpha=0} = \int_{t_0}^{t_1} [(\partial F/\partial x)w(t) + (\partial F/\partial \dot{x})\dot{w}(t)]dt$$

Integrating by parts

$$\int_{t_0}^{t_1} (\partial F/\partial \dot{x})\dot{w}(t)dt = [(\partial F/\partial \dot{x})w(t)]_{t_0}^{t_1} - \int_{t_0}^{t_1} w(t)[d(\partial F/\partial \dot{x})/dt]dt$$

so that

$$\partial J\,|_{\alpha=0} = \int_{t_0}^{t_1} \{[(\partial F/\partial x)w(t) - w(t)[d(\partial F/\partial \dot{x})/dt]\}dt + [(\partial F/\partial \dot{x})w(t)]_{t_0}^{t_1} = 0$$

The boundary conditions $x(t_0) = x^*(t_0)$ and $x(t_1) = x^*(t_1)$ for $\alpha > 0$ imply $w(t_0) = w(t_1) = 0$. Thus $[(\partial F/\partial x)w(t)]_{t_0}^{t_1} = 0$. Therefore at extremal function we must have

$$\partial J\,|_{\alpha=0} = \int_{t_0}^{t_1} [(\partial F/\partial x) - d(\partial F/\partial \dot{x})/dt]w(t)\}dt = 0$$

which, for any $w(t)$, implies

$$(\partial F/\partial x) - d(\partial F/\partial \dot{x})/dt = 0$$

which is Euler's equation.

C.3 Some other necessary conditions for the extremal points

Euler's condition for an extremal function refers either to a minimum or to a maximum. Moreover it has a local character. We are interested in verifying if there are conditions that allow us to distinguish if an extremal is a minimum or a maximum. By analogy to the case of maximization of functions, we observe that a maximum for a functional must satisfy $\partial^2 J \leq 0$, where $\partial^2 J$ is the second-order variation of functional. This requires $(\partial^2 F/\partial \dot{x}^2) \leq 0$. Moreover if $(\partial^2 F/\partial \dot{x}^2) < 0$, this is sufficient condition for a maximum.

Another necessary condition for a maximum is obtained using

Definition C.5

For some $z(t) \epsilon M$, the function

$$E(x, \dot{x}, \dot{z}, t) = F(x, \dot{z}, t) - F(x, \dot{x}, t) - (\partial F/\partial \dot{x})(\dot{z} - \dot{x})$$

is the Weierstrass or excess function.

The Weierstrass function is interesting because a restriction on $E(\cdot)$ is also a restriction on $F(\cdot)$ and becomes a global restriction on $F(\cdot)$. We know that when the maximand is a function, a maximum requires that the function be concave at that point. When the maximand is a functional $J(\cdot)$, the integrand function $F(\cdot)$ must be concave at a maximum. By defining the new variable $h = \dot{z} - \dot{x}$, we can set

$$E(x, \dot{x}, \dot{z}, t) = E(x, \dot{x}, \dot{x} + h, t) = F(x, \dot{x} + h, t) - F(x, \dot{x}, t)(\partial F/\partial \dot{x})h$$

When the integrand function $F(\cdot)$ is concave in x, it follows that $E(x, \dot{x}, \dot{z}, t) \leq 0$, where $E(\cdot) < 0$ if $F(\cdot)$ is strict concave. Therefore $E(\cdot) \leq 0$, together with Euler's equation, is a necessary condition for a maximum, or a sufficient condition if $E(\cdot) < 0$. Note that the latter is automatically true when $(\partial^2 F/\partial \dot{x}^2) < 0$.

C.4 Constrained maxima and minima and the optimal control problem as a specific constrained variational problem

In this section we examine some constrained variational problems. We shall distinguish two cases, depending on whether the constraints are equalities or inequalities. To simplify we limit our attention to the case of only one constraint, but the analysis can be extended to vectors of constraints.

1. Equality constraints

A constrained problem of the calculus of variations frequently encountered in the applications is

$$\max J = \int_{t_0}^{t_1} F[t, x(t), \dot{x}(t)]dt$$

sub $g[t, x(t), \dot{x}(t)] = b$

$x(t) \in M; x(t_0) = x_0; x(t_1) = x_1$

where b is a constant. We assume $\partial g/\partial \dot{x}(t) \neq 0$, so that the constraint can always be reduced to the first-order ordinary differential equation $\dot{x}(t) = h[x(t), b]$. By direct substitution of $h(\cdot)$ into the integrand function, the problem can be transformed into one of free maximum. However it is preferable to adopt the more general solution which considers the Lagrangian

$$L[t, x(t), \dot{x}(t), \lambda(t)] = F[t, x(t), \dot{x}(t)] + \lambda(t)\{b - g[t, x(t), \dot{x}(t)]\}$$

as integrand function, where the costate variable $\lambda(t)$ is the equivalent of Lagrange's multiplier of the constrained maximum problem of functions. The variational problem becomes

$$\max J[x(t), \lambda(t)] = \int_{t_0}^{t_1} L[t, x(t), \dot{x}(t), \lambda(t)]dt$$

$$x(t), \lambda(t) \in M; x(t_0) = x_0; x(t_1) = x_1$$

Euler's equations are

$$\frac{\partial L}{\partial x} - \frac{d}{dt}(\partial L/\partial \dot{x}) = 0$$

$$\frac{\partial L}{\partial \lambda} = 0 = b - g[t, x(t), \dot{x}(t)]$$

2. Inequality constraints

In this case the constrained maximum problem is

$$\max J = \int_{t_0}^{t_1} F[t, x(t), \dot{x}(t)]dt$$

$$\text{sub} \quad g[t, x(t), \dot{x}(t)] \leq b;$$

$$x(t) \in M; x(t_0) = x_0; x(t_1) = x_1$$

Necessary conditions for a maximum now integrate Euler's equation with Kuhn-Tucker and complementary slackness conditions. Therefore necessary conditions are

$$\partial L/\partial x - \frac{d}{dt}(\partial L/\partial \dot{x}) = 0$$

$$\frac{\partial L}{\partial \lambda} = b - g[t, x(t), \dot{x}(t)] \geq 0; \lambda(t) \geq 0$$

$$\lambda(t)\{b - g[t, x(t), \dot{x}(t)]\} = 0$$

An important implication is that if some conditions are met, an optimal control problem can be considered a specific constrained problem of the calculus of variations. To verify this, let us refer to the following constrained maximum problem

$$\max J = \int_{t_0}^{t_1} F[t, x(t), u(t)]dt$$

$$\text{sub} \quad \dot{x}(t) = f[(x(t), u(t)]$$

$$x(t) \in M; x(t_0) = x_0; x(t_1) = x_1$$

As a variational problem this formulation has the following peculiarities. Firstly the integrand function does not depend on the variable $\dot{x}$. This dependence, on the contrary, does appear in the constraint as an equation of motion for the state variable $x(t)$. Secondly, the constraint and the integrand function both depend on a trajectory (a control variable) which is also one of the unknowns in the problem. For solving the variational constrained problems we can form a Lagrangian

$$L[t, x(t), \dot{x}(t), u(t), \lambda(t)] = F[t, x(t), u(t)] + \lambda(t)[f(x(t), u(t) - \dot{x}(t)]$$
$$= H[t, x(t), u(t), \lambda(t)] - \lambda(t)\dot{x}(t)$$

The function $H[t, x(t), u(t), \lambda(t)] = F[t, x(t), u(t)] + \lambda(t) [f(x(t), u(t)]$ is called the Hamiltonian function which, as we shall see, performs a fundamental role in Pontryagin's maximum principle for the problem of optimal control.

We can formulate the following problem of the calculus of variations

$$\max J = \int_{t_0}^{t_1} \{H[t, x(t), u(t), \lambda(t)] - \lambda(t)\dot{x}(t)\}dt$$
$$x(t_0) = x_0; x(t_1) = x_1$$

Since the functional is maximized for unknown trajectories $u(t)$, $x(t)$, $\lambda(t)$, the Euler equations are

$$\frac{\partial L}{\partial u} - \frac{d}{dt}(\partial L/\partial \dot{u}) = \frac{\partial H}{\partial u} = 0$$
$$\frac{\partial L}{\partial x} - \frac{d}{dt}(\partial L/\partial \dot{x}) = \frac{\partial H}{\partial x} + \dot{\lambda} = 0$$
$$\frac{\partial L}{\partial \lambda} - \frac{d}{dt}(\partial L/\partial \dot{\lambda}) = \frac{\partial H}{\partial \lambda} - \dot{x} = 0$$

These conditions are exactly the same as those required by Pontryagins maximum principle for the optimal control. Moreover, if we assume the constraint $f[x(t), u(t)]$ to be invertible, so that $u = g [x(t), \dot{x}(t)]$, and substitute this into the integrand function, with some manipulation the necessary conditions for the constrained problem can be reduced to those of the canonical variational problem with integrand function $F[t, x(t), \dot{x}(t)]$.

C.5 The Transversality condition and constraints on the terminal point

In the previous versions of the calculus of variations both terminal time $t = t_1$ and terminal value $x(t_1) = x_1$ were given. However, terminal time can be assumed to run forever or terminal value can be seen as a mobile point along a given terminal trajectory. In particular the condition for terminal state to belong to a given trajectory at the instant $t = t_1$ can appear as the condition

$$T[x(t), t] = 0 \text{ at } t = t_1$$

To obtain the necessary conditions for problems of the calculus of variations with terminal conditions we can consider the terminal instant as the limit of paths $t_1(\alpha) = t_1 + \alpha\Delta t$ which are in a neighbourhood of terminal time. These paths have the property $t_1 + \alpha\Delta t \to t_1$ as $\alpha \to 0$. Every trajectories $x(t)$ which reaches terminal surface at $t_1(\alpha)$ stays in a neighbourhood of the extremal if $x(t) = x(t)^* + \alpha w(t)$. With this approximation, the functional objective can be rewritten as

$$J(\alpha) = \int_{t_0}^{t_1(\alpha)} F[t, x(t)^* + \alpha w(t), \dot{x}(t)^* + \alpha\dot{w}(t)]dt$$

Since at a maximum $\partial J|_{\alpha=0} = 0$, by virtue of Leibinitz's rule for derivatives, the necessary condition for a maximum becomes

$$dJ/d\alpha = 0 = F[t, x(t), \dot{x}(t)][dt_1(\alpha)/d\alpha] + \int_{t_0}^{t_1} [(\partial F/\partial x)w(t)dt + \int_{t_0}^{t_1} (\partial F/\partial \dot{x})\dot{w}(t)]dt$$

Integrating the third term on the right side by parts, and substituting we get

$$F[t, x(t), \dot{x}(t)][dt_1(\alpha)/d\alpha] + \int_{t_0}^{t_1} \{[(\partial F/\partial x) - d[(\partial F/\partial \dot{x})]/dt]\}dt = 0$$

The magnitude $[dt_1(\alpha)/d\alpha]$ which appears in the first term is obtained by differentiating for α the condition $T[x(t_1(\alpha)), t_1(\alpha)] = 0$. If we adopt the resulting expressions when $\alpha \to 0$, we get the following necessary condition for a maximum

$$(\partial F/\partial x) - \{d[(\partial F/\partial \dot{x})]/dt]\} = 0$$
$$\{F[t, x(t), \dot{x}(t)] - (\partial F/\partial x)\dot{x}\}_{t=t_1} + [(\partial F/\partial \dot{x})]_{t=t_1} [\dot{x}]_{T[x(t),t]=0} = 0$$

Another condition is now added to Euler's equation. It is the transversality condition. It says that the line tangent to the extremal trajectory at the terminal instant must be normal to the terminal surface. Sometimes by extension every other condition on the terminal point is called a transversality condition. In particular instead of the condition $x(t_1) = x_1$ we can have one of the following condition

a) with $t= t_1$ finite,
1. the terminal value must satisfy the inequality $x(t_1) \geq x_1$.
    In this case the constraint gives rise to an appropriate slackness condition

    $$\lambda(t) \geq 0 \quad \lambda(t)[x(t) - x_1] = 0 \text{ at } t = t_1$$

2. the extremal trajectory must intersect a given curve $g(t)$ at terminal time.
    In this case the terminal condition is $x(t) - g(t) = 0$ at $t = t_1$
b) with infinite horizon $t \to \infty$.
    The previous conditions (equality, inequality or intersection of extremal trajectory with a curve) are replaced by the respective limiting conditions

    $$\lim_{t\to\infty} x(t) = x_1; \lim_{t\to\infty} \lambda(t) \geq 0 \text{ and } \lim_{t\to\infty} \lambda(t)[x(t) - x_1] = 0; \lim \lim_{t\to\infty}[x(t) - g(t)] = 0$$

C.6   The maximum principle for the optimal control: The canonical conditions

We are now ready to examine the optimal control problem. From a general point of view this problem deals with the efficient regulation of a system moving over time between two states (initial and terminal) according to a law of motion for the state variable. A problem of optimal control has the form

$$\max J = \int_{t_0}^{t_1} F[t, x(t), u(t)]dt + S(x_1, t_1)$$

$$\text{sub} \quad \dot{x}(t) = f[x(t), u(t)]$$

$$x(t) \in M; x(t_0) = x_0; x(t_1) = x_1$$

Functional $J(\cdot)$ is the measure of the performance of the system. The efficiency criterium is to maximize the index of performance. Trajectory $x(t)$ indicates the state of the system and trajectory $u(t)$ is the control variable. The values x_0 and x_1 are respectively initial and terminal conditions. The function $S(x_1, t_1)$ is the terminal 'scrap value' of the functional objective which indicates the value of terminal point. M is the space of functions defined in R_+. Pontryagin's maximum principle states the necessary conditions for optimal control. Mathematical proof for these conditions will be given in the next section. They are obtained by the following procedure

1. The Hamiltonian function is formulated

    $$H[t, x(t), u(t), \lambda(t)] = F[t, x(t), u(t)] + \lambda(t)[f(x(t), u(t)]$$

2. The trajectories $u(t)$, $x(t)$, $\lambda(t)$ which solve the optimal control are chosen so that they satisfy the following conditions
    a) $\max\limits_{\{u(t)\}} H[t, x(t), u(t), \lambda(t)]$ for $t \in [t_0, t_1]$
    b) $\dot{x} = \partial H / \partial \lambda(t) = f[x(t), u(t)]$ with the initial condition $x(t_0) = x_0$
    c) $\dot{\lambda} = -\partial H / \partial x(t) = -[\partial F / \partial x(t) + \lambda(t)\partial f / \partial x(t)]$ with the terminal condition $\lambda(t_1) = \partial S / \partial x_1$.

When the Hamiltonian $H(\cdot)$ is differentiable with respect to $u(t)$, condition (a) for regular maxima becomes

$$\partial H / \partial u(t) = [\partial F / \partial u(t) + \lambda(t)\partial f / \partial u(t)] = 0$$

C.7 The maximum principle for the optimal control: Determination of necessary conditions

Necessary conditions for optimal control (the maximum principle) can be obtained following the Lagrange procedure for constrained maximization of functions. Let us consider the Lagrangian

$$L[x(t), u(t), \lambda(t), t] = J[\cdot] + \int_{t_0}^{t_1} \lambda(t)[f(x(t), u(t) - \dot{x}]dt$$
$$= \int_{t_0}^{t_1} \{F[t, x(t), u(t)] + \lambda(t)[f(x(t), u(t)) - \dot{x}]\}dt + S(x_1, t_1)$$

Integrating the term relative to $\lambda(t)\dot{x}$ by parts and substituting the result into L we have

$$L[x(t), u(t), \lambda(t), t] = \int_{t_0}^{t_1} \{F[t, x(t), u(t)] + \lambda(t)[f(x(t), u(t)] + \dot{\lambda}x(t)]\}dt$$
$$+ \lambda(t_0)x_0 - \lambda(t_1)x_1 + S(x_1, t_1)$$

By forming the Hamiltonian $H[t, x(t), u(t), \lambda(t)] = F[t, x(t), u(t)] + \lambda(t)[f(x(t), u(t)]$ we can write $L(\cdot)$

$$L[x(t), u(t), \lambda(t), t] = \int_{t_0}^{t_1} \{H[t, x(t), u(t), (t)] + \dot{\lambda}x(t)\}dt + \lambda(t_0)x_0 - \lambda(t_1)x_1 + S(x_1, t_1)$$

The Lagrangian variation is

$$\partial L = \int_{t_0}^{t_1} \{[(\partial H/\partial x) + \dot{\lambda}]\partial x(t) + (\partial H/\partial u)\partial u(t)\}dt + [-\lambda(t_1) + (\partial S/\partial x_1)]\partial x_1$$

The necessary condition for maximizing the Lagrangian, $\partial L = 0$, requires

$$(\partial H/\partial x) + \dot{\lambda} = 0; (\lambda H/\lambda u) = 0; -\lambda(t_1) + (\partial S/\partial x_1) = 0$$

Moreover partial variation of $L(\cdot)$ for the co-state variable $\lambda(t)$ is

$$\partial L = \int_{t_0}^{t_1} [(\partial H/\partial \lambda) - \dot{x}]\partial \lambda(t)]dt$$

from which we obtain another necessary condition

$$(\partial H/\partial \lambda) - \dot{x} = 0$$

The latter condition can also be obtained if the Lagrangian is written as

$$L^*[x(t), u(t), \lambda(t), t] = \int_{t_0}^{t_1} \{H[t, x(t), u(t), \lambda(t)] - \lambda(t)\dot{x}]\}dt + \lambda(t_0)x_0 - \lambda(t_1)x_1 + S(x_1, t_1)$$

Indeed, the previous condition is the partial variation ∂L^* with respect to $\lambda(t)$. This justifies the procedure which obtains the necessary conditions for optimal control by considering the variation ∂L with respect to $x(t)$ and $u(t)$ and then the variation ∂L^* with respect to $\lambda(t)$.

In the optimal control problem with terminal condition $T(x(t), t) = 0$ at $t = t_1$, when t_1 is variable along a terminal surface the partial variation of the Lagrangian is

$$\partial L = (\partial L/\partial t_1)\partial t_1$$

The rule of derivatives for a variable under an integral sign gives

$$(\partial L/\partial t_1) = [H(\cdot) - \lambda(t)\dot{x}]_{t=t_1} + (\partial S/\partial t_1) - [\lambda(t)\dot{x} + \dot{\lambda}x(t)]_{t=t_1} + (\partial S/\partial x_1)(dx_1/dt_1)$$

Since a maximum also requires $(\partial L/\partial t_1) = 0$ we obtain the transversality condition

$$[H(\cdot)_{t_1} + (\partial S/\partial t_1)] + [(\partial S/\partial x_1) - \lambda(t)](dx/dt)_{T(\cdot)=0} = 0$$

C.8   Optimal control problems with discounted Hamiltonian

Often in economics the maximizing functional depends on the integrand function of type

$$e^{-\beta t}F[t, x(t), u(t)]$$

where the function is discounted by a factor $e^{-\beta t}$. This type of problem is called an optimal control problem with a current value Hamiltonian. It qualifies as a class of optimal control problems for which a specific version of Pontryagin's maximum principle can be formulated. Here we shall deal only with problems with no scrap value function. For current value Hamiltonian problems the maximum principle consists of the following procedure

1. Current value costate variable $\mu(t) = \lambda(t)e^{\beta t}$ and current value Hamiltonian $H_c(\cdot) = e^{\beta t}H(\cdot)$ are defined

$$H_c[t, x(t), u(t), \mu(t)] = F[t, x(t), u(t)] + \mu(t)[f(x(t), u(t)]$$

2. The solutions to the optimal control are selected among the trajectories u(t), x(t), $\mu(t)$ which, for an internal maximum, satisfy the following conditions
   a) $\partial H_c/\partial u(t) = [\partial F/\partial u(t) + \mu(t)\partial f/\partial u(t)] = 0$
   b) $\dot{x} = \partial H_c/\partial \mu(t) = f[x(t), u(t)]$ with the initial condition $x(t_0) = x_0$
   c) $\dot{\lambda} = -\partial H/\partial x(t)$

The last condition (c) refers to the original costate variable and to the discounted Hamiltonian. To formulate this condition symmetrically we must take into account that

$$\dot{\lambda} = e^{-\beta t}\dot{\mu} - \beta e^{-\beta t}\mu(t); \; -\partial H/\partial x(t) = -e^{-\beta t}\partial H_c/\partial x(t)$$

so that we obtain

c') $\dot{\mu} = \beta\mu(t) - \partial H_c/\partial x(t)$

Therefore, maximum principle for problems with the current value Hamiltonian $H_c(\cdot)$ can be stated as the above conditions a, b and c').

C.9 An extension of maximum principle to optimal control with discrete time

When time is discrete, Pontryagin's maximum principle musts be reformulated. The problem

$$\max \sum_{t=1}^{T} F[t, x_t, u_t]$$
$$x_{t+1} - x_t = f(x_t, u_t)$$
$$x_{t0} = x_0; x_T = \tilde{x}_T$$

can be solved as a sequence of constrained maximum problems. The Lagrangian at t is

$$L(t, x_t, u_t, \lambda_{t+1}) = \sum_{t=1}^{T} F[t, x_t, u_t] + \lambda_{t+1}[f(x_t, u_t) - x_{t+1} + x_t]$$

For $t = 1, \ldots, T$, maximization of the Lagrangian requires the following necessary conditions

$(\partial L/u_t) = (\partial F/\partial u_t) + \lambda_{t+1}(\partial f/\partial u_t) = 0$
$(\partial L/x_t) = (\partial F/\partial x_t) + \lambda_{t+1}(\partial f/\partial x_t) + (\lambda_{t+1} - \lambda_t) = 0$
$(\partial L/\lambda_{t+1}) = f(x_t, u_t) - x_{t+1} + x_t = 0$
$(\partial L/\lambda_T) = -\lambda_T = 0$

In this case the maximum principle consists of the following procedure

1. Write the equation for the motion explicitly as the difference equation $x_{t+1} = x_t + f(x_t, u_t)$ so that the following Hamiltonian can be formed

   $$H(t, x_t, u_t, x_{t+1}, \lambda_{t+1}) = F[t, x_t, u_t] + \lambda_{t+1}[x_t + f(x_t, u_t)] = F[t, x_t, u_t] + \lambda_{t+1}x_{t+1}$$

2. The solutions to the optimal control are chosen among the sequences u_t, x_t, λ_t which, for internal maxima, satisfy the following conditions

   a) $\max\limits_{\{u_t\}} H(t, x_t, u_t, \lambda_{t+1})$ for t $[t_0, T]$

   b) $x_{t+1} = \partial H/\partial \lambda_{t+1} = x_t + f[x_t, u_t]$ with the initial condition $x_{t0} = x_0$

   c) $\lambda_{t+1} = \partial H/\partial x_{t+1}$ with the terminal condition $\lambda_T = 0$.

   When the Hamiltonian $H(\cdot)$ is differentiable with respect to u_t, condition a) for internal maximum sets

   $$\partial H/\partial u_t = [\partial F/\partial u_t + \lambda_{t+1}\partial f/\partial u_t] = 0$$

These conditions are necessary because between the Hamiltonian and the Lagrangian there is the trivial relationship

$$H(t, x_t, u_t, x_{t+1}, \lambda_{t+1}) = L(t, x_t, u_t, \lambda_{t+1}) + \lambda_{t+1}x_{t+1}$$

so that

$$\partial H/\partial u_t = \partial L/\partial u_t$$
$$\partial H/\partial x_t = \partial L/\partial x_t + \lambda_t$$
$$\partial H/\partial \lambda_{t+1} = \partial L/\partial \lambda_{t+1} + x_{t+1}$$

If we enforce the necessary conditions for maximizing the Lagrangian, we obtain the above conditions a, b and c stated by Pontryagins' maximum principle.

References

Arrow, K. and M. Kurz (1970) *Public Investment, The Rate of Return and Optimal Fiscal Policy* (Baltimore: Johns Hopkins).

Chiang, A. (1992) *Elements of Dynamic Optimization* (Singapore: McGraw-Hill).

Chirichiello, G. (1992) *Ottimizzazione Dinamica e Modelli di Teoria Economica (Dynamic Optimization and Models in Economics)* (Rome: OCSM).

Elsgots, L. (1978) *Differential Equations and Calculus of Variations*, (Moscow: Mir Publisher).

Gandolfo, G. (1996) *Economic Dynamics* (Berlin: Springer-Verlag).

Hadley, G. and M. Kemp (1971) *Variational Methods in Economics* (New York: North-Holland).

Intriligator, M. (1971) *Mathematical Optimization and Economic Theory* (Englewood Cliffs, N..J.: Prentice-Hall)

Kamien, M. and N. Schwartz (1985) *Dynamic Optimization. The Calculus of Variations and Optimal Control in Economics and Management* (New York: North-Holland).

Luenberger, D. (1979) *Introduction to Dynamic Systems* (New York: Wiley).

Stanpacchia, G. (1973) *Lezioni di Analisi Matematica (Lectures on Mathematical Analysis)*, Vol. II (Naples, Italy: Liguori).

Index

Woodford M., 156, 162

Yip C., 137, 166, 182
Young A., 190

Younes Y., 136

Zilcha I., 142

1